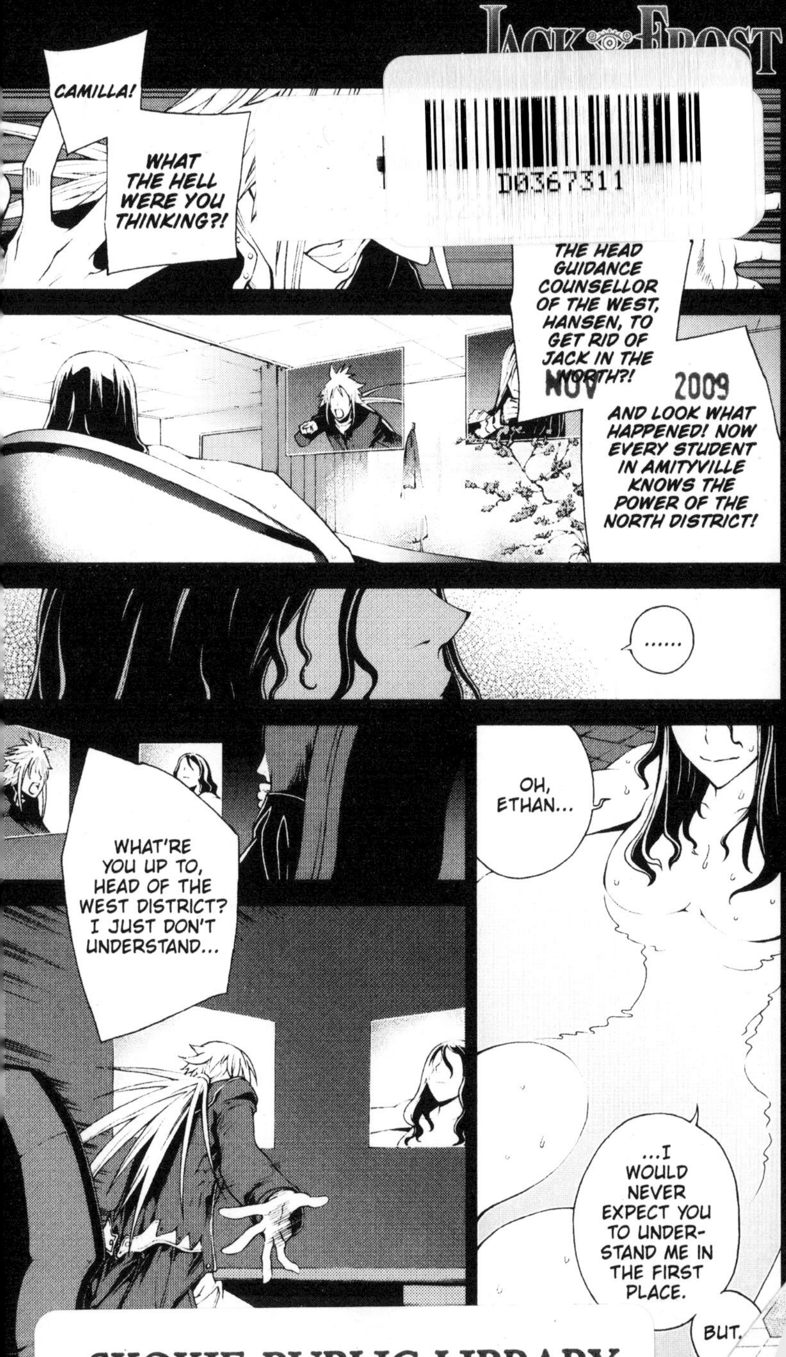
CAMILLA!
WHAT THE HELL WERE YOU THINKING?!
THE HEAD GUIDANCE COUNSELLOR OF THE WEST, HANSEN, TO GET RID OF JACK IN THE NORTH?!
AND LOOK WHAT HAPPENED! NOW EVERY STUDENT IN AMITYVILLE KNOWS THE POWER OF THE NORTH DISTRICT!
......
WHAT'RE YOU UP TO, HEAD OF THE WEST DISTRICT? I JUST DON'T UNDERSTAND...
OH, ETHAN...
...I WOULD NEVER EXPECT YOU TO UNDERSTAND ME IN THE FIRST PLACE.
BUT.

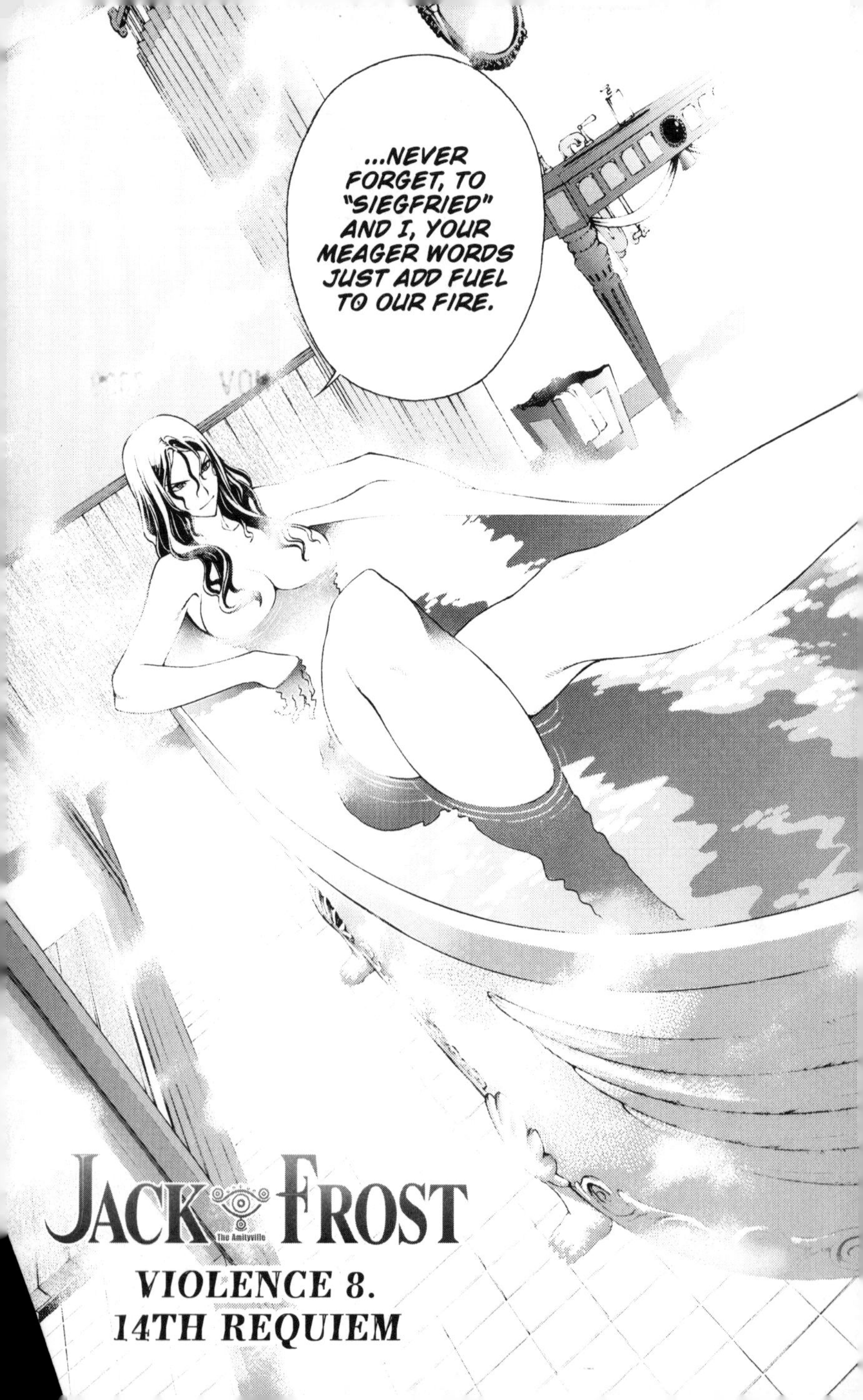
...NEVER FORGET, TO "SIEGFRIED" AND I, YOUR MEAGER WORDS JUST ADD FUEL TO OUR FIRE.
JACK FROST
The Amityville
VIOLENCE 8.
14TH REQUIEM

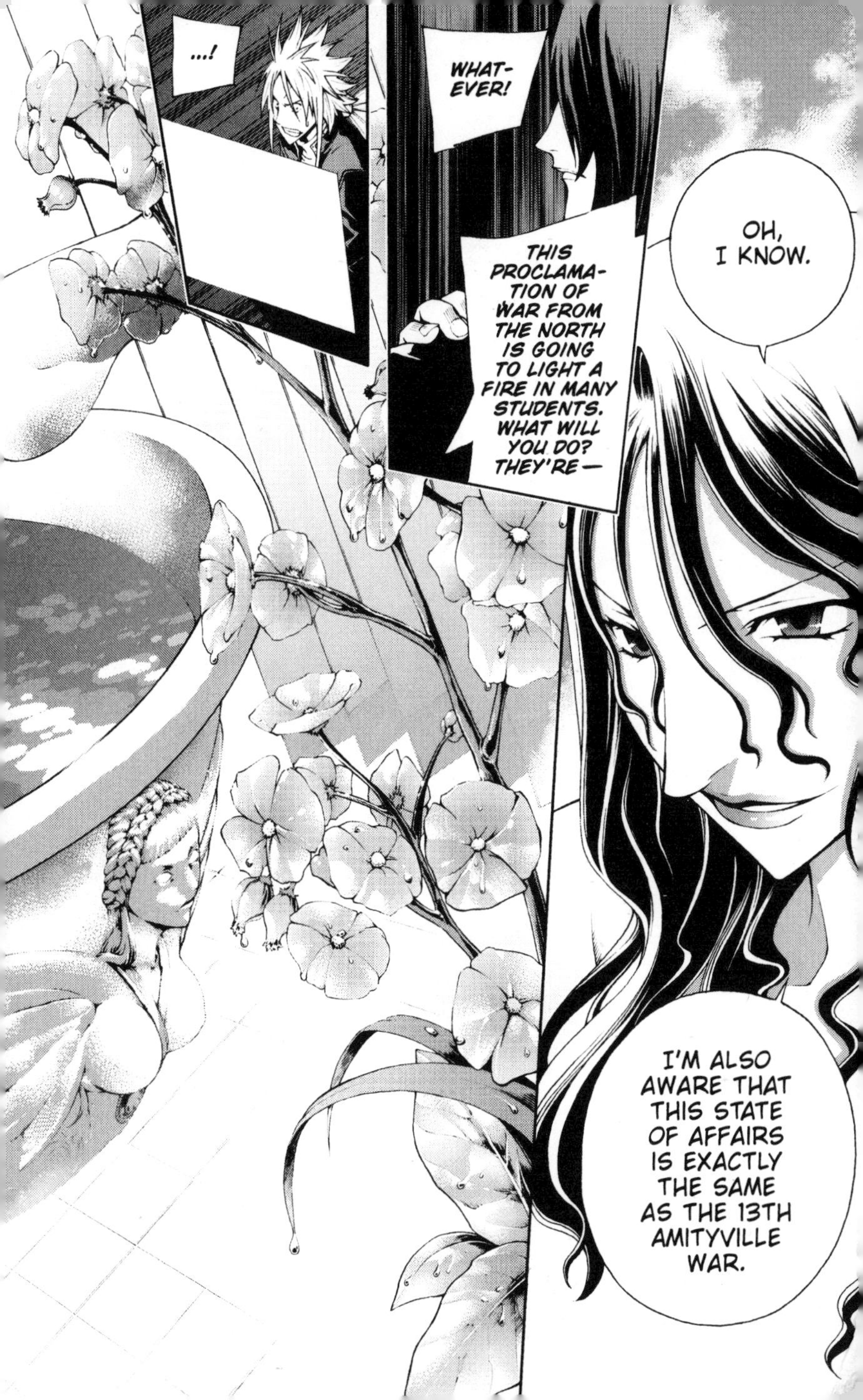
...!
WHAT-EVER!
THIS PROCLAMATION OF WAR FROM THE NORTH IS GOING TO LIGHT A FIRE IN MANY STUDENTS. WHAT WILL YOU DO? THEY'RE—
OH, I KNOW.
I'M ALSO AWARE THAT THIS STATE OF AFFAIRS IS EXACTLY THE SAME AS THE 13TH AMITYVILLE WAR.

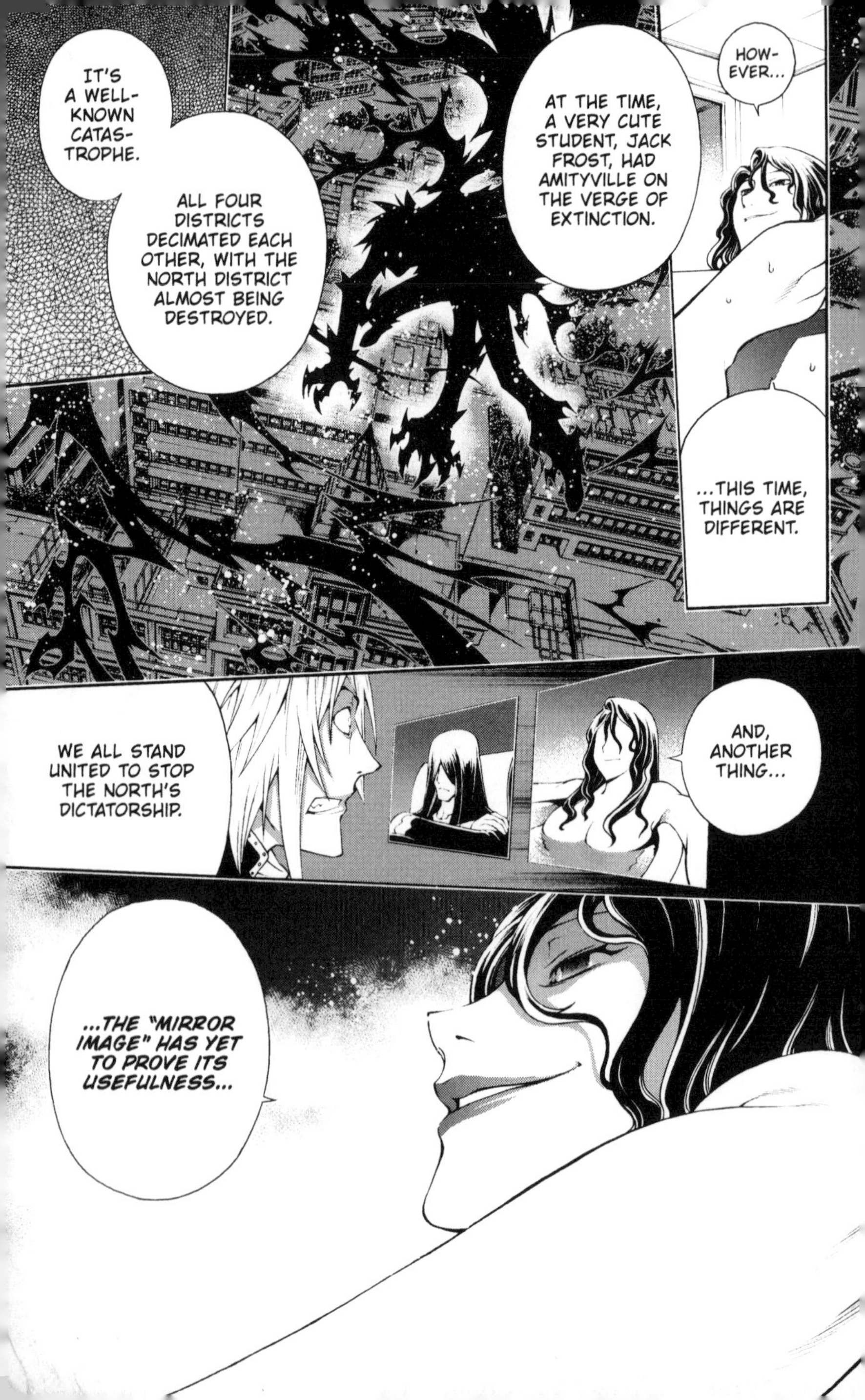
IT'S A WELL-KNOWN CATAS-TROPHE.
ALL FOUR DISTRICTS DECIMATED EACH OTHER, WITH THE NORTH DISTRICT ALMOST BEING DESTROYED.
AT THE TIME, A VERY CUTE STUDENT, JACK FROST, HAD AMITYVILLE ON THE VERGE OF EXTINCTION.
HOW-EVER...
...THIS TIME, THINGS ARE DIFFERENT.
WE ALL STAND UNITED TO STOP THE NORTH'S DICTATORSHIP.
AND, ANOTHER THING...
...THE "MIRROR IMAGE" HAS YET TO PROVE ITS USEFULNESS...

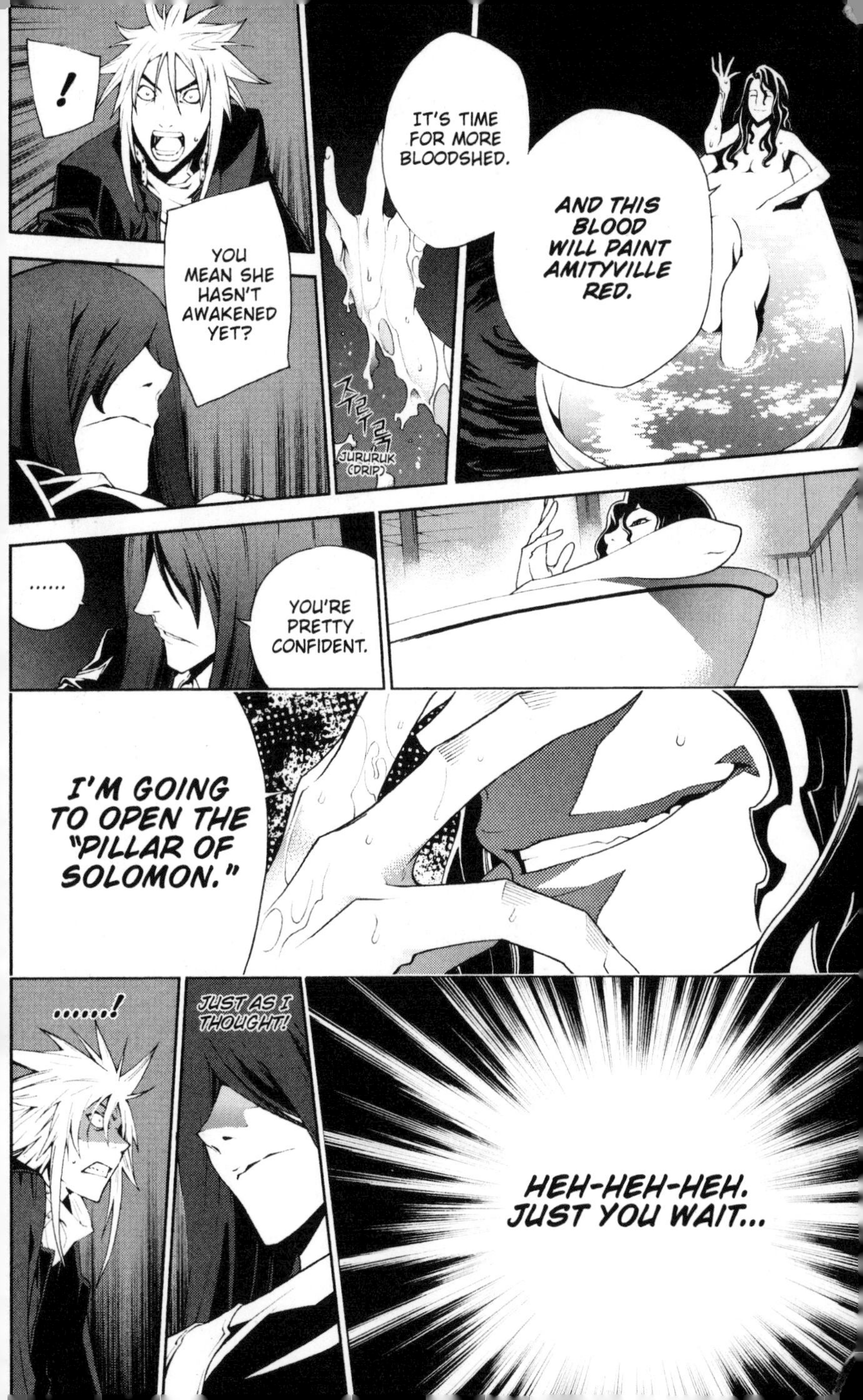
!
YOU MEAN SHE HASN'T AWAKENED YET?
IT'S TIME FOR MORE BLOODSHED.
JURURUK (DRIP)
AND THIS BLOOD WILL PAINT AMITYVILLE RED.
......
YOU'RE PRETTY CONFIDENT.
I'M GOING TO OPEN THE "PILLAR OF SOLOMON."
......!
JUST AS I THOUGHT!
HEH-HEH-HEH. JUST YOU WAIT...

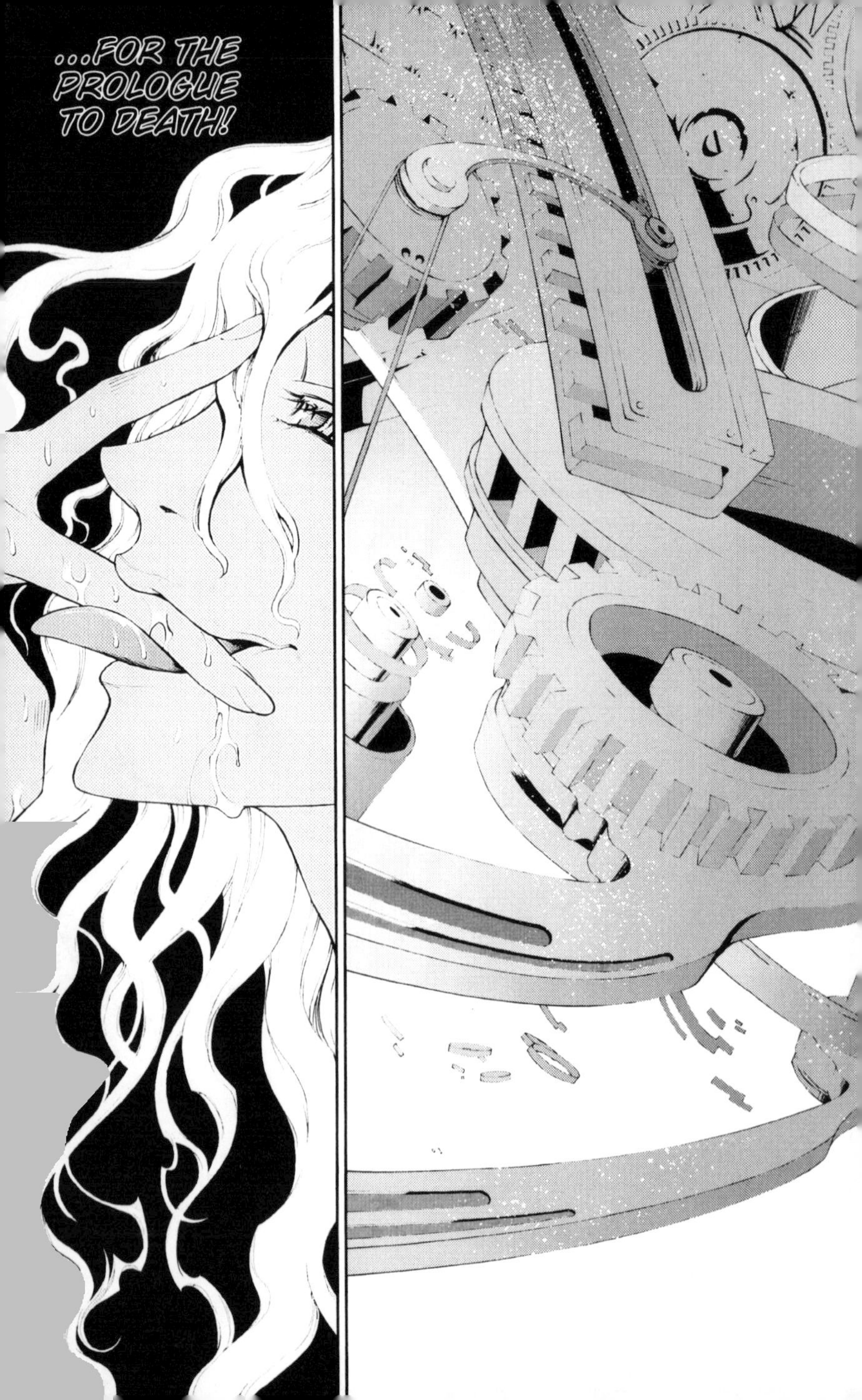
...FOR THE PROLOGUE TO DEATH!

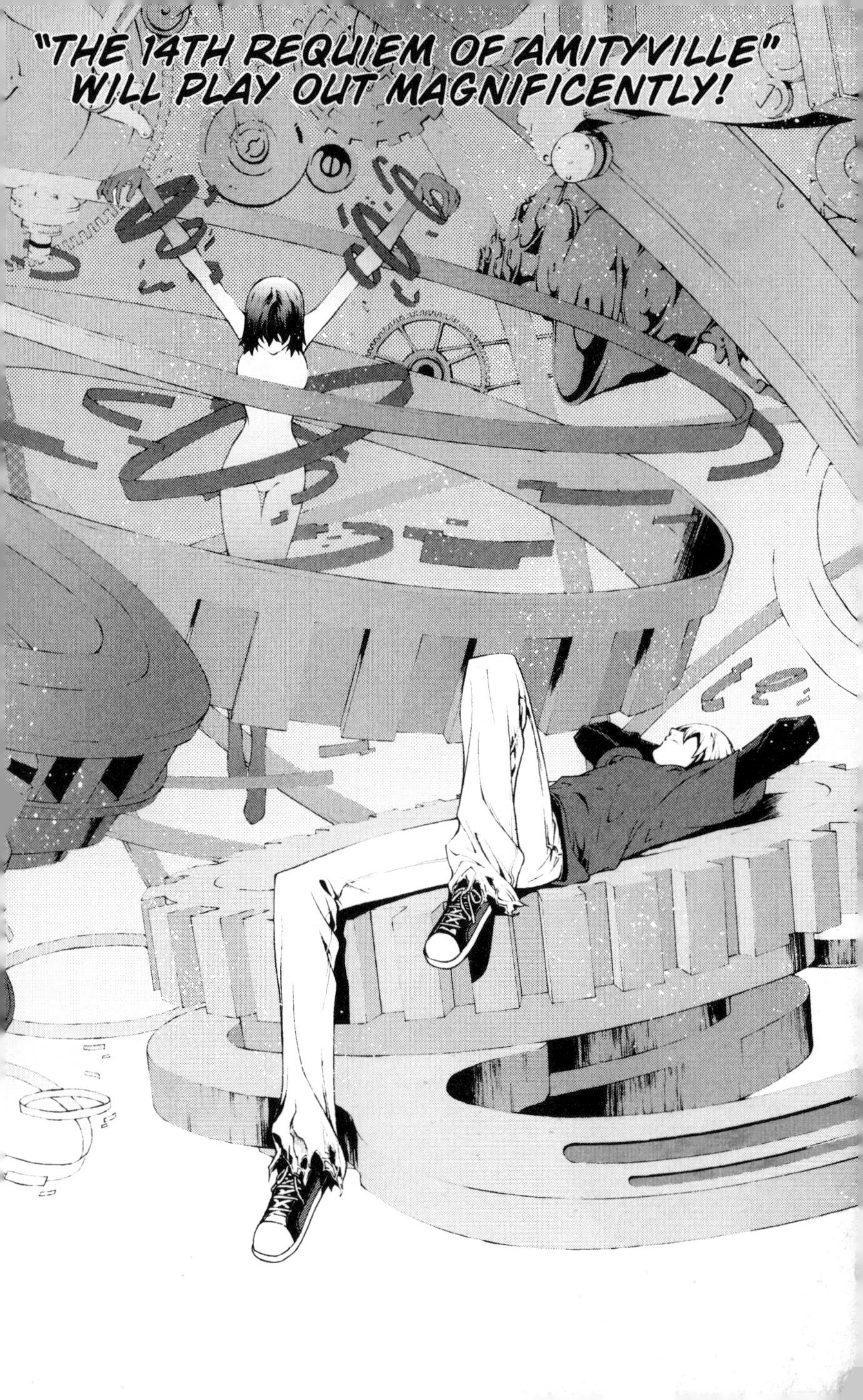
"THE 14TH REQUIEM OF AMITYVILLE"
WILL PLAY OUT MAGNIFICENTLY!

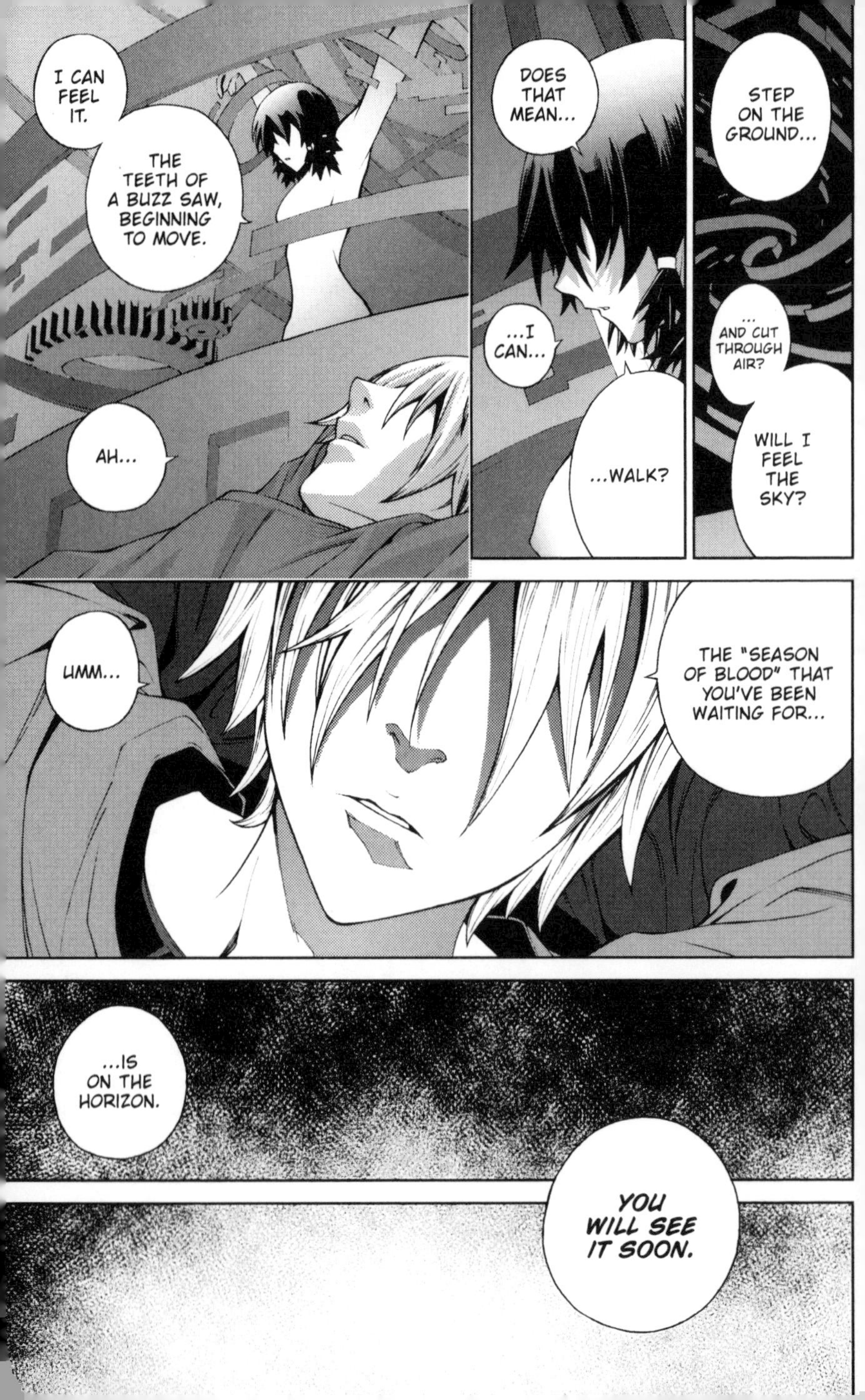
I CAN FEEL IT.
THE TEETH OF A BUZZ SAW, BEGINNING TO MOVE.
AH...
DOES THAT MEAN...
...I CAN...
...WALK?
STEP ON THE GROUND...
...AND CUT THROUGH AIR?
WILL I FEEL THE SKY?
UMM...
THE "SEASON OF BLOOD" THAT YOU'VE BEEN WAITING FOR...
...IS ON THE HORIZON.
YOU WILL SEE IT SOON.

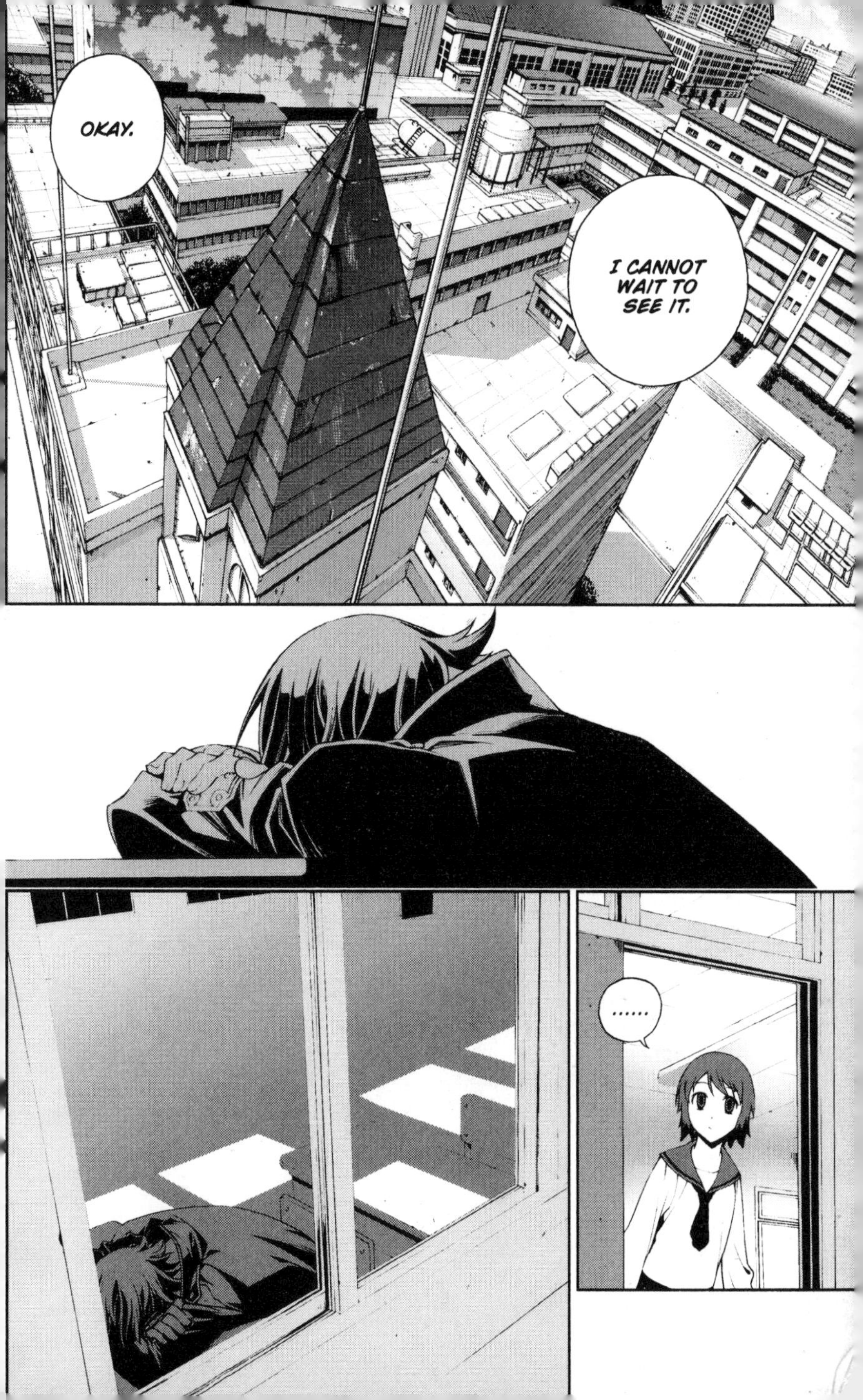
OKAY.
I CANNOT WAIT TO SEE IT.
......

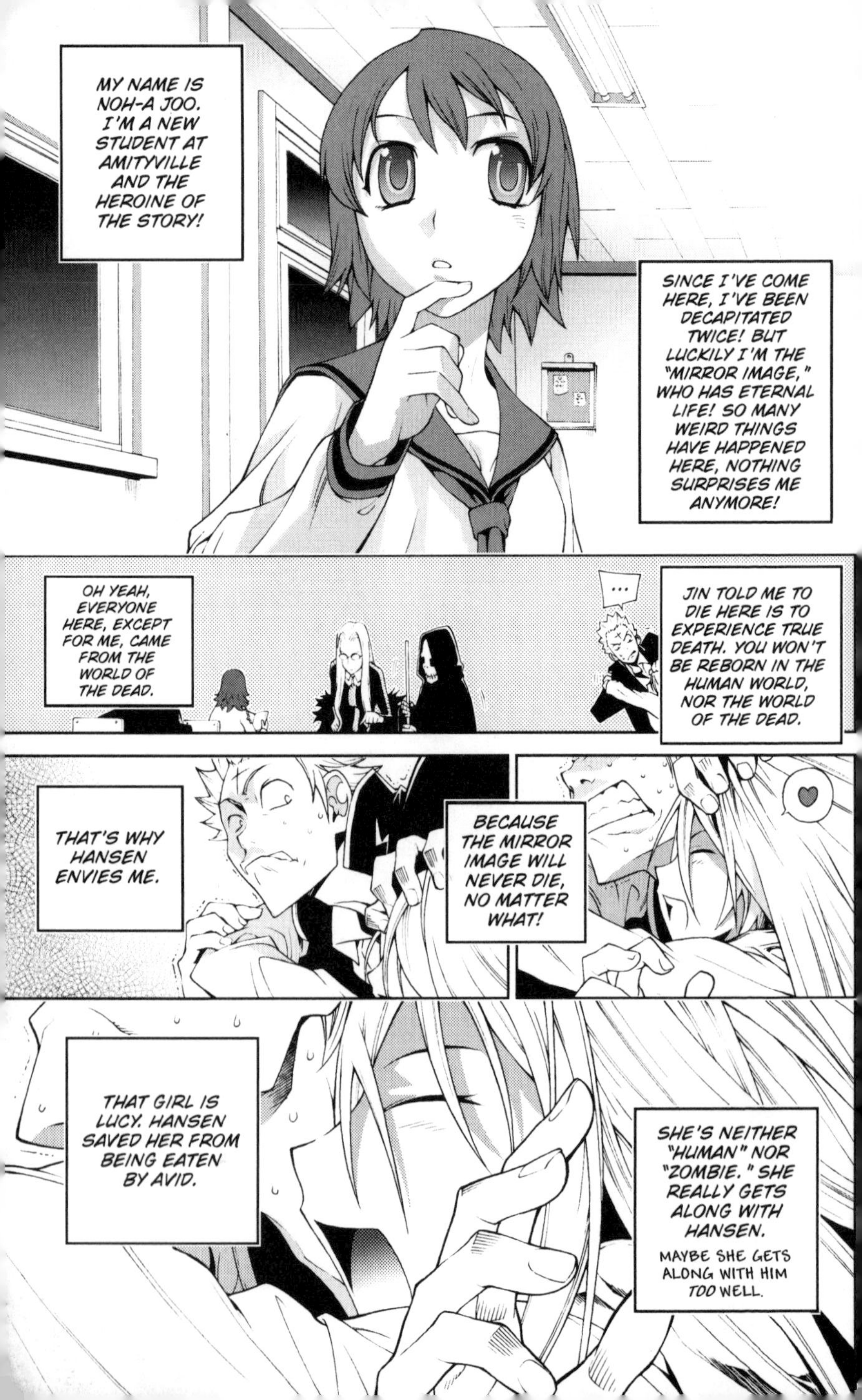
MY NAME IS NOH-A JOO. I'M A NEW STUDENT AT AMITYVILLE AND THE HEROINE OF THE STORY!
SINCE I'VE COME HERE, I'VE BEEN DECAPITATED TWICE! BUT LUCKILY I'M THE "MIRROR IMAGE," WHO HAS ETERNAL LIFE! SO MANY WEIRD THINGS HAVE HAPPENED HERE, NOTHING SURPRISES ME ANYMORE!
OH YEAH, EVERYONE HERE, EXCEPT FOR ME, CAME FROM THE WORLD OF THE DEAD.
...
JIN TOLD ME TO DIE HERE IS TO EXPERIENCE TRUE DEATH. YOU WON'T BE REBORN IN THE HUMAN WORLD, NOR THE WORLD OF THE DEAD.
THAT'S WHY HANSEN ENVIES ME.
BECAUSE THE MIRROR IMAGE WILL NEVER DIE, NO MATTER WHAT!
THAT GIRL IS LUCY. HANSEN SAVED HER FROM BEING EATEN BY AVID.
SHE'S NEITHER "HUMAN" NOR "ZOMBIE." SHE REALLY GETS ALONG WITH HANSEN.
MAYBE SHE GETS ALONG WITH HIM TOO WELL.

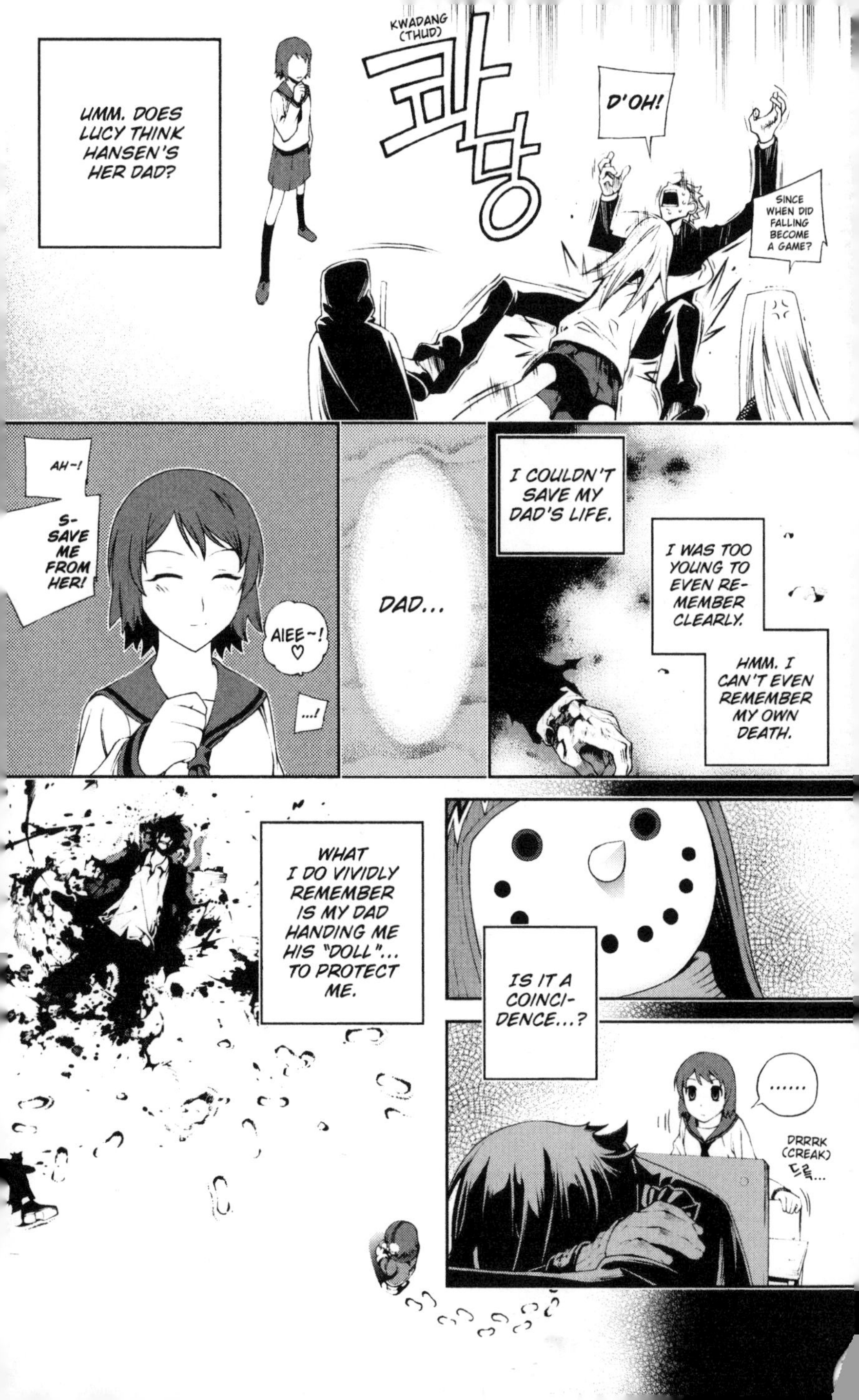
UMM. DOES LUCY THINK HANSEN'S HER DAD?
KWADANG (THUD)
콰당
D'OH!
SINCE WHEN DID FALLING BECOME A GAME?
AH~!
S-SAVE ME FROM HER!
AIEE~! ♡
...!
DAD...
I COULDN'T SAVE MY DAD'S LIFE.
I WAS TOO YOUNG TO EVEN RE-MEMBER CLEARLY.
HMM. I CAN'T EVEN REMEMBER MY OWN DEATH.
WHAT I DO VIVIDLY REMEMBER IS MY DAD HANDING ME HIS "DOLL"... TO PROTECT ME.
IS IT A COINCI-DENCE...?
......
DRRRK (CREAK)
드륵...

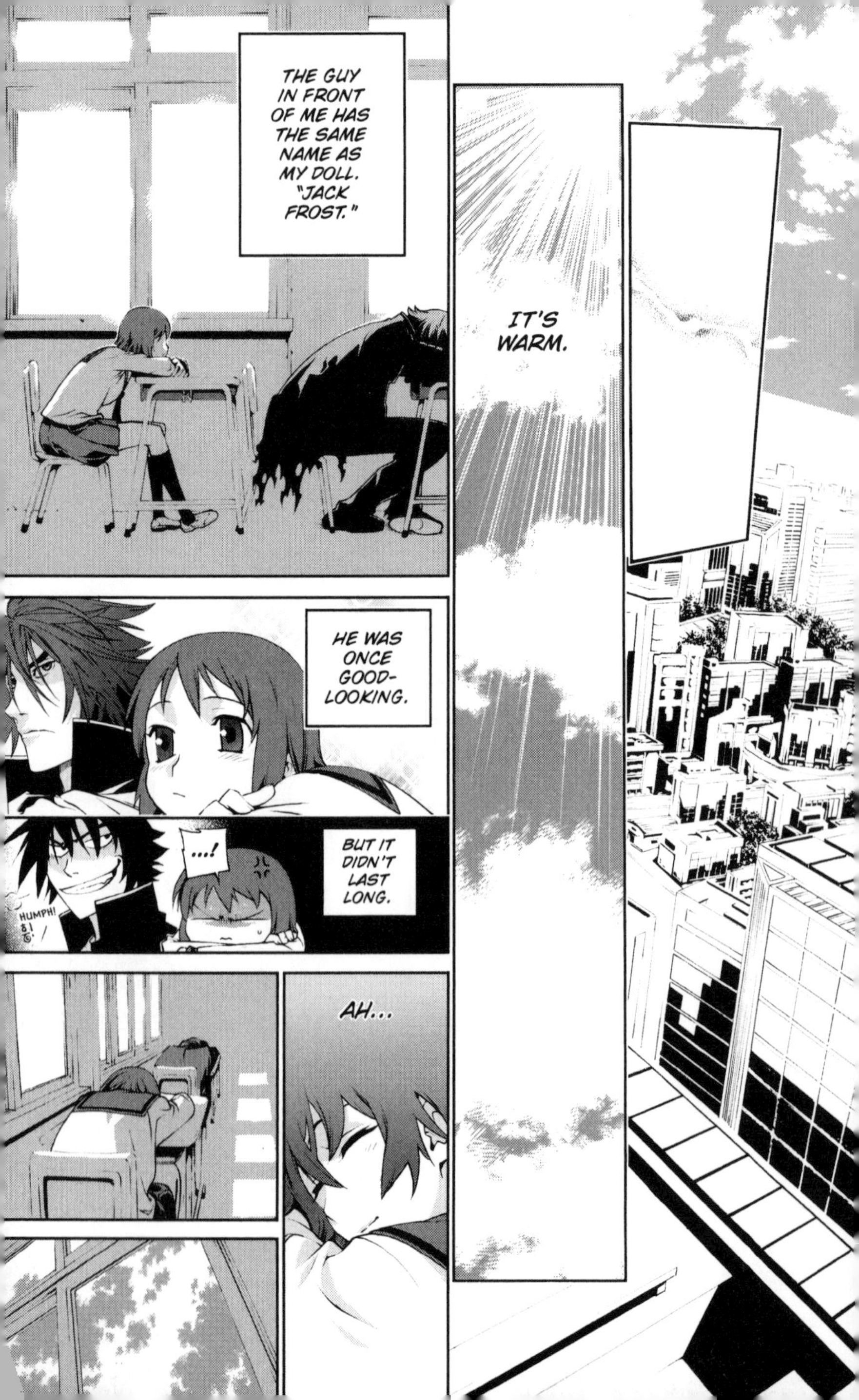
THE GUY IN FRONT OF ME HAS THE SAME NAME AS MY DOLL. "JACK FROST."
HE WAS ONCE GOOD-LOOKING.
HUMPH!
...!
BUT IT DIDN'T LAST LONG.
AH...
IT'S WARM.

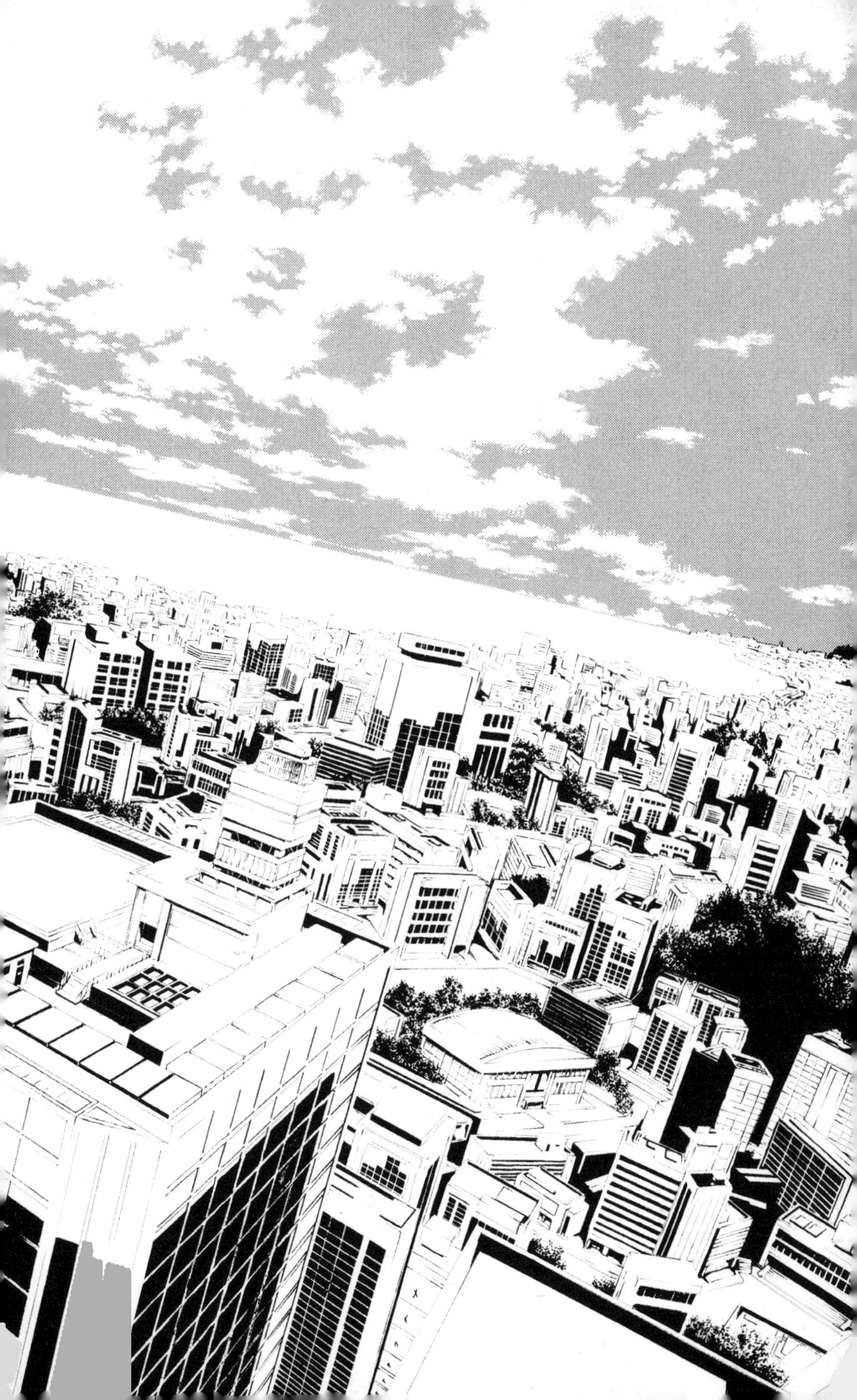

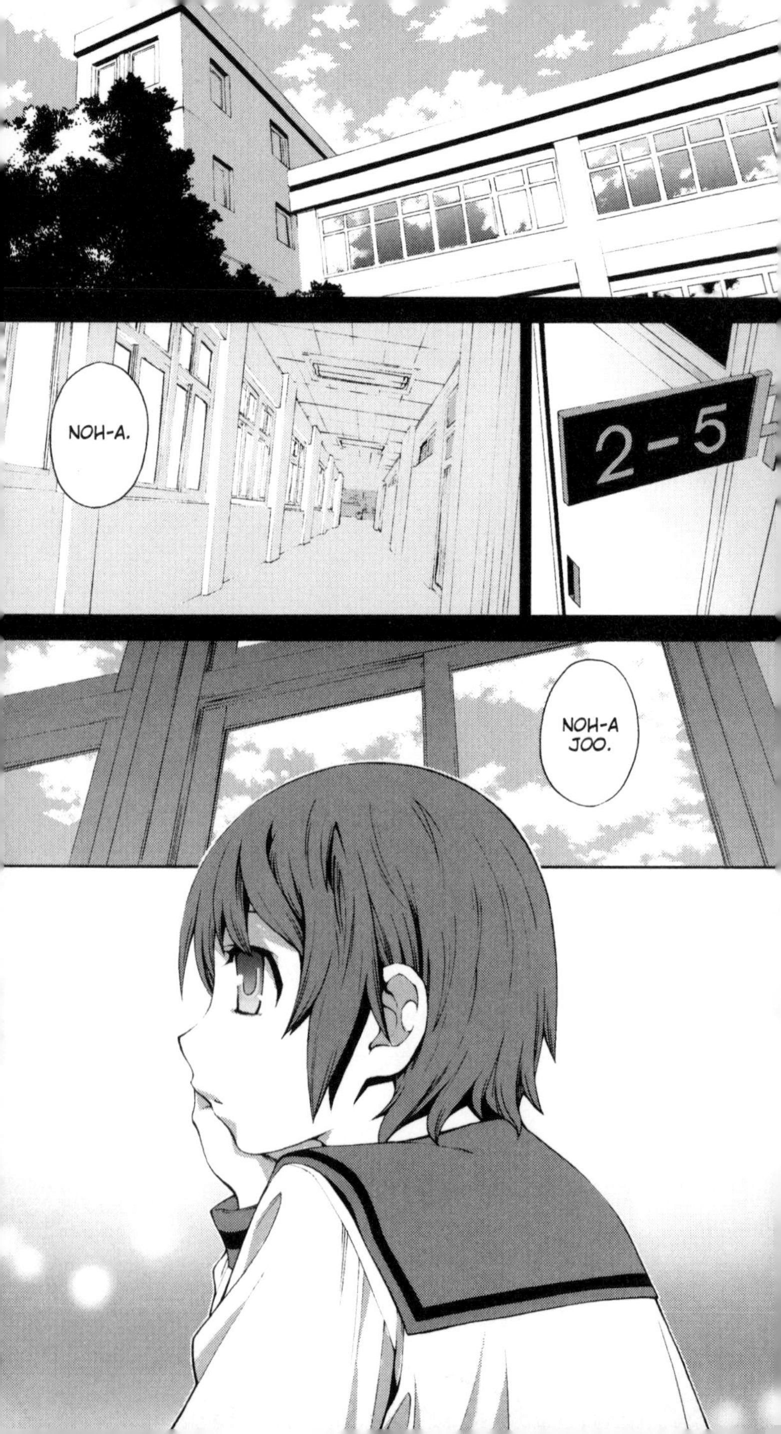
NOH-A.
2-5
NOH-A JOO.

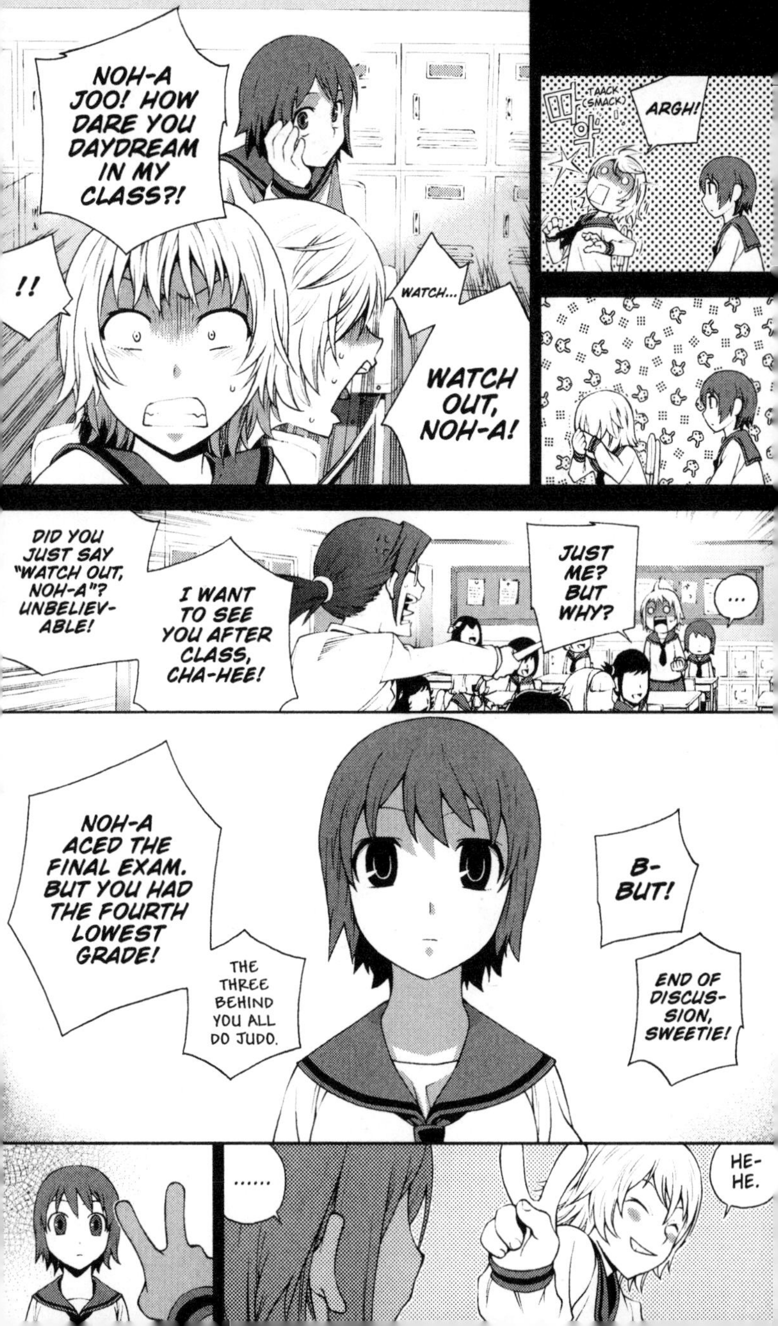
NOH-A JOO! HOW DARE YOU DAYDREAM IN MY CLASS?!
!!
WATCH...
WATCH OUT, NOH-A!
TAACK (SMACK)
ARGH!
DID YOU JUST SAY "WATCH OUT, NOH-A"? UNBELIEV-ABLE!
I WANT TO SEE YOU AFTER CLASS, CHA-HEE!
JUST ME? BUT WHY?
...
NOH-A ACED THE FINAL EXAM. BUT YOU HAD THE FOURTH LOWEST GRADE!
THE THREE BEHIND YOU ALL DO JUDO.
B-BUT!
END OF DISCUSSION, SWEETIE!
......
HE-HE.

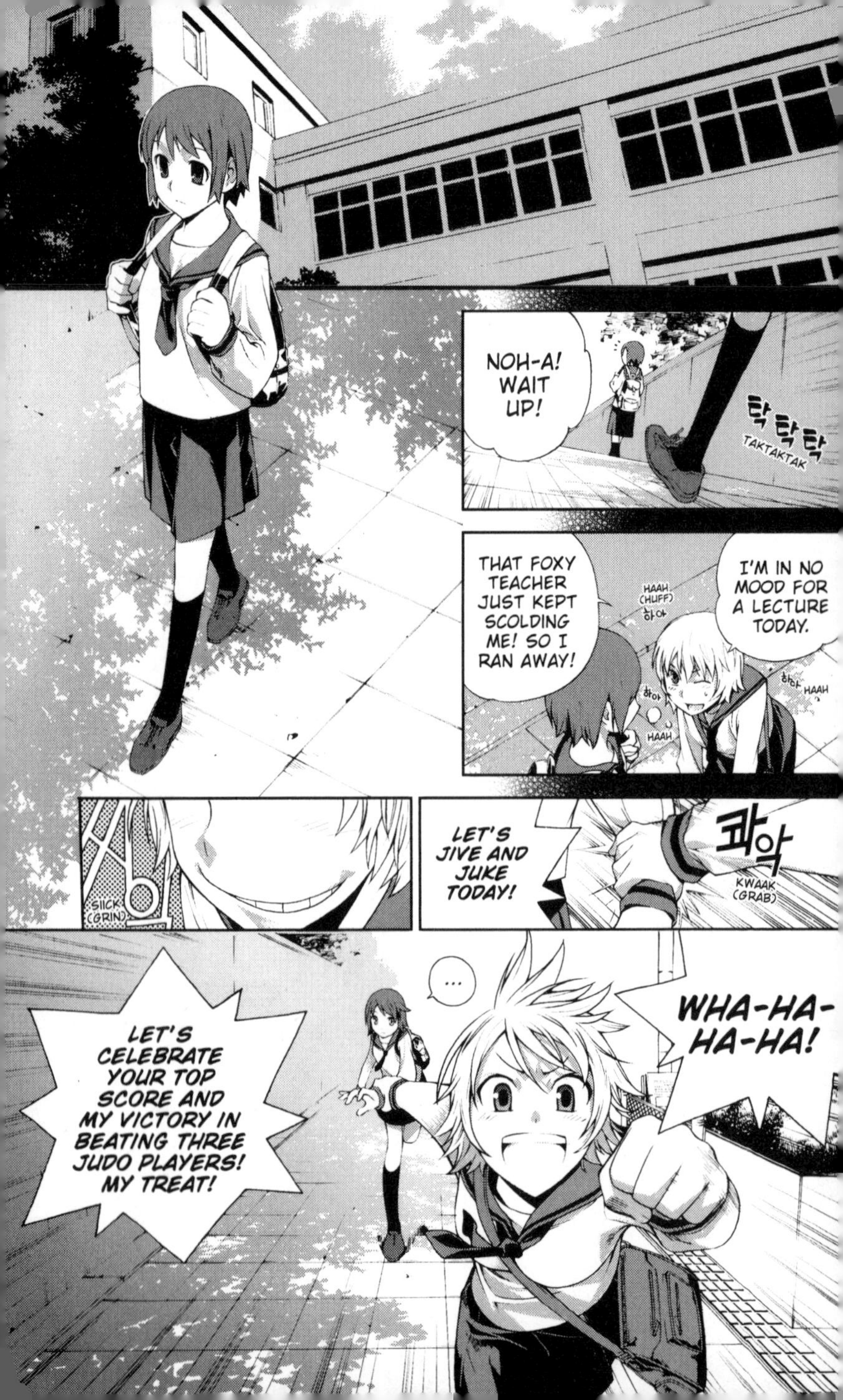

NOH-A! WAIT UP!
탁탁탁
TAKTAKTAK
THAT FOXY TEACHER JUST KEPT SCOLDING ME! SO I RAN AWAY!
HAAH (HUFF)
하아
I'M IN NO MOOD FOR A LECTURE TODAY.
하아
HAAH
하아
HAAH
SIICK (GRIN)
LET'S JIVE AND JUKE TODAY!
콰악
KWAAK (GRAB)
LET'S CELEBRATE YOUR TOP SCORE AND MY VICTORY IN BEATING THREE JUDO PLAYERS! MY TREAT!
...
WHA-HA-HA-HA!

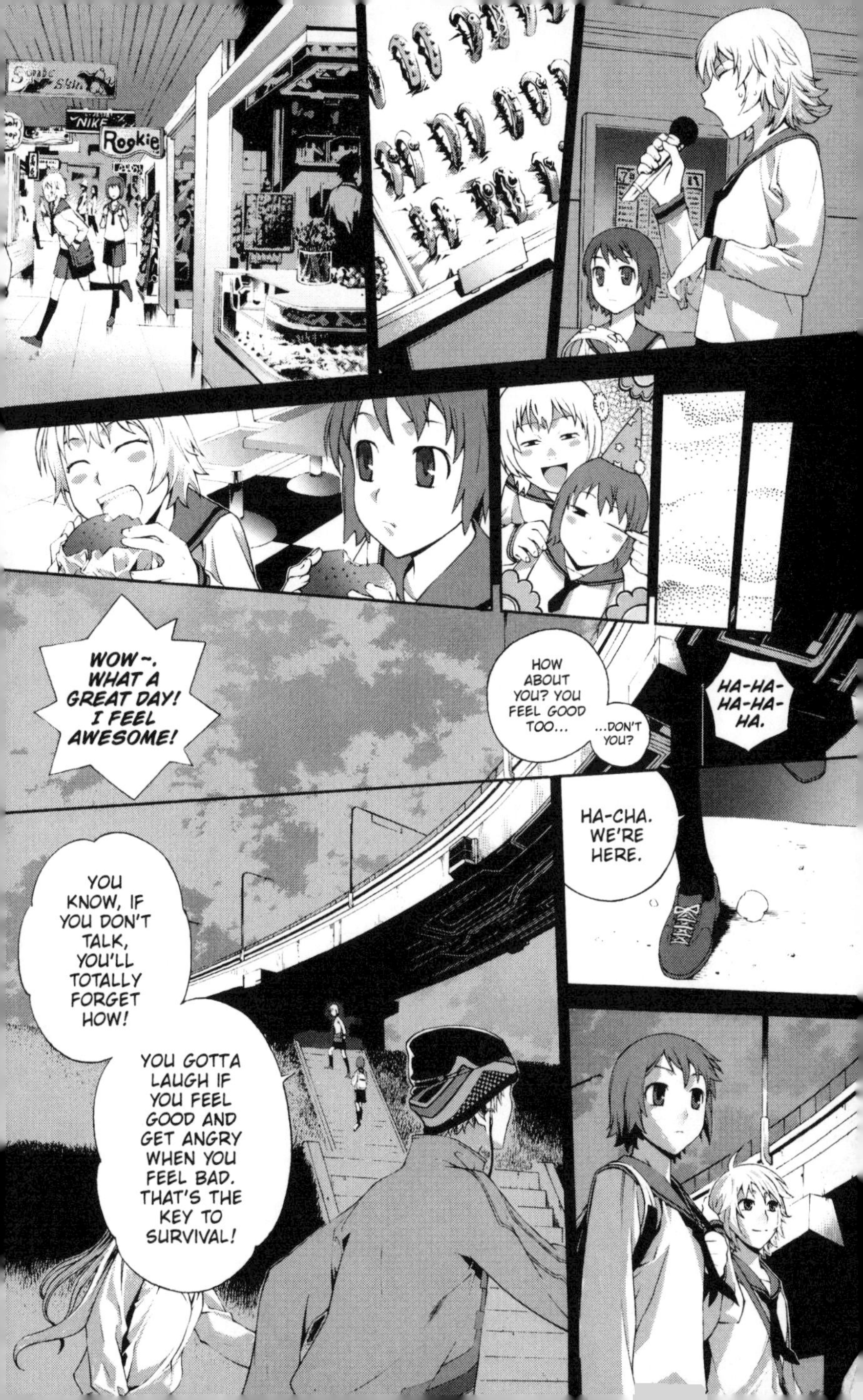
NIKE
Rookie
WOW~. WHAT A GREAT DAY! I FEEL AWESOME!
HOW ABOUT YOU? YOU FEEL GOOD TOO...
...DON'T YOU?
HA-HA-HA-HA-HA.
YOU KNOW, IF YOU DON'T TALK, YOU'LL TOTALLY FORGET HOW!
YOU GOTTA LAUGH IF YOU FEEL GOOD AND GET ANGRY WHEN YOU FEEL BAD. THAT'S THE KEY TO SURVIVAL!
HA-CHA. WE'RE HERE.

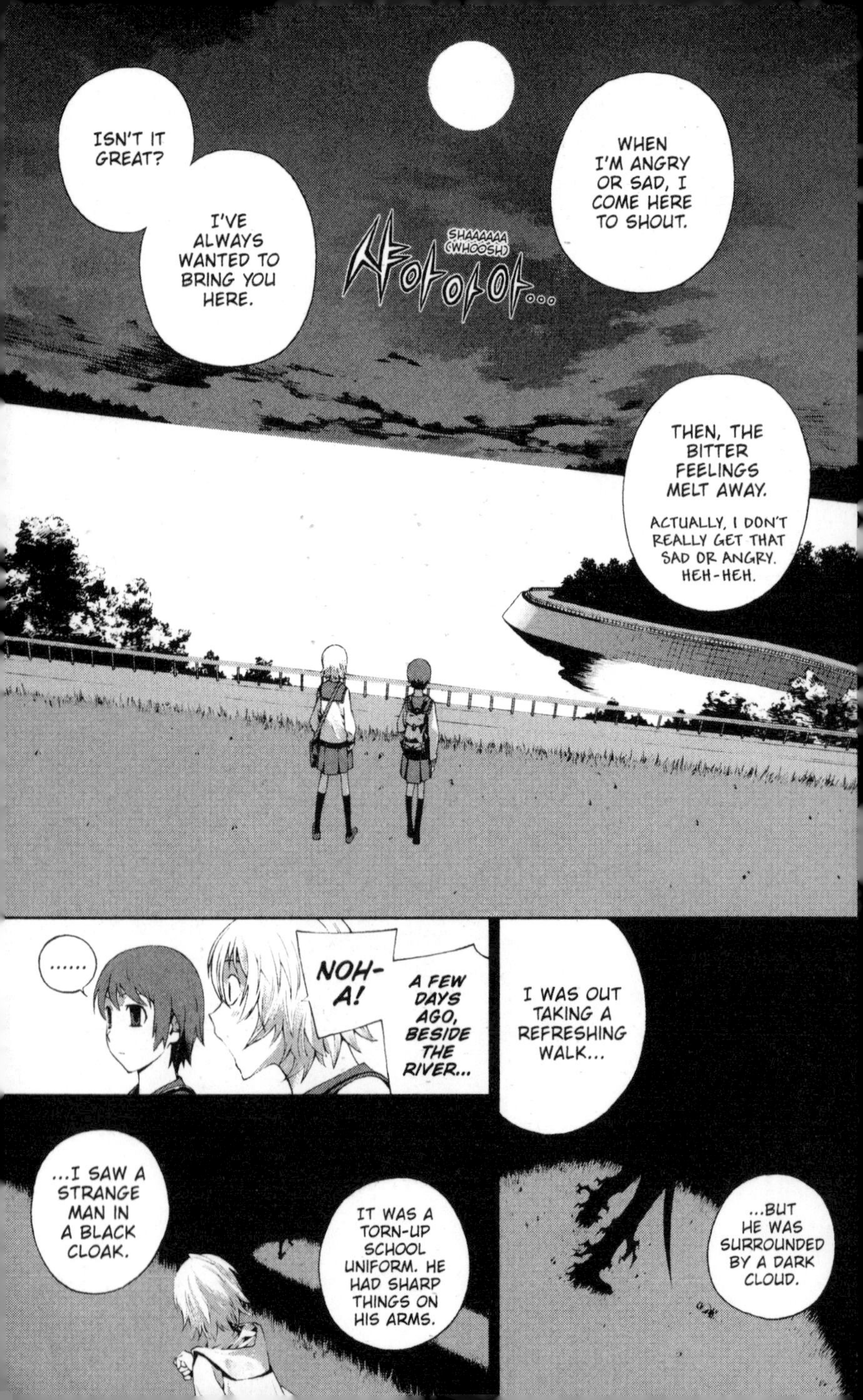
ISN'T IT GREAT?
I'VE ALWAYS WANTED TO BRING YOU HERE.
샤아아아...
SHAAAAAA (WHOOSH)
WHEN I'M ANGRY OR SAD, I COME HERE TO SHOUT.
THEN, THE BITTER FEELINGS MELT AWAY.
ACTUALLY, I DON'T REALLY GET THAT SAD OR ANGRY. HEH-HEH.
......
NOH-A!
A FEW DAYS AGO, BESIDE THE RIVER...
I WAS OUT TAKING A REFRESHING WALK...
...I SAW A STRANGE MAN IN A BLACK CLOAK.
IT WAS A TORN-UP SCHOOL UNIFORM. HE HAD SHARP THINGS ON HIS ARMS.
...BUT HE WAS SURROUNDED BY A DARK CLOUD.

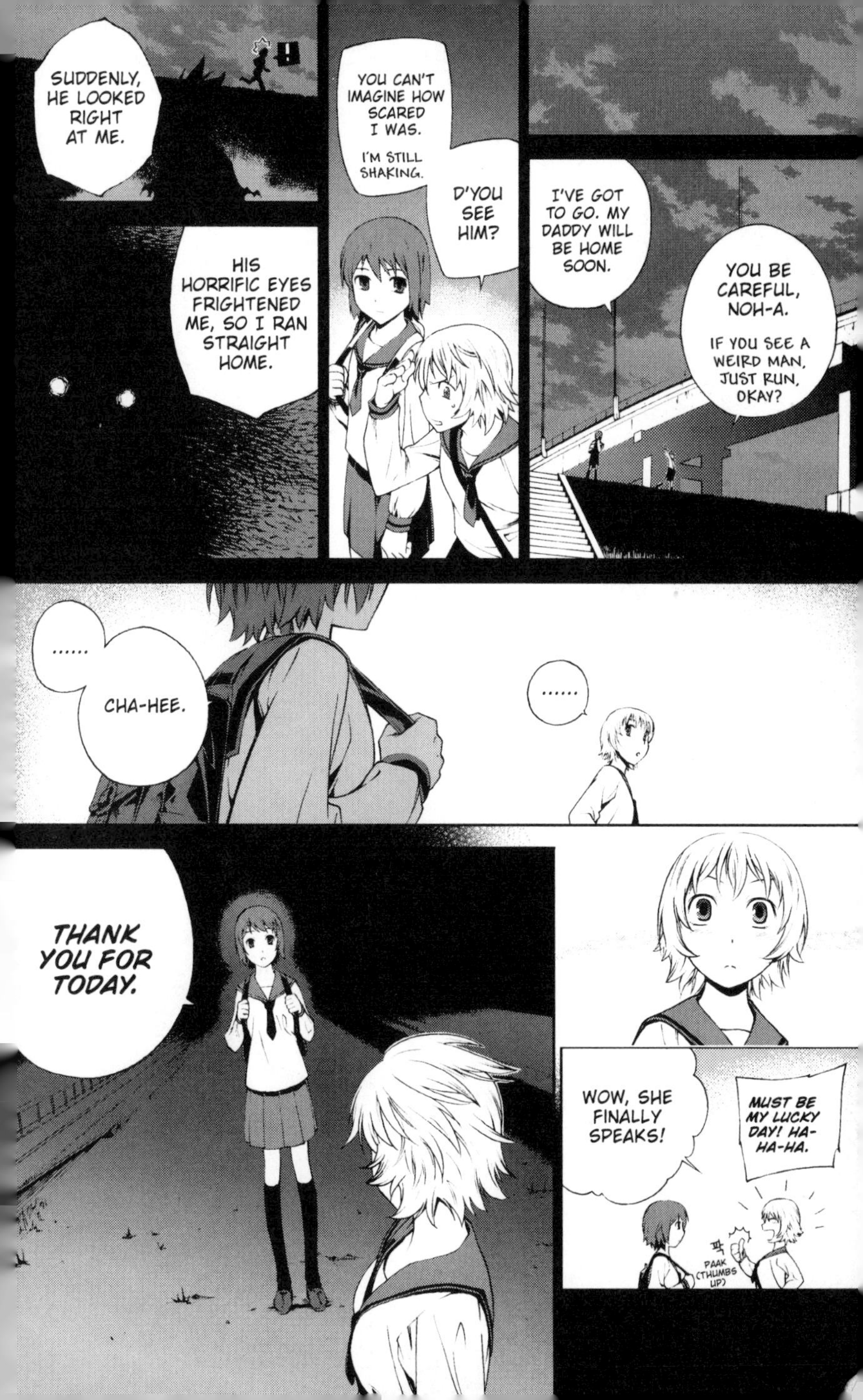
SUDDENLY, HE LOOKED RIGHT AT ME.
!
HIS HORRIFIC EYES FRIGHTENED ME, SO I RAN STRAIGHT HOME.
YOU CAN'T IMAGINE HOW SCARED I WAS.
I'M STILL SHAKING.
D'YOU SEE HIM?
I'VE GOT TO GO. MY DADDY WILL BE HOME SOON.
YOU BE CAREFUL, NOH-A.
IF YOU SEE A WEIRD MAN, JUST RUN, OKAY?
......
CHA-HEE.
......
THANK YOU FOR TODAY.
WOW, SHE FINALLY SPEAKS!
MUST BE MY LUCKY DAY! HA-HA-HA.
팍
PAAK (THUMBS UP)

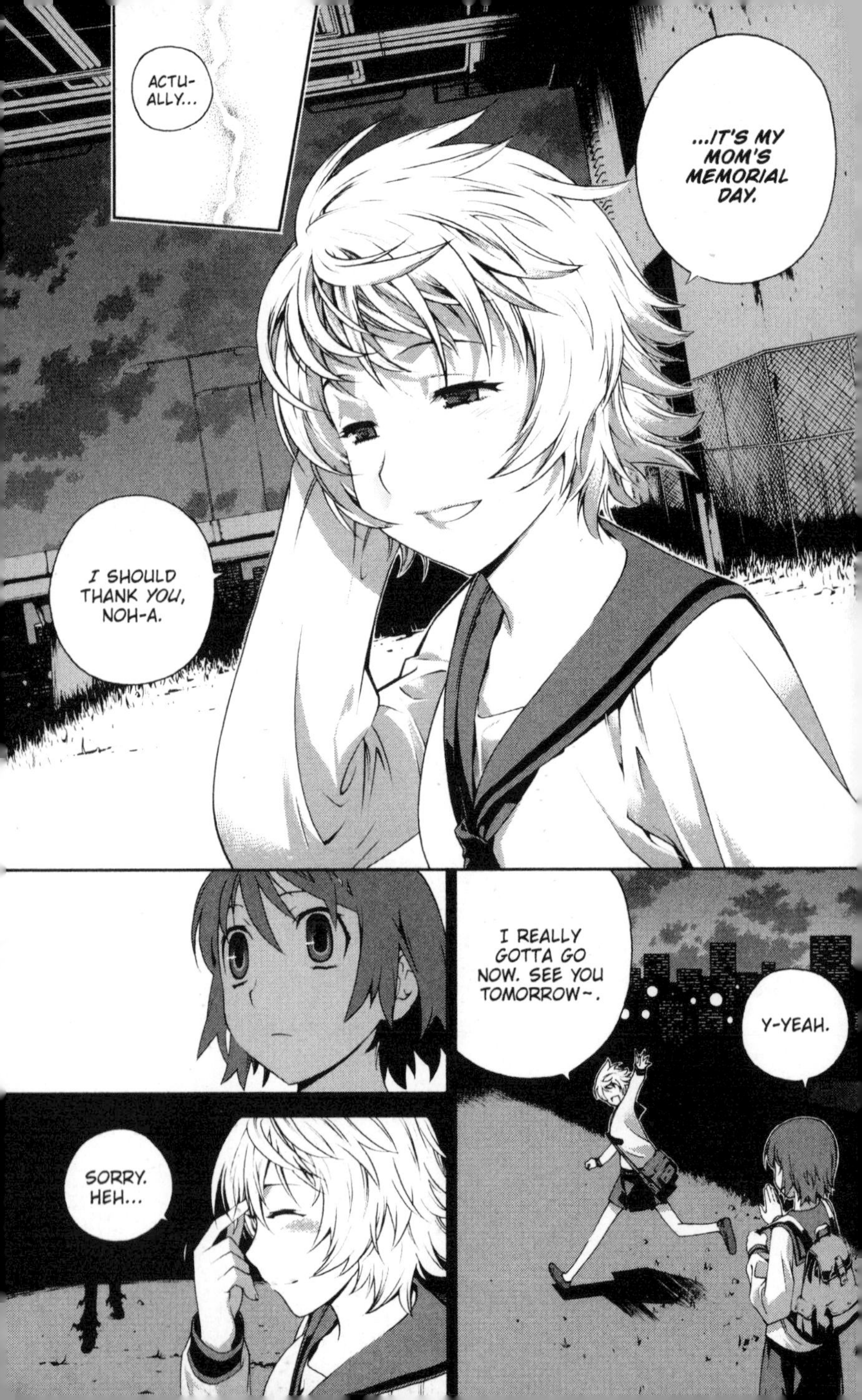
ACTU-ALLY...
...IT'S MY MOM'S MEMORIAL DAY.
I SHOULD THANK YOU, NOH-A.
SORRY. HEH...
I REALLY GOTTA GO NOW. SEE YOU TOMORROW~.
Y-YEAH.

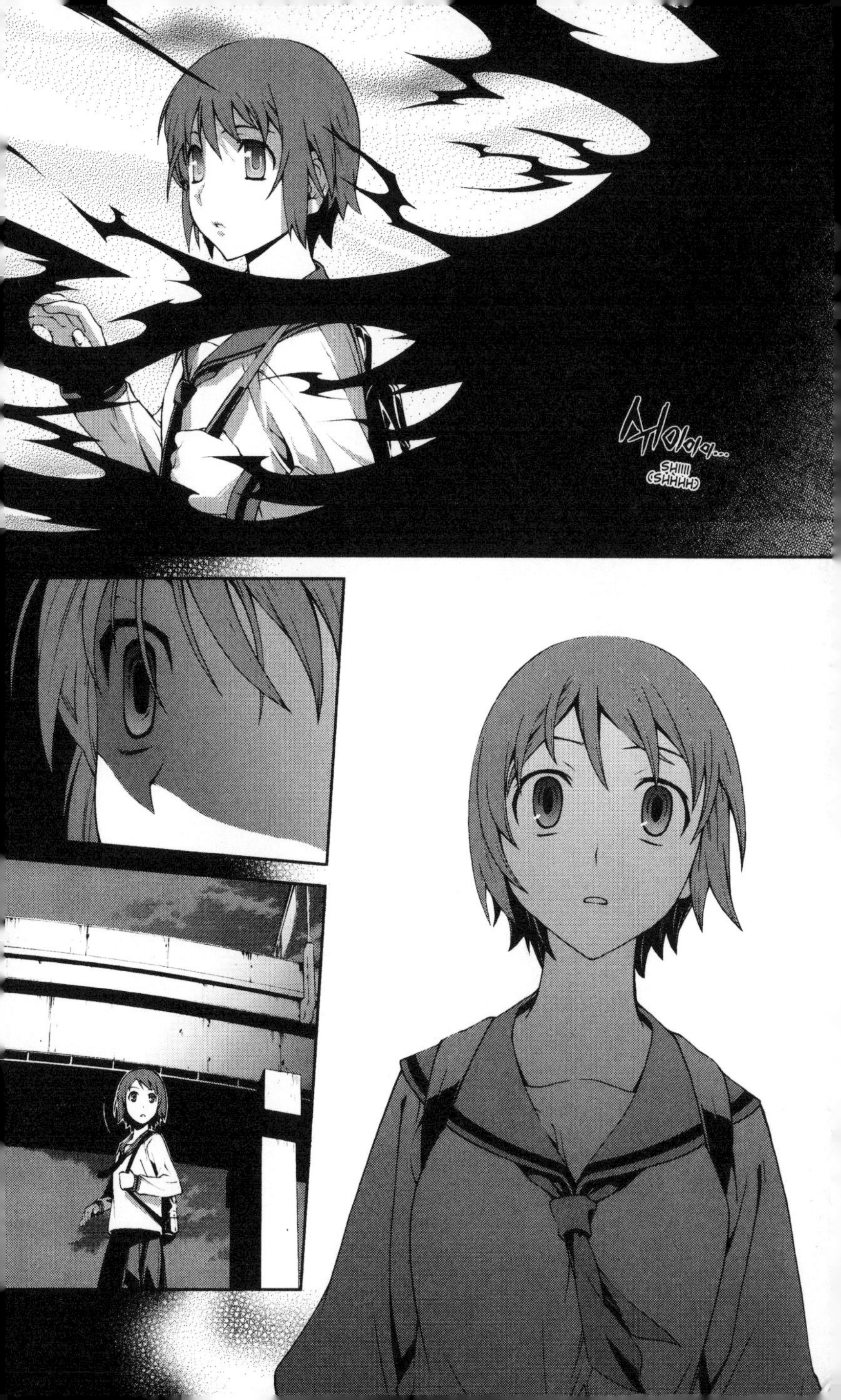
SHIIII
(SHHHH)

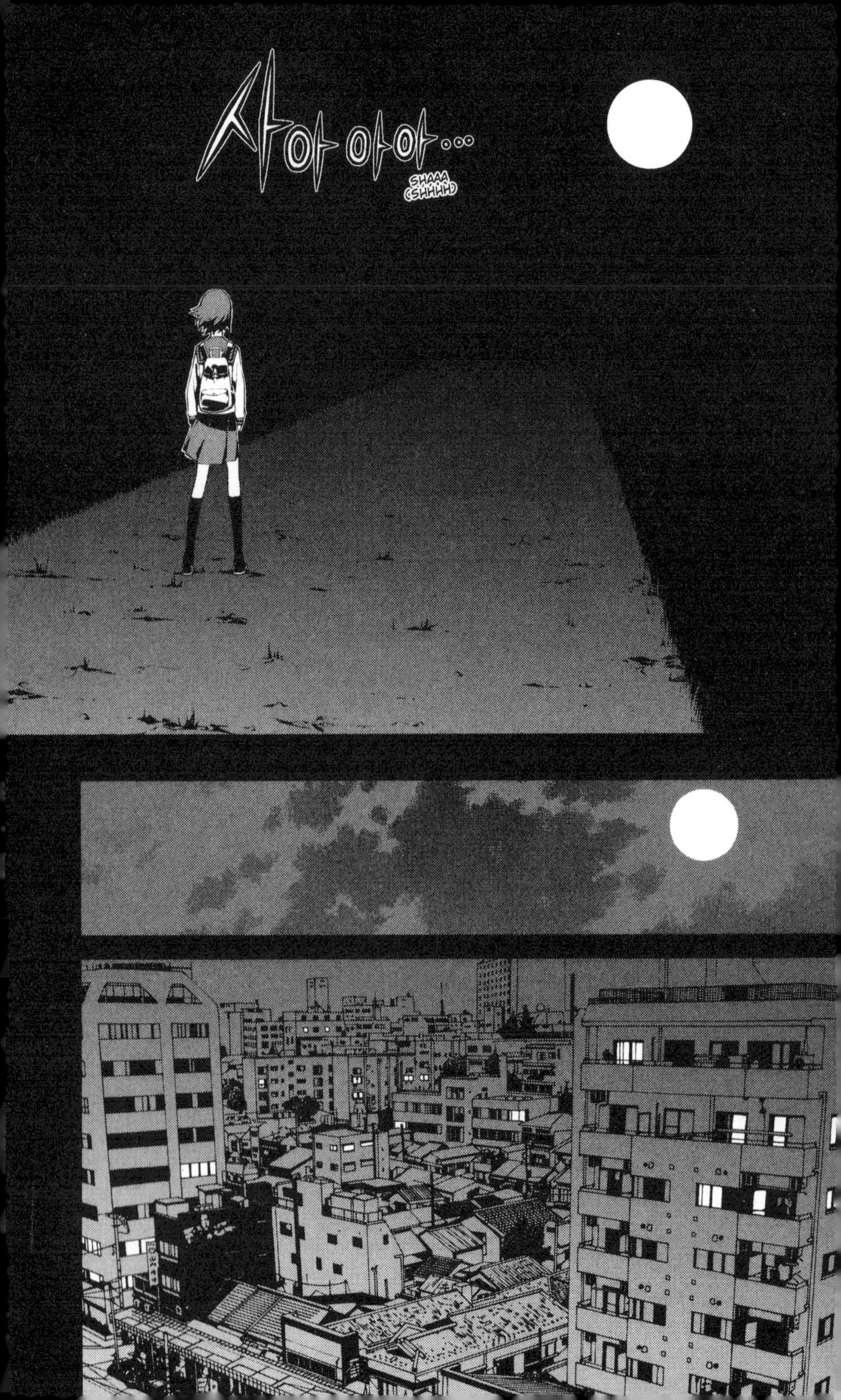
사아 아아...
SHAAA (SHHHH)

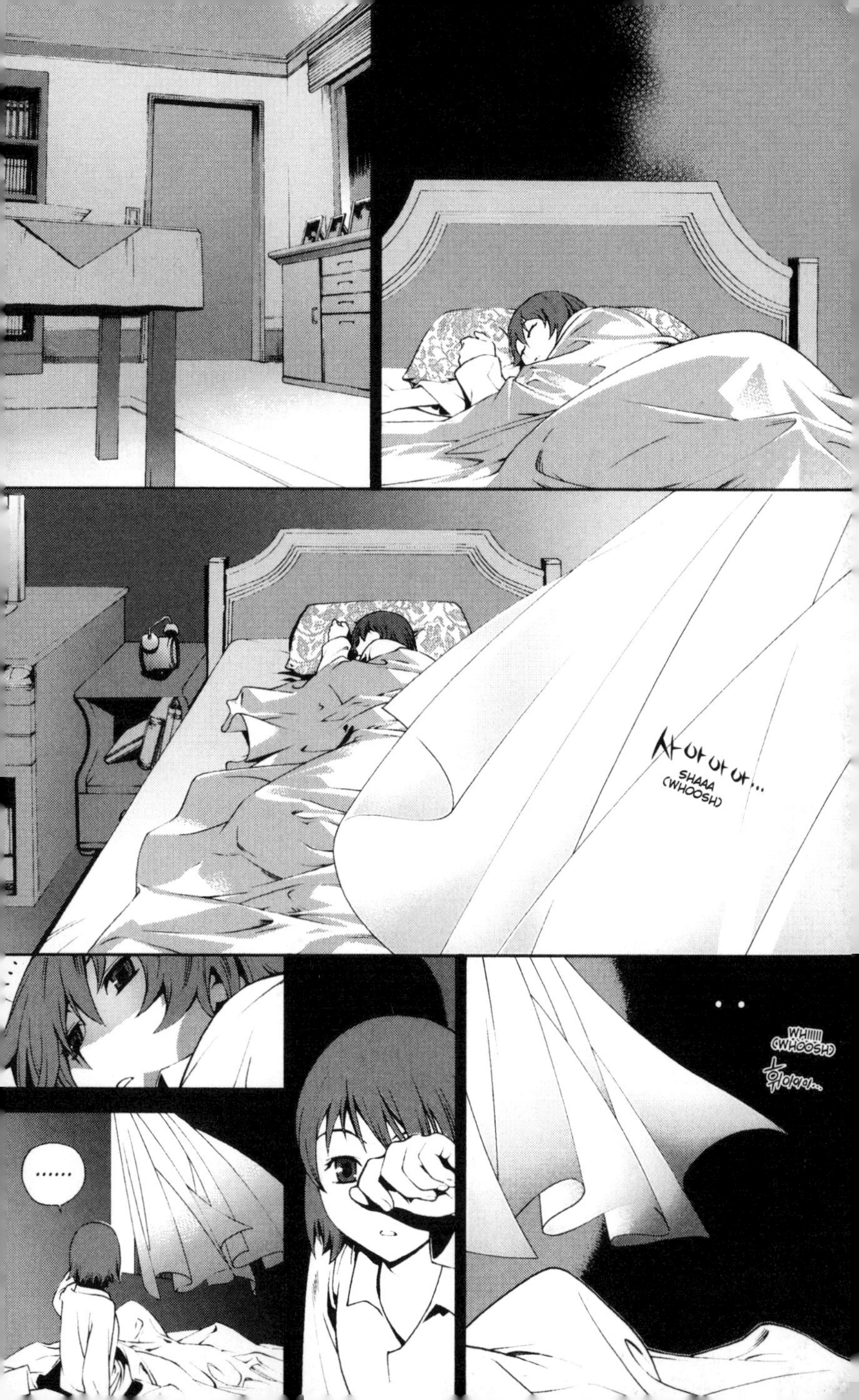
샤아아아...
SHAAA (WHOOSH)
....
......
• •
WHIIIII (WHOOSH)
휘이이이...

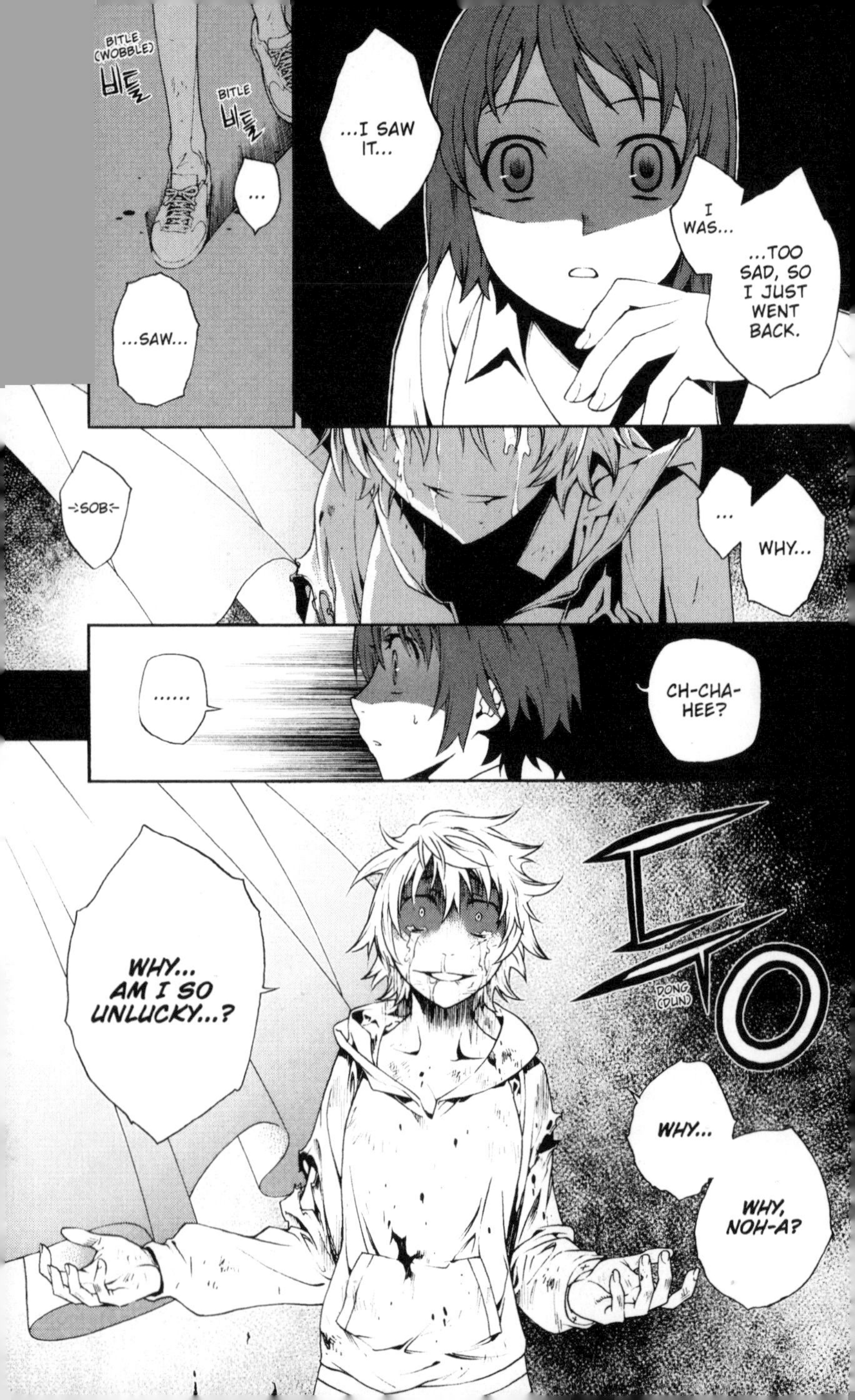
BITLE (WOBBLE)
비틀
BITLE
비틀
...
...SAW...
...I SAW IT...
I WAS...
...TOO SAD, SO I JUST WENT BACK.
-SOB-
... WHY...
......
CH-CHA-HEE?
WHY... AM I SO UNLUCKY...?
DONG (DUN)
WHY...
WHY, NOH-A?

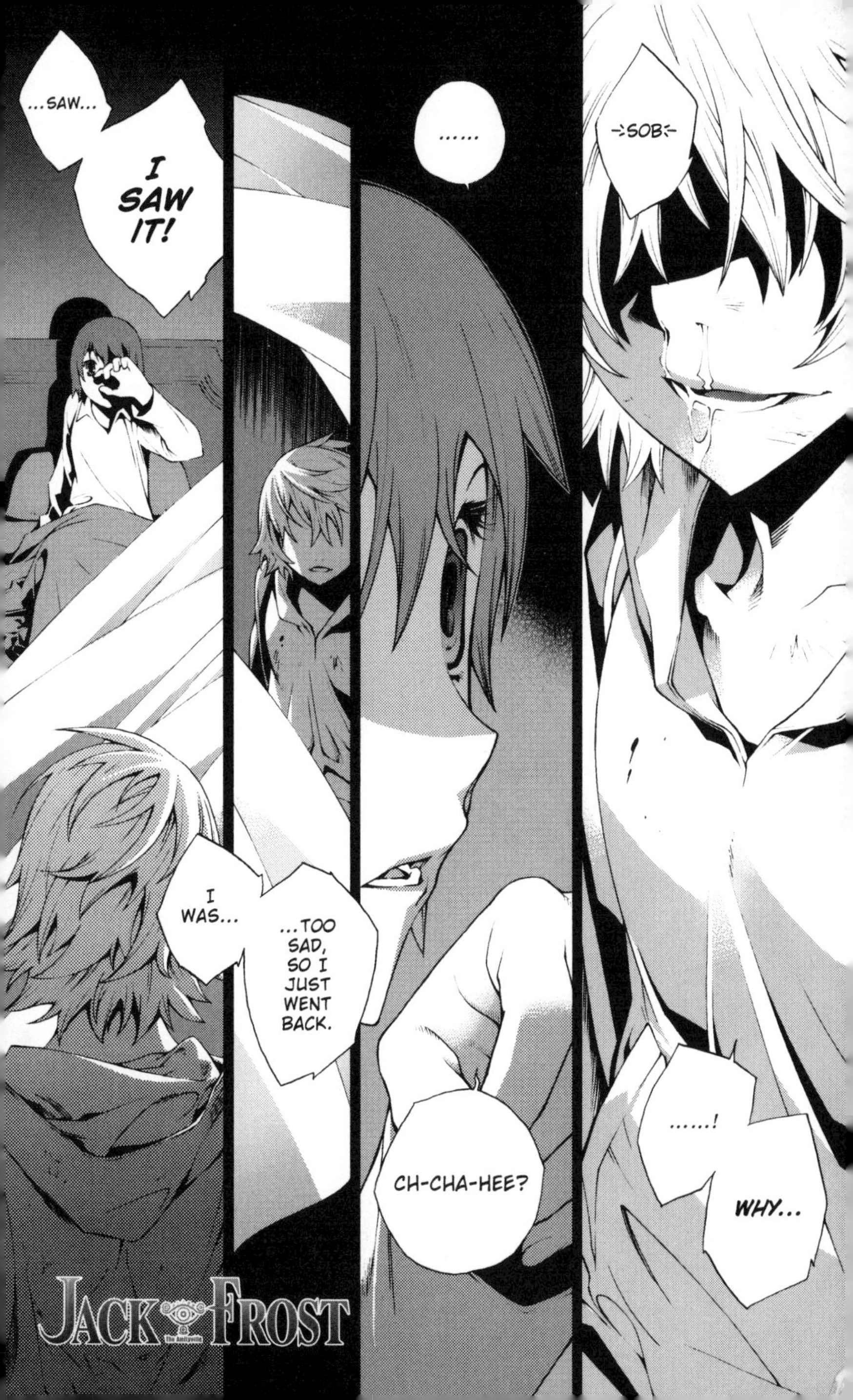
...SAW...
I SAW IT!
I WAS...
...TOO SAD, SO I JUST WENT BACK.
......
CH-CHA-HEE?
SOB
......!
WHY...
JACK FROST

WHY DID IT HAPPEN TO ME?
WHY...
WHY, NOH-A?
JACK FROST
The Amityville
VIOLENCE 9.
LOST LAKE

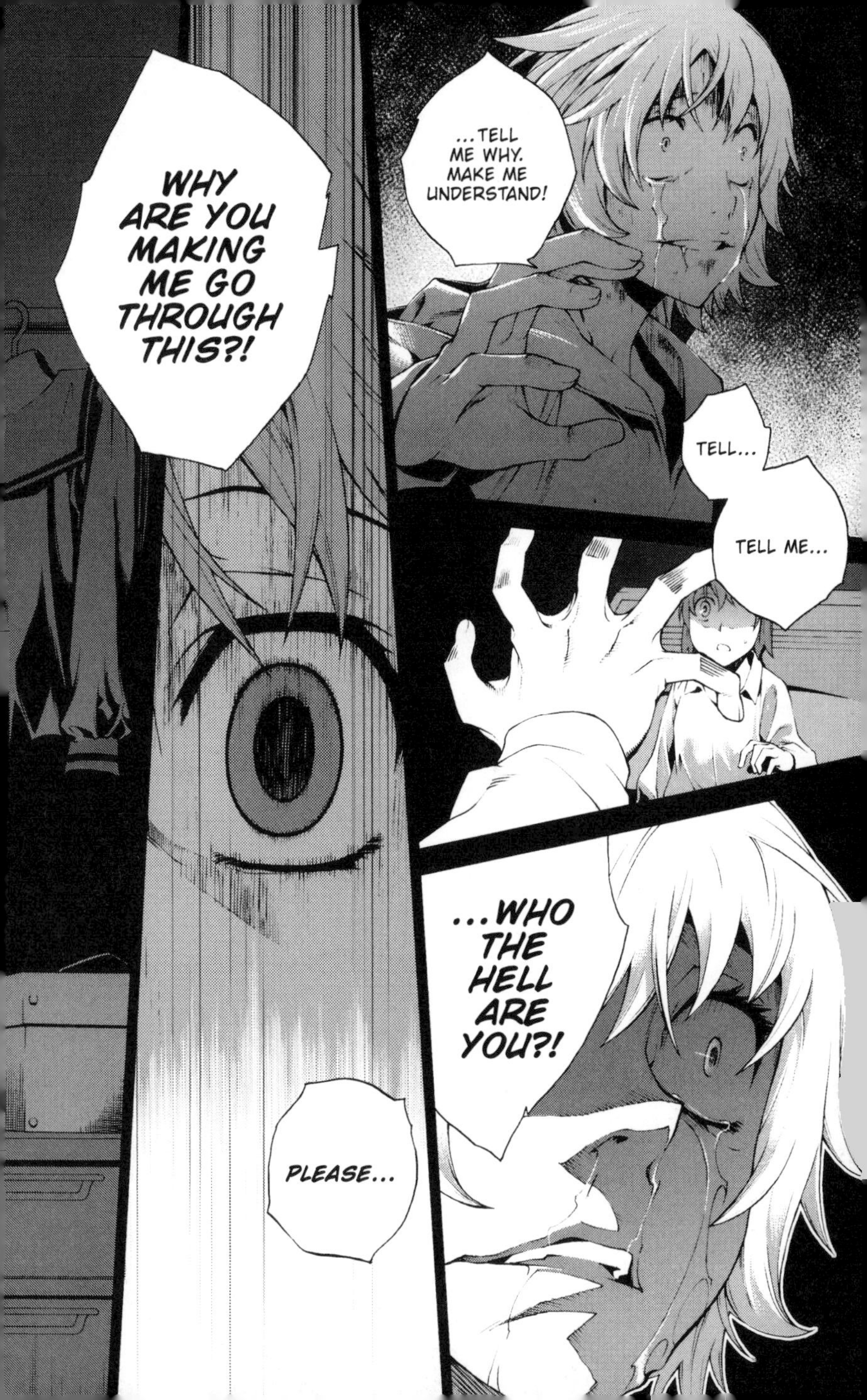
WHY ARE YOU MAKING ME GO THROUGH THIS?!
...TELL ME WHY. MAKE ME UNDERSTAND!
TELL...
TELL ME...
...WHO THE HELL ARE YOU?!
PLEASE...

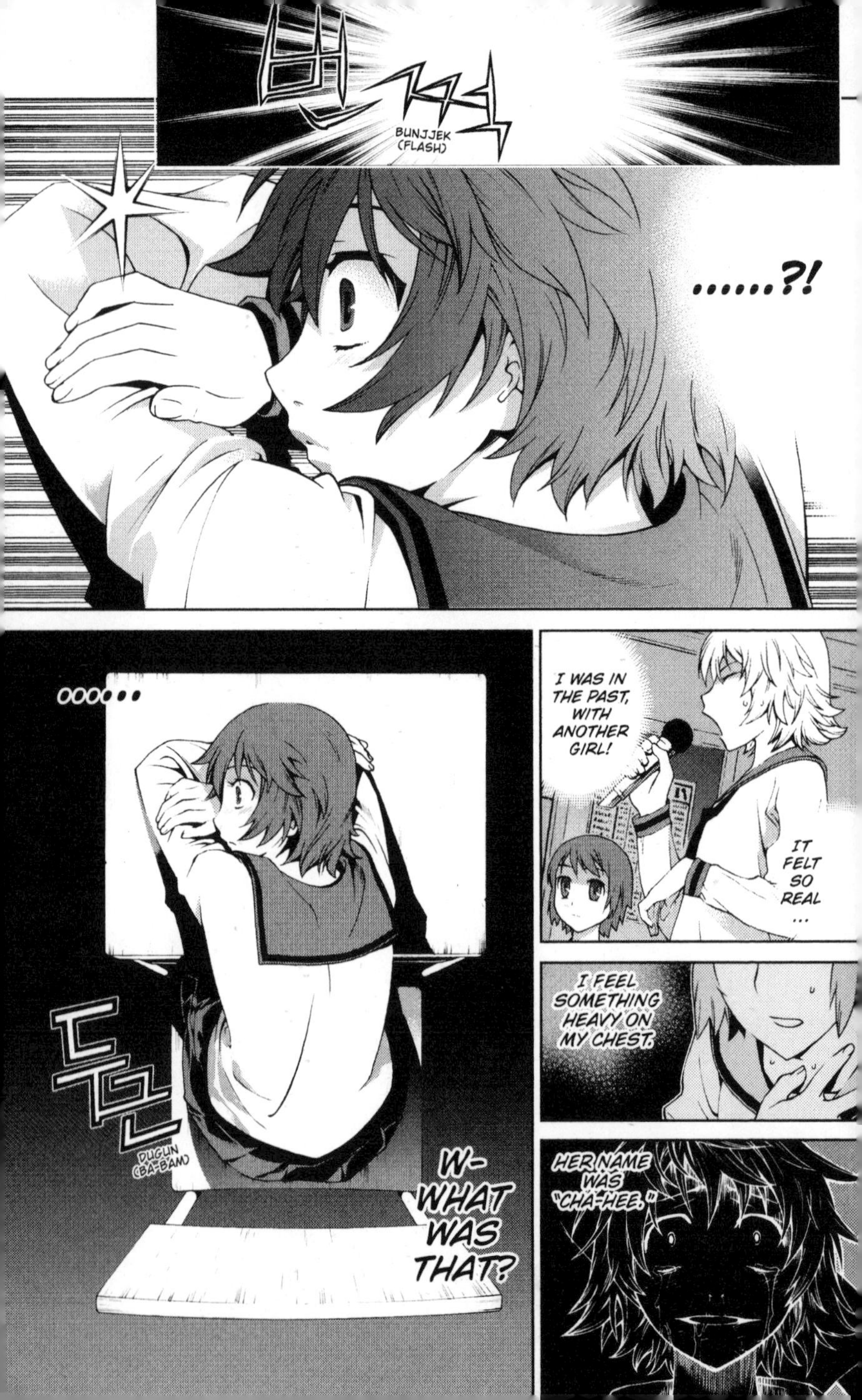
BUNJJEK (FLASH)
......?!
OOOO...
DUGUN (BA-BAM)
W-WHAT WAS THAT?
I WAS IN THE PAST, WITH ANOTHER GIRL!
IT FELT SO REAL...
I FEEL SOMETHING HEAVY ON MY CHEST.
HER NAME WAS "CHA-HEE."

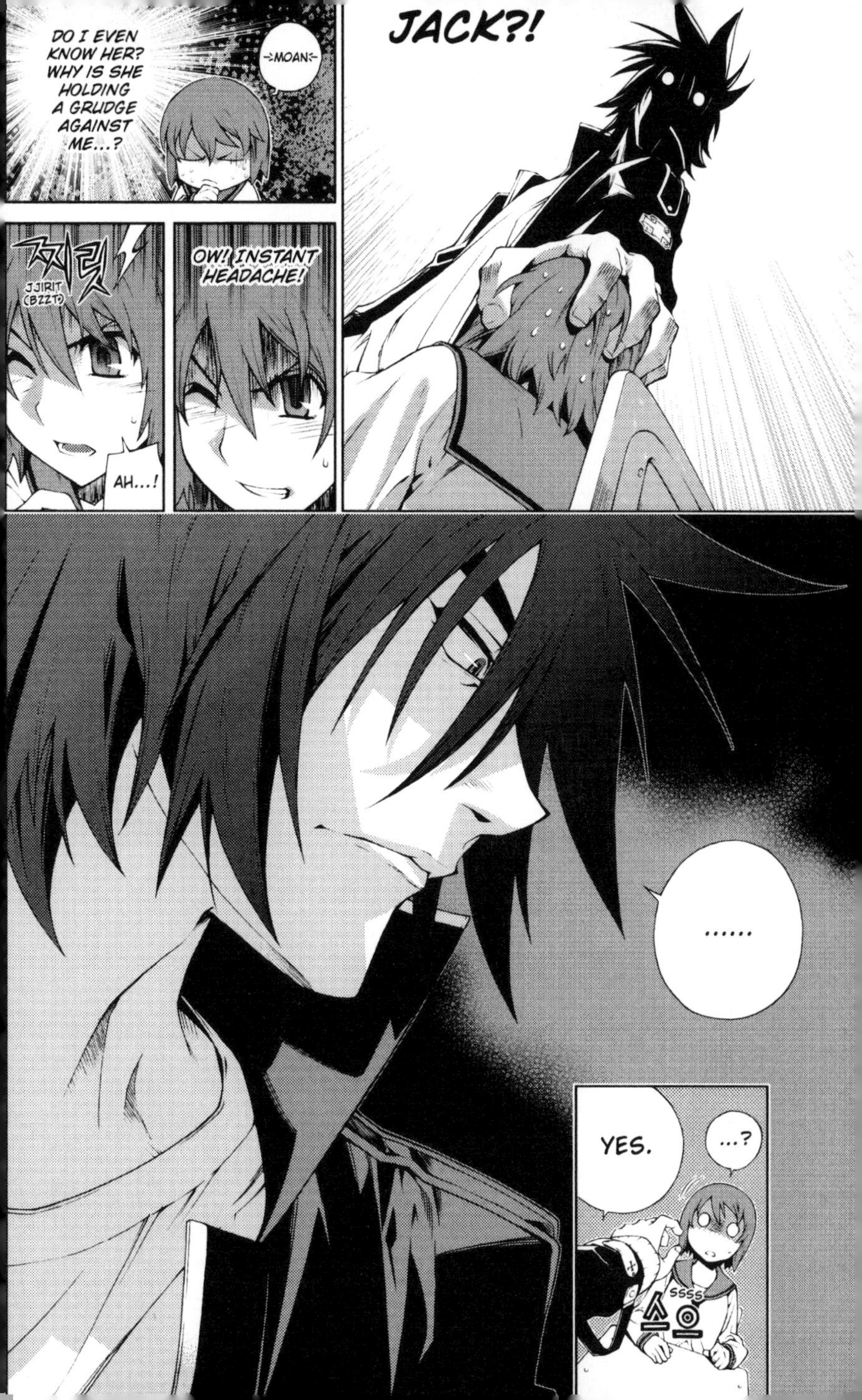
DO I EVEN KNOW HER? WHY IS SHE HOLDING A GRUDGE AGAINST ME...?
MOAN
JACK?!
쯔지릿
JJIRIT (BZZT)
AH...!
OW! INSTANT HEADACHE!
......
YES.
...?
SSSS

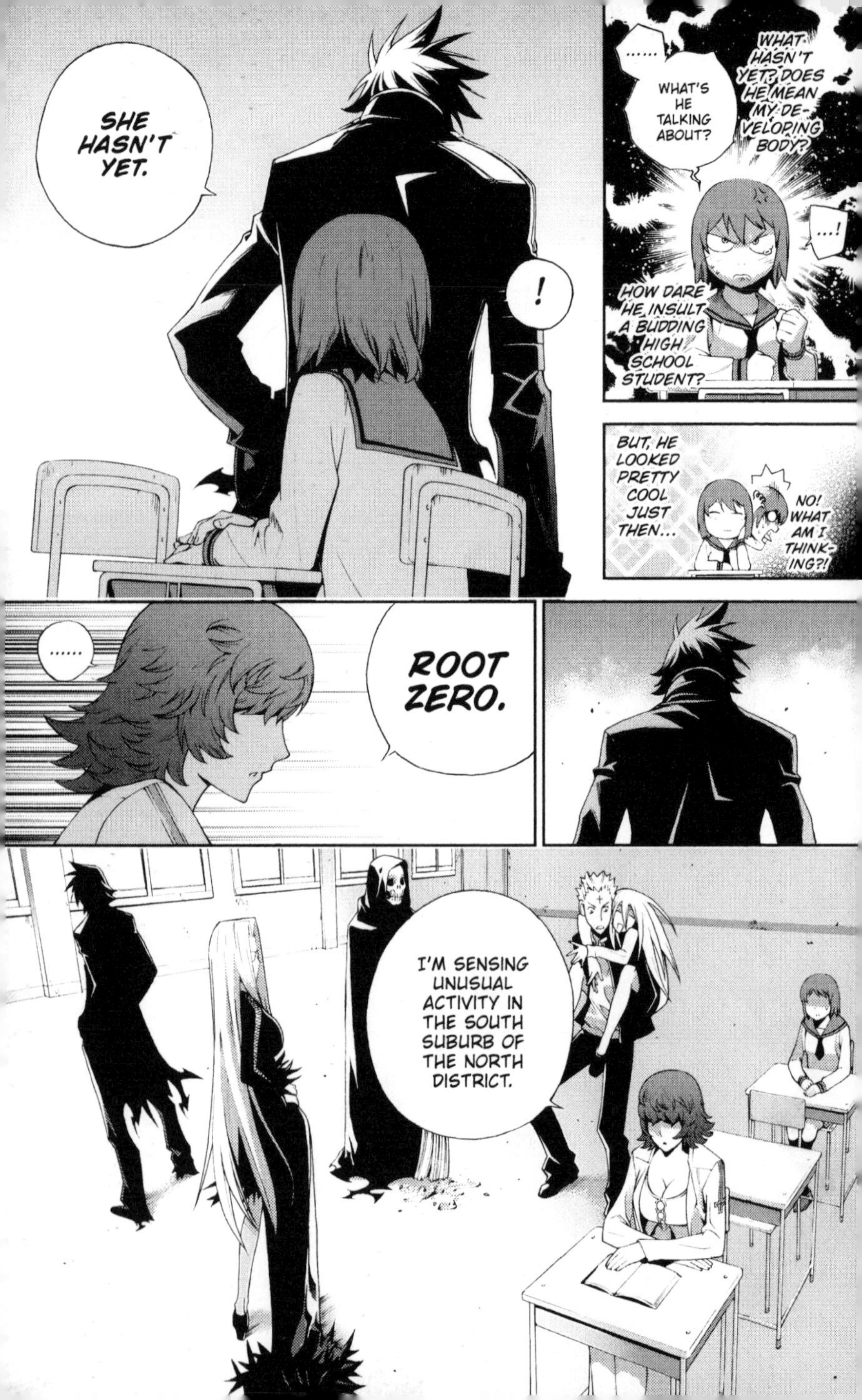
SHE HASN'T YET.
!
......
WHAT'S HE TALKING ABOUT?
WHAT HASN'T YET? DOES HE MEAN MY DE-VELOPING BODY?
...!
HOW DARE HE INSULT A BUDDING HIGH SCHOOL STUDENT?
BUT, HE LOOKED PRETTY COOL JUST THEN...
NO! WHAT AM I THINK-ING?!
......
ROOT ZERO.
I'M SENSING UNUSUAL ACTIVITY IN THE SOUTH SUBURB OF THE NORTH DISTRICT.

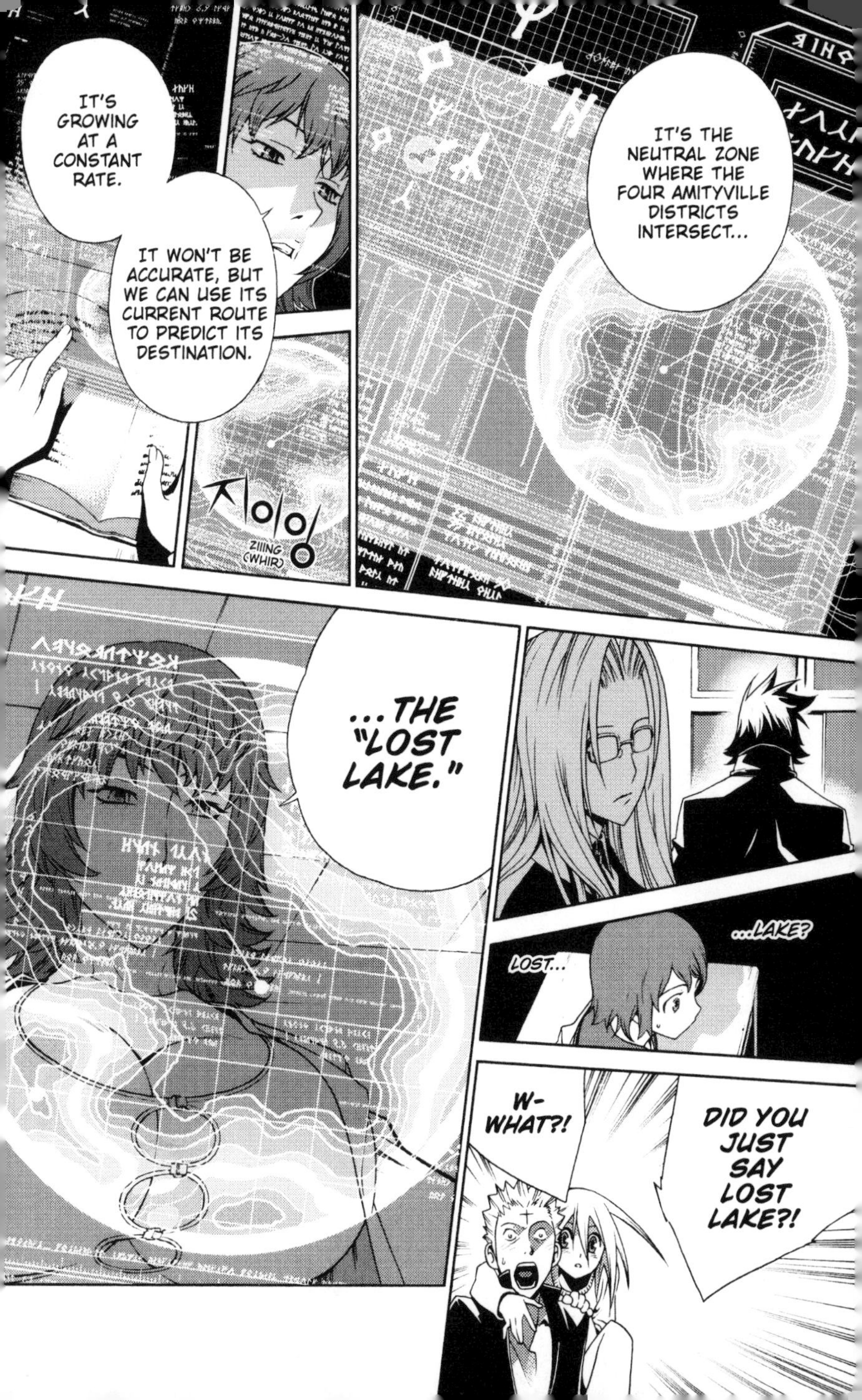
IT'S GROWING AT A CONSTANT RATE.
IT WON'T BE ACCURATE, BUT WE CAN USE ITS CURRENT ROUTE TO PREDICT ITS DESTINATION.
ZIIING (WHIR)
IT'S THE NEUTRAL ZONE WHERE THE FOUR AMITYVILLE DISTRICTS INTERSECT...
...THE "LOST LAKE."
LOST...
...LAKE?
W-WHAT?!
DID YOU JUST SAY LOST LAKE?!

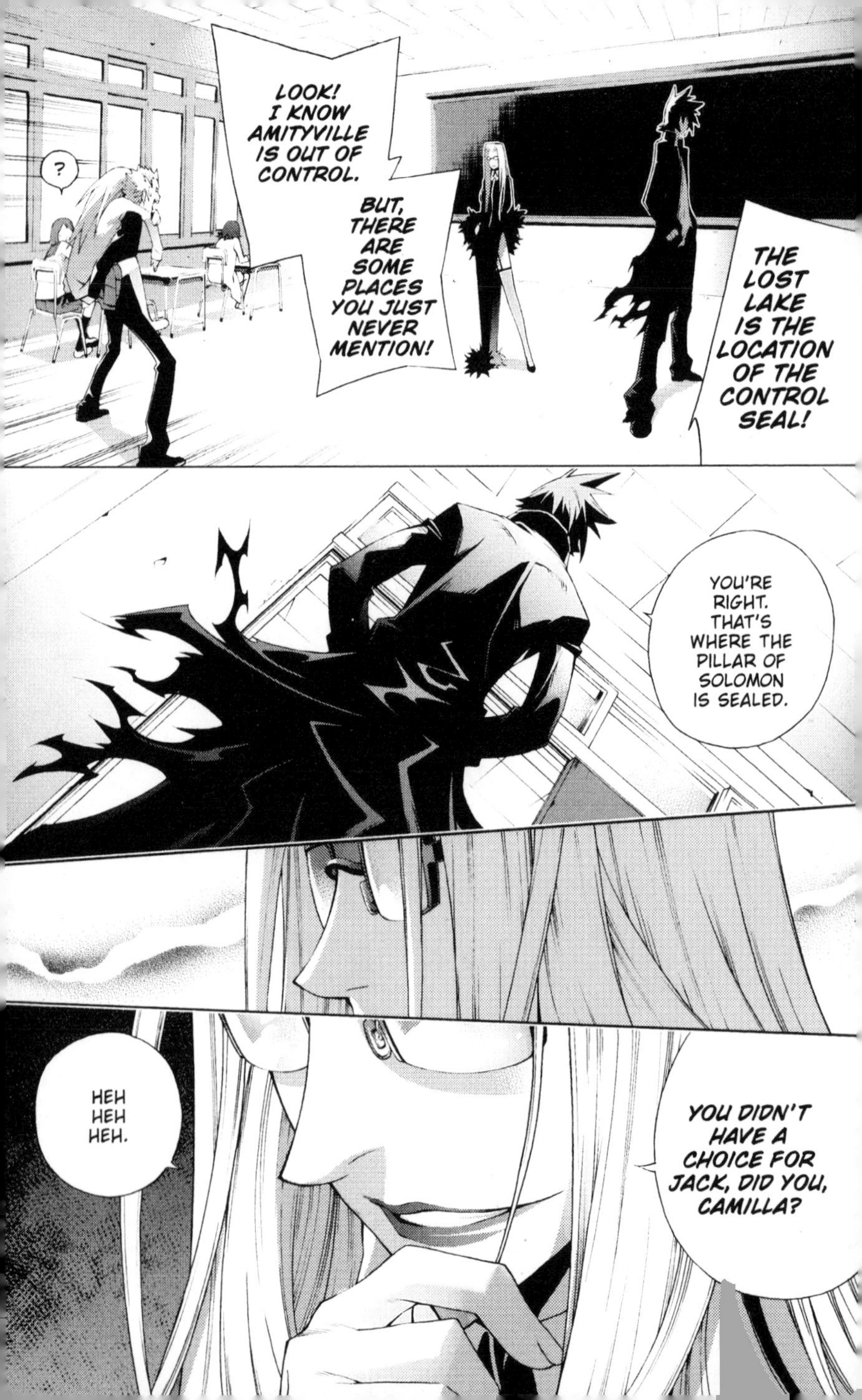
?
LOOK! I KNOW AMITYVILLE IS OUT OF CONTROL.
BUT, THERE ARE SOME PLACES YOU JUST NEVER MENTION!
THE LOST LAKE IS THE LOCATION OF THE CONTROL SEAL!
YOU'RE RIGHT. THAT'S WHERE THE PILLAR OF SOLOMON IS SEALED.
HEH HEH HEH.
YOU DIDN'T HAVE A CHOICE FOR JACK, DID YOU, CAMILLA?

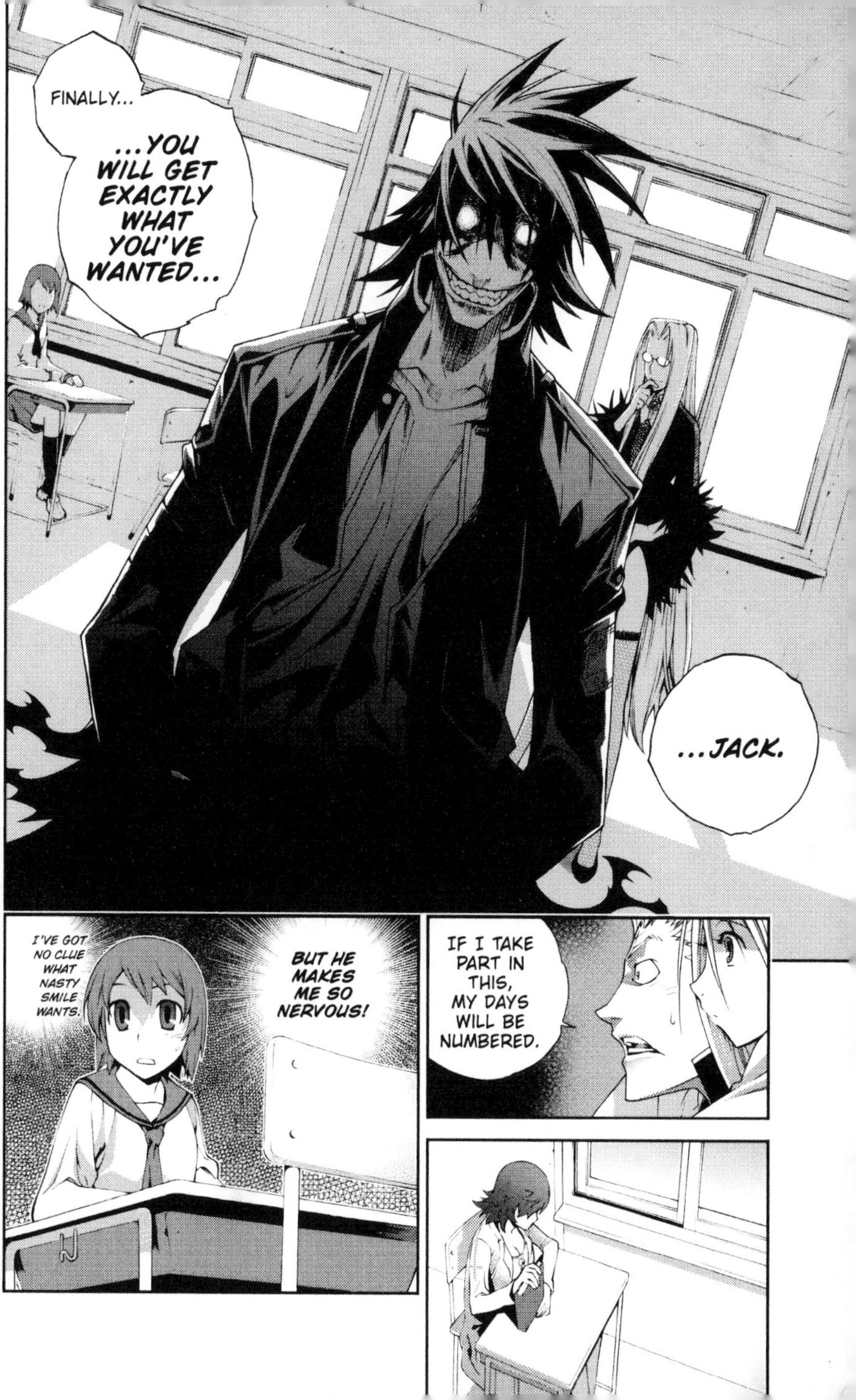
FINALLY...
...YOU WILL GET EXACTLY WHAT YOU'VE WANTED...
...JACK.
I'VE GOT NO CLUE WHAT NASTY SMILE WANTS.
BUT HE MAKES ME SO NERVOUS!
IF I TAKE PART IN THIS, MY DAYS WILL BE NUMBERED.

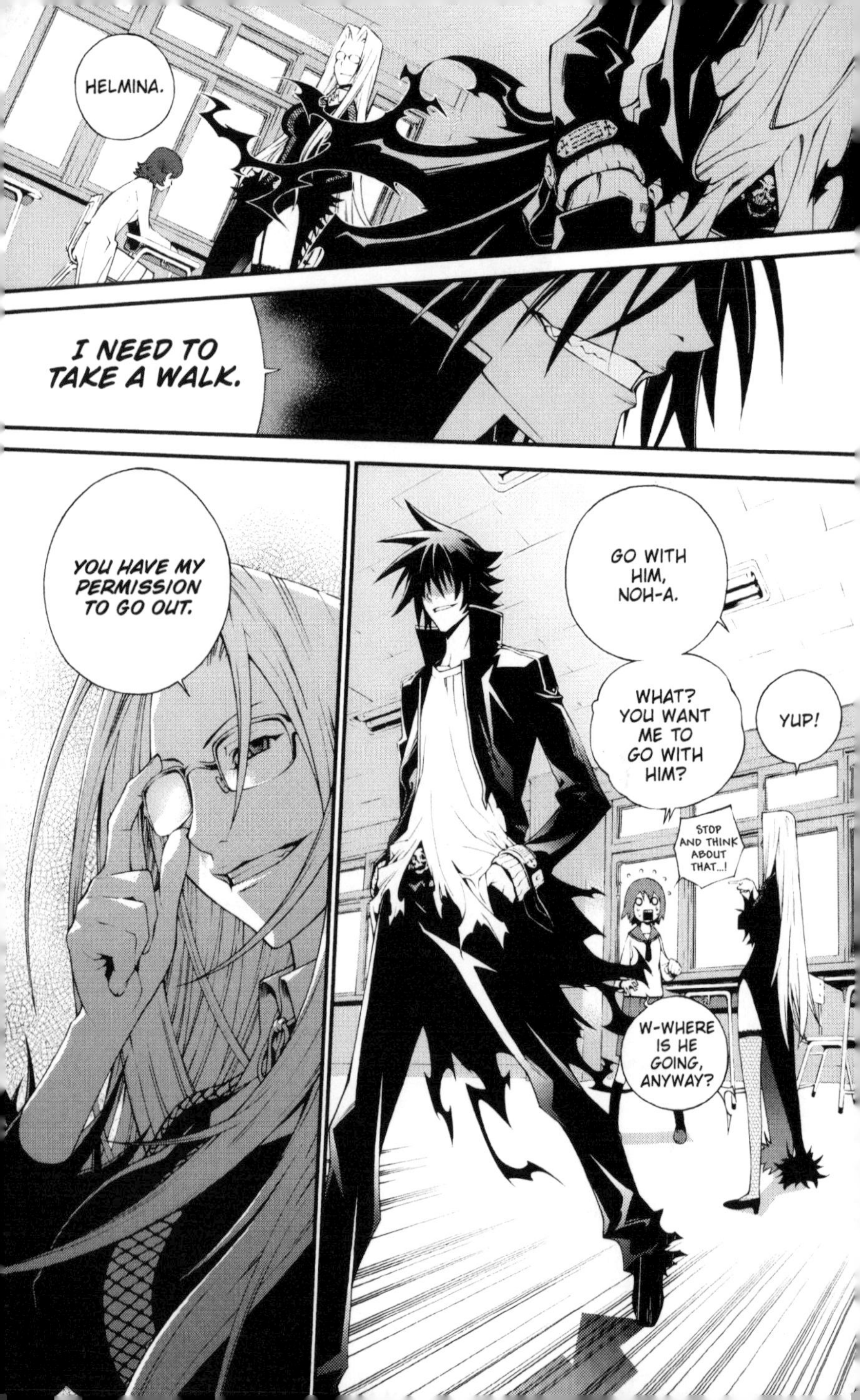
HELMINA.
I NEED TO TAKE A WALK.
YOU HAVE MY PERMISSION TO GO OUT.
GO WITH HIM, NOH-A.
WHAT? YOU WANT ME TO GO WITH HIM?
YUP!
STOP AND THINK ABOUT THAT...!
W-WHERE IS HE GOING, ANYWAY?

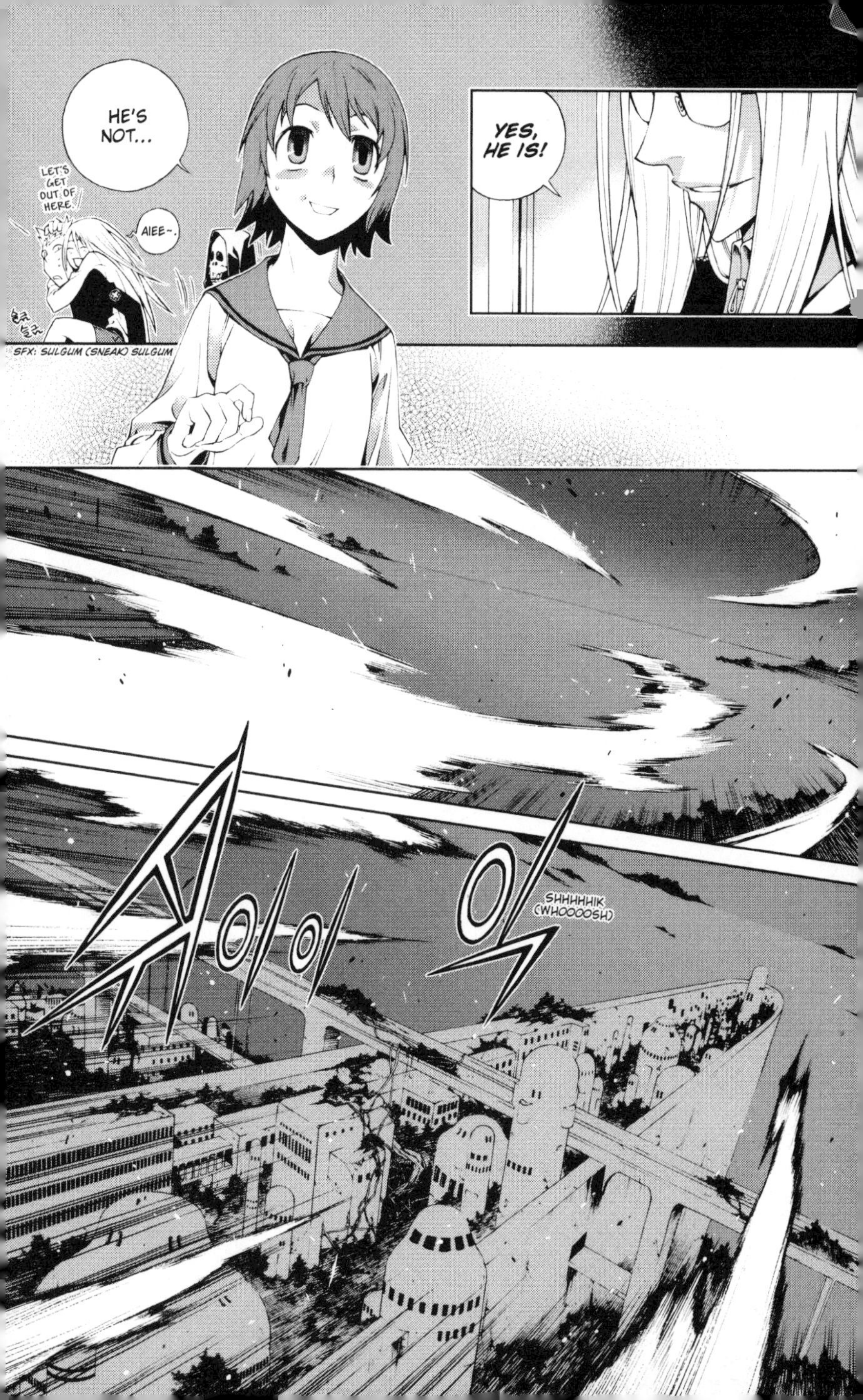
HE'S NOT...
LET'S GET OUT OF HERE.
AIEE~.
SFX: SULGUM (SNEAK) SULGUM
YES, HE IS!
SHHHHHIK (WHOOOOSH)

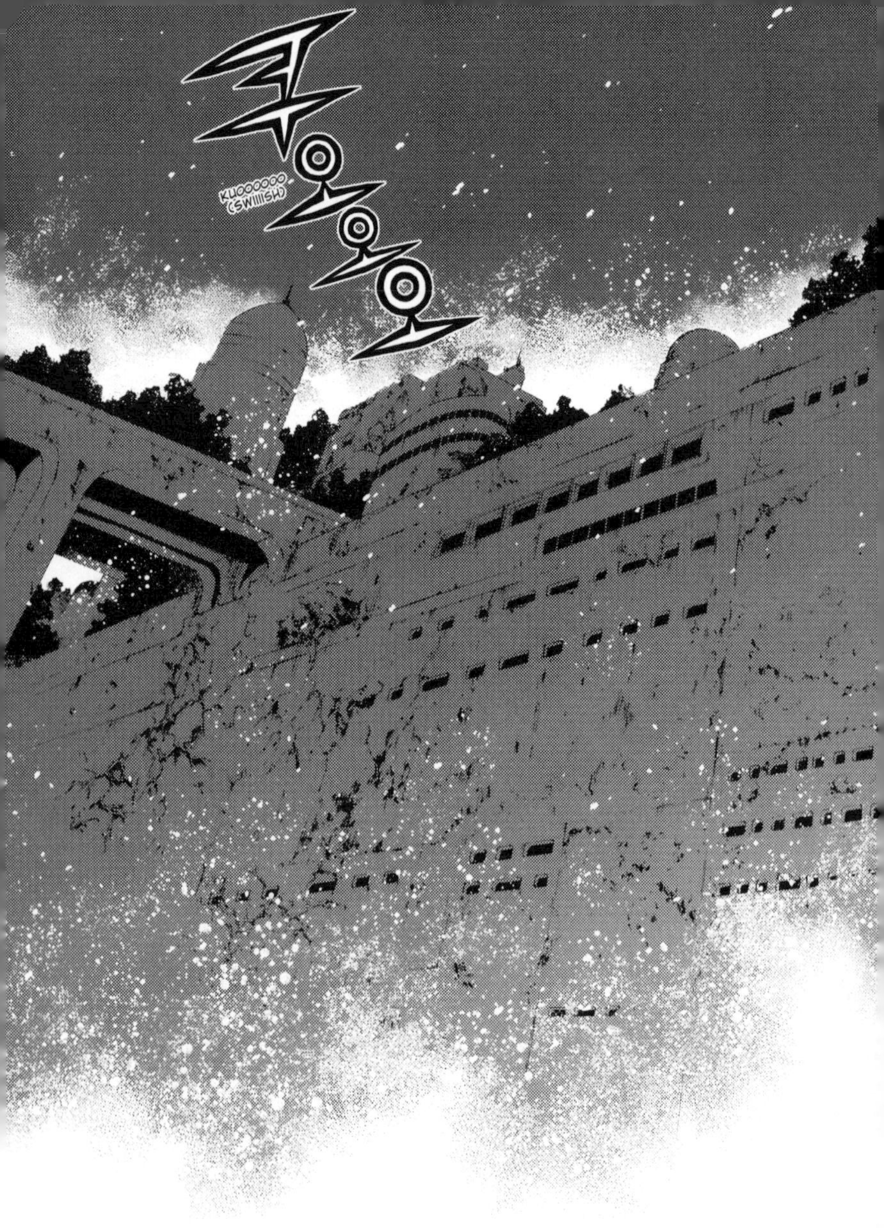
KUOOOOOO
(SWIIIISH)

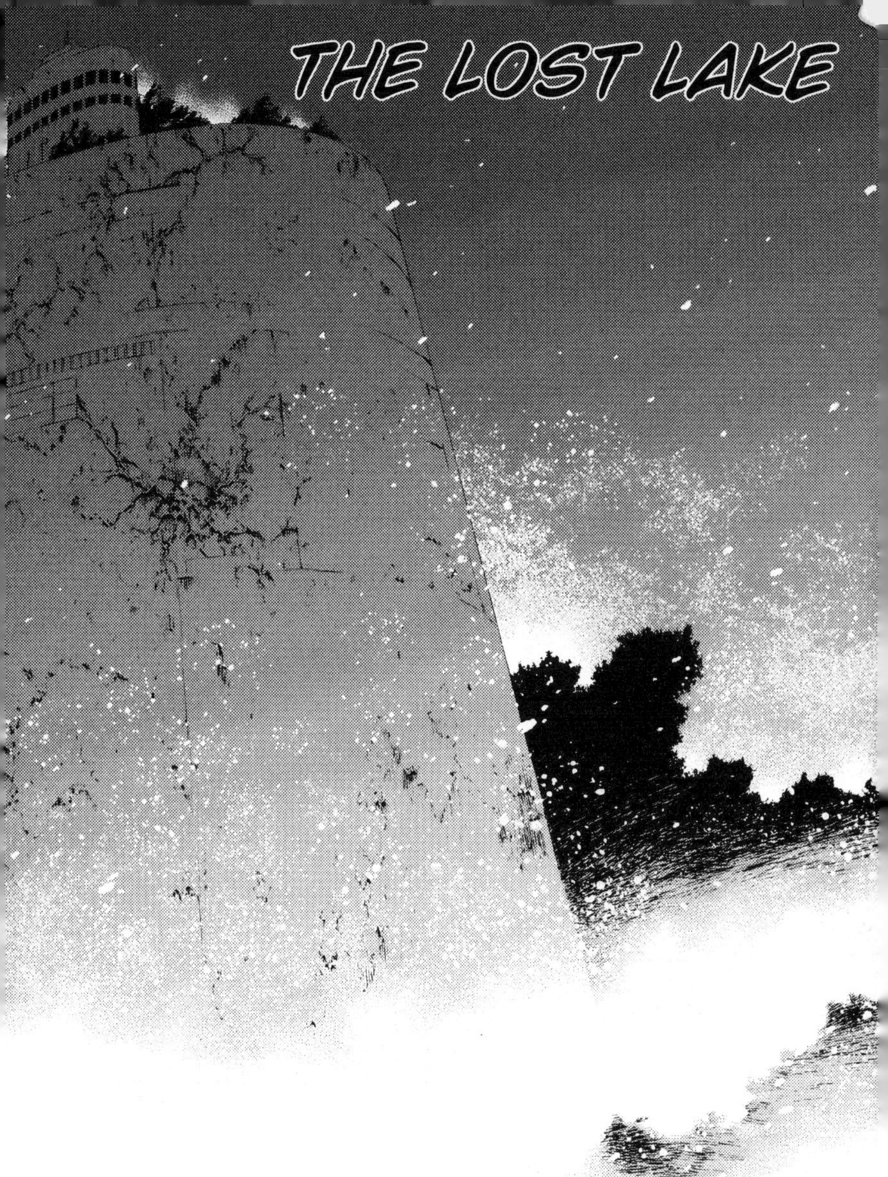
THE LOST LAKE

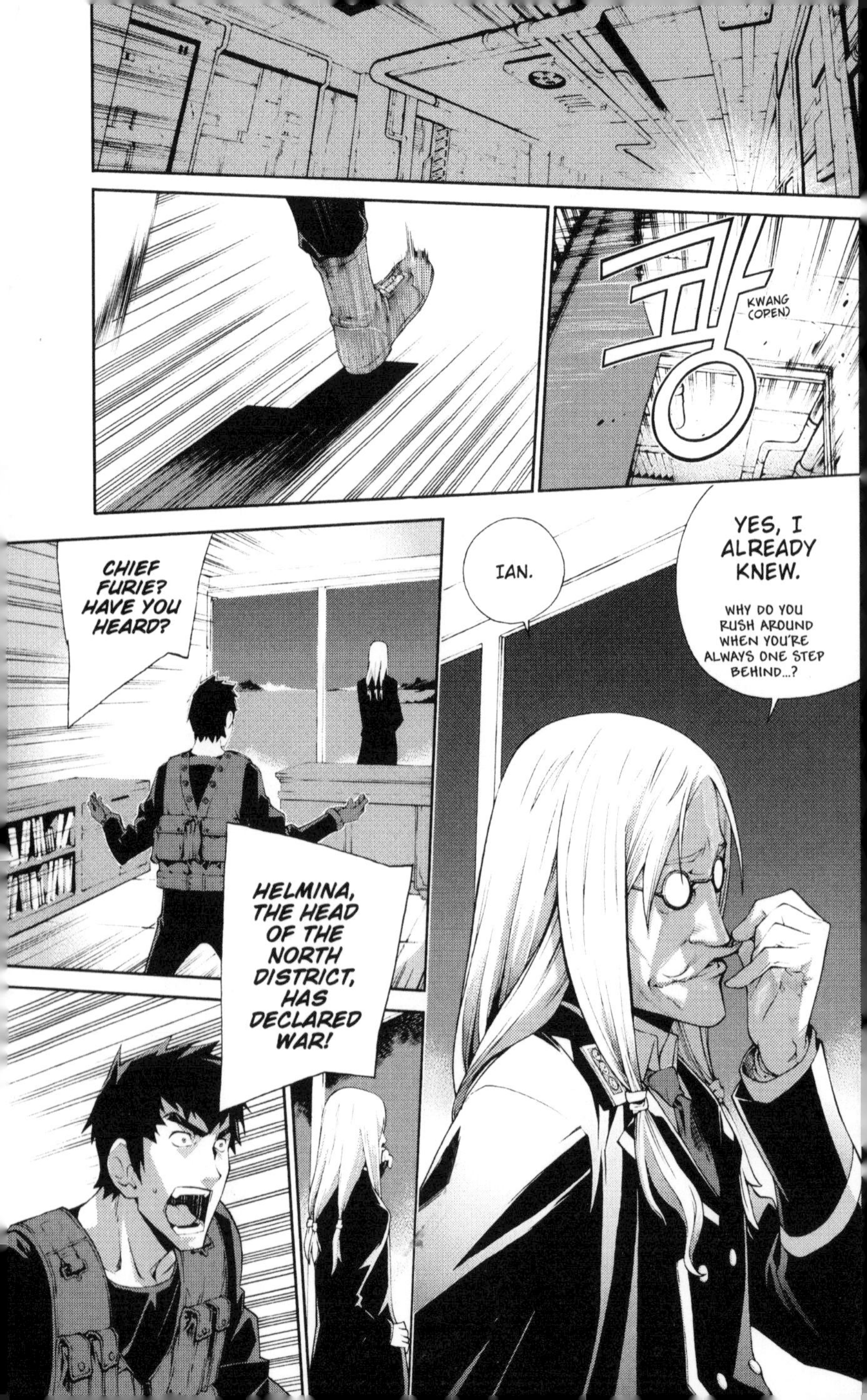

쾅
KWANG (OPEN)
CHIEF FURIE? HAVE YOU HEARD?
HELMINA, THE HEAD OF THE NORTH DISTRICT, HAS DECLARED WAR!
IAN.
YES, I ALREADY KNEW.
WHY DO YOU RUSH AROUND WHEN YOU'RE ALWAYS ONE STEP BEHIND...?

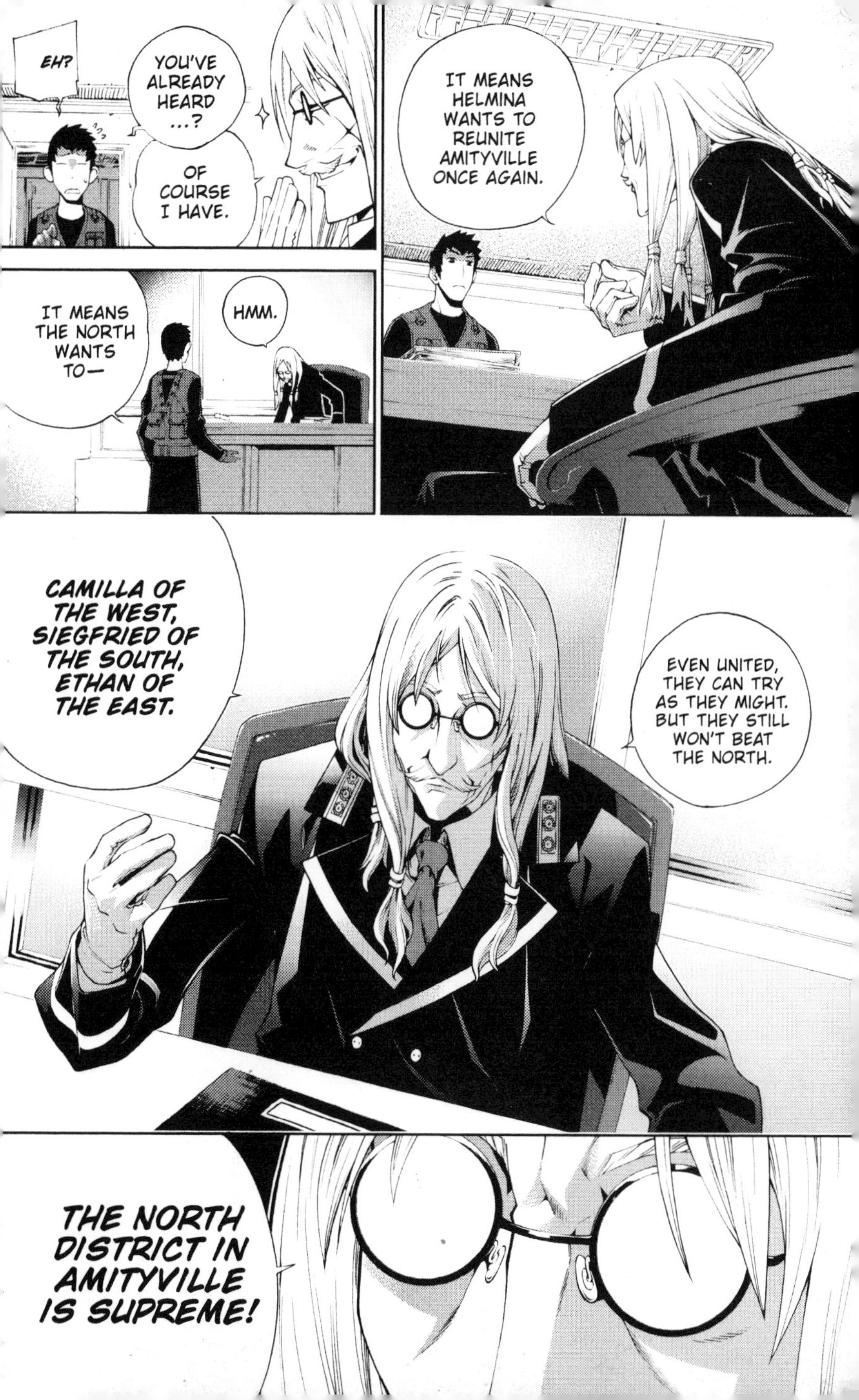
EH?
YOU'VE ALREADY HEARD ...?
OF COURSE I HAVE.
IT MEANS HELMINA WANTS TO REUNITE AMITYVILLE ONCE AGAIN.
IT MEANS THE NORTH WANTS TO—
HMM.
CAMILLA OF THE WEST, SIEGFRIED OF THE SOUTH, ETHAN OF THE EAST.
EVEN UNITED, THEY CAN TRY AS THEY MIGHT. BUT THEY STILL WON'T BEAT THE NORTH.
THE NORTH DISTRICT IN AMITYVILLE IS SUPREME!

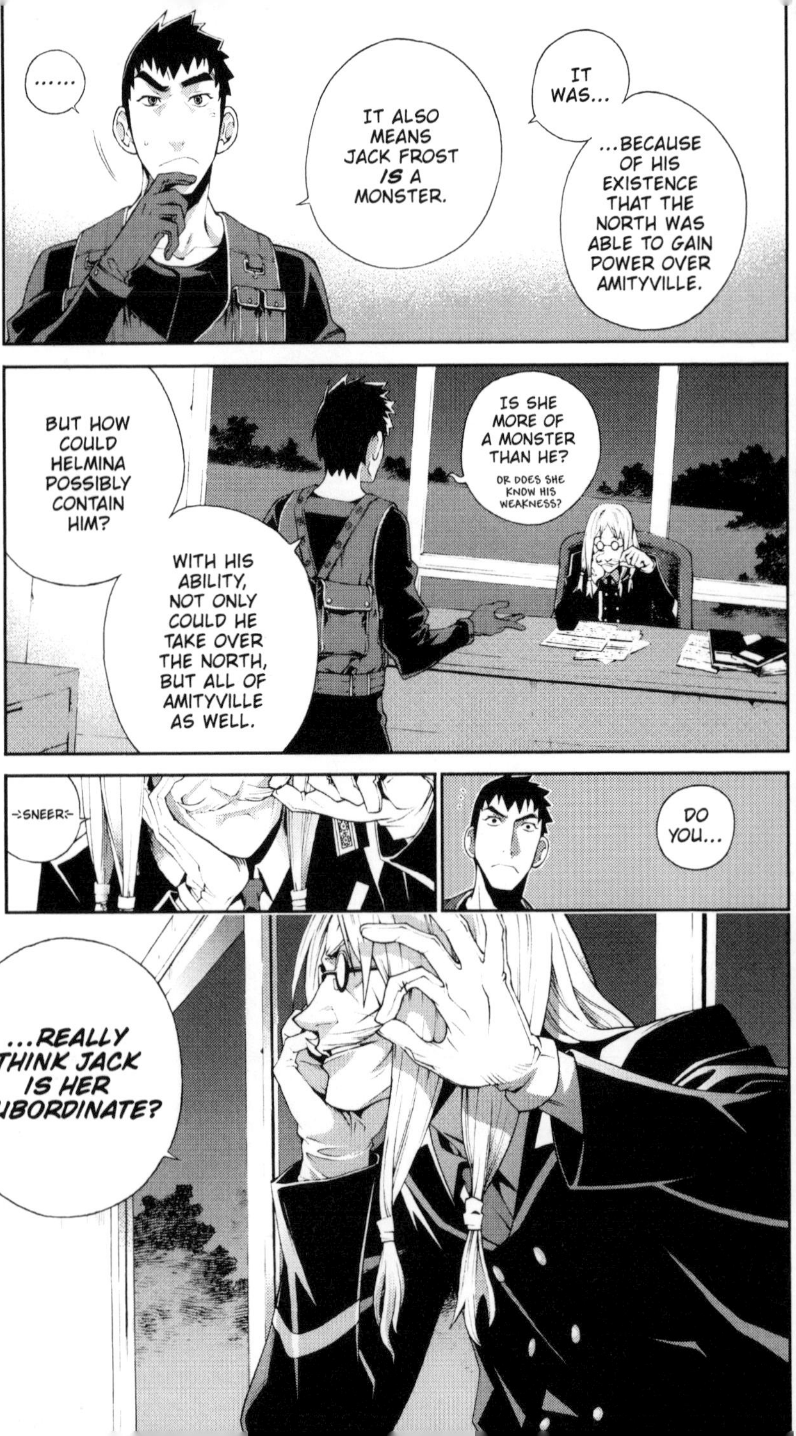
......
IT ALSO MEANS JACK FROST IS A MONSTER.
IT WAS...
...BECAUSE OF HIS EXISTENCE THAT THE NORTH WAS ABLE TO GAIN POWER OVER AMITYVILLE.
BUT HOW COULD HELMINA POSSIBLY CONTAIN HIM?
WITH HIS ABILITY, NOT ONLY COULD HE TAKE OVER THE NORTH, BUT ALL OF AMITYVILLE AS WELL.
IS SHE MORE OF A MONSTER THAN HE?
OR DOES SHE KNOW HIS WEAKNESS?
-›SNEER‹-
DO YOU...
...REALLY THINK JACK IS HER SUBORDINATE?

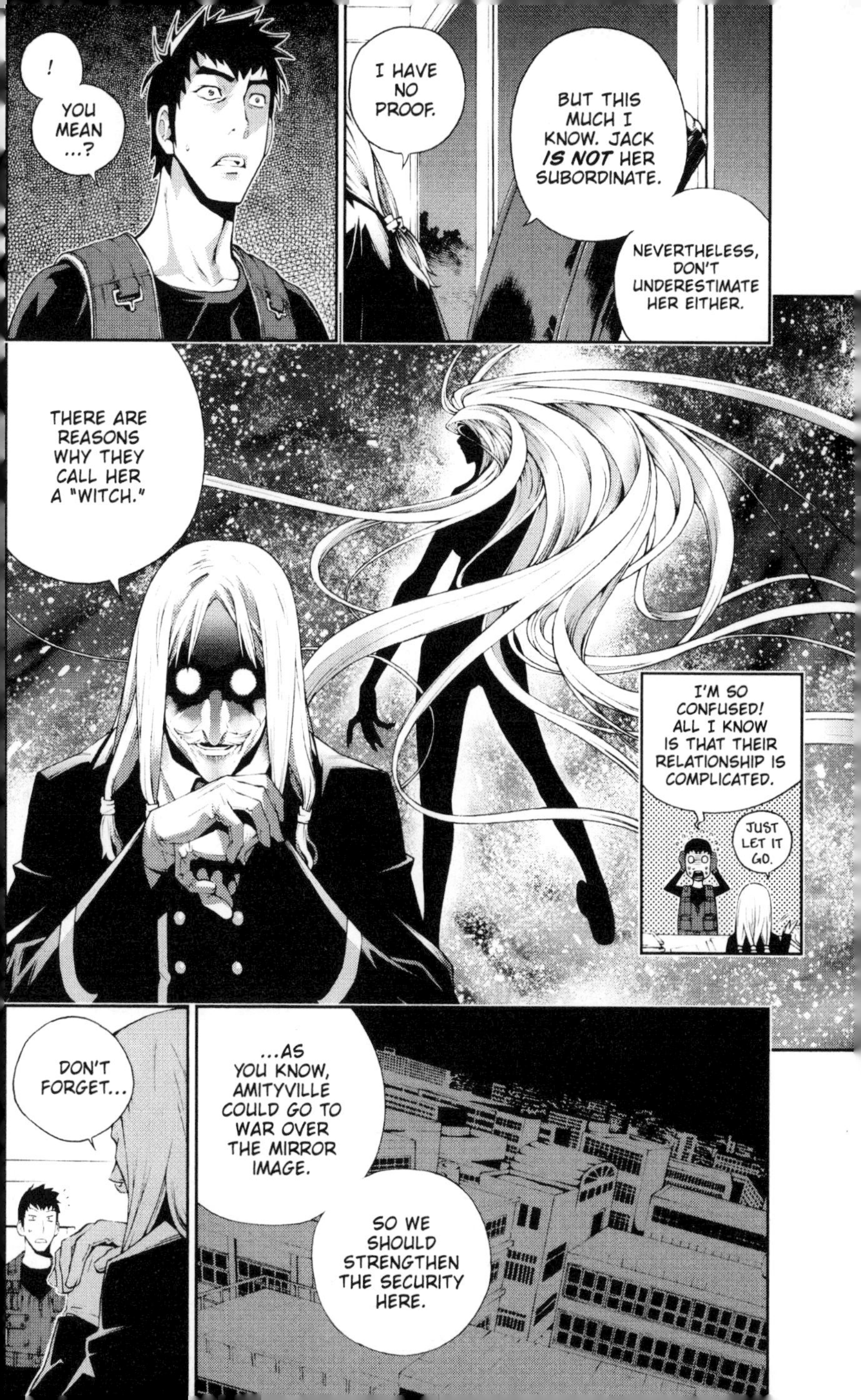
!
YOU MEAN ...?
I HAVE NO PROOF.
BUT THIS MUCH I KNOW. JACK IS NOT HER SUBORDINATE.
NEVERTHELESS, DON'T UNDERESTIMATE HER EITHER.
THERE ARE REASONS WHY THEY CALL HER A "WITCH."
I'M SO CONFUSED! ALL I KNOW IS THAT THEIR RELATIONSHIP IS COMPLICATED.
JUST LET IT GO.
DON'T FORGET...
...AS YOU KNOW, AMITYVILLE COULD GO TO WAR OVER THE MIRROR IMAGE.
SO WE SHOULD STRENGTHEN THE SECURITY HERE.

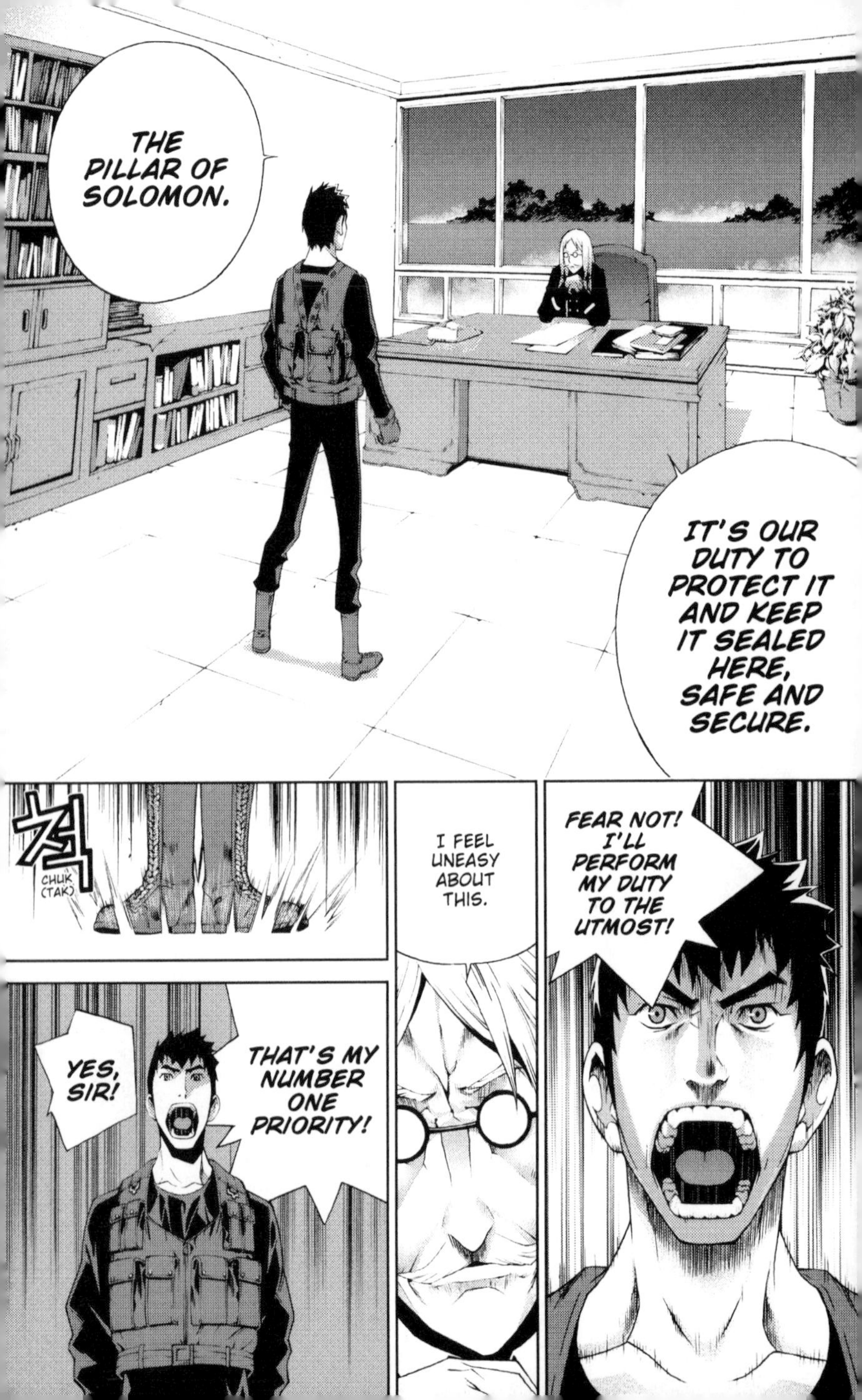
THE PILLAR OF SOLOMON.
IT'S OUR DUTY TO PROTECT IT AND KEEP IT SEALED HERE, SAFE AND SECURE.
CHUK (TAK)
YES, SIR!
THAT'S MY NUMBER ONE PRIORITY!
I FEEL UNEASY ABOUT THIS.
FEAR NOT! I'LL PERFORM MY DUTY TO THE UTMOST!

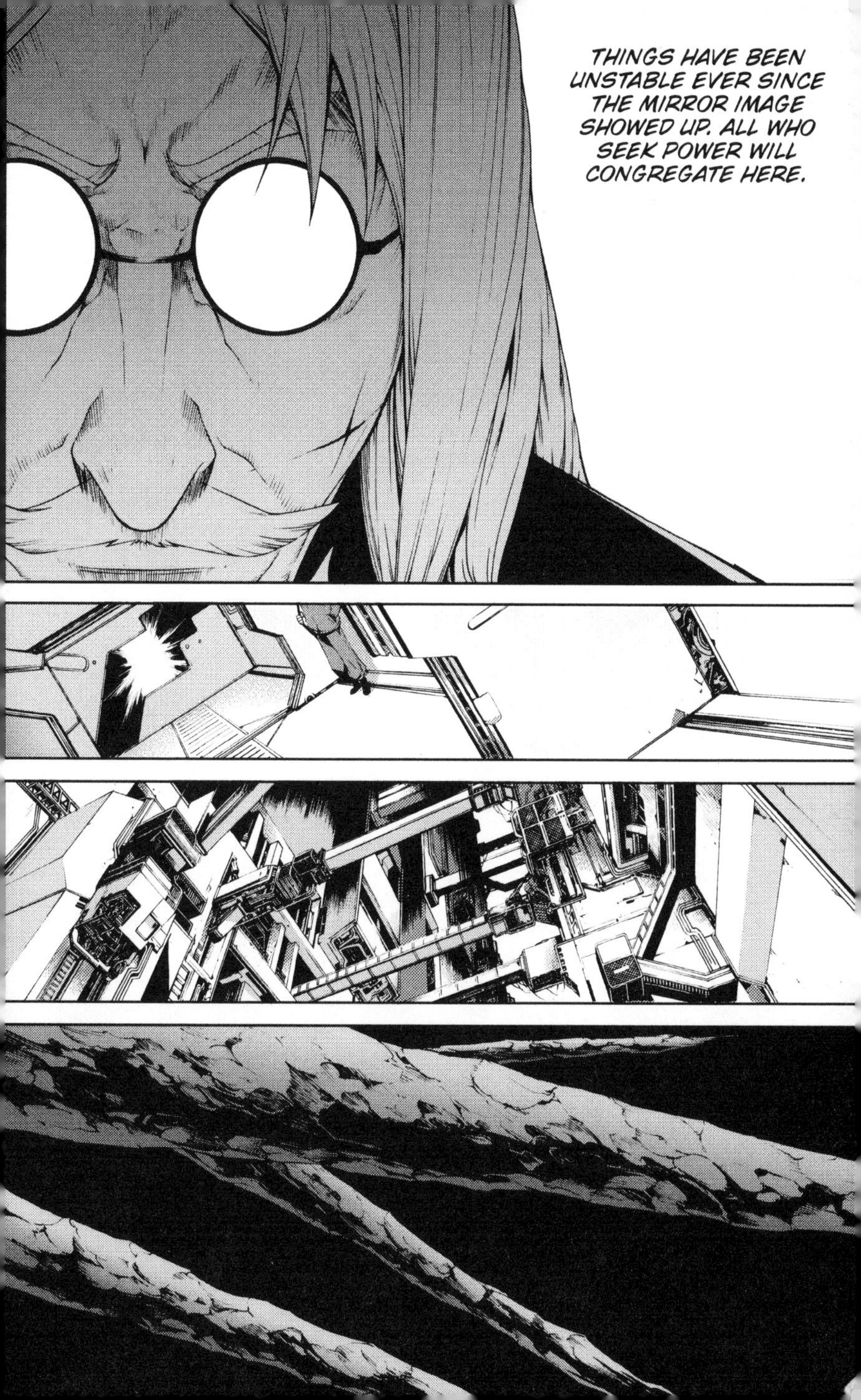
THINGS HAVE BEEN UNSTABLE EVER SINCE THE MIRROR IMAGE SHOWED UP. ALL WHO SEEK POWER WILL CONGREGATE HERE.

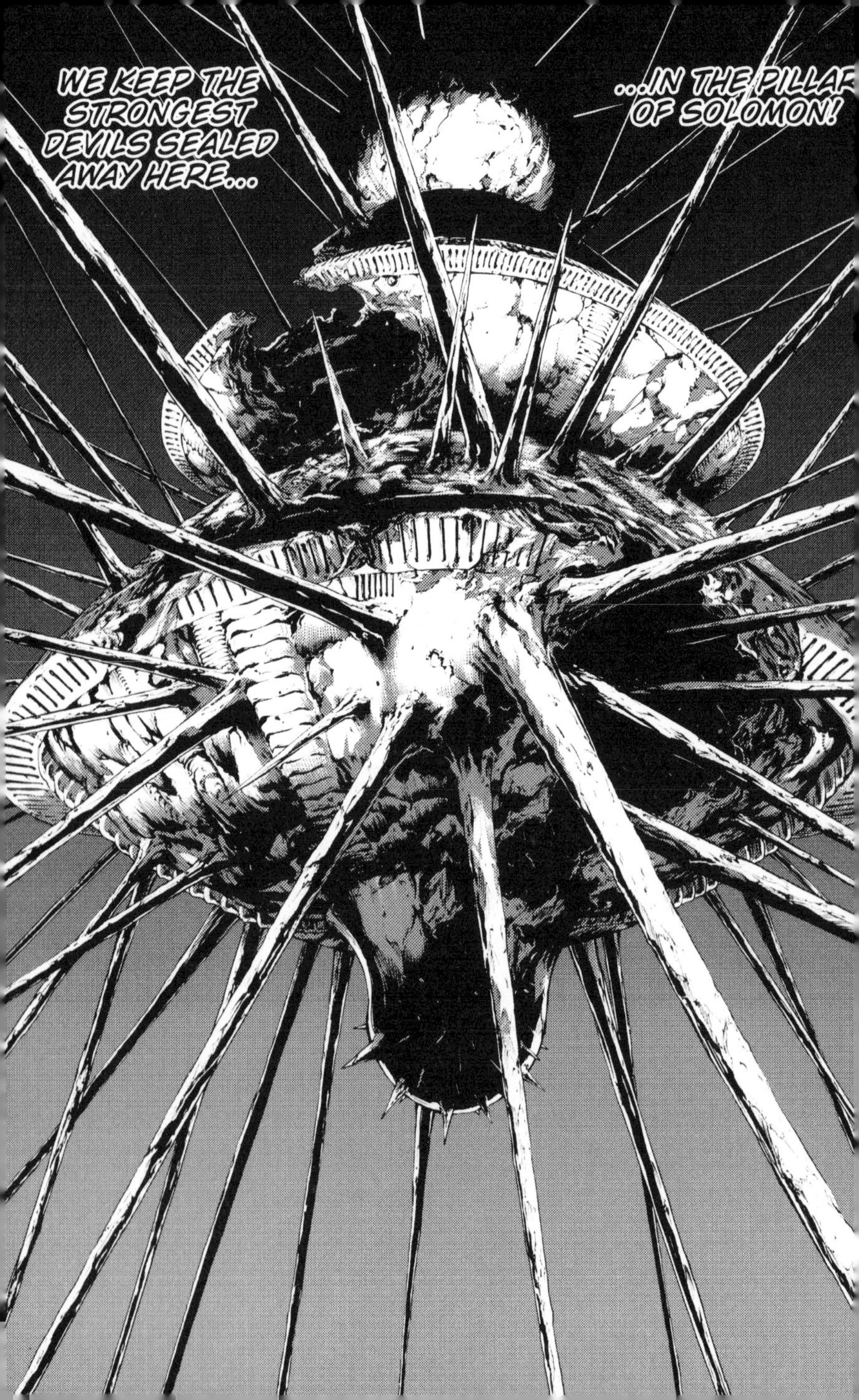
WE KEEP THE STRONGEST DEVILS SEALED AWAY HERE...
...IN THE PILLAR OF SOLOMON!

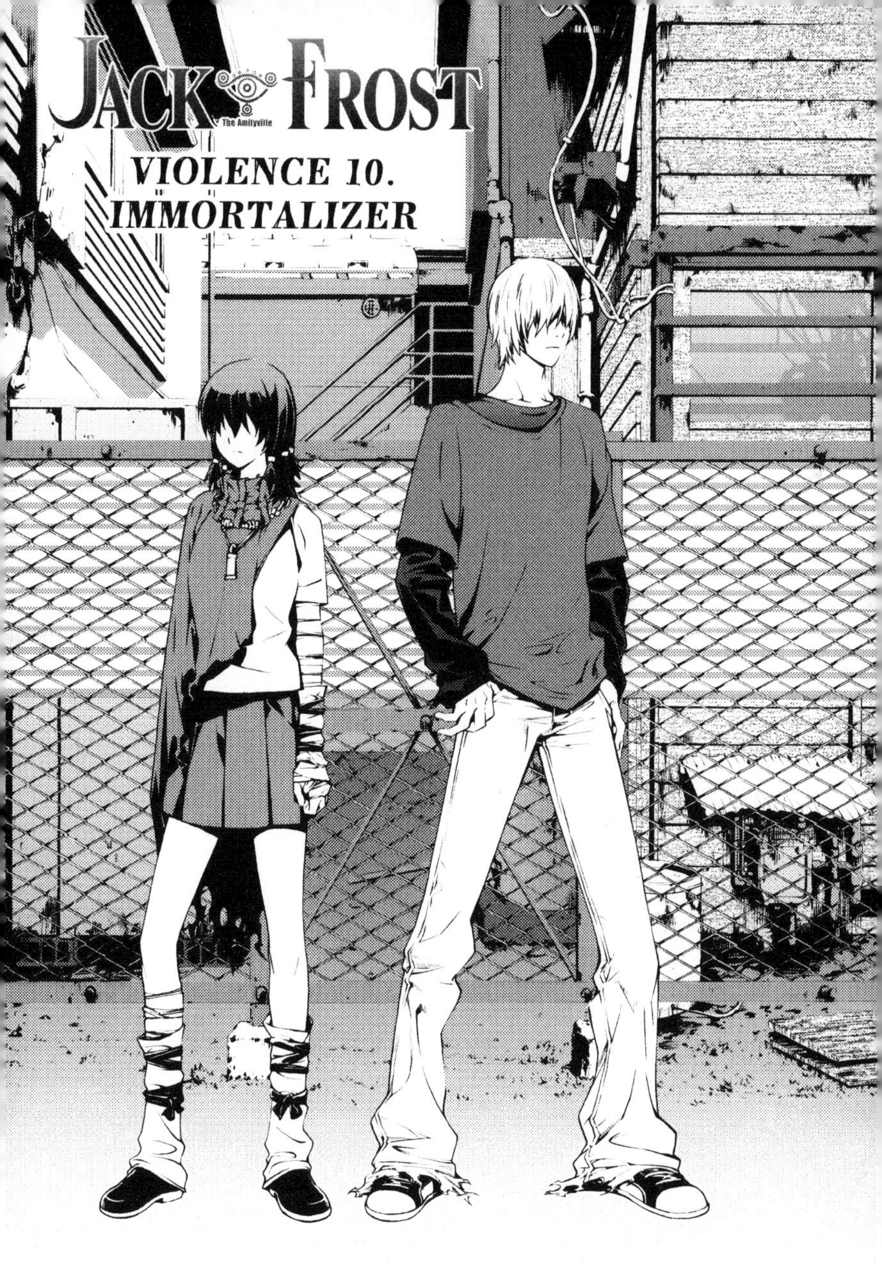
JACK FROST
The Amityville
VIOLENCE 10.
IMMORTALIZER

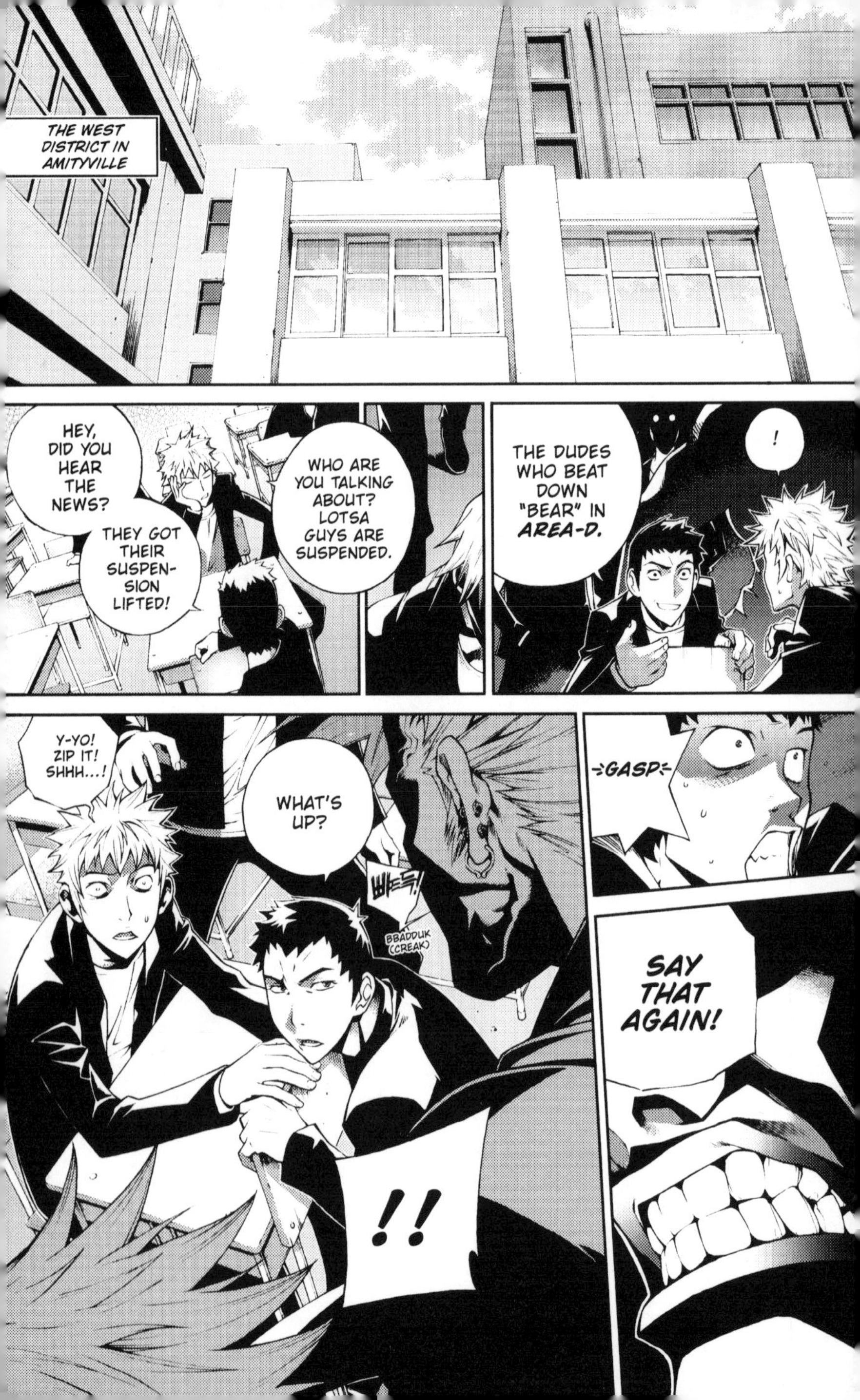
THE WEST DISTRICT IN AMITYVILLE
HEY, DID YOU HEAR THE NEWS?
THEY GOT THEIR SUSPENSION LIFTED!
WHO ARE YOU TALKING ABOUT? LOTSA GUYS ARE SUSPENDED.
THE DUDES WHO BEAT DOWN "BEAR" IN AREA-D.
!
Y-YO! ZIP IT! SHHH...!
WHAT'S UP?
빠득!
BBADDUK (CREAK)
!!
GASP
SAY THAT AGAIN!

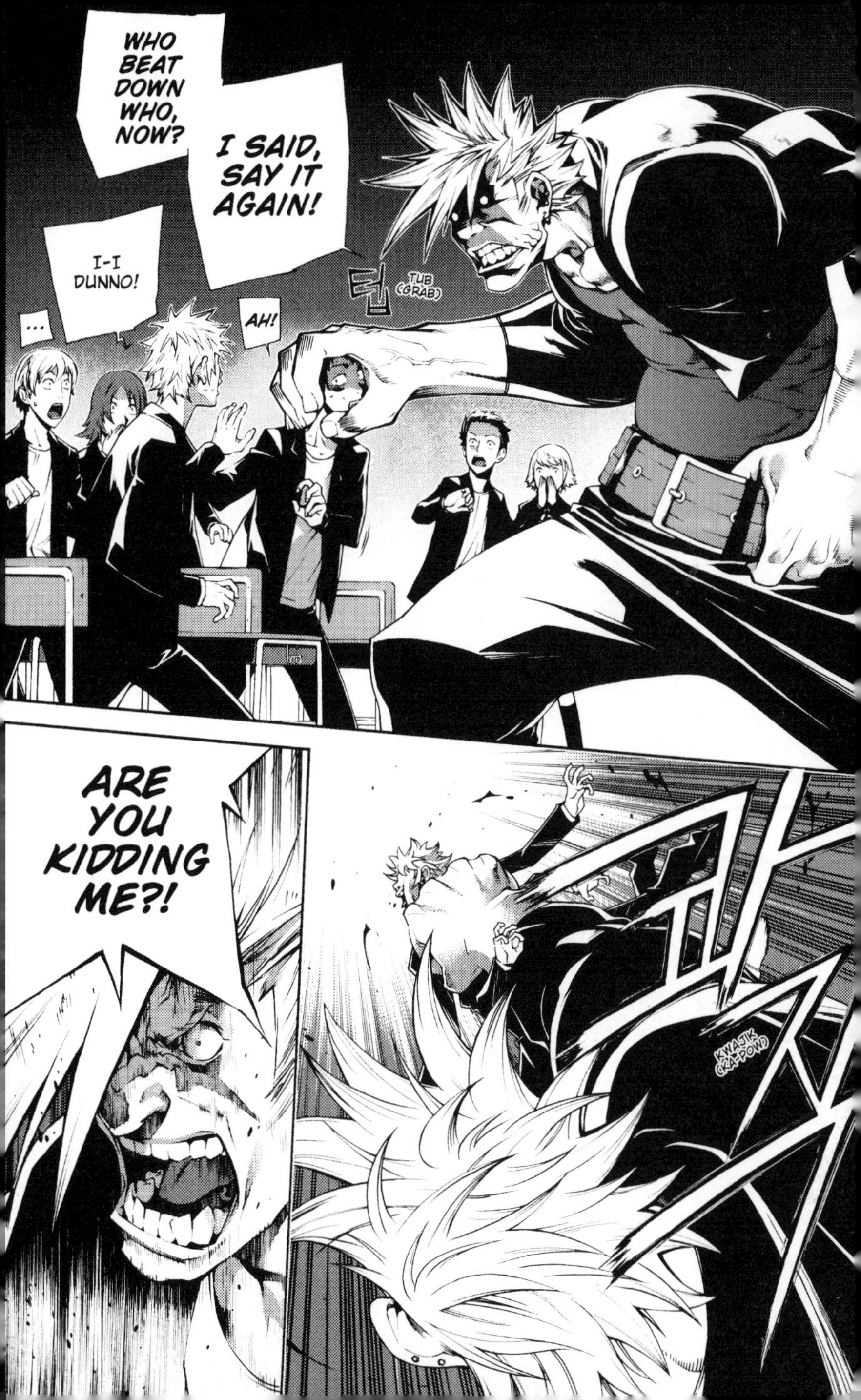
WHO BEAT DOWN WHO, NOW?
I SAID, SAY IT AGAIN!
I-I DUNNO!
...
AH!
TUB (GRAB)
ARE YOU KIDDING ME?!
KWAJIK (KA-POW)

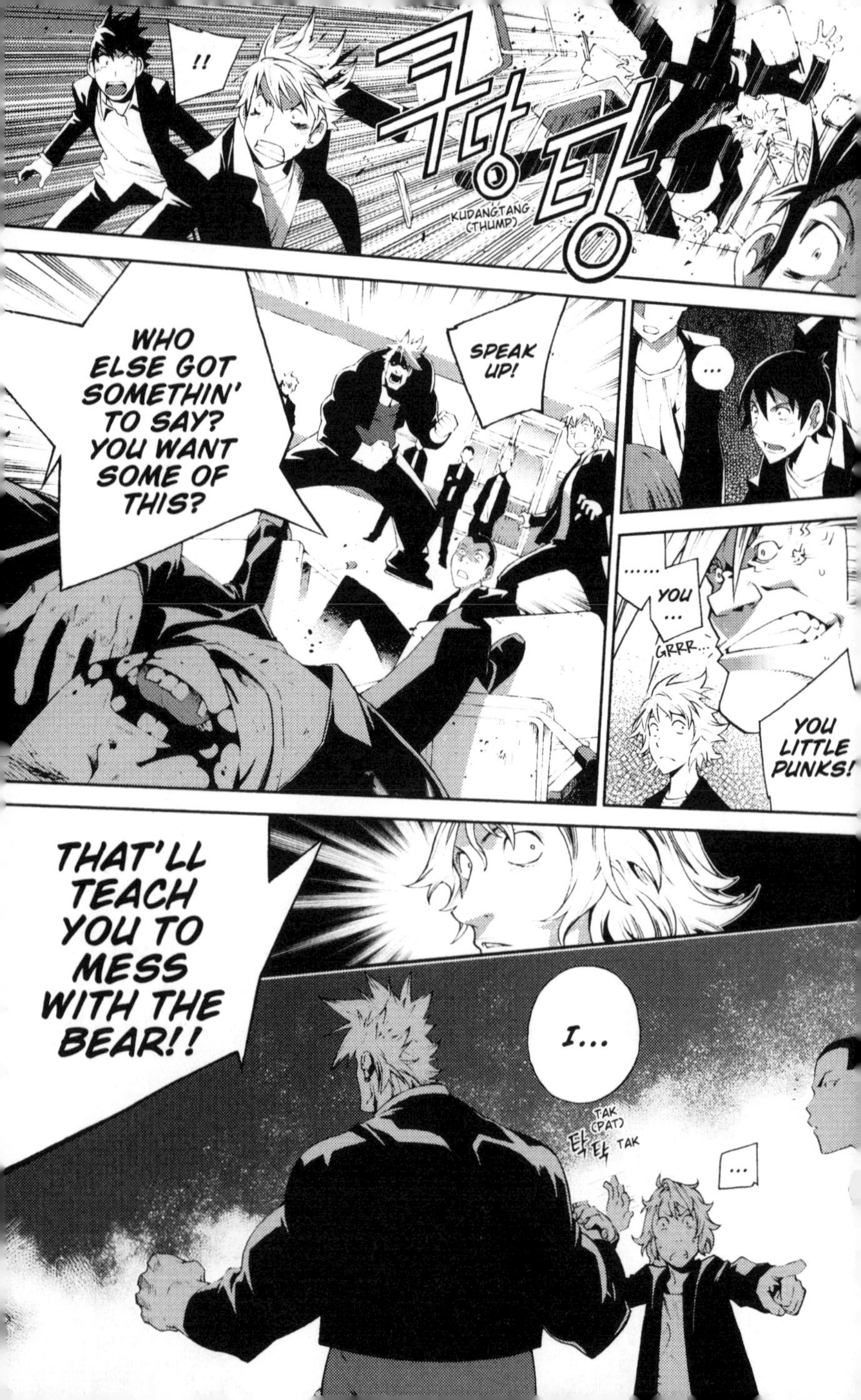
!!
쿠당탕
KUDANGTANG (THUMP)
WHO ELSE GOT SOMETHIN' TO SAY? YOU WANT SOME OF THIS?
SPEAK UP!
...
......
YOU ...
GRRR...
YOU LITTLE PUNKS!
THAT'LL TEACH YOU TO MESS WITH THE BEAR!!
I...
TAK (PAT) 탁 탁 TAK
...

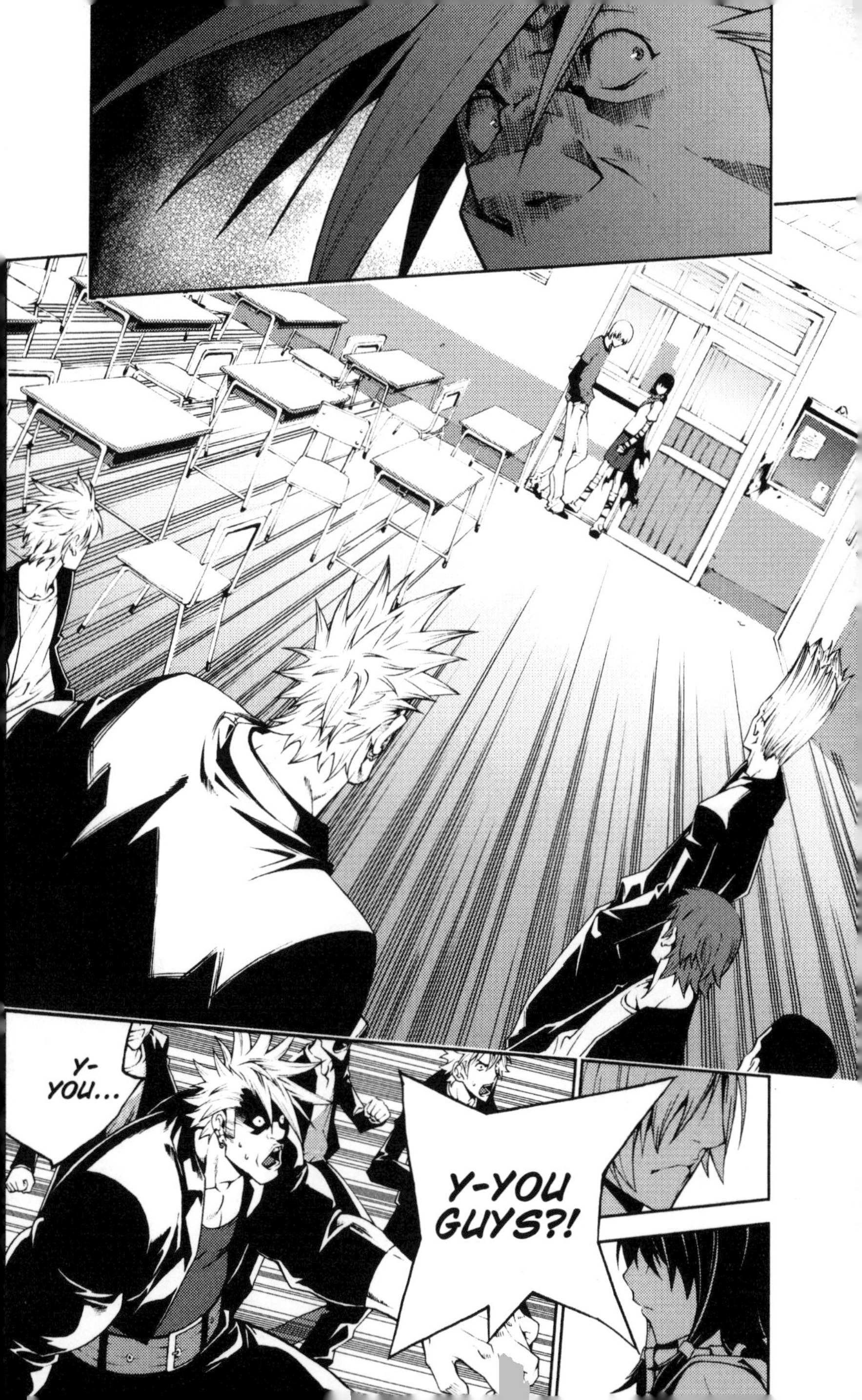
Y-
YOU...
Y-YOU
GUYS?!

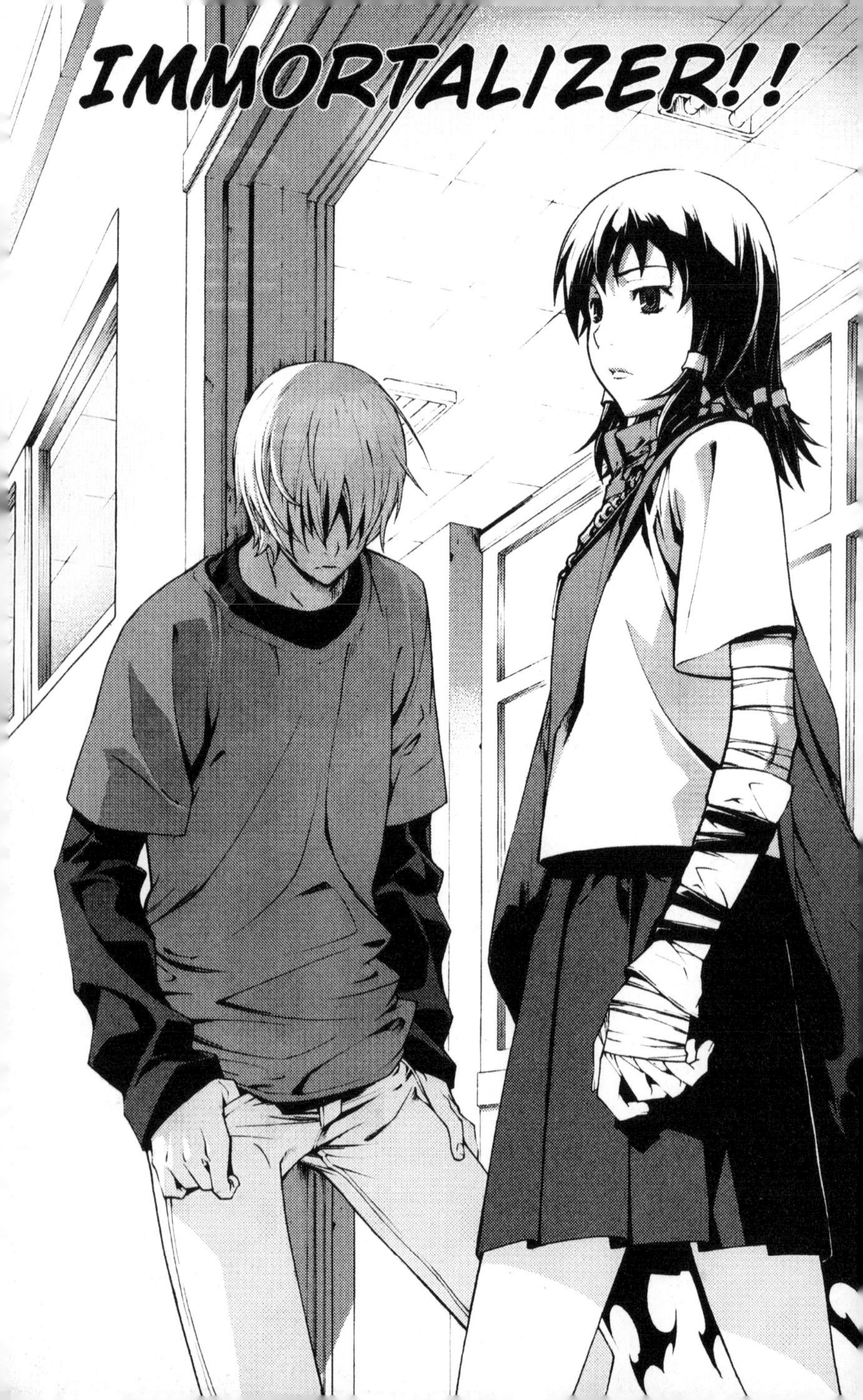
IMMORTALIZER!!

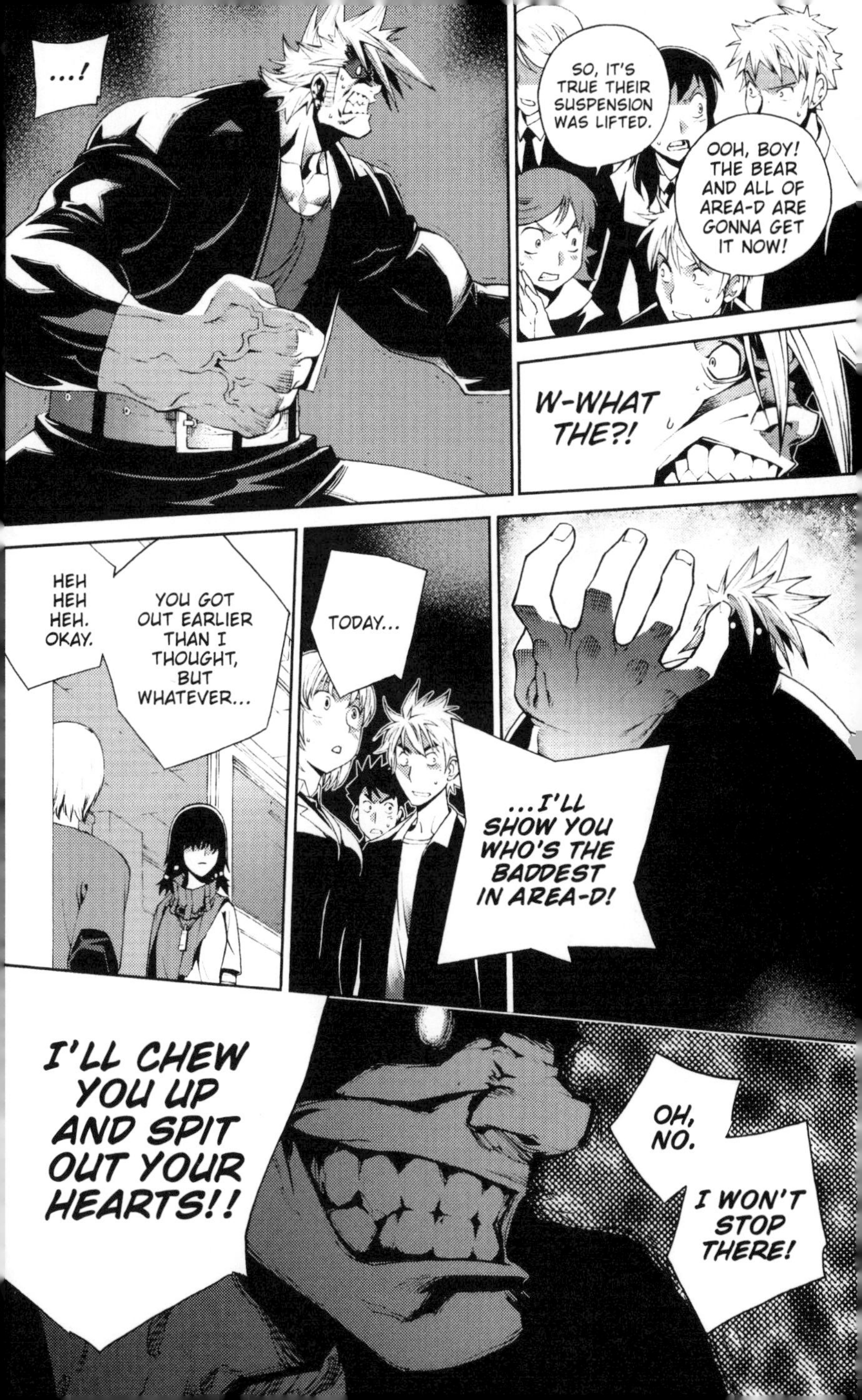
...!
SO, IT'S TRUE THEIR SUSPENSION WAS LIFTED.
OOH, BOY! THE BEAR AND ALL OF AREA-D ARE GONNA GET IT NOW!
W-WHAT THE?!
HEH HEH HEH. OKAY.
YOU GOT OUT EARLIER THAN I THOUGHT, BUT WHATEVER...
TODAY...
...I'LL SHOW YOU WHO'S THE BADDEST IN AREA-D!
I'LL CHEW YOU UP AND SPIT OUT YOUR HEARTS!!
OH, NO.
I WON'T STOP THERE!

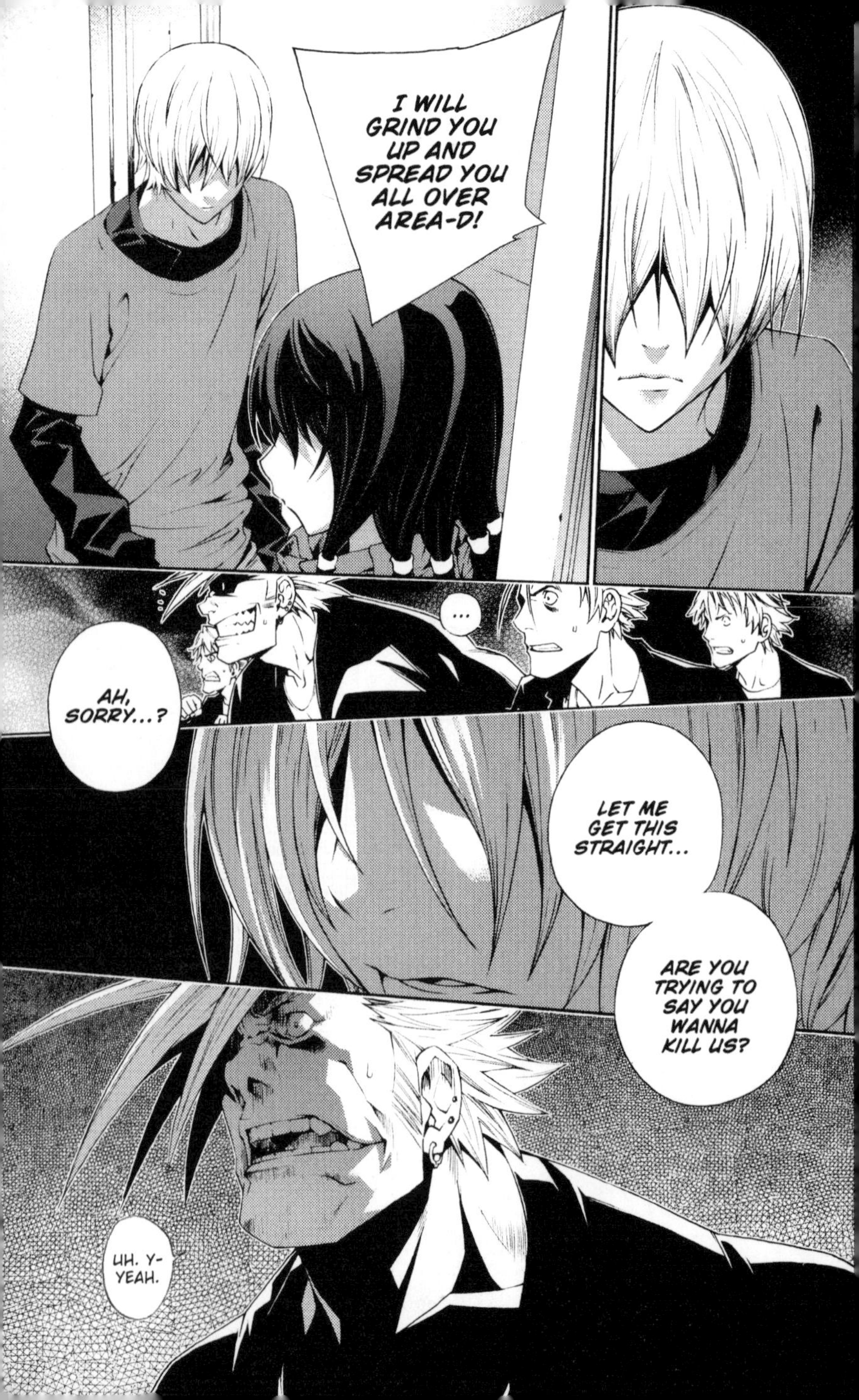

I WILL GRIND YOU UP AND SPREAD YOU ALL OVER AREA-D!
AH, SORRY...?
...
LET ME GET THIS STRAIGHT...
ARE YOU TRYING TO SAY YOU WANNA KILL US?
UH. Y-YEAH.

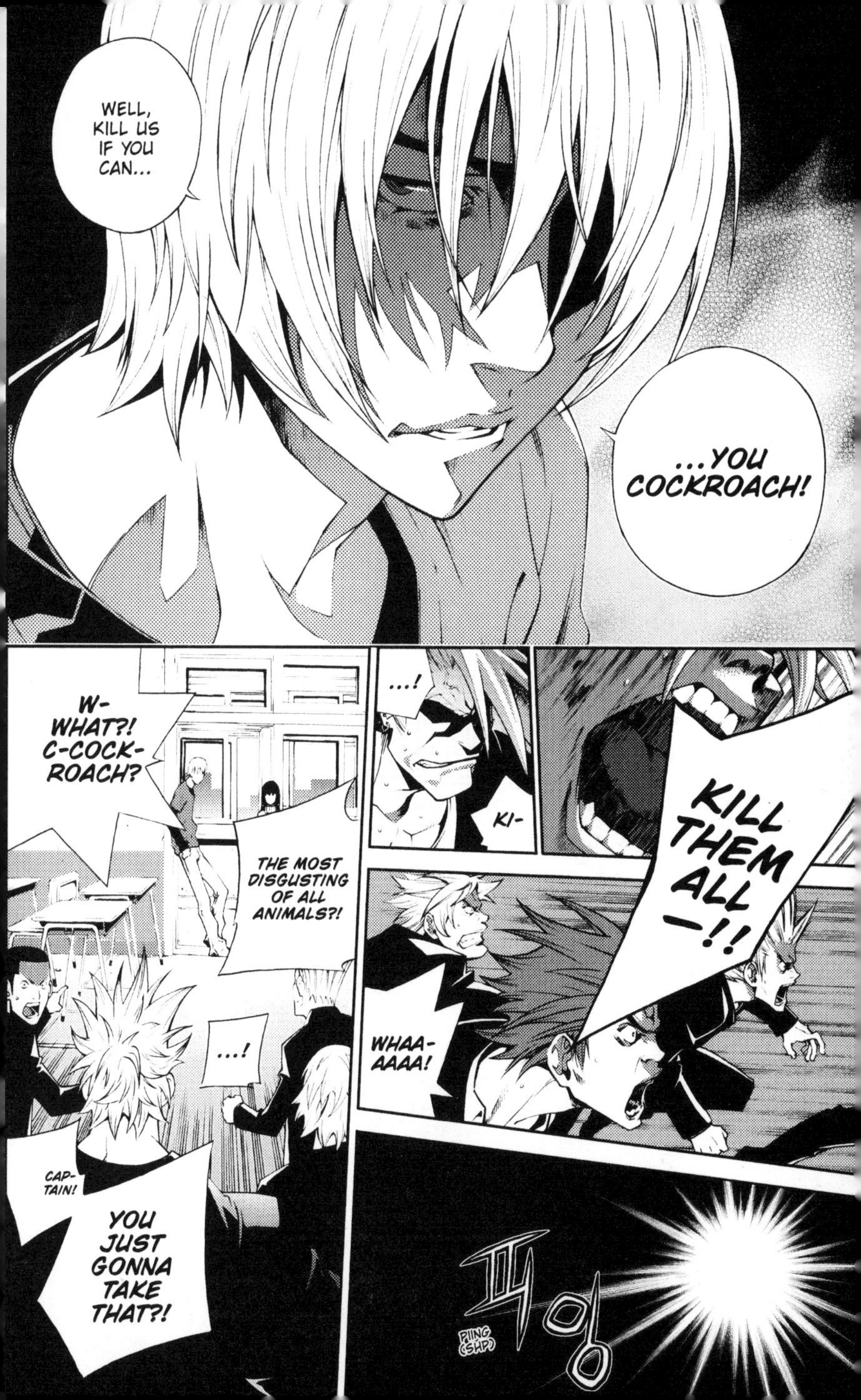
WELL, KILL US IF YOU CAN...
...YOU COCKROACH!
W-WHAT?! C-COCK-ROACH?
THE MOST DISGUSTING OF ALL ANIMALS?!
...!
CAP-TAIN!
YOU JUST GONNA TAKE THAT?!
...!
KI-
KILL THEM ALL—!!
WHAA-AAAA!
PIING (SHP)

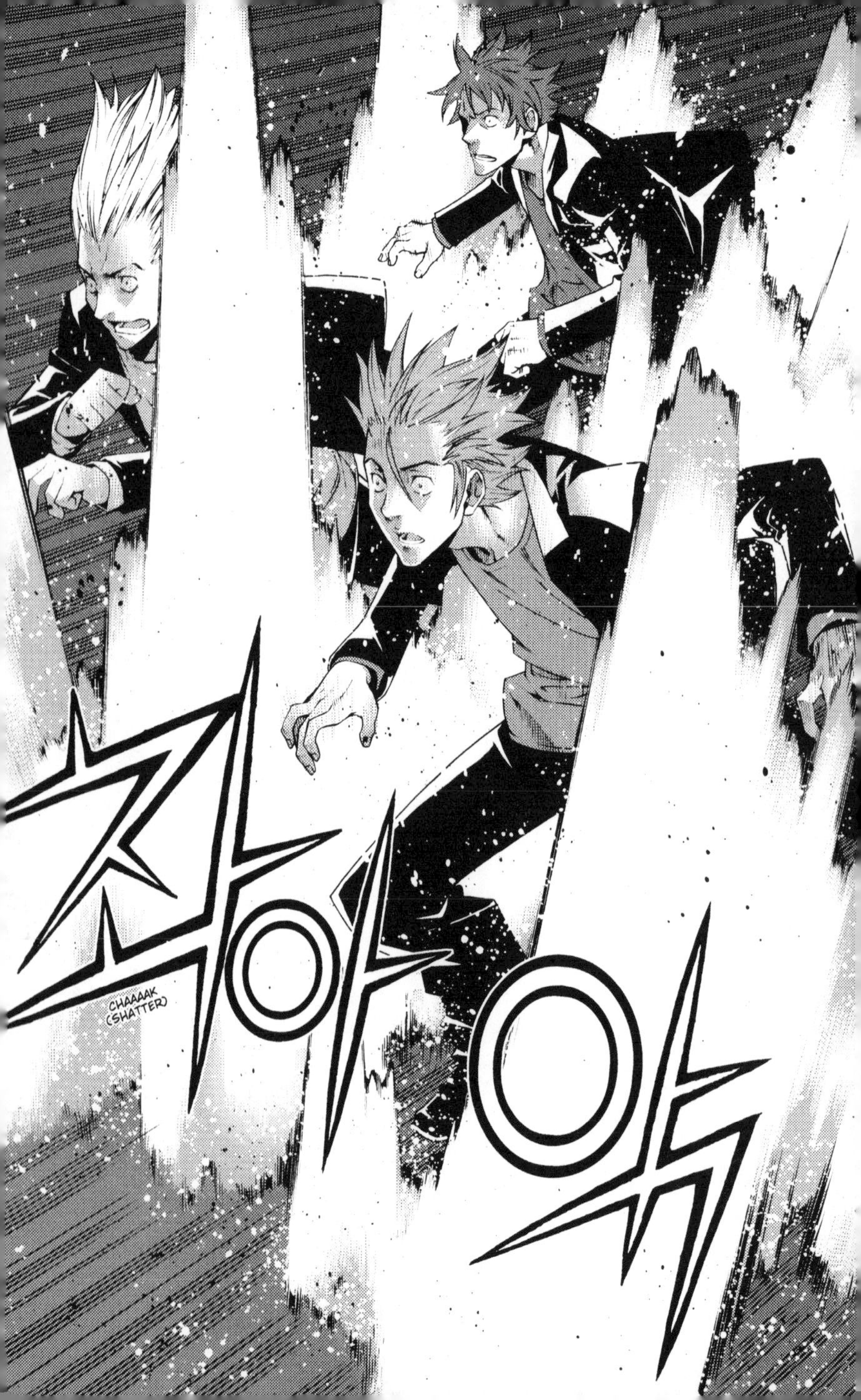
CHAAAAK
(SHATTER)

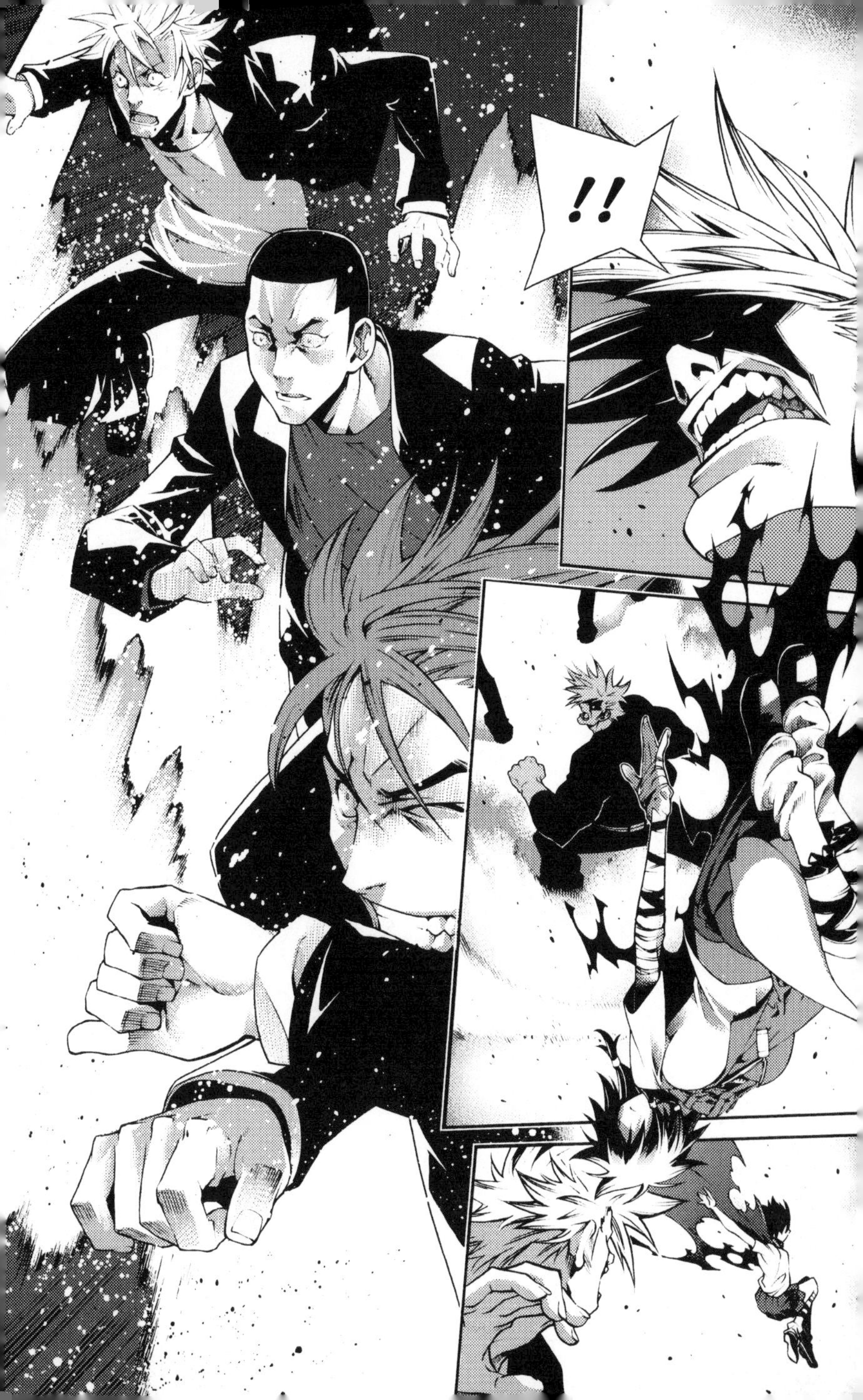
!!

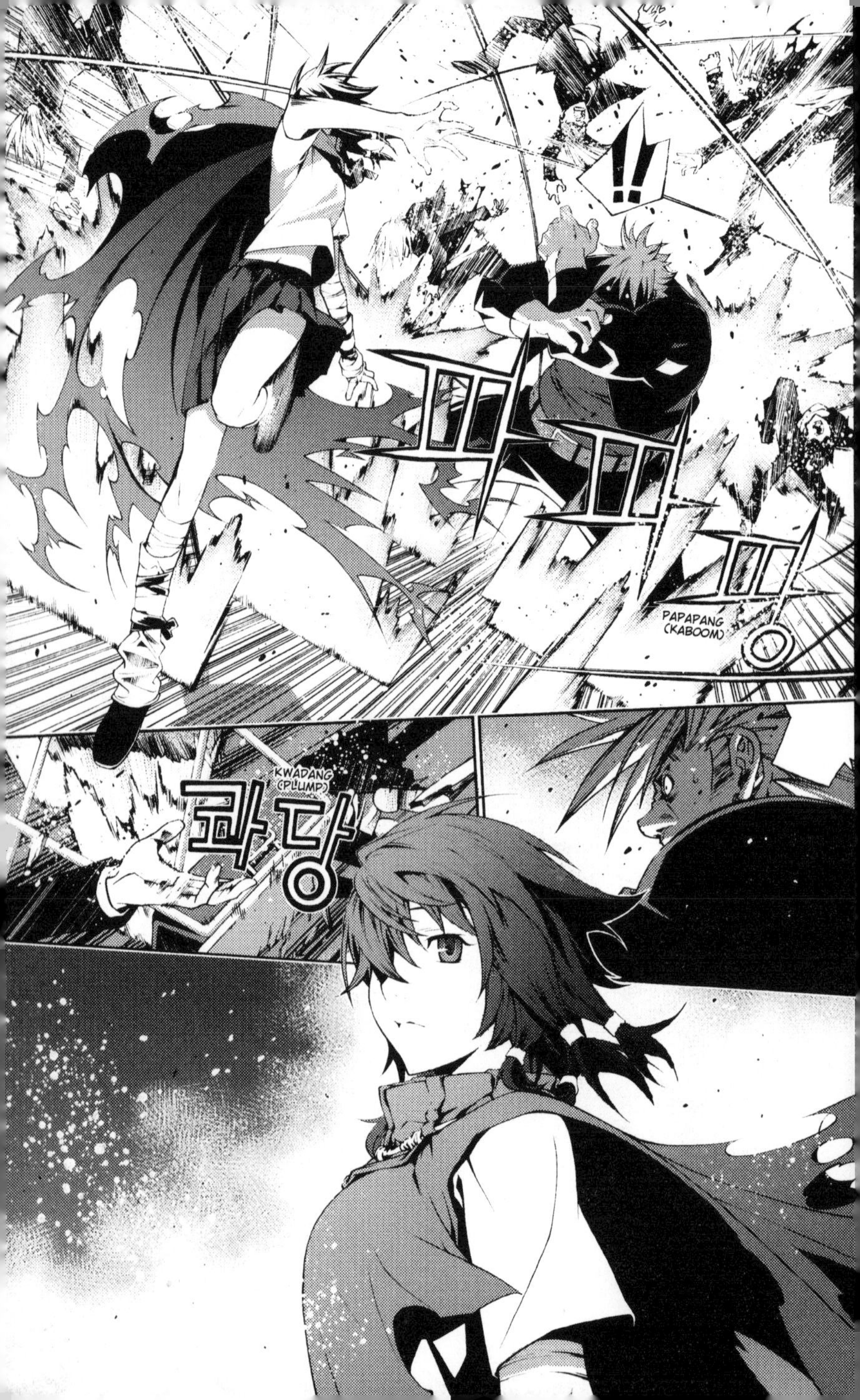
!!
파파팡
PAPAPANG (KABOOM)
KWADANG (PLUMP)
콰당

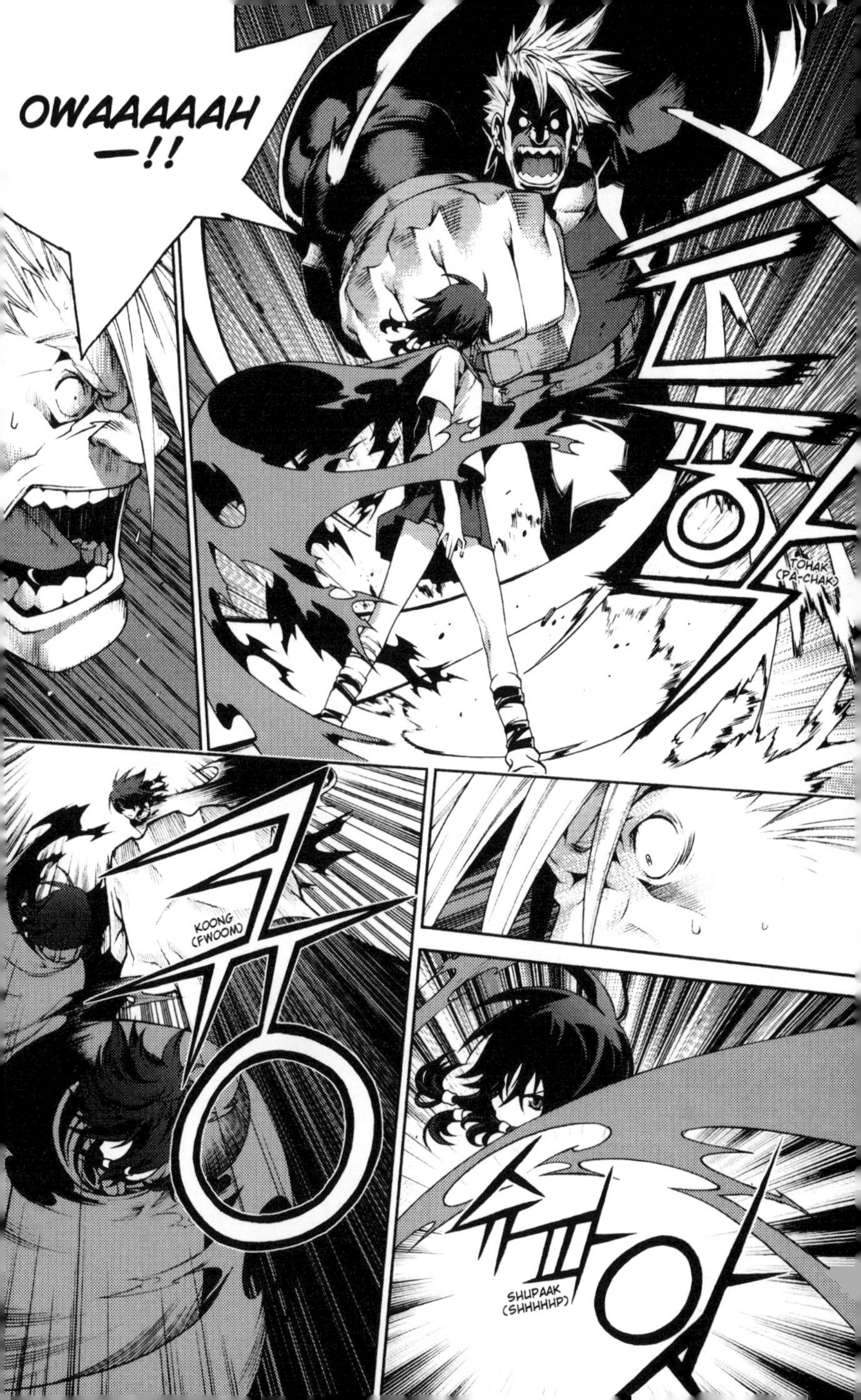
OWAAAAAH
—!!
TOHAK
(PA-CHAK)
KOONG
(FWOOM)
SHUPAAK
(SHHHHHP)

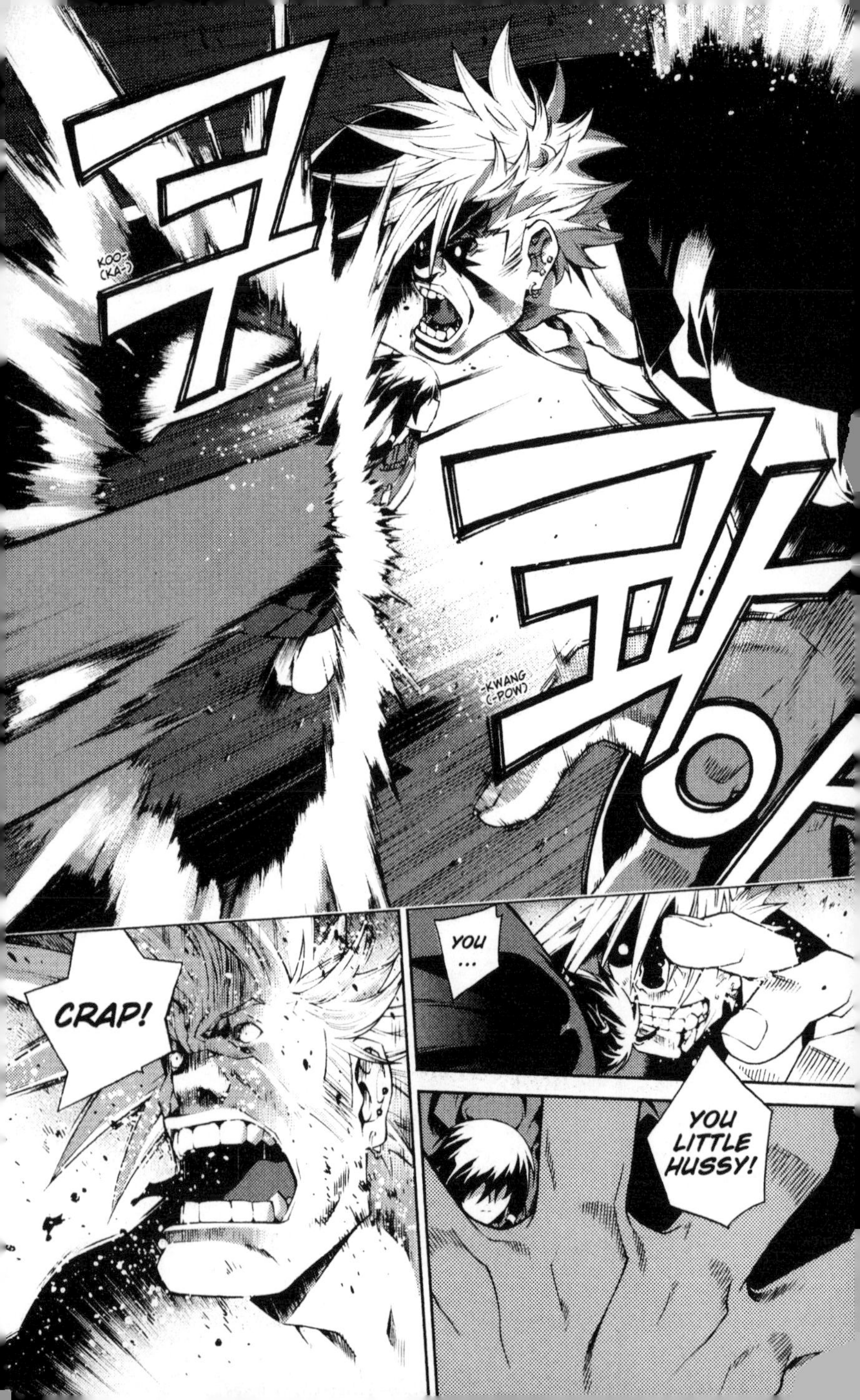
KOO- (KA-)
-KWANG (-POW)
CRAP!
YOU ...
YOU LITTLE HUSSY!

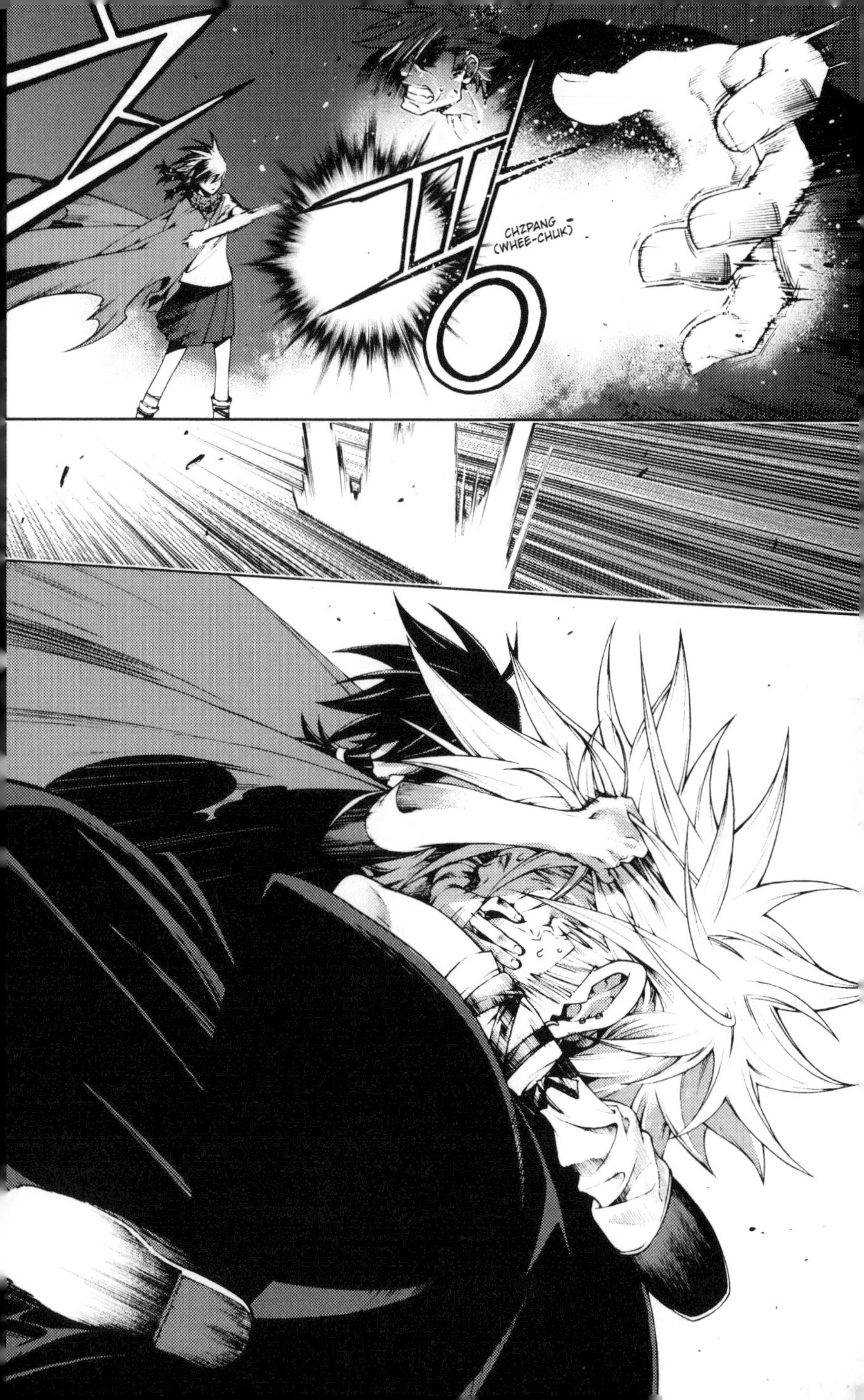
CHZPANG
(WHEE-CHUK)

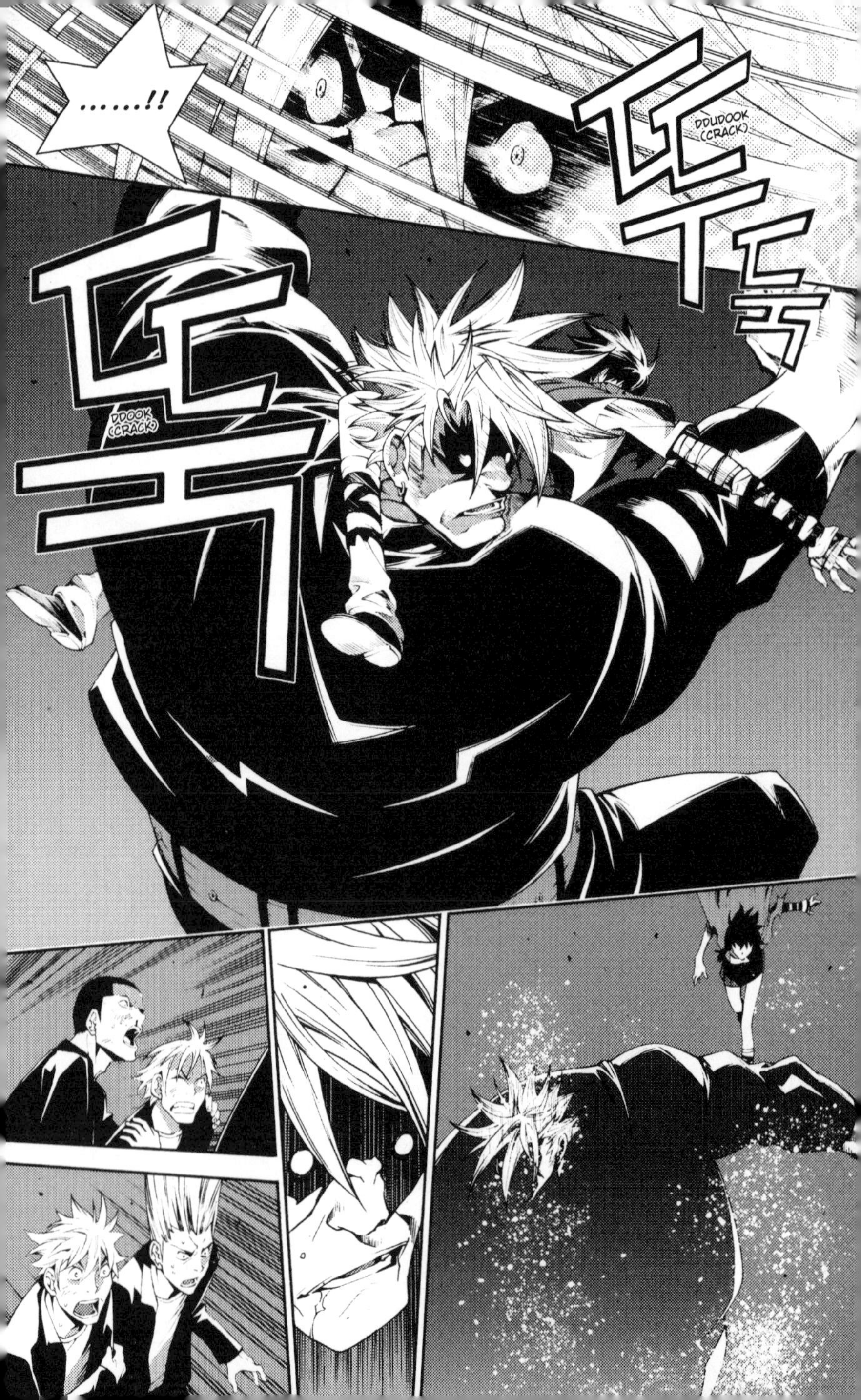
......!!
DDUDOOK (CRACK)
DDOOK (CRACK)

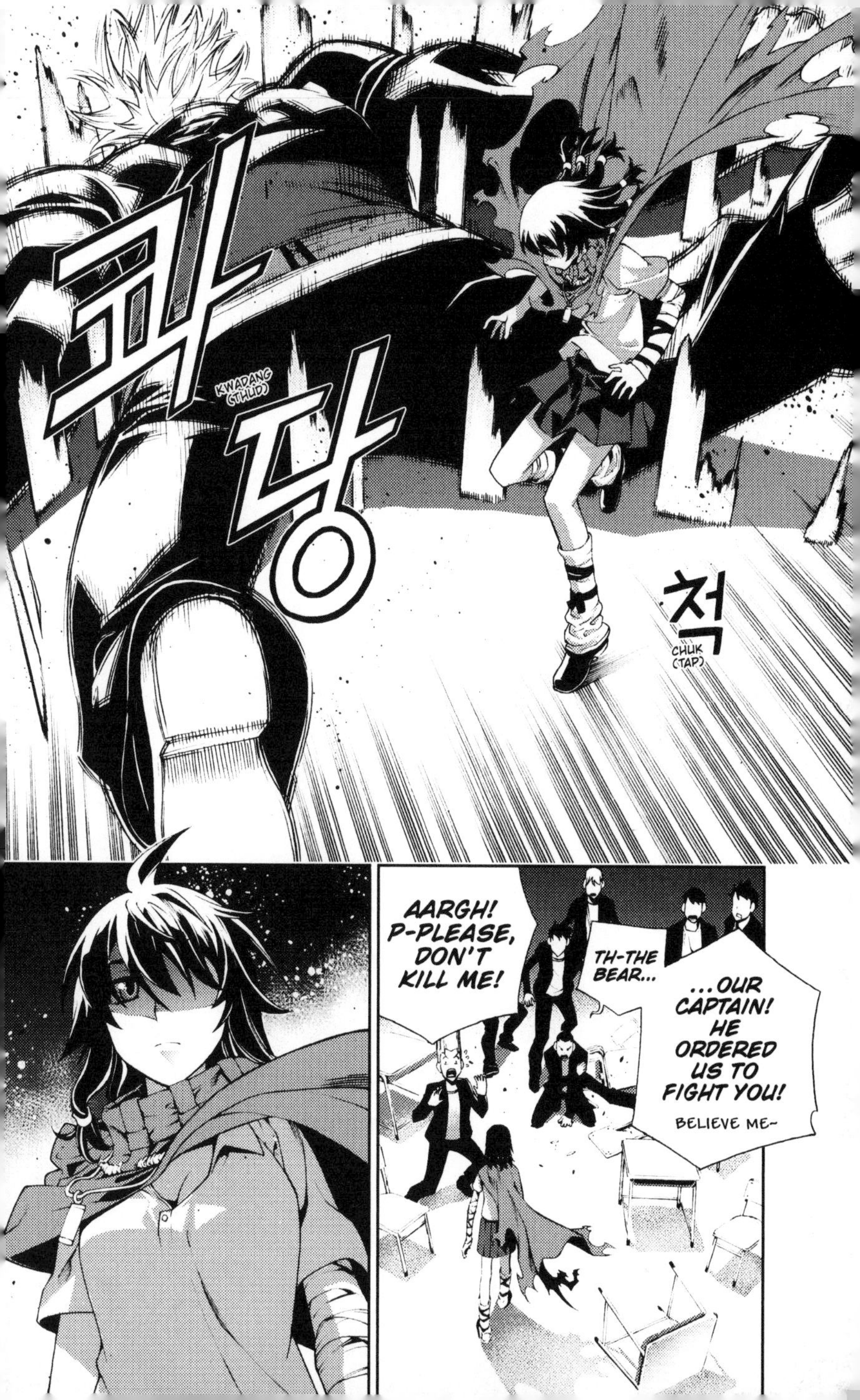
콰당
KWADANG (THUD)
척
CHUK (TAP)
AARGH! P-PLEASE, DON'T KILL ME!
TH-THE BEAR...
...OUR CAPTAIN! HE ORDERED US TO FIGHT YOU!
BELIEVE ME~

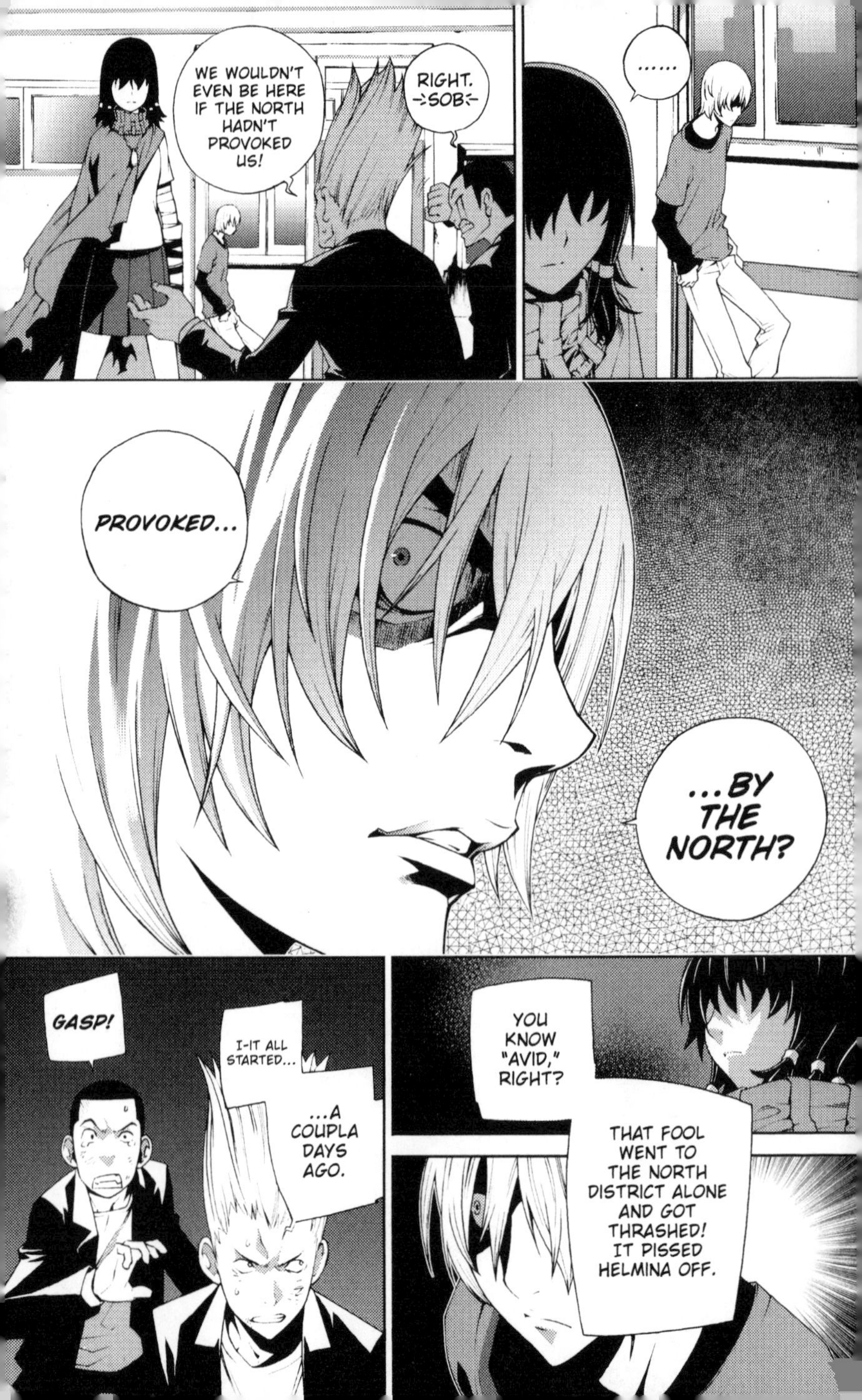
WE WOULDN'T EVEN BE HERE IF THE NORTH HADN'T PROVOKED US!
RIGHT. -SOB-
......
PROVOKED...
...BY THE NORTH?
GASP!
I-IT ALL STARTED...
...A COUPLA DAYS AGO.
YOU KNOW "AVID," RIGHT?
THAT FOOL WENT TO THE NORTH DISTRICT ALONE AND GOT THRASHED! IT PISSED HELMINA OFF.

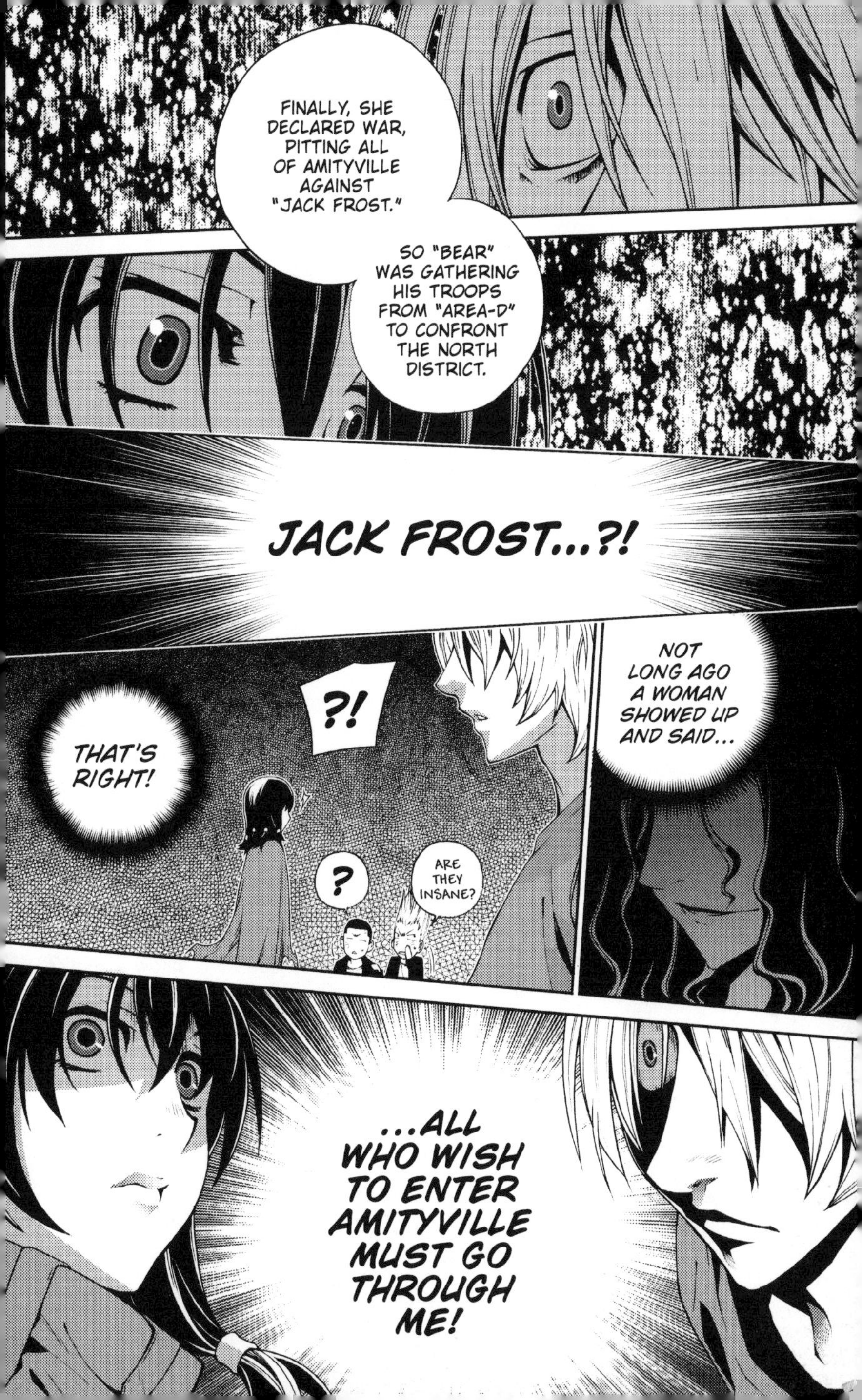
FINALLY, SHE DECLARED WAR, PITTING ALL OF AMITYVILLE AGAINST "JACK FROST."
SO "BEAR" WAS GATHERING HIS TROOPS FROM "AREA-D" TO CONFRONT THE NORTH DISTRICT.
JACK FROST...?!
THAT'S RIGHT!
?!
?
ARE THEY INSANE?
NOT LONG AGO A WOMAN SHOWED UP AND SAID...
...ALL WHO WISH TO ENTER AMITYVILLE MUST GO THROUGH ME!

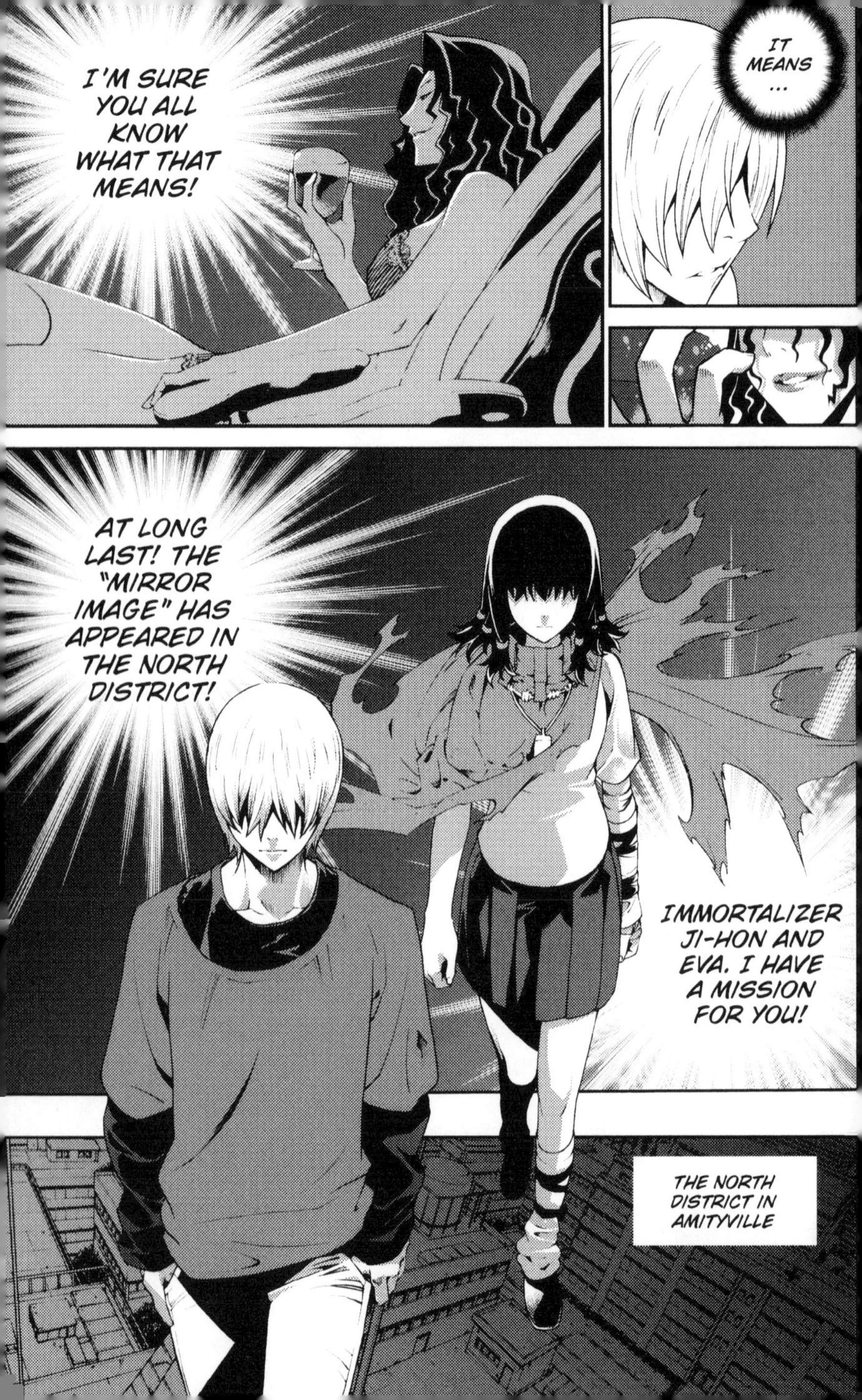
I'M SURE YOU ALL KNOW WHAT THAT MEANS!
IT MEANS ...
AT LONG LAST! THE "MIRROR IMAGE" HAS APPEARED IN THE NORTH DISTRICT!
IMMORTALIZER JI-HON AND EVA. I HAVE A MISSION FOR YOU!
THE NORTH DISTRICT IN AMITYVILLE

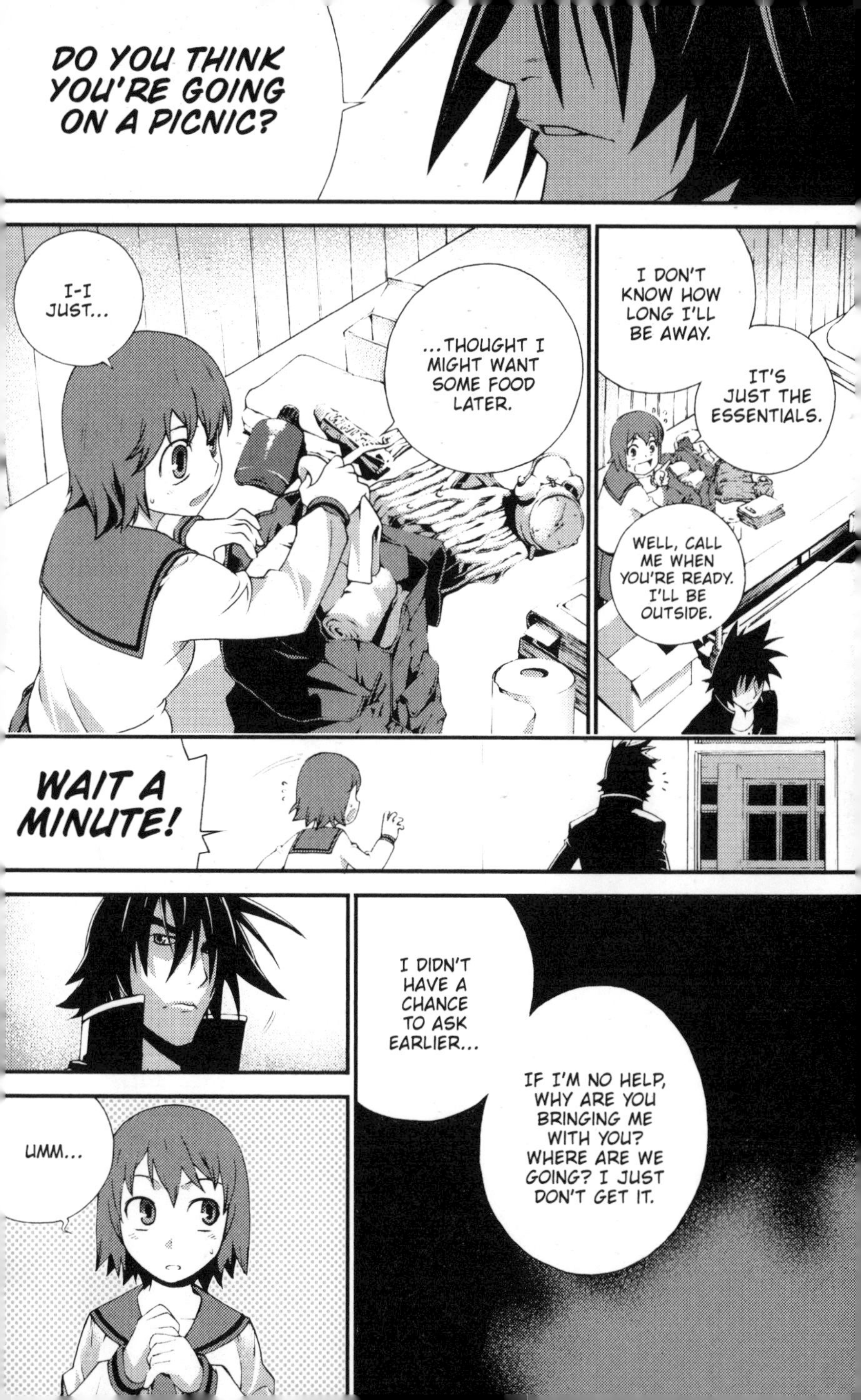
DO YOU THINK YOU'RE GOING ON A PICNIC?
I-I JUST...
...THOUGHT I MIGHT WANT SOME FOOD LATER.
I DON'T KNOW HOW LONG I'LL BE AWAY.
IT'S JUST THE ESSENTIALS.
WELL, CALL ME WHEN YOU'RE READY. I'LL BE OUTSIDE.
WAIT A MINUTE!
I DIDN'T HAVE A CHANCE TO ASK EARLIER...
UMM...
IF I'M NO HELP, WHY ARE YOU BRINGING ME WITH YOU? WHERE ARE WE GOING? I JUST DON'T GET IT.

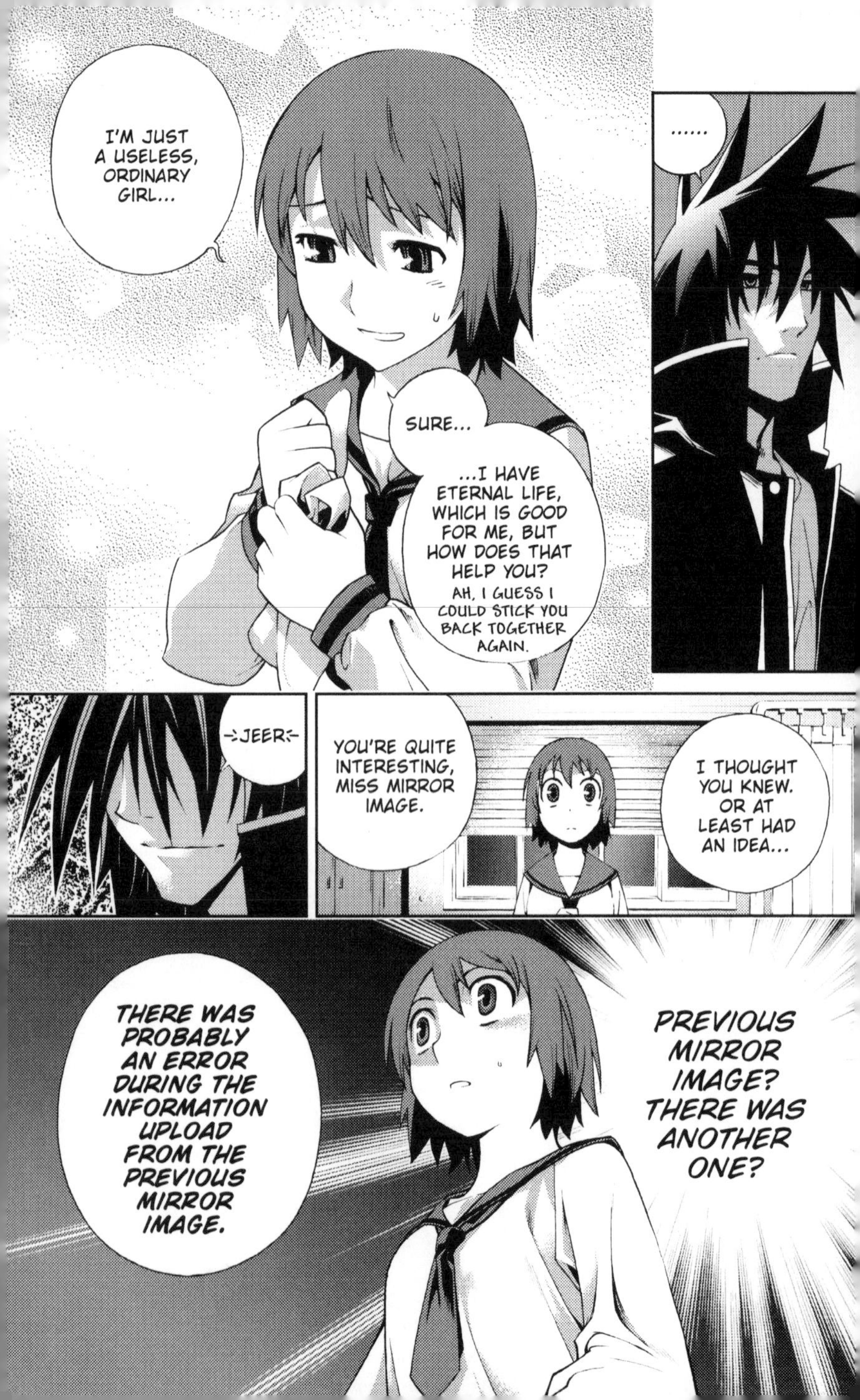
I'M JUST A USELESS, ORDINARY GIRL...
SURE...
...I HAVE ETERNAL LIFE, WHICH IS GOOD FOR ME, BUT HOW DOES THAT HELP YOU?
AH, I GUESS I COULD STICK YOU BACK TOGETHER AGAIN.
......
-JEER-
YOU'RE QUITE INTERESTING, MISS MIRROR IMAGE.
I THOUGHT YOU KNEW. OR AT LEAST HAD AN IDEA...
THERE WAS PROBABLY AN ERROR DURING THE INFORMATION UPLOAD FROM THE PREVIOUS MIRROR IMAGE.
PREVIOUS MIRROR IMAGE? THERE WAS ANOTHER ONE?

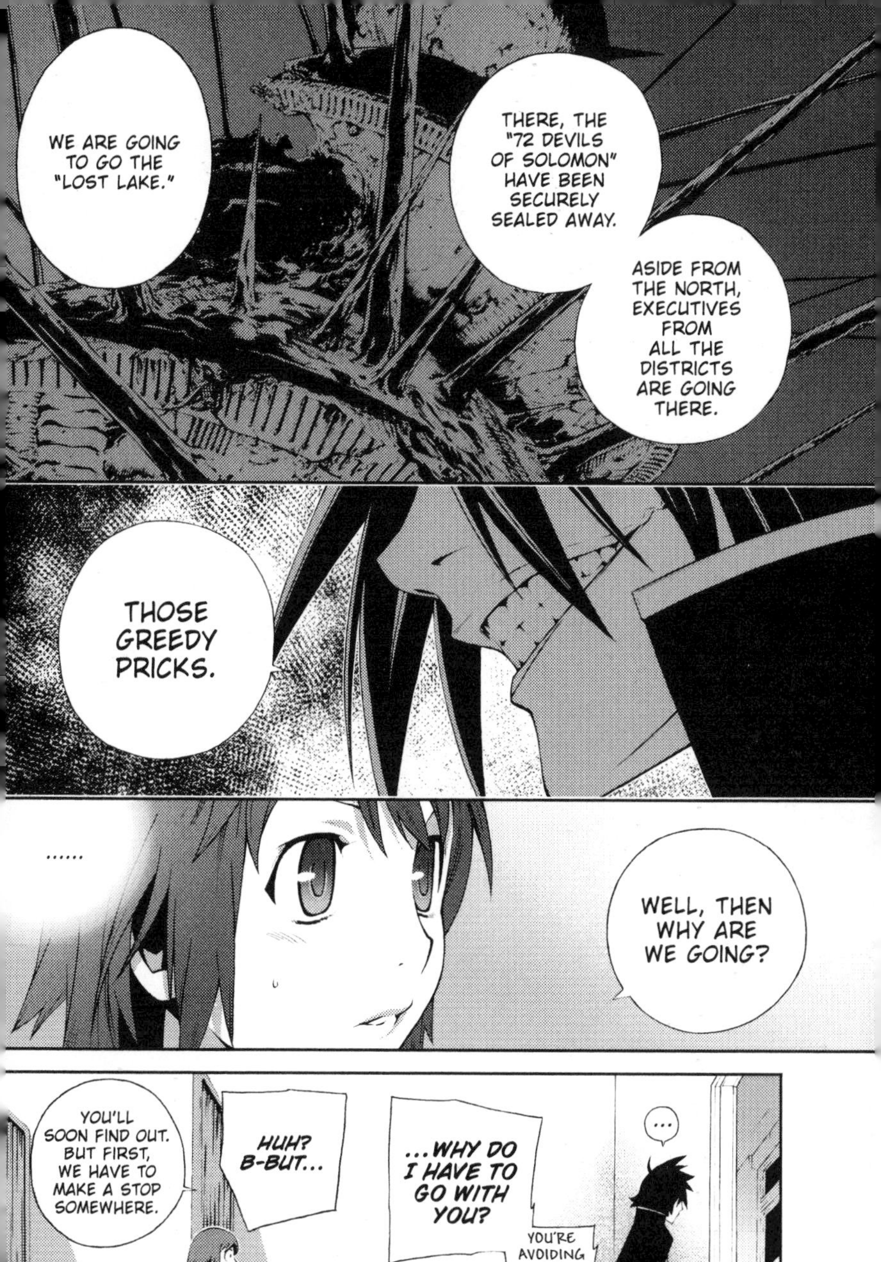
WE ARE GOING TO GO THE "LOST LAKE."
THERE, THE "72 DEVILS OF SOLOMON" HAVE BEEN SECURELY SEALED AWAY.
ASIDE FROM THE NORTH, EXECUTIVES FROM ALL THE DISTRICTS ARE GOING THERE.
THOSE GREEDY PRICKS.
......
WELL, THEN WHY ARE WE GOING?
YOU'LL SOON FIND OUT. BUT FIRST, WE HAVE TO MAKE A STOP SOMEWHERE.
HUH? B-BUT...
...WHY DO I HAVE TO GO WITH YOU?
...
YOU'RE AVOIDING THE QUES-TION!

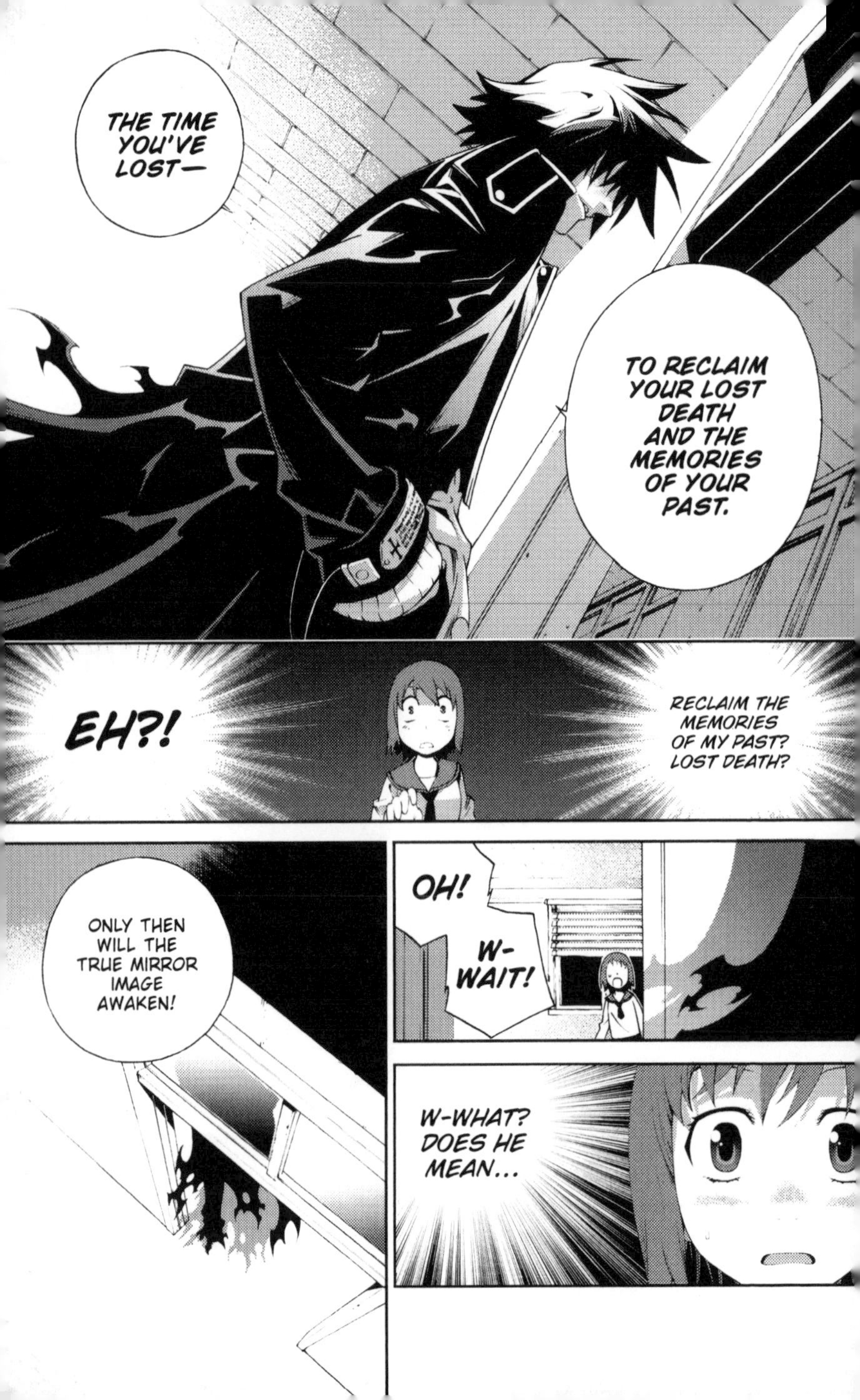
THE TIME YOU'VE LOST—
TO RECLAIM YOUR LOST DEATH AND THE MEMORIES OF YOUR PAST.
EH?!
RECLAIM THE MEMORIES OF MY PAST? LOST DEATH?
ONLY THEN WILL THE TRUE MIRROR IMAGE AWAKEN!
OH!
W-WAIT!
W-WHAT? DOES HE MEAN...

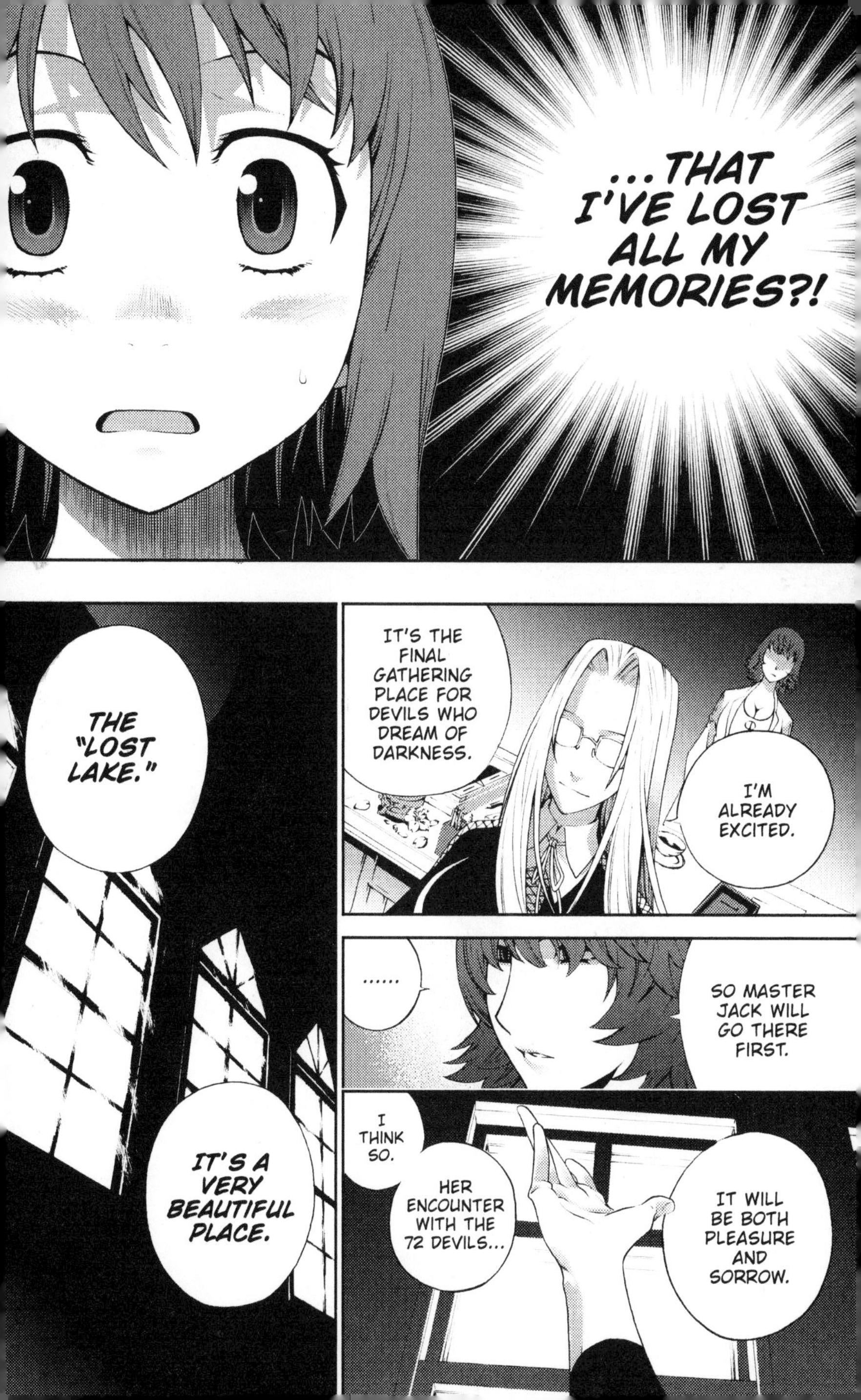
...THAT I'VE LOST ALL MY MEMORIES?!
THE "LOST LAKE."
IT'S A VERY BEAUTIFUL PLACE.
IT'S THE FINAL GATHERING PLACE FOR DEVILS WHO DREAM OF DARKNESS.
I'M ALREADY EXCITED.
......
SO MASTER JACK WILL GO THERE FIRST.
I THINK SO.
HER ENCOUNTER WITH THE 72 DEVILS...
IT WILL BE BOTH PLEASURE AND SORROW.

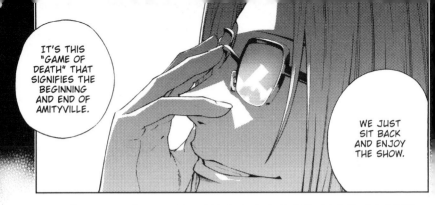

IT'S THIS "GAME OF DEATH" THAT SIGNIFIES THE BEGINNING AND END OF AMITYVILLE.

WE JUST SIT BACK AND ENJOY THE SHOW.

IT'S A SPECIAL PRESENT FROM "JACK" AND THE "MIRROR IMAGE."

HEY!

WAIT FOR ME.

WHAT A SNOB!

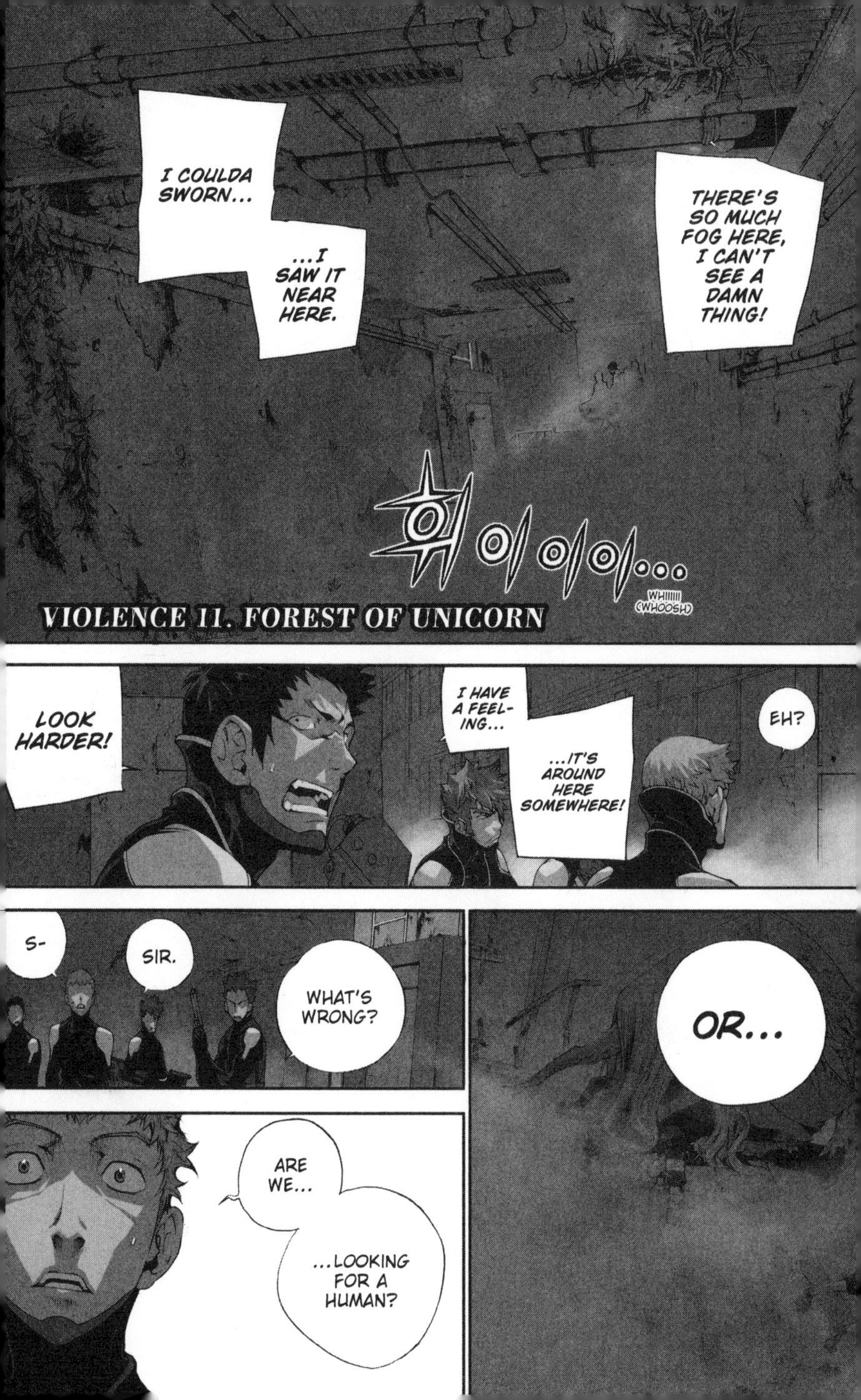

I COULDA SWORN...
...I SAW IT NEAR HERE.
THERE'S SO MUCH FOG HERE, I CAN'T SEE A DAMN THING!
휘이이이이...
WHIIIIII (WHOOSH)
VIOLENCE 11. FOREST OF UNICORN
LOOK HARDER!
I HAVE A FEEL-ING...
...IT'S AROUND HERE SOMEWHERE!
EH?
S-
SIR.
WHAT'S WRONG?
ARE WE...
...LOOKING FOR A HUMAN?
OR...

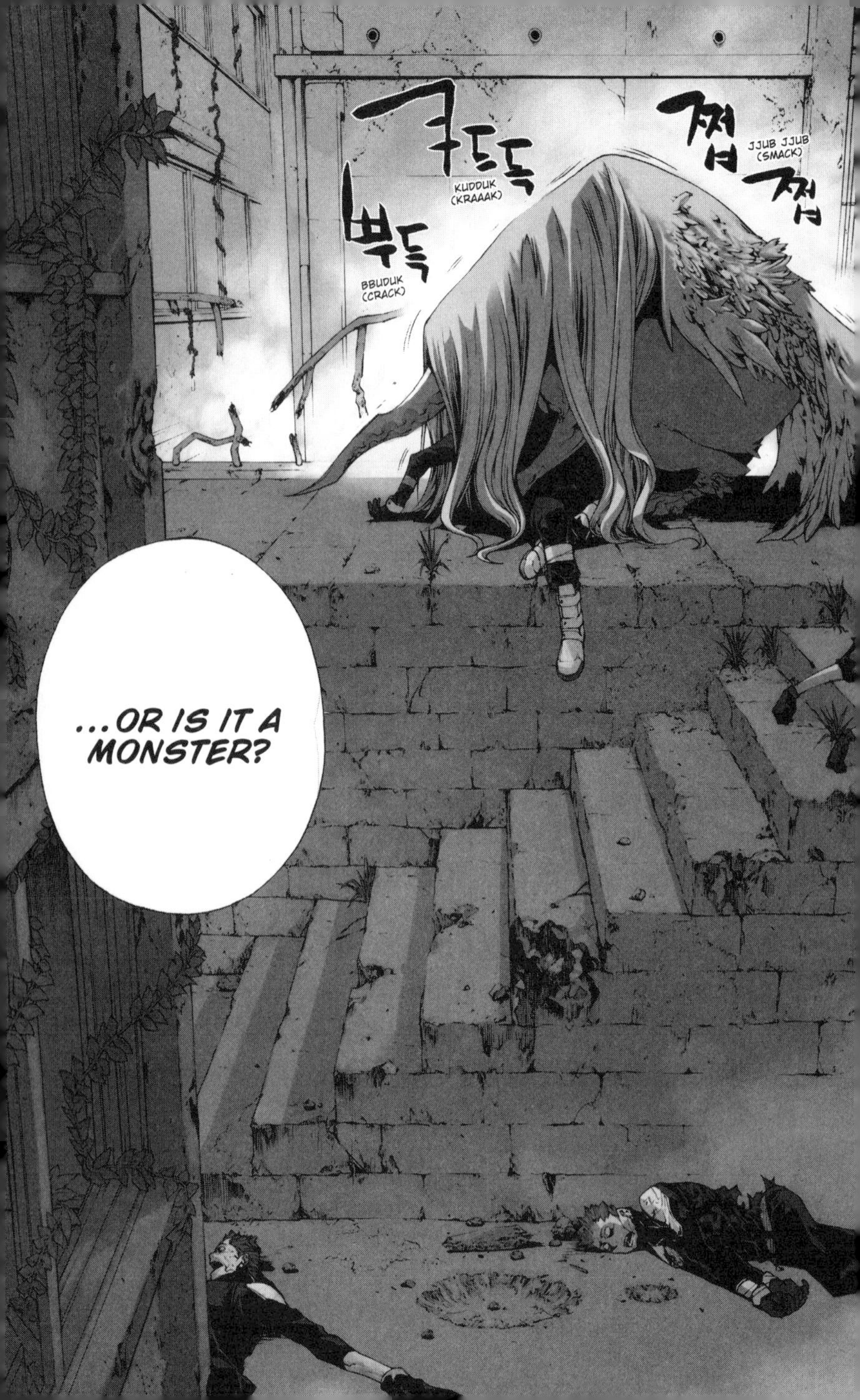
쿠드득
KUDDUK (KRAAAK)
뿌드득
BBUDUK (CRACK)
쩝 쩝
JJUB JJUB (SMACK)
...OR IS IT A MONSTER?

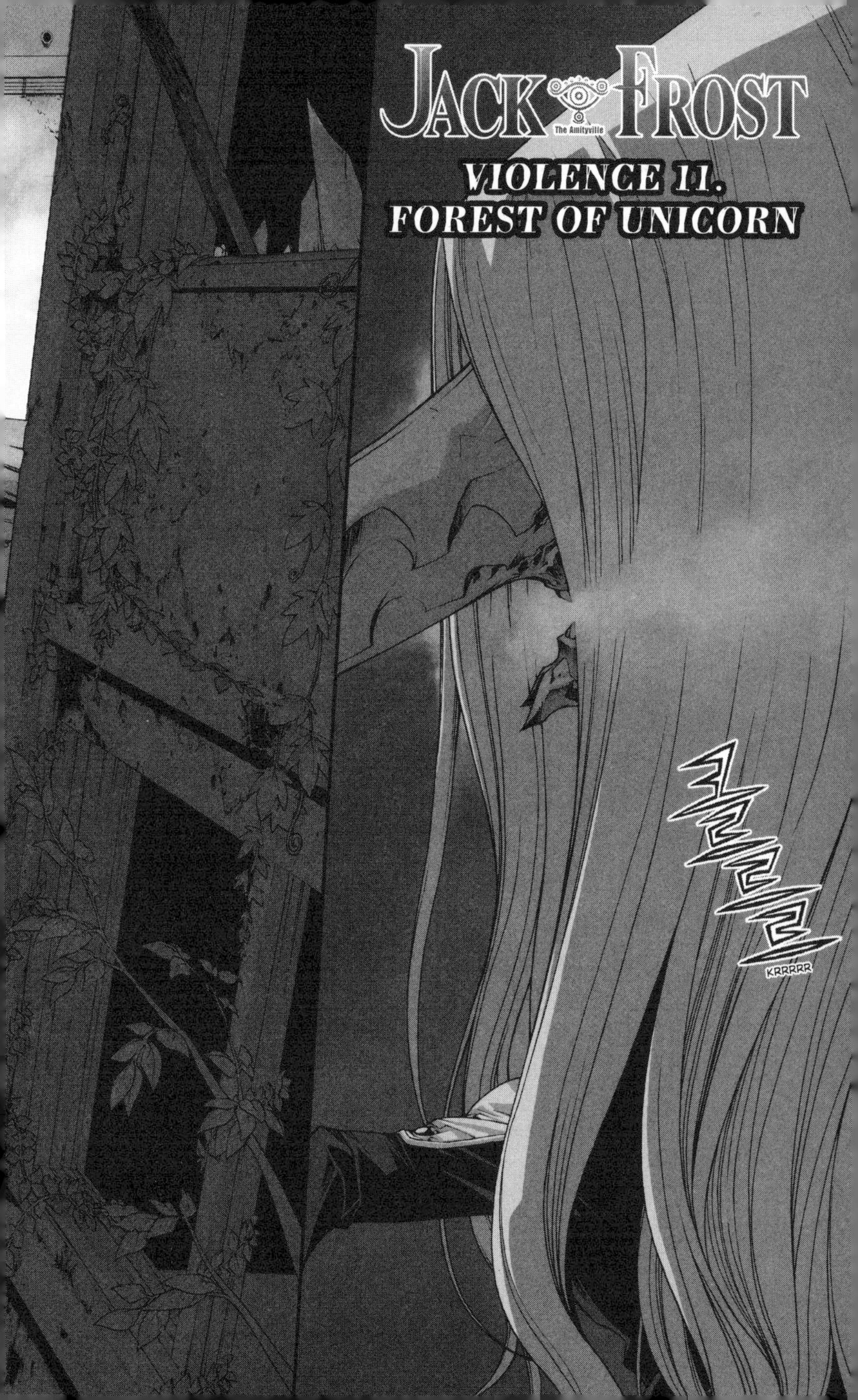
JACK FROST
The Amityville
VIOLENCE 11.
FOREST OF UNICORN
KRRRRR

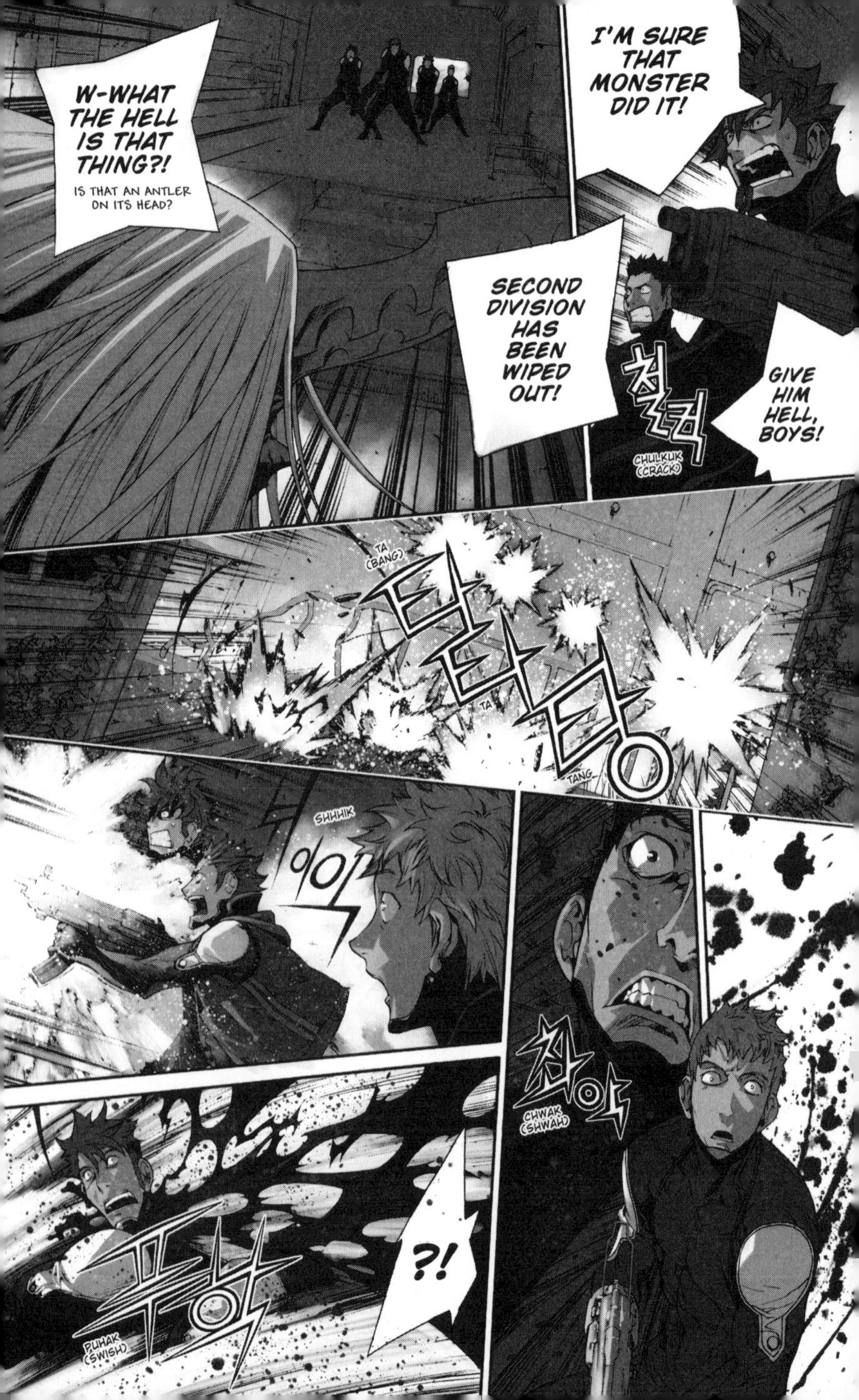
W-WHAT THE HELL IS THAT THING?!
IS THAT AN ANTLER ON ITS HEAD?
I'M SURE THAT MONSTER DID IT!
SECOND DIVISION HAS BEEN WIPED OUT!
CHULKUK (CRACK)
GIVE HIM HELL, BOYS!
TA (BANG)
TA
TANG
SHHHIK
?!
PUHAK (SWISH)
CHWAK (SHWAH)

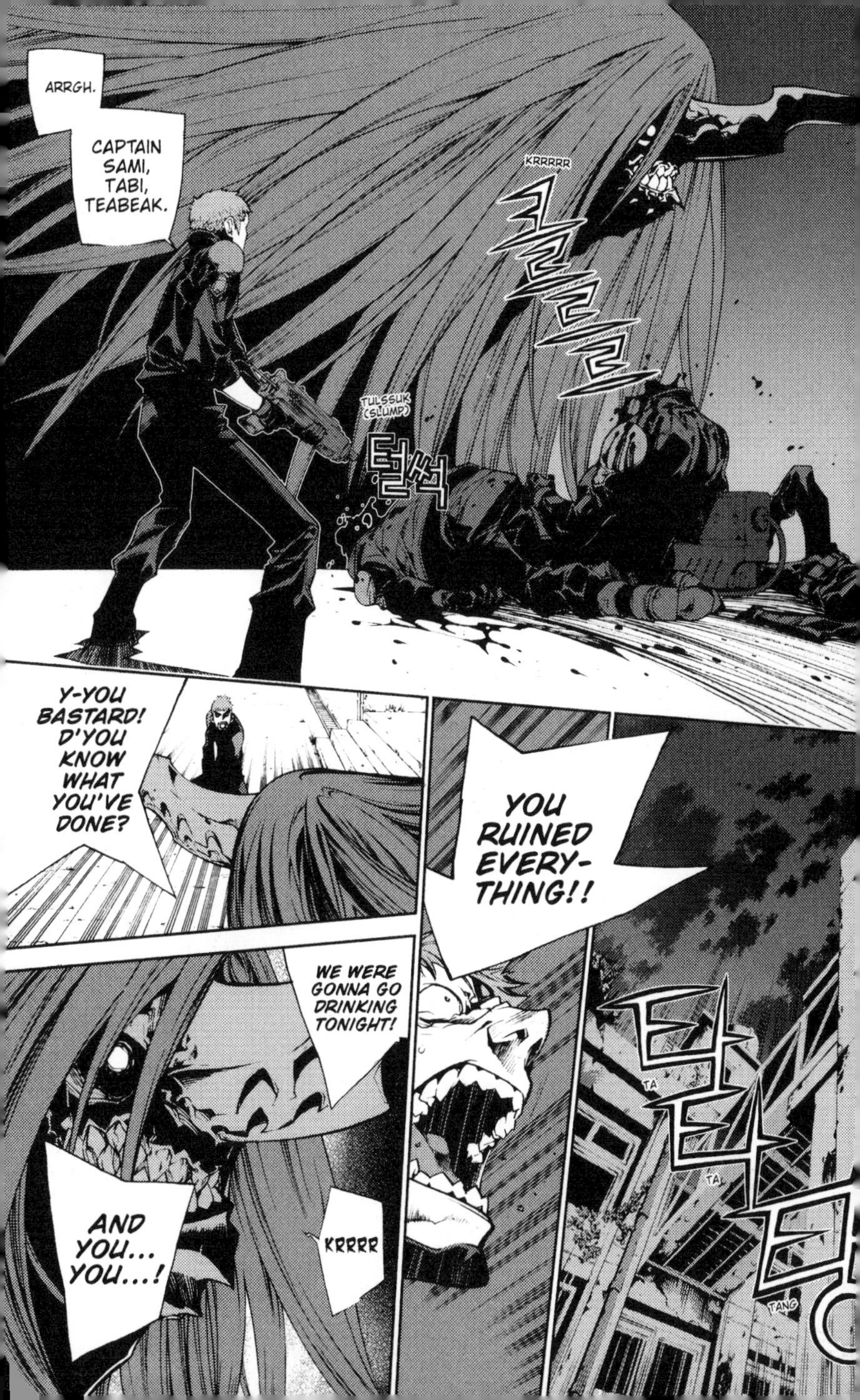

ARRGH.
CAPTAIN SAMI, TABI, TEABEAK.
KRRRRR
TULSSUK (SLUMP)
Y-YOU BASTARD! D'YOU KNOW WHAT YOU'VE DONE?
YOU RUINED EVERY-THING!!
WE WERE GONNA GO DRINKING TONIGHT!
AND YOU... YOU...!
KRRRR
TA
TA
TANG

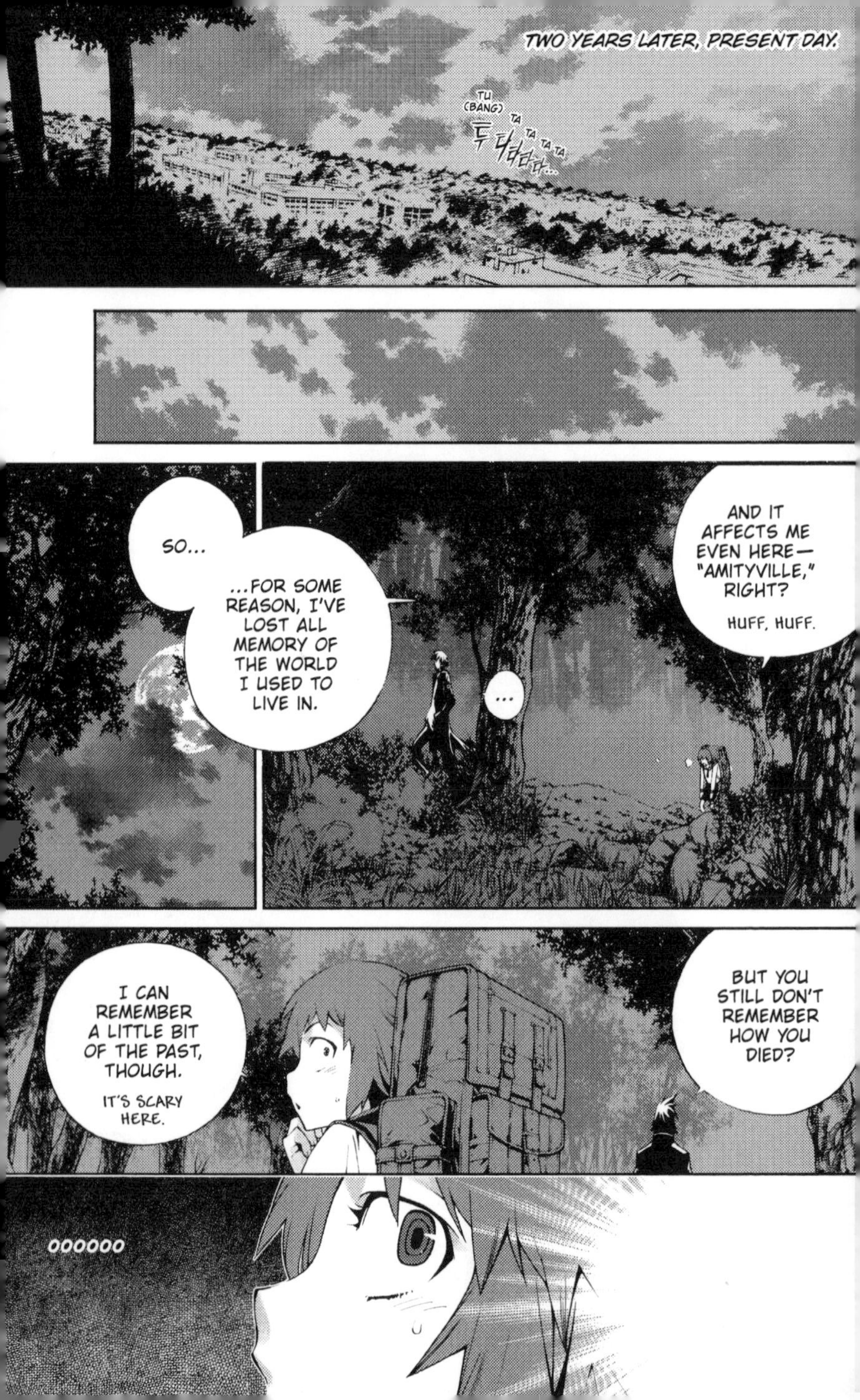
TWO YEARS LATER, PRESENT DAY.
TU (BANG) TA TA TA TA
SO...
...FOR SOME REASON, I'VE LOST ALL MEMORY OF THE WORLD I USED TO LIVE IN.
...
AND IT AFFECTS ME EVEN HERE—"AMITYVILLE," RIGHT?
HUFF, HUFF.
I CAN REMEMBER A LITTLE BIT OF THE PAST, THOUGH.
IT'S SCARY HERE.
BUT YOU STILL DON'T REMEMBER HOW YOU DIED?
OOOOOO

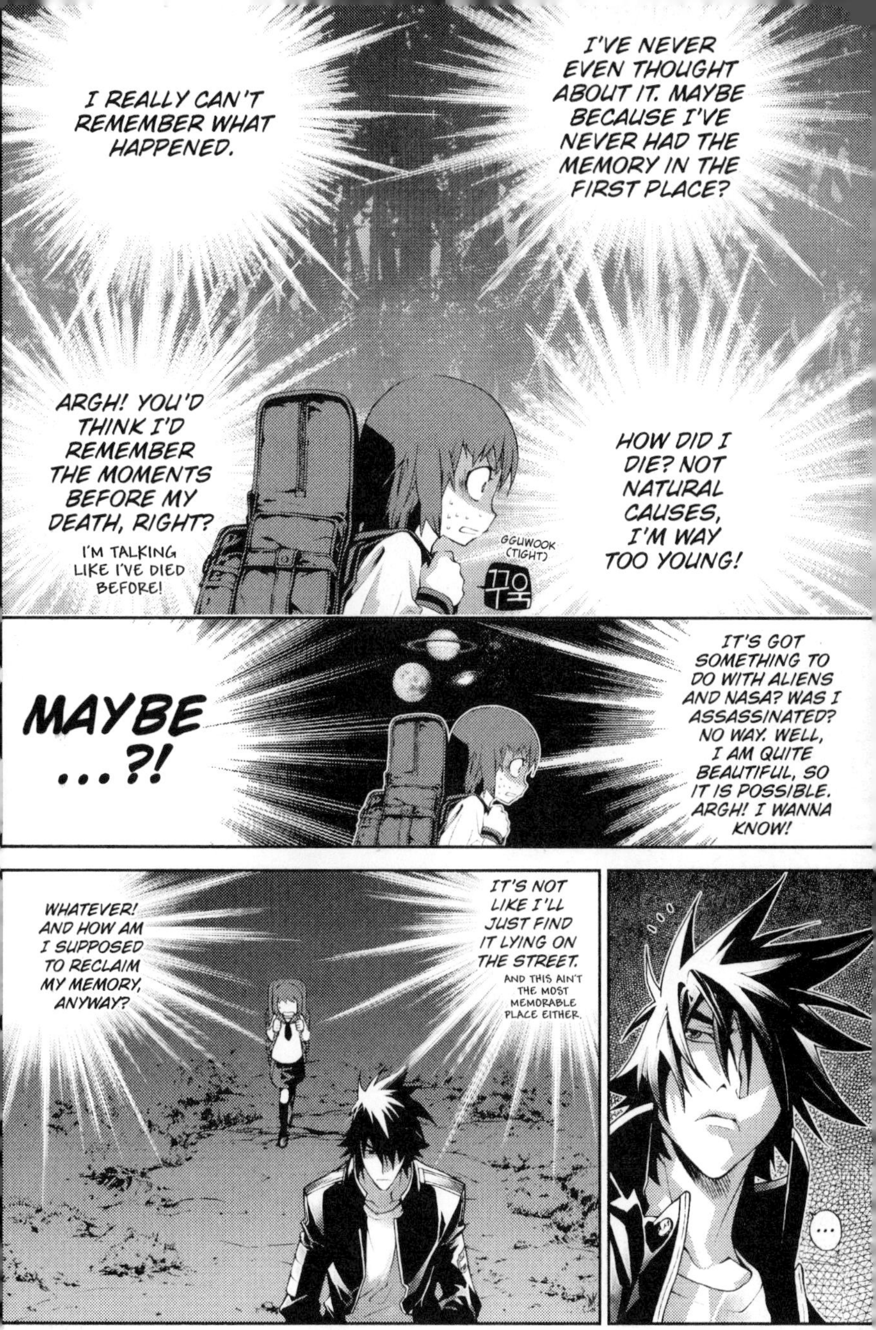
I REALLY CAN'T REMEMBER WHAT HAPPENED.
I'VE NEVER EVEN THOUGHT ABOUT IT. MAYBE BECAUSE I'VE NEVER HAD THE MEMORY IN THE FIRST PLACE?
ARGH! YOU'D THINK I'D REMEMBER THE MOMENTS BEFORE MY DEATH, RIGHT?
I'M TALKING LIKE I'VE DIED BEFORE!
GGUWOOK (TIGHT)
HOW DID I DIE? NOT NATURAL CAUSES, I'M WAY TOO YOUNG!
MAYBE ...?!
IT'S GOT SOMETHING TO DO WITH ALIENS AND NASA? WAS I ASSASSINATED? NO WAY. WELL, I AM QUITE BEAUTIFUL, SO IT IS POSSIBLE. ARGH! I WANNA KNOW!
WHATEVER! AND HOW AM I SUPPOSED TO RECLAIM MY MEMORY, ANYWAY?
IT'S NOT LIKE I'LL JUST FIND IT LYING ON THE STREET.
AND THIS AIN'T THE MOST MEMORABLE PLACE EITHER.
...

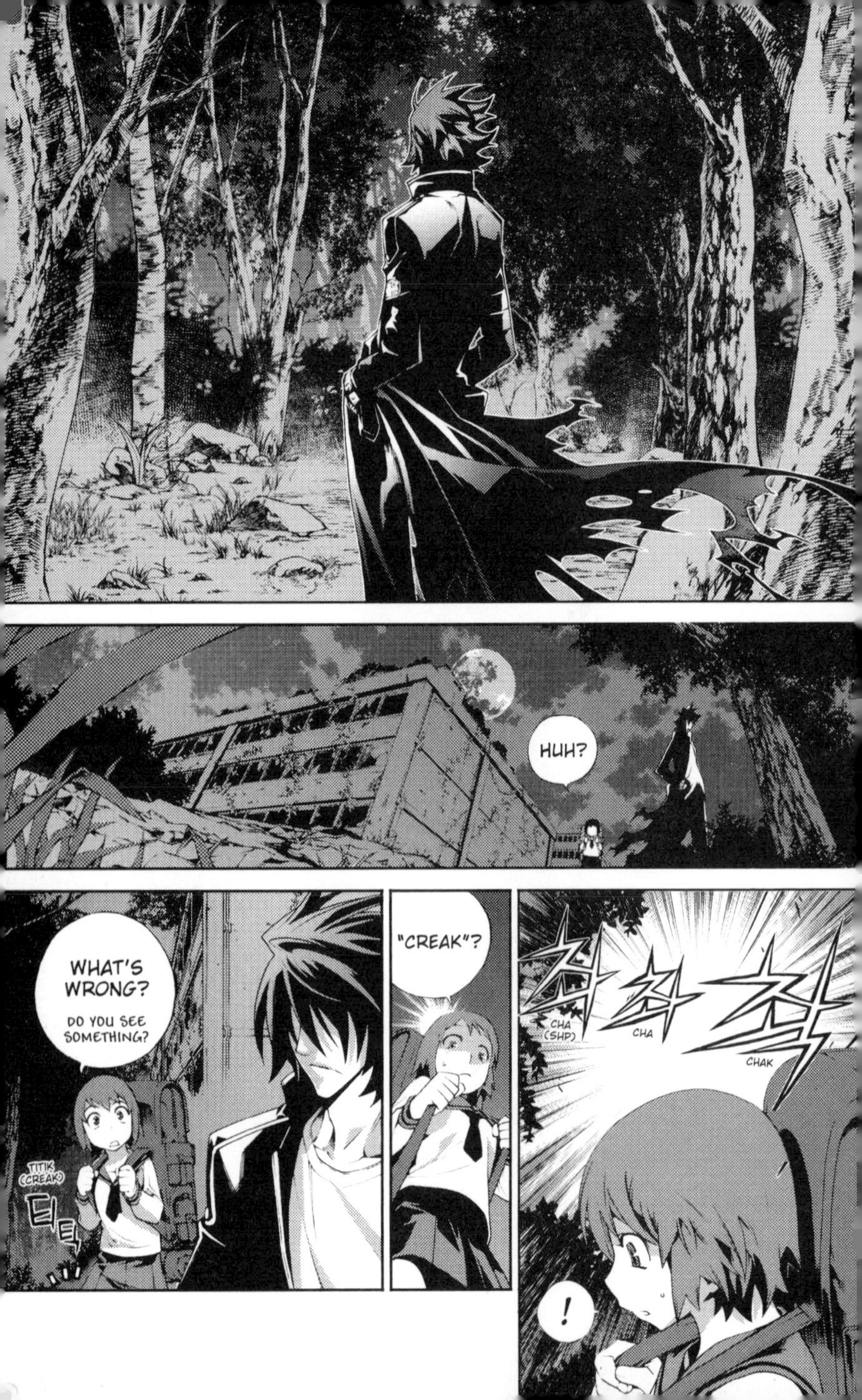
HUH?
WHAT'S WRONG?
DO YOU SEE SOMETHING?
TITIK (CREAK)
"CREAK"?
CHA (SHP)
CHA
CHAK
!

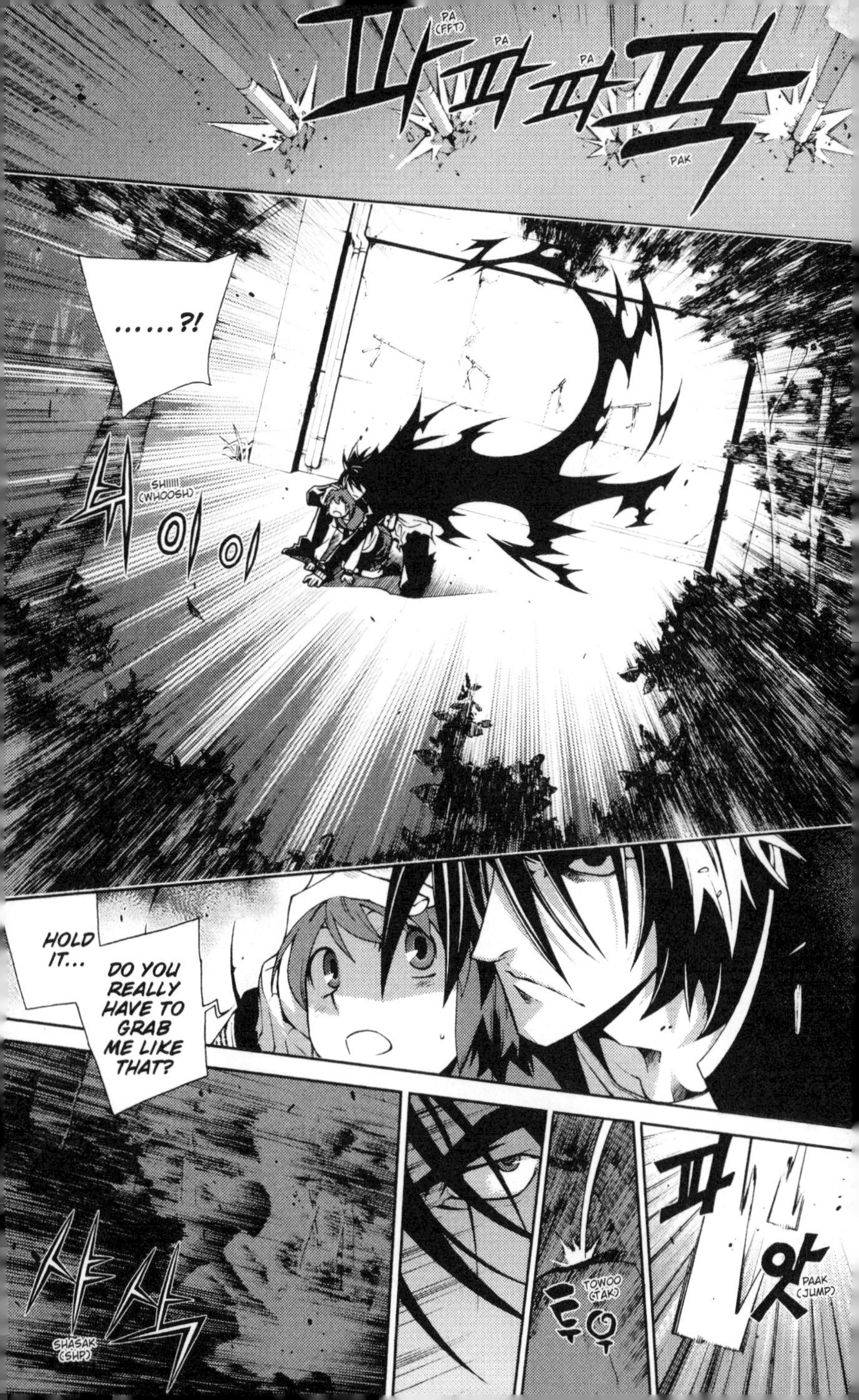
PA (FFT)
PA
PA
PAK
......?!
SHIIIII (WHOOSH)
HOLD IT...
DO YOU REALLY HAVE TO GRAB ME LIKE THAT?
SHASAK (SHP)
TOWOO (TAK)
PAAK (JUMP)

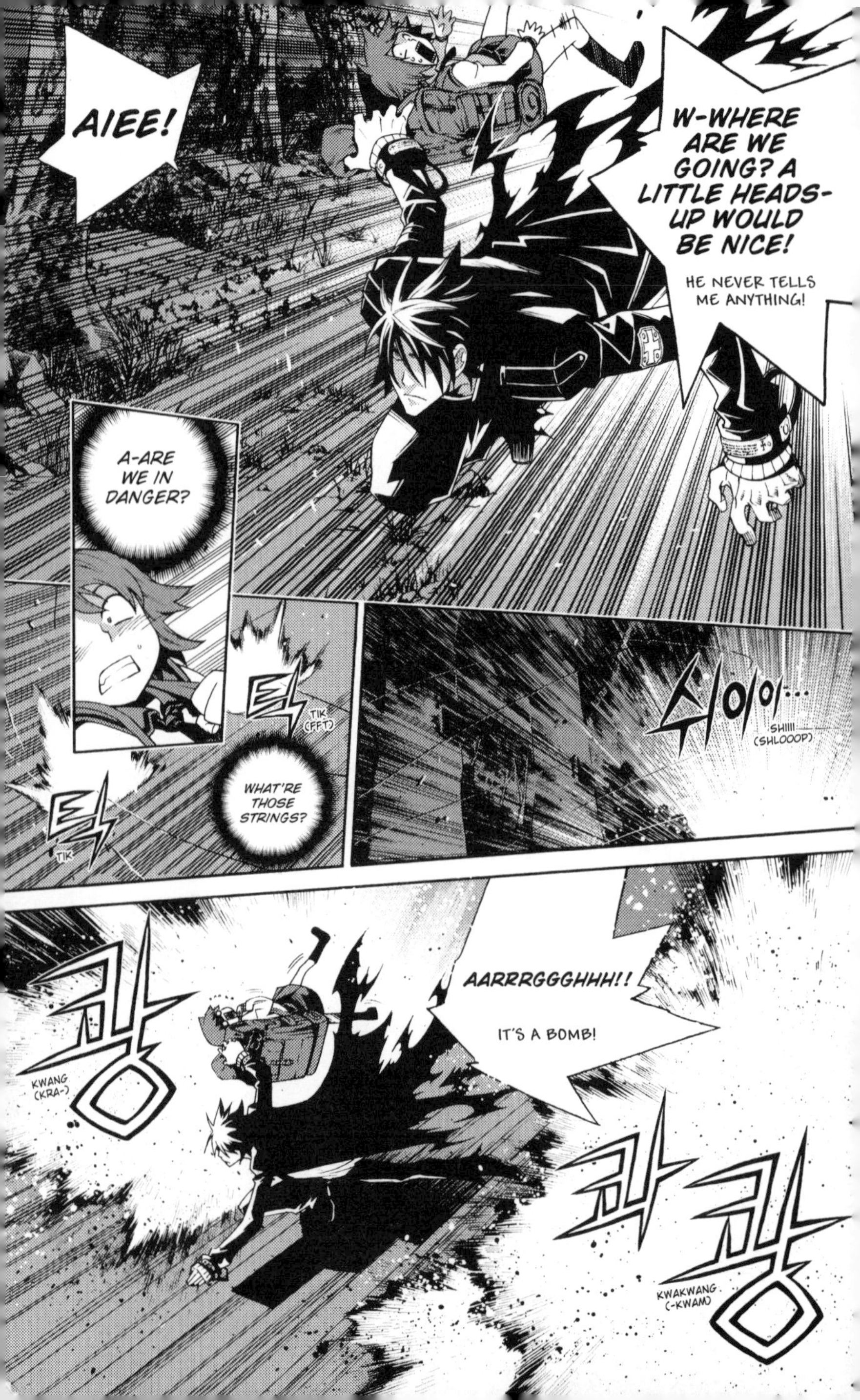
AIEE!
W-WHERE ARE WE GOING? A LITTLE HEADS-UP WOULD BE NICE!
HE NEVER TELLS ME ANYTHING!
A-ARE WE IN DANGER?
티
TIK (FFT)
WHAT'RE THOSE STRINGS?
티
TIK
쉬이이...
SHIIII (SHLOOOP)
콰앙
KWANG (KRA-)
AARRRGGGHHH!!
IT'S A BOMB!
콰콰앙
KWAKWANG (-KWAM)

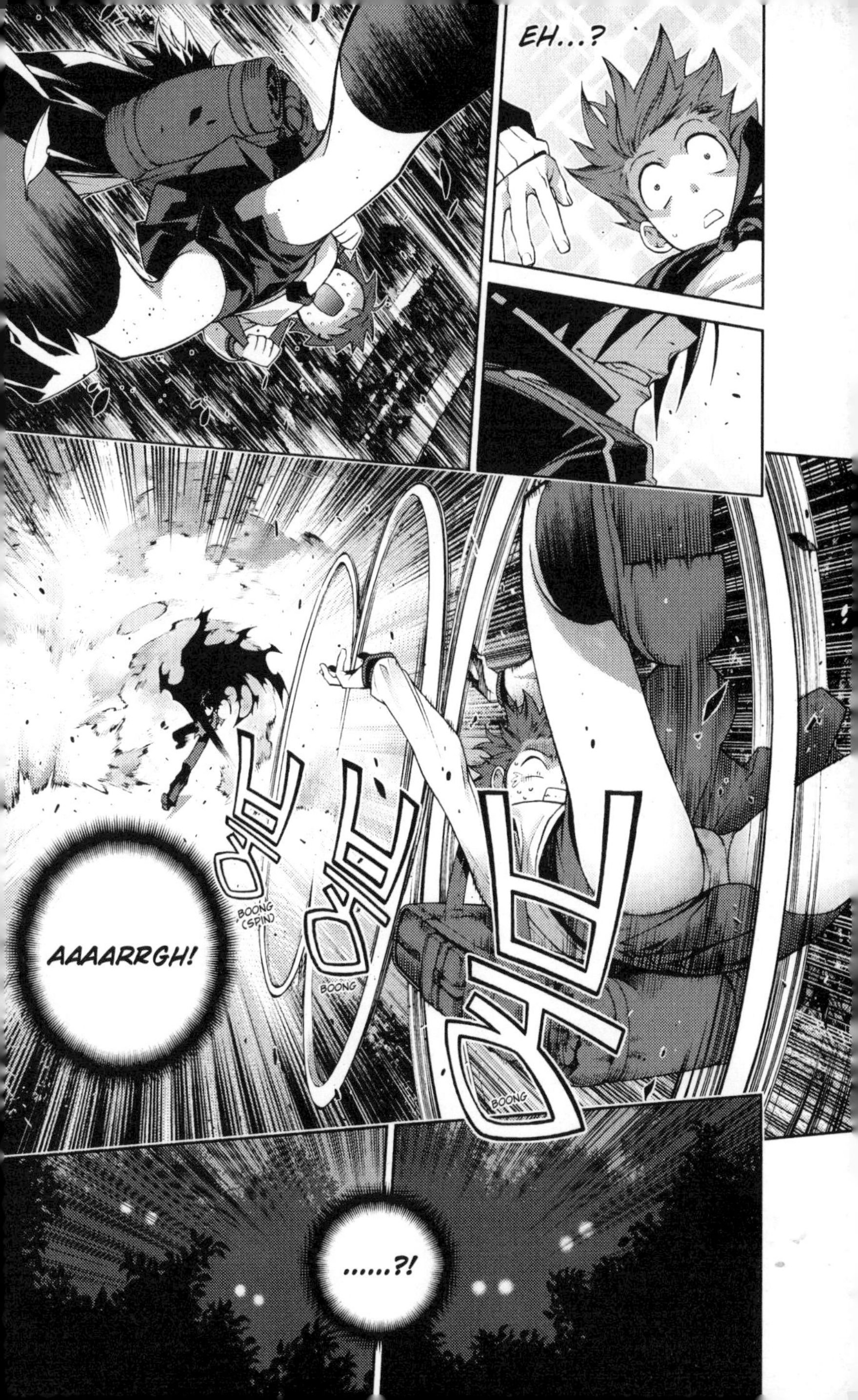
EH...?
AAAARRGH!
BOONG (SPIN)
BOONG
BOONG
......?!

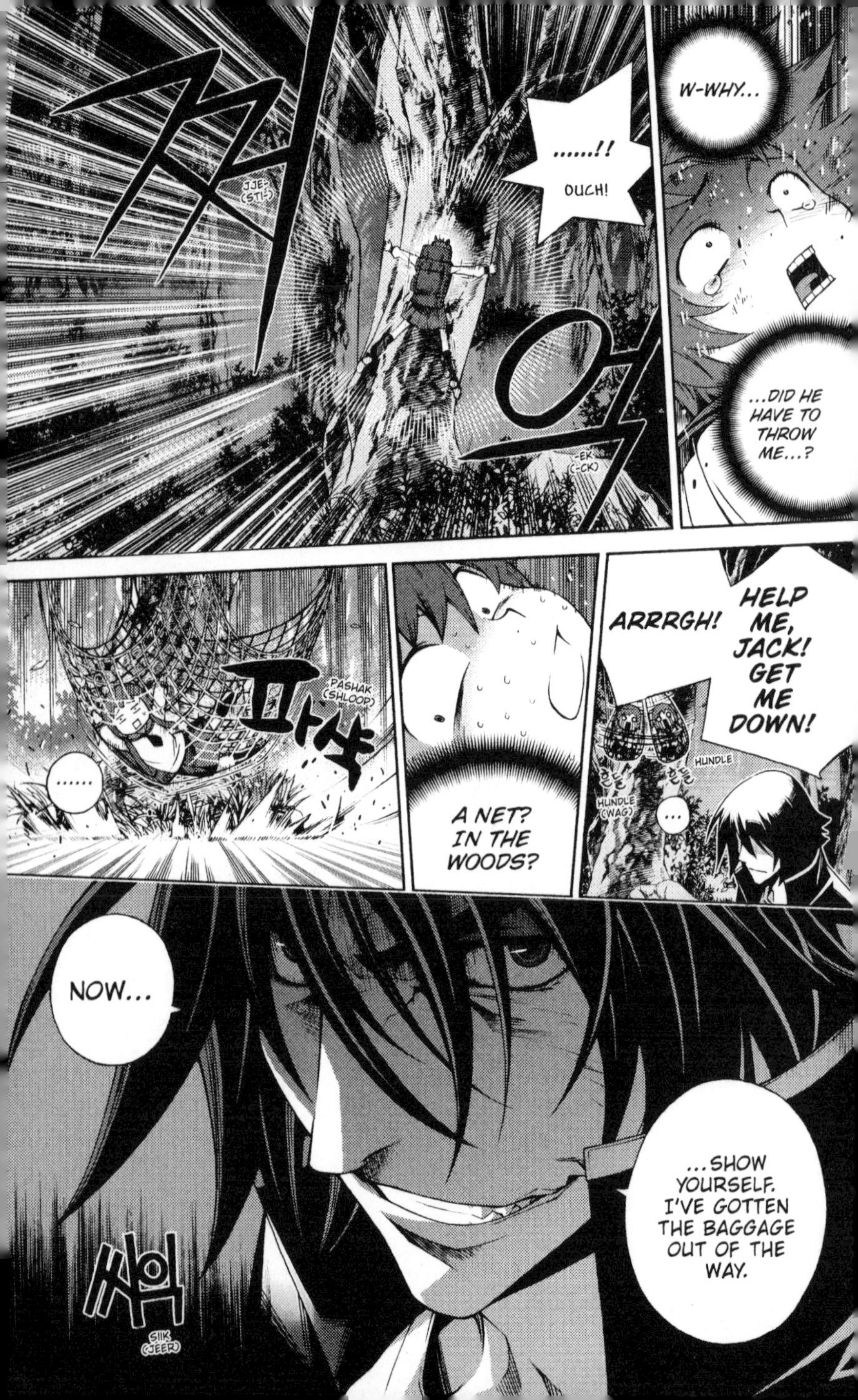
JJE-
(STI-)
......!!
OUCH!
-EK
(-CK)
W-WHY...
...DID HE HAVE TO THROW ME...?
PASHAK
(SHLOOP)
......
A NET? IN THE WOODS?
ARRRGH!
HELP ME, JACK! GET ME DOWN!
HUNDLE
HUNDLE
(WAG)
...
NOW...
...SHOW YOURSELF. I'VE GOTTEN THE BAGGAGE OUT OF THE WAY.
SIIK
(JEER)

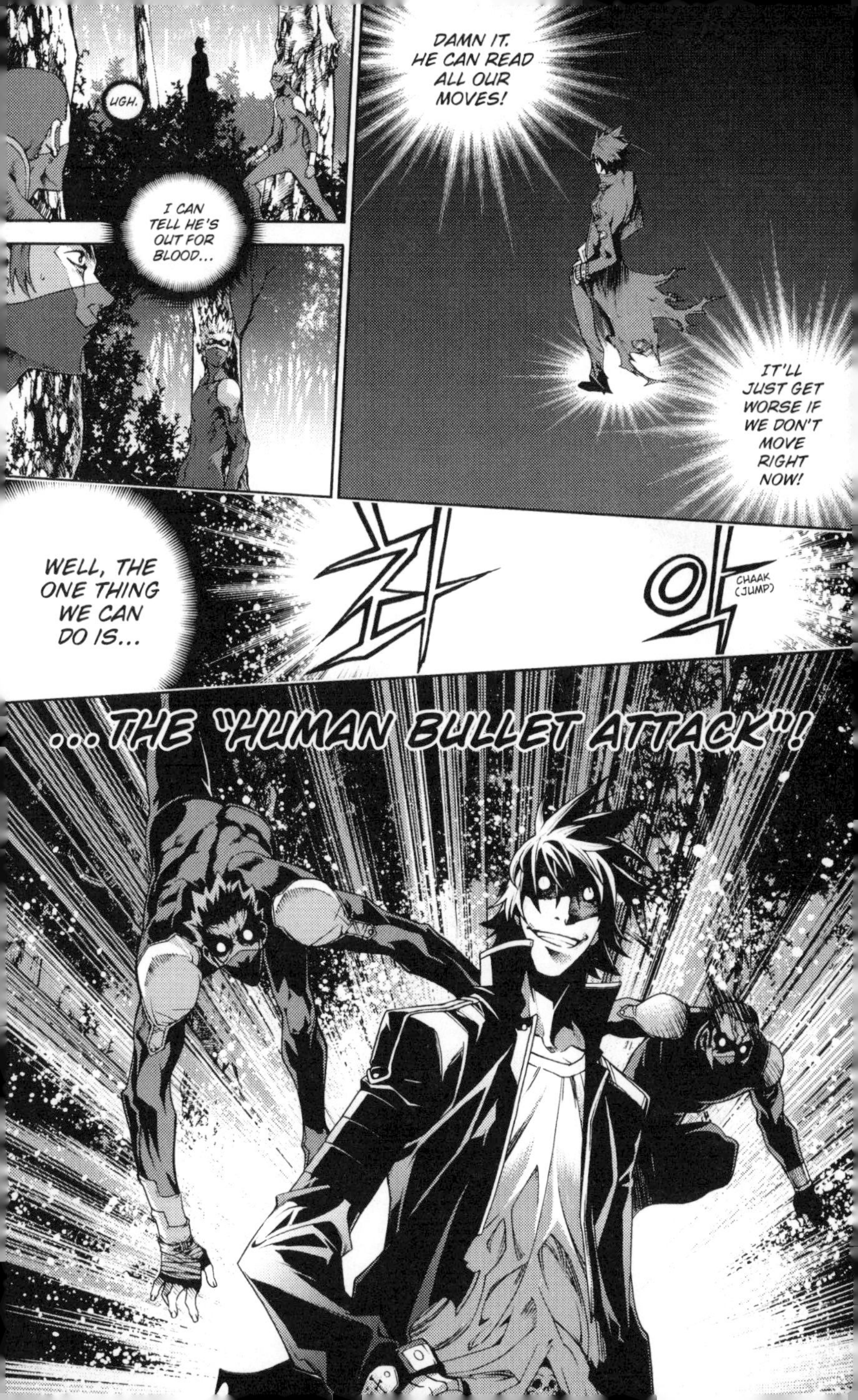
UGH.
I CAN TELL HE'S OUT FOR BLOOD...
DAMN IT. HE CAN READ ALL OUR MOVES!
IT'LL JUST GET WORSE IF WE DON'T MOVE RIGHT NOW!
WELL, THE ONE THING WE CAN DO IS...
착
CHAAK (JUMP)
...THE "HUMAN BULLET ATTACK"!

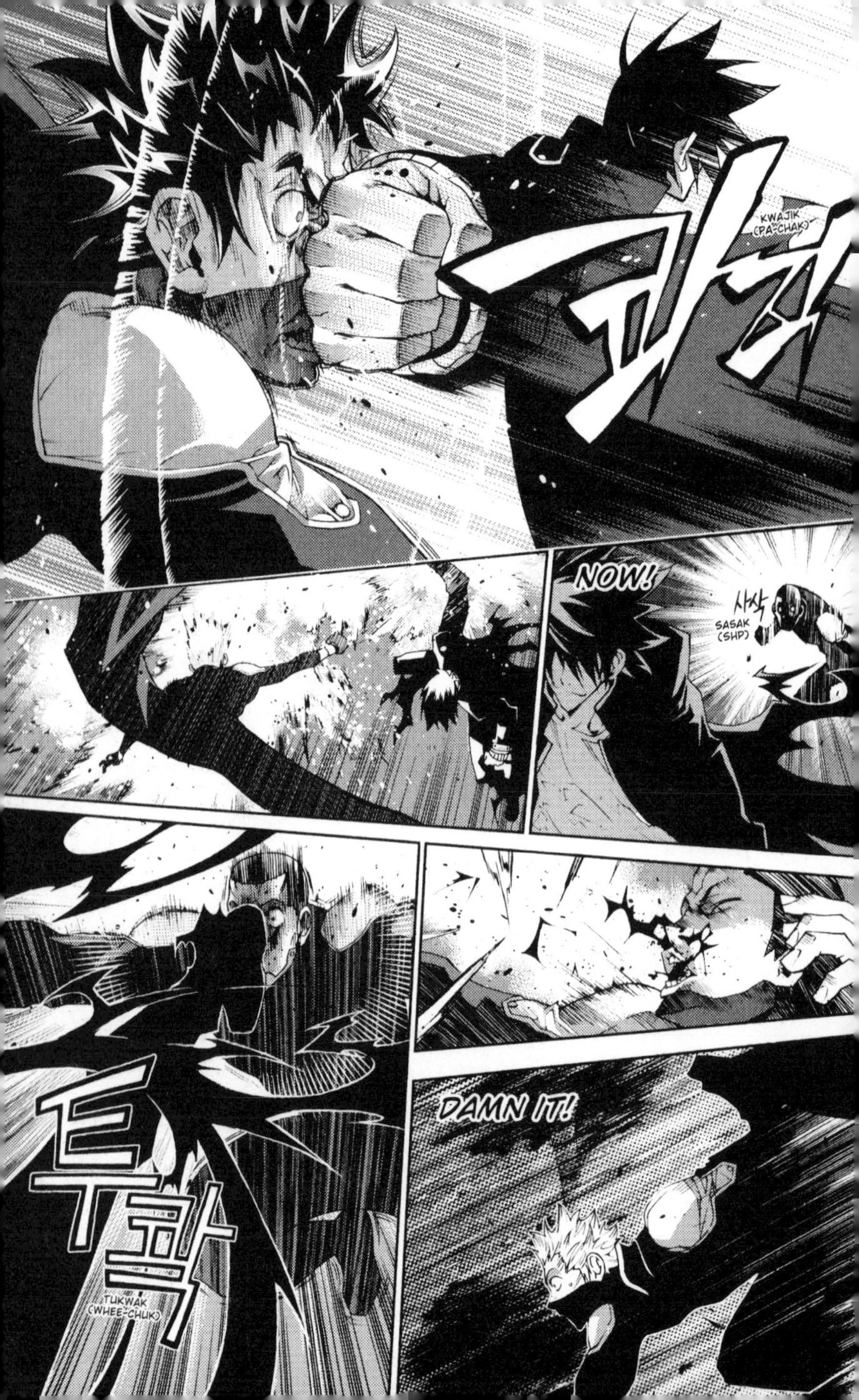

콰직
KWAJIK
(PA-CHAK)
NOW!
사삭
SASAK
(SHP)
투콱
TUKWAK
(WHEE-CHUK)
DAMN IT!

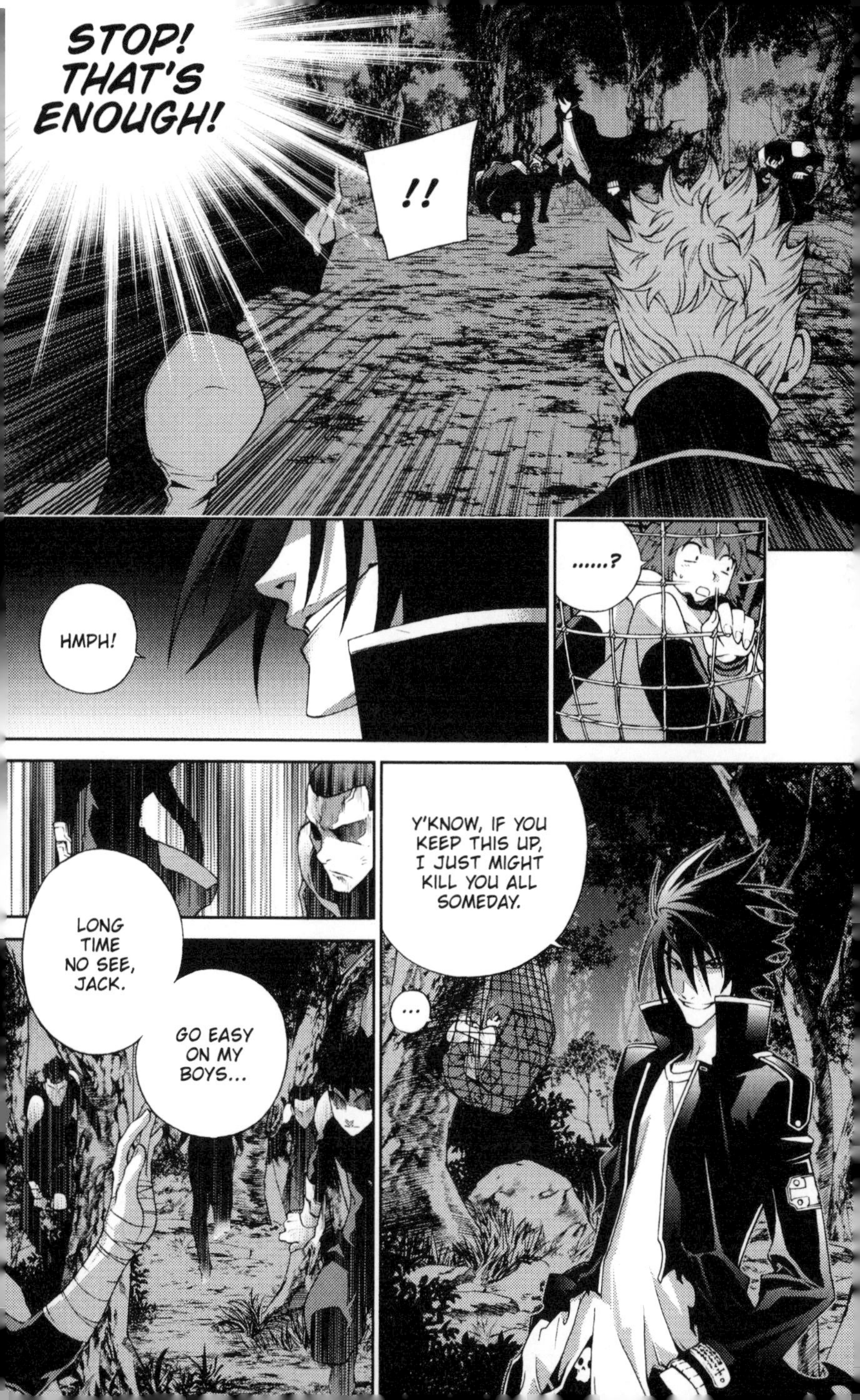
STOP! THAT'S ENOUGH!
!!
HMPH!
......?
Y'KNOW, IF YOU KEEP THIS UP, I JUST MIGHT KILL YOU ALL SOMEDAY.
LONG TIME NO SEE, JACK.
GO EASY ON MY BOYS...
...

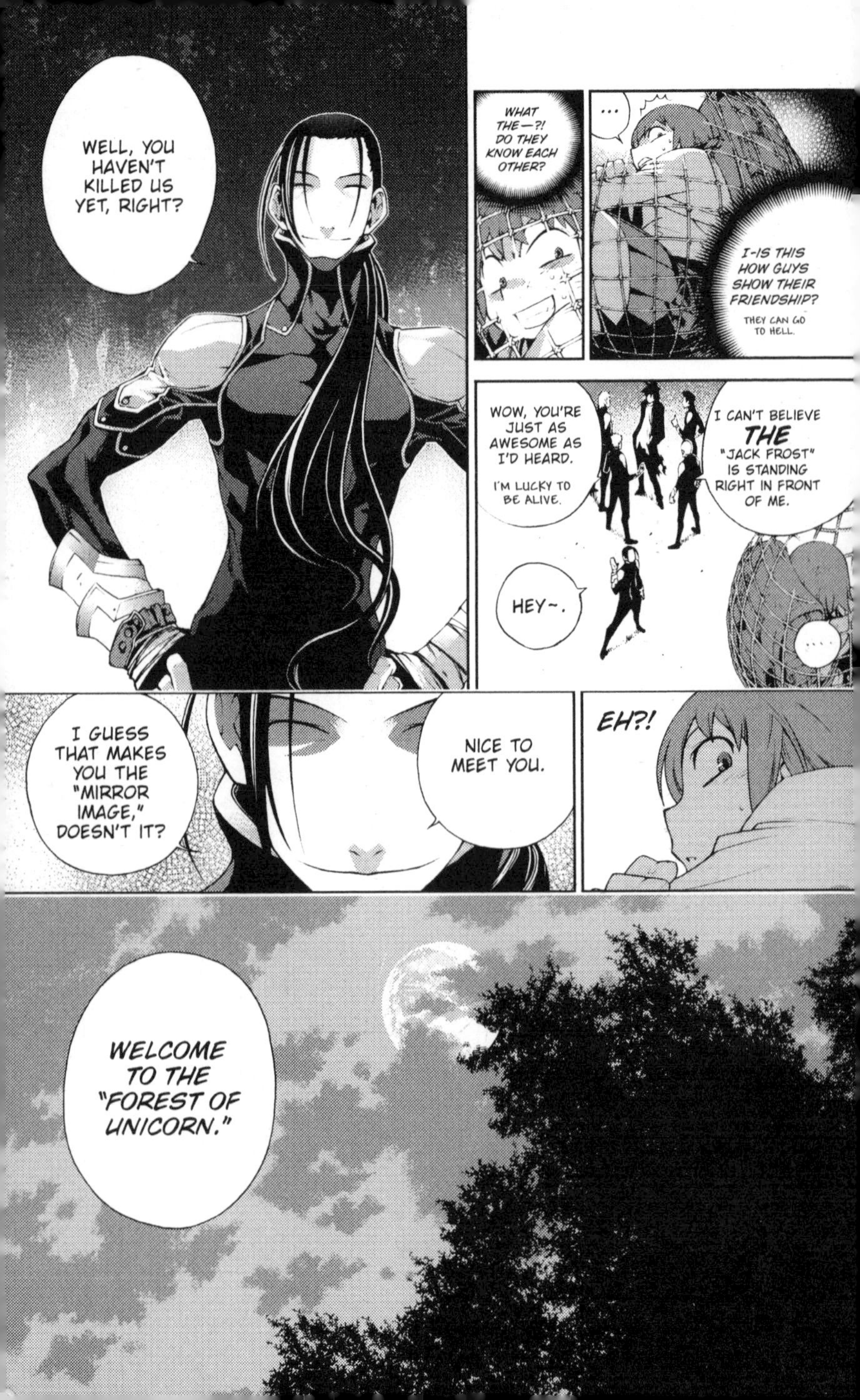

WELL, YOU HAVEN'T KILLED US YET, RIGHT?
WHAT THE—?! DO THEY KNOW EACH OTHER?
...
I-IS THIS HOW GUYS SHOW THEIR FRIENDSHIP?
THEY CAN GO TO HELL.
WOW, YOU'RE JUST AS AWESOME AS I'D HEARD.
I'M LUCKY TO BE ALIVE.
I CAN'T BELIEVE THE "JACK FROST" IS STANDING RIGHT IN FRONT OF ME.
HEY~.
....
I GUESS THAT MAKES YOU THE "MIRROR IMAGE," DOESN'T IT?
NICE TO MEET YOU.
EH?!
WELCOME TO THE "FOREST OF UNICORN."

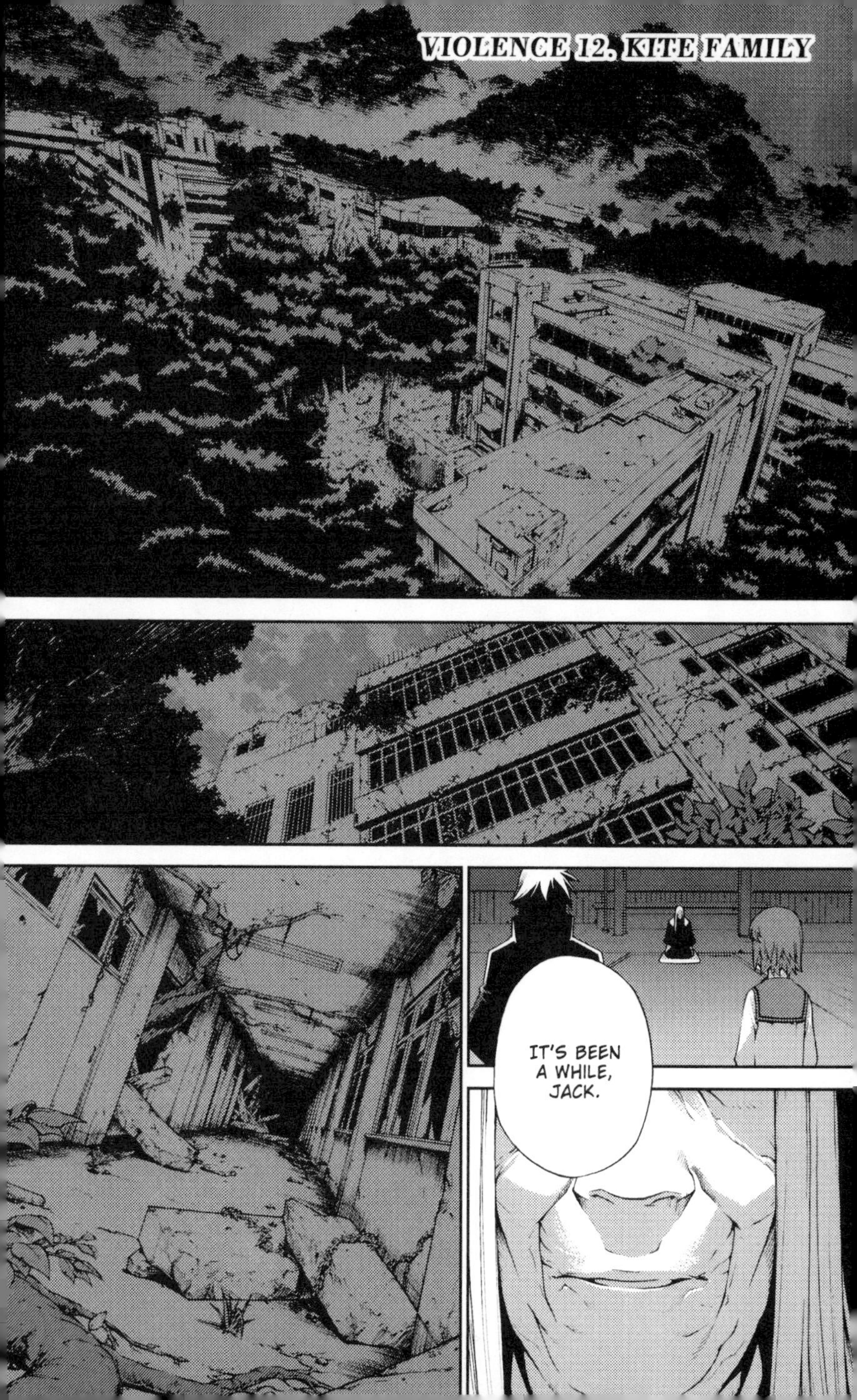
VIOLENCE 12. KITE FAMILY
IT'S BEEN A WHILE, JACK.

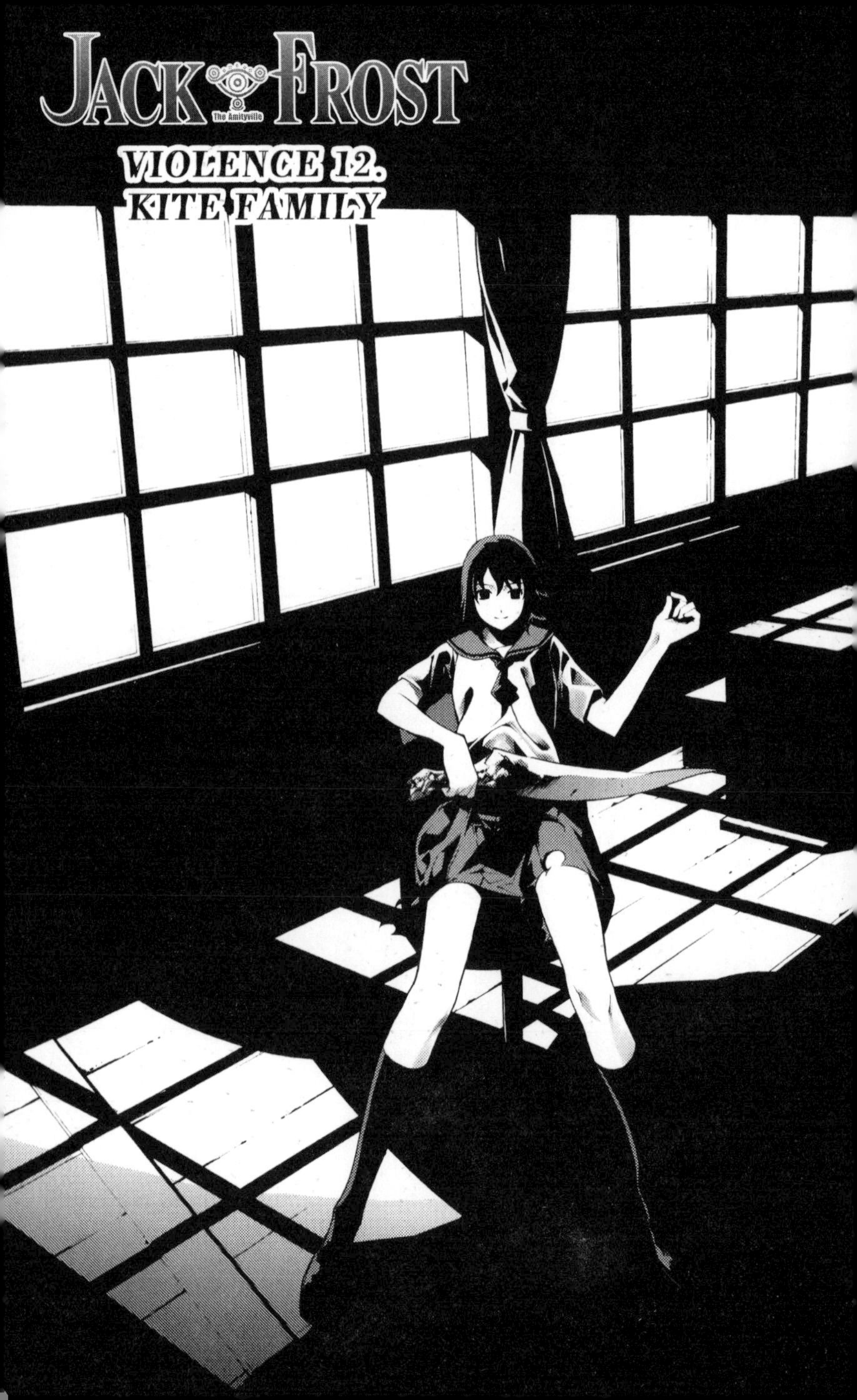
JACK FROST
The Amityville
VIOLENCE 12.
KITE FAMILY

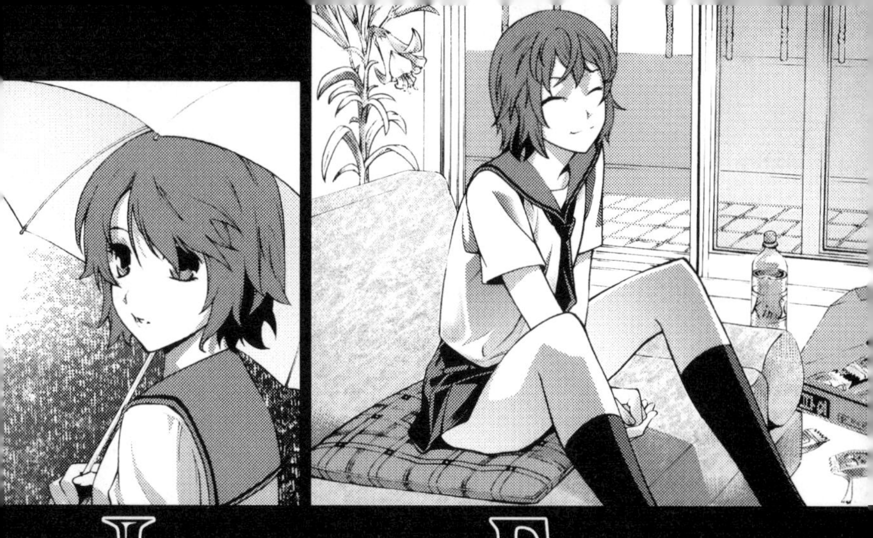

JACK FROST
The Amityville

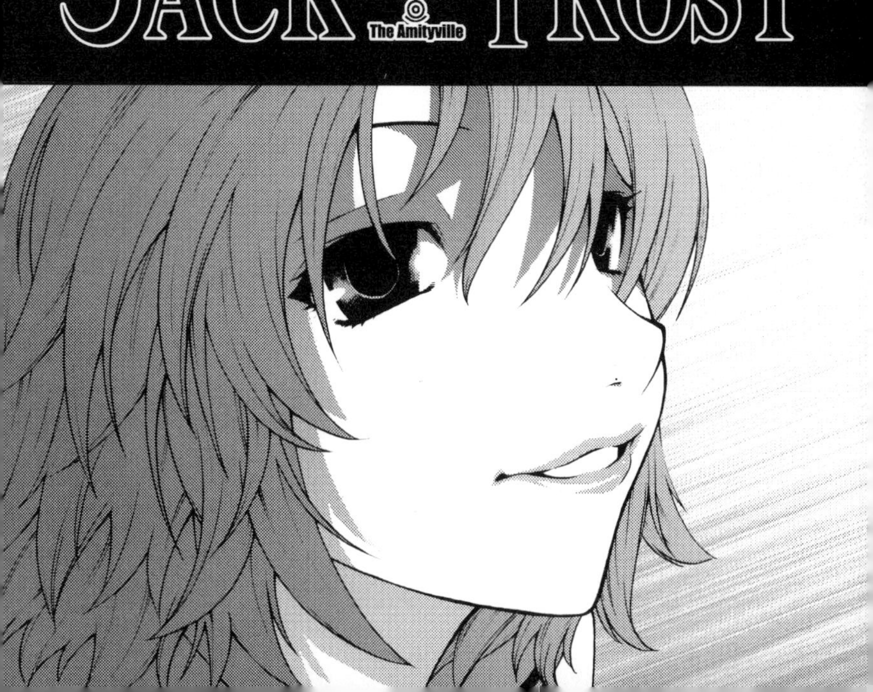

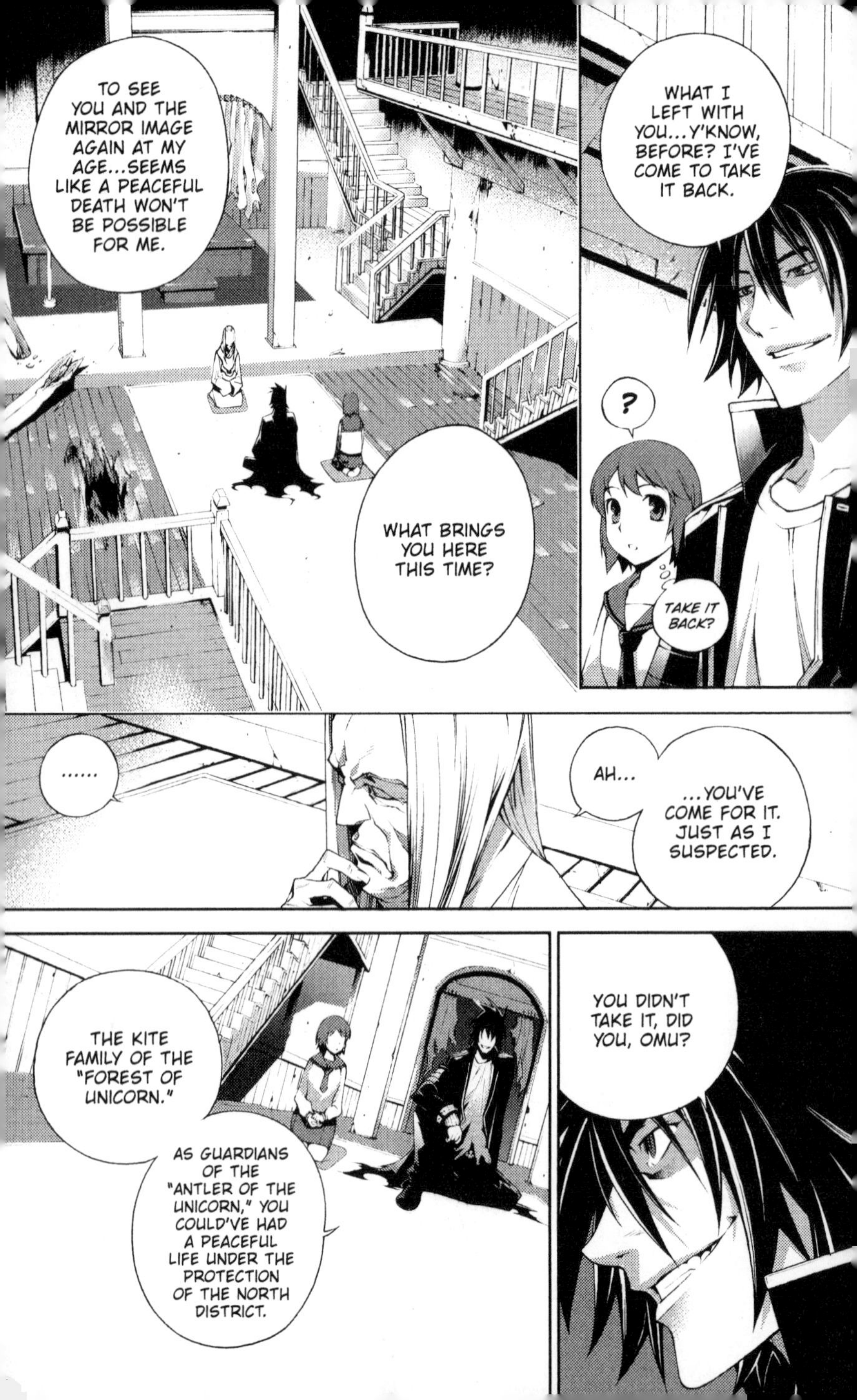
TO SEE YOU AND THE MIRROR IMAGE AGAIN AT MY AGE...SEEMS LIKE A PEACEFUL DEATH WON'T BE POSSIBLE FOR ME.
WHAT BRINGS YOU HERE THIS TIME?
WHAT I LEFT WITH YOU...Y'KNOW, BEFORE? I'VE COME TO TAKE IT BACK.
?
TAKE IT BACK?
......
AH...
...YOU'VE COME FOR IT. JUST AS I SUSPECTED.
THE KITE FAMILY OF THE "FOREST OF UNICORN."
AS GUARDIANS OF THE "ANTLER OF THE UNICORN," YOU COULD'VE HAD A PEACEFUL LIFE UNDER THE PROTECTION OF THE NORTH DISTRICT.
YOU DIDN'T TAKE IT, DID YOU, OMU?

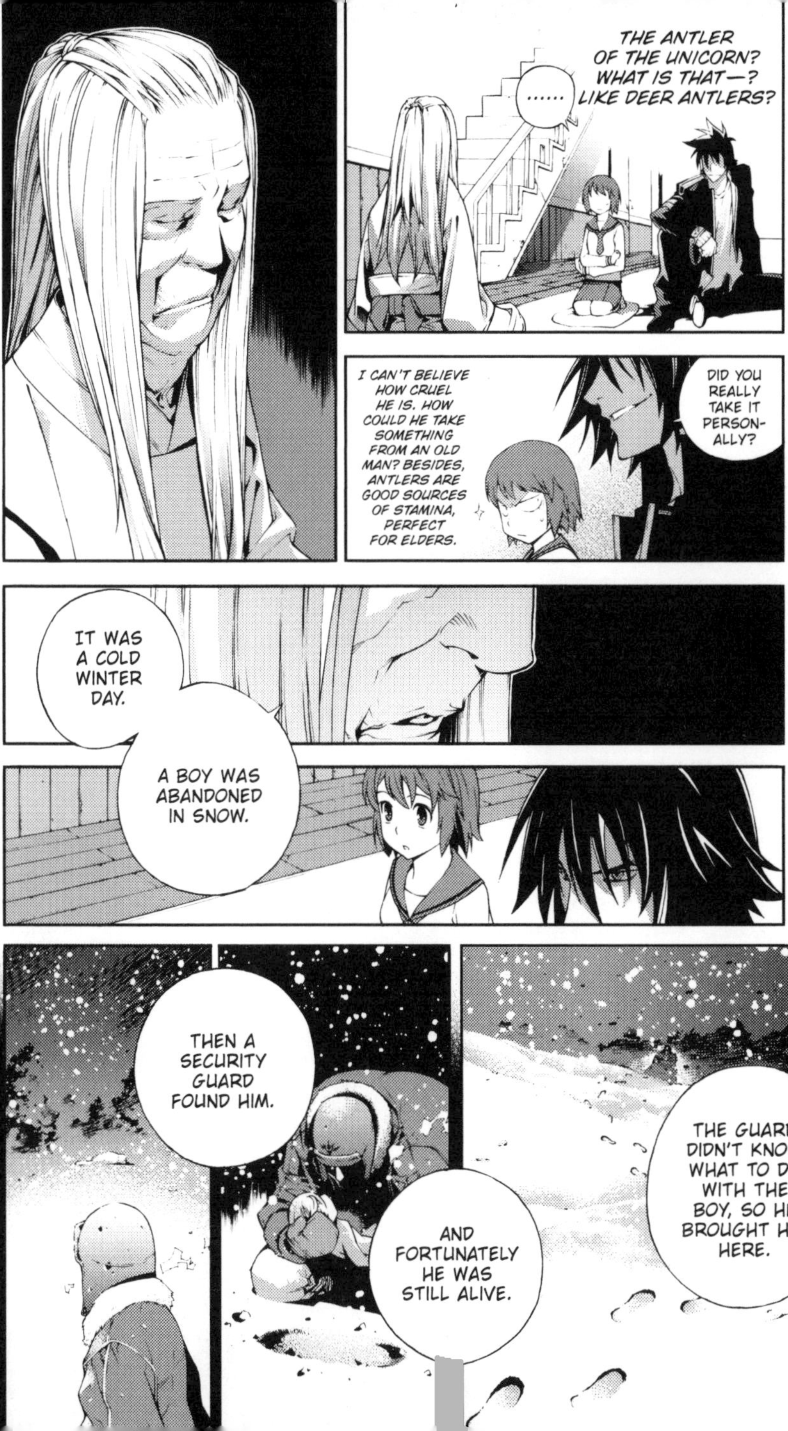
THE ANTLER OF THE UNICORN? WHAT IS THAT—? LIKE DEER ANTLERS?
......
I CAN'T BELIEVE HOW CRUEL HE IS. HOW COULD HE TAKE SOMETHING FROM AN OLD MAN? BESIDES, ANTLERS ARE GOOD SOURCES OF STAMINA, PERFECT FOR ELDERS.
DID YOU REALLY TAKE IT PERSON-ALLY?
IT WAS A COLD WINTER DAY.
A BOY WAS ABANDONED IN SNOW.
THEN A SECURITY GUARD FOUND HIM.
AND FORTUNATELY HE WAS STILL ALIVE.
THE GUARD DIDN'T KNOW WHAT TO DO WITH THE BOY, SO HE BROUGHT HIM HERE.

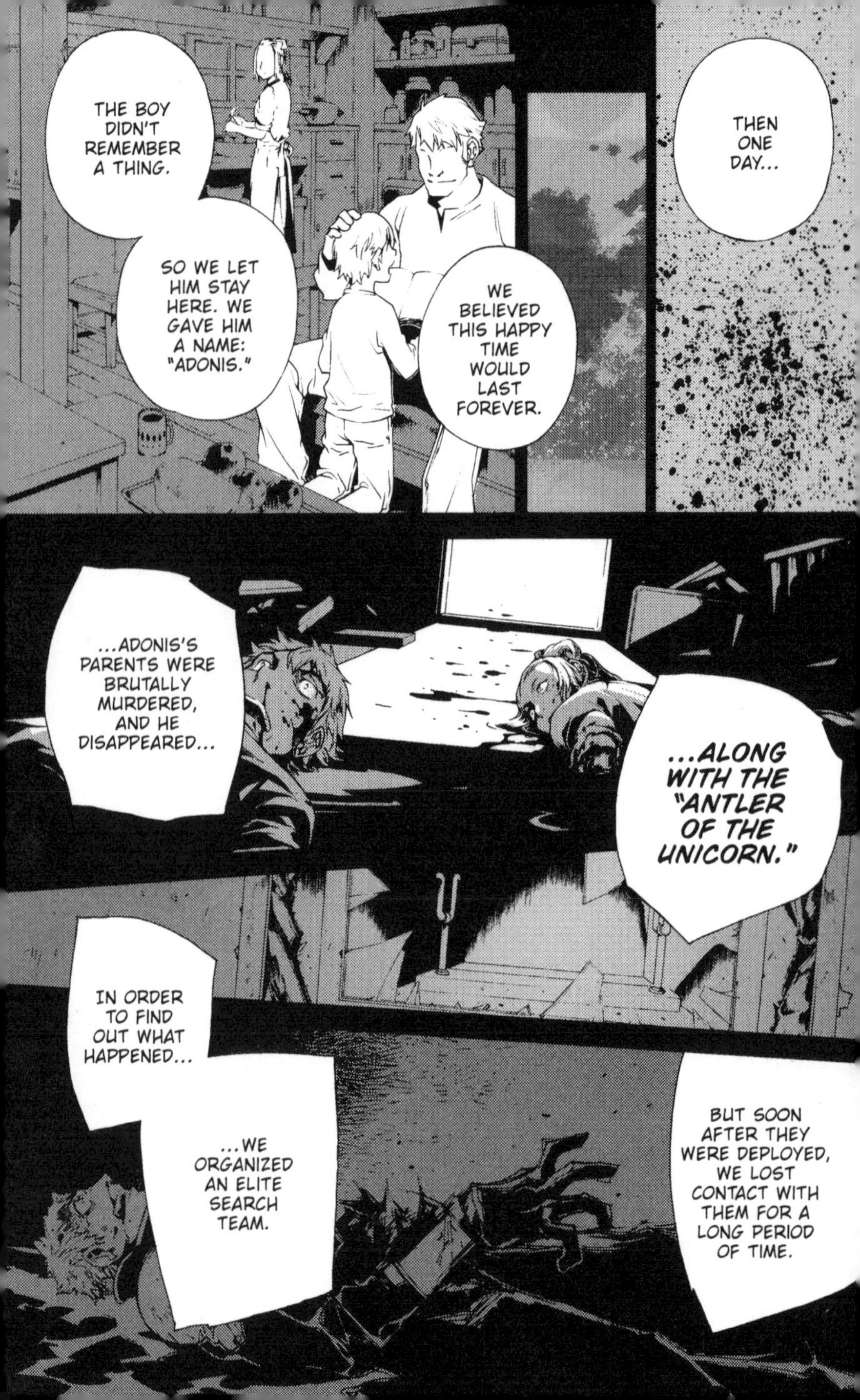
THE BOY DIDN'T REMEMBER A THING.
SO WE LET HIM STAY HERE. WE GAVE HIM A NAME: "ADONIS."
WE BELIEVED THIS HAPPY TIME WOULD LAST FOREVER.
THEN ONE DAY...
...ADONIS'S PARENTS WERE BRUTALLY MURDERED, AND HE DISAPPEARED...
...ALONG WITH THE "ANTLER OF THE UNICORN."
IN ORDER TO FIND OUT WHAT HAPPENED...
...WE ORGANIZED AN ELITE SEARCH TEAM.
BUT SOON AFTER THEY WERE DEPLOYED, WE LOST CONTACT WITH THEM FOR A LONG PERIOD OF TIME.

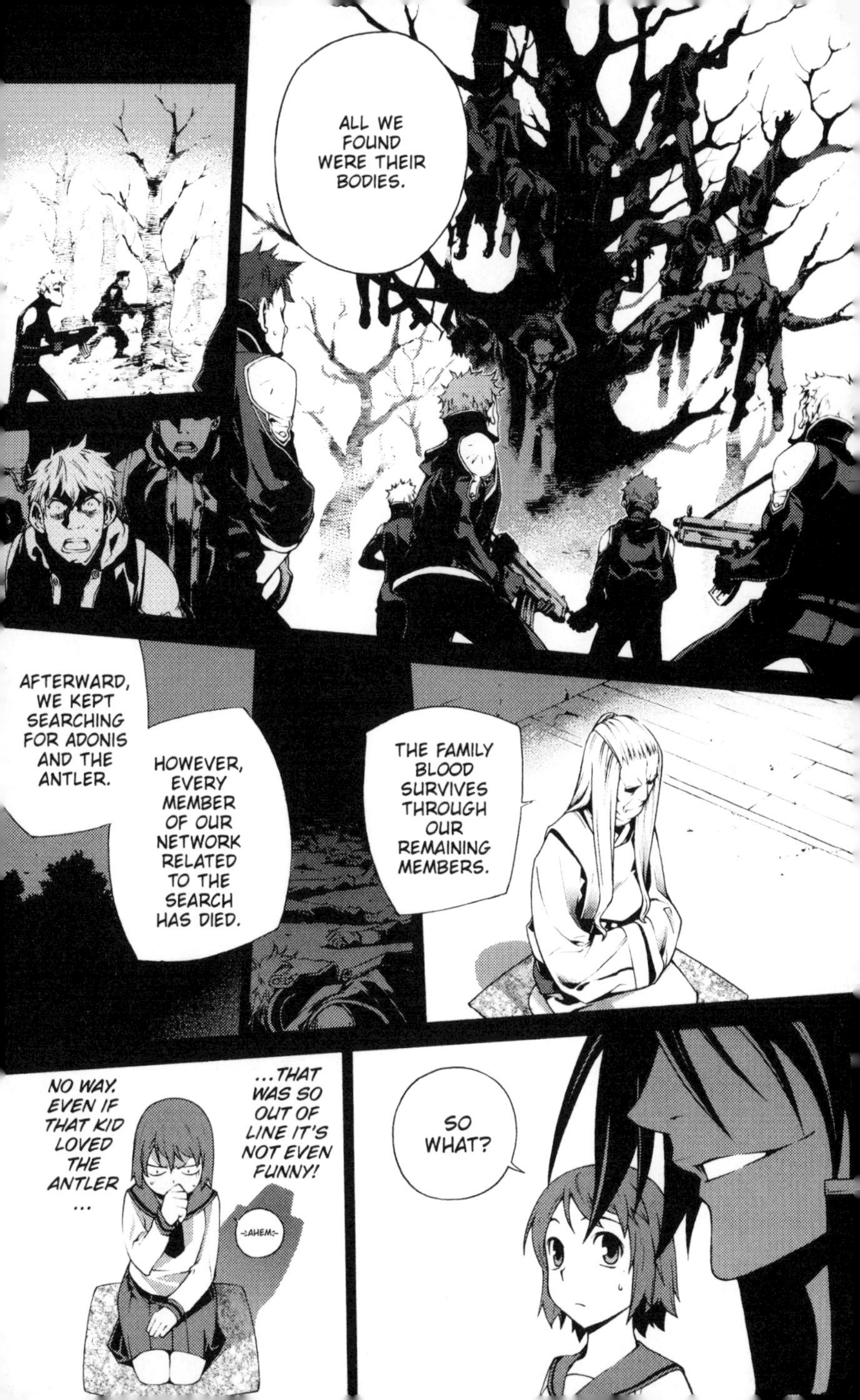
ALL WE FOUND WERE THEIR BODIES.
AFTERWARD, WE KEPT SEARCHING FOR ADONIS AND THE ANTLER.
HOWEVER, EVERY MEMBER OF OUR NETWORK RELATED TO THE SEARCH HAS DIED.
THE FAMILY BLOOD SURVIVES THROUGH OUR REMAINING MEMBERS.
NO WAY. EVEN IF THAT KID LOVED THE ANTLER ...
...THAT WAS SO OUT OF LINE IT'S NOT EVEN FUNNY!
AHEM
SO WHAT?

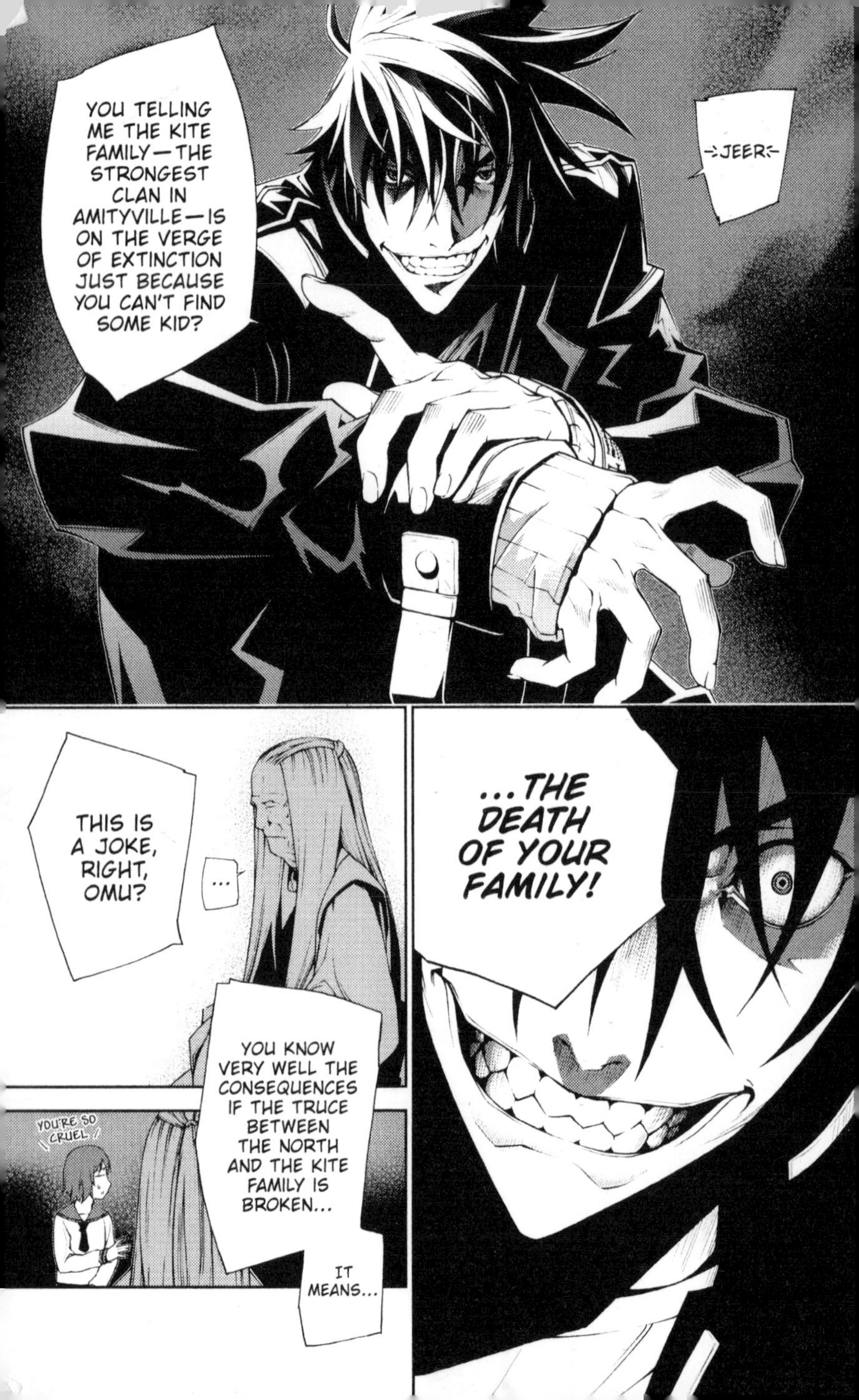
YOU TELLING ME THE KITE FAMILY—THE STRONGEST CLAN IN AMITYVILLE—IS ON THE VERGE OF EXTINCTION JUST BECAUSE YOU CAN'T FIND SOME KID?
⊰JEER⊱
THIS IS A JOKE, RIGHT, OMU?
...
YOU'RE SO CRUEL
YOU KNOW VERY WELL THE CONSEQUENCES IF THE TRUCE BETWEEN THE NORTH AND THE KITE FAMILY IS BROKEN...
IT MEANS...
...THE DEATH OF YOUR FAMILY!

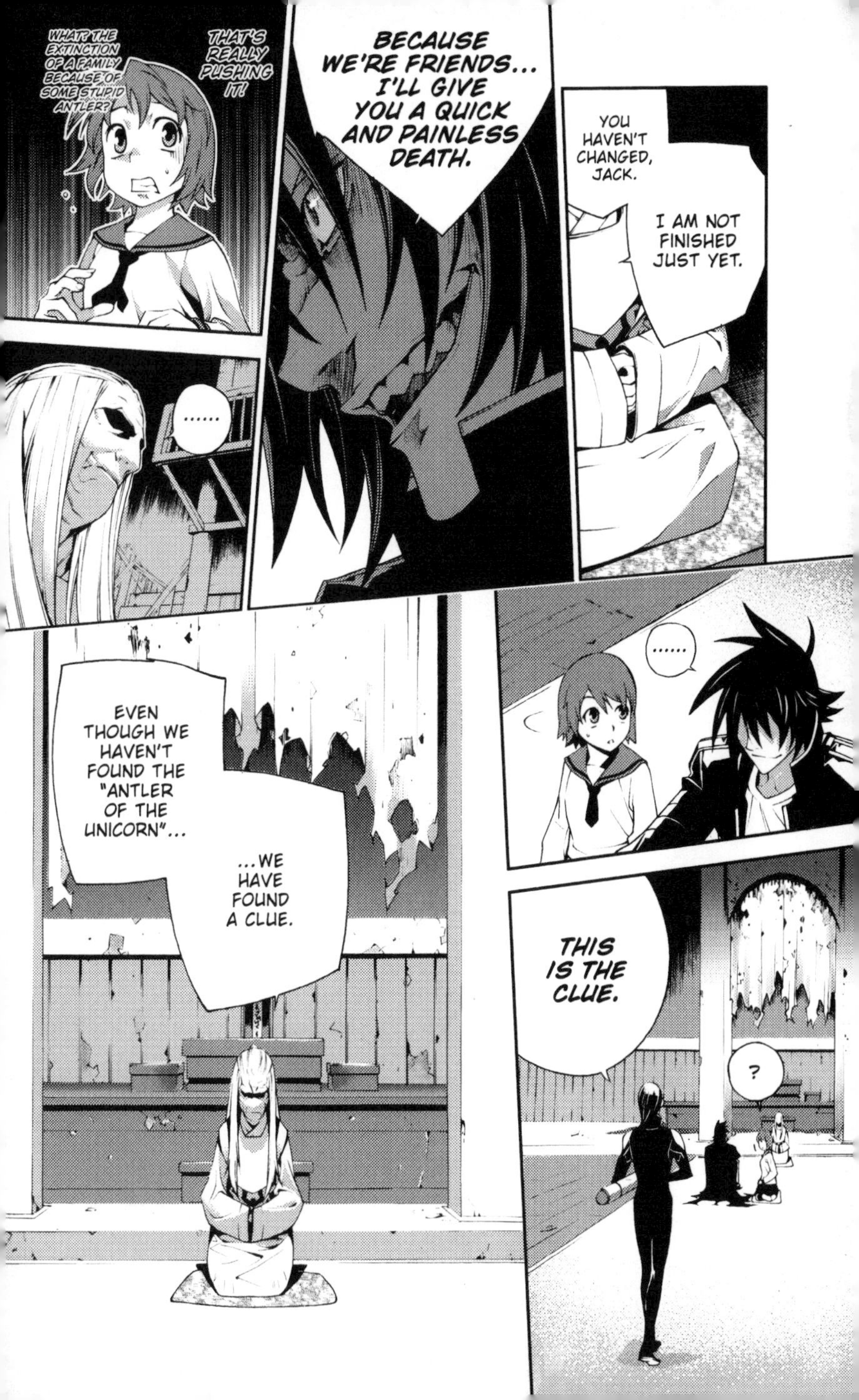
WHAT? THE EXTINCTION OF A FAMILY BECAUSE OF SOME STUPID ANTLER?
THAT'S REALLY PUSHING IT!
BECAUSE WE'RE FRIENDS... I'LL GIVE YOU A QUICK AND PAINLESS DEATH.
YOU HAVEN'T CHANGED, JACK.
I AM NOT FINISHED JUST YET.
......
EVEN THOUGH WE HAVEN'T FOUND THE "ANTLER OF THE UNICORN"...
...WE HAVE FOUND A CLUE.
......
THIS IS THE CLUE.
?

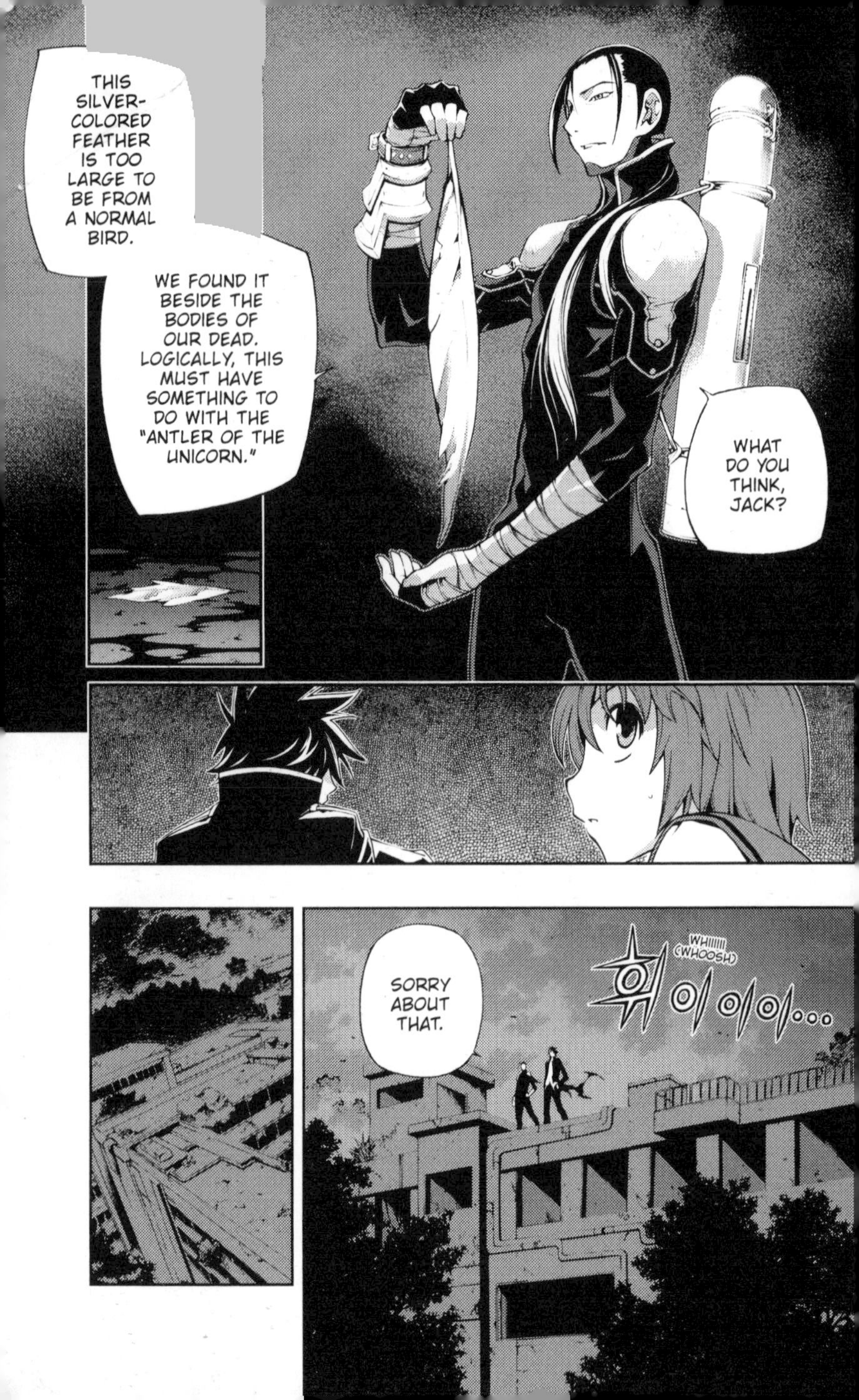
THIS SILVER-COLORED FEATHER IS TOO LARGE TO BE FROM A NORMAL BIRD.
WE FOUND IT BESIDE THE BODIES OF OUR DEAD. LOGICALLY, THIS MUST HAVE SOMETHING TO DO WITH THE "ANTLER OF THE UNICORN."
WHAT DO YOU THINK, JACK?
SORRY ABOUT THAT.
휘이이이...
WHIIIIII (WHOOSH)

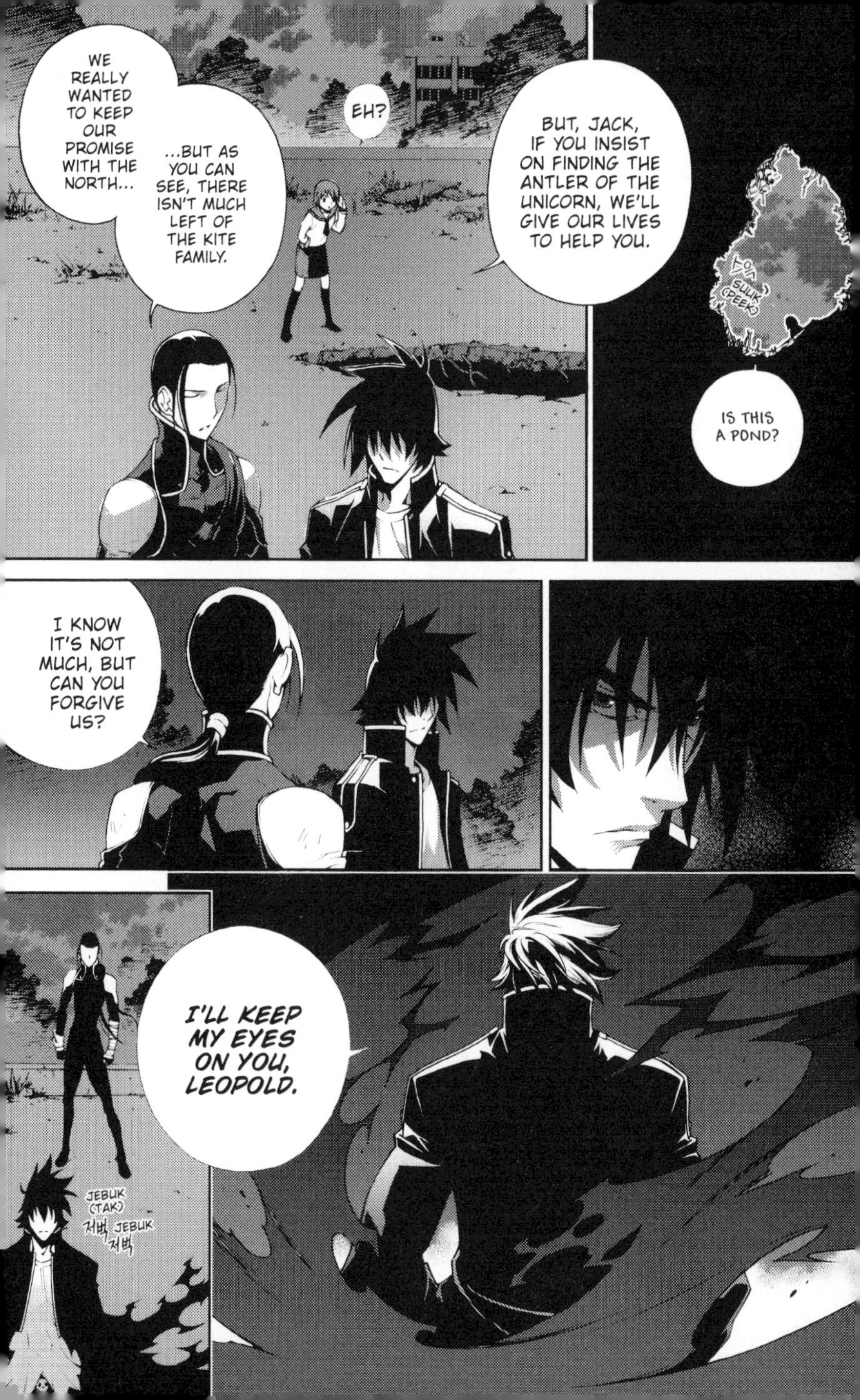
WE REALLY WANTED TO KEEP OUR PROMISE WITH THE NORTH...
...BUT AS YOU CAN SEE, THERE ISN'T MUCH LEFT OF THE KITE FAMILY.
EH?
BUT, JACK, IF YOU INSIST ON FINDING THE ANTLER OF THE UNICORN, WE'LL GIVE OUR LIVES TO HELP YOU.
스윽 SUUK (PEEK)
IS THIS A POND?
I KNOW IT'S NOT MUCH, BUT CAN YOU FORGIVE US?
JEBUK (TAK)
저벅 JEBUK
저벅
I'LL KEEP MY EYES ON YOU, LEOPOLD.

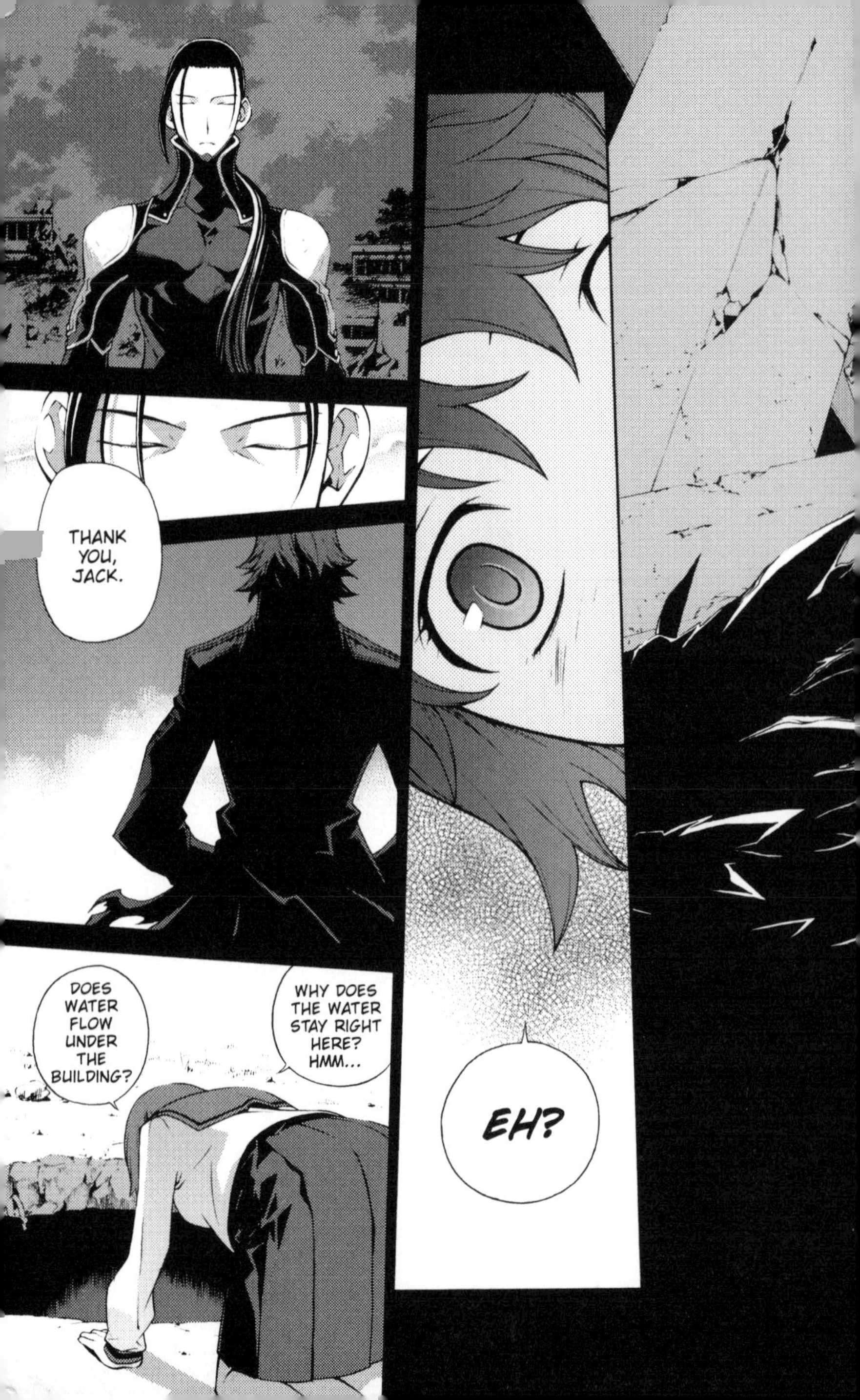
THANK YOU, JACK.
DOES WATER FLOW UNDER THE BUILDING?
WHY DOES THE WATER STAY RIGHT HERE? HMM...
EH?

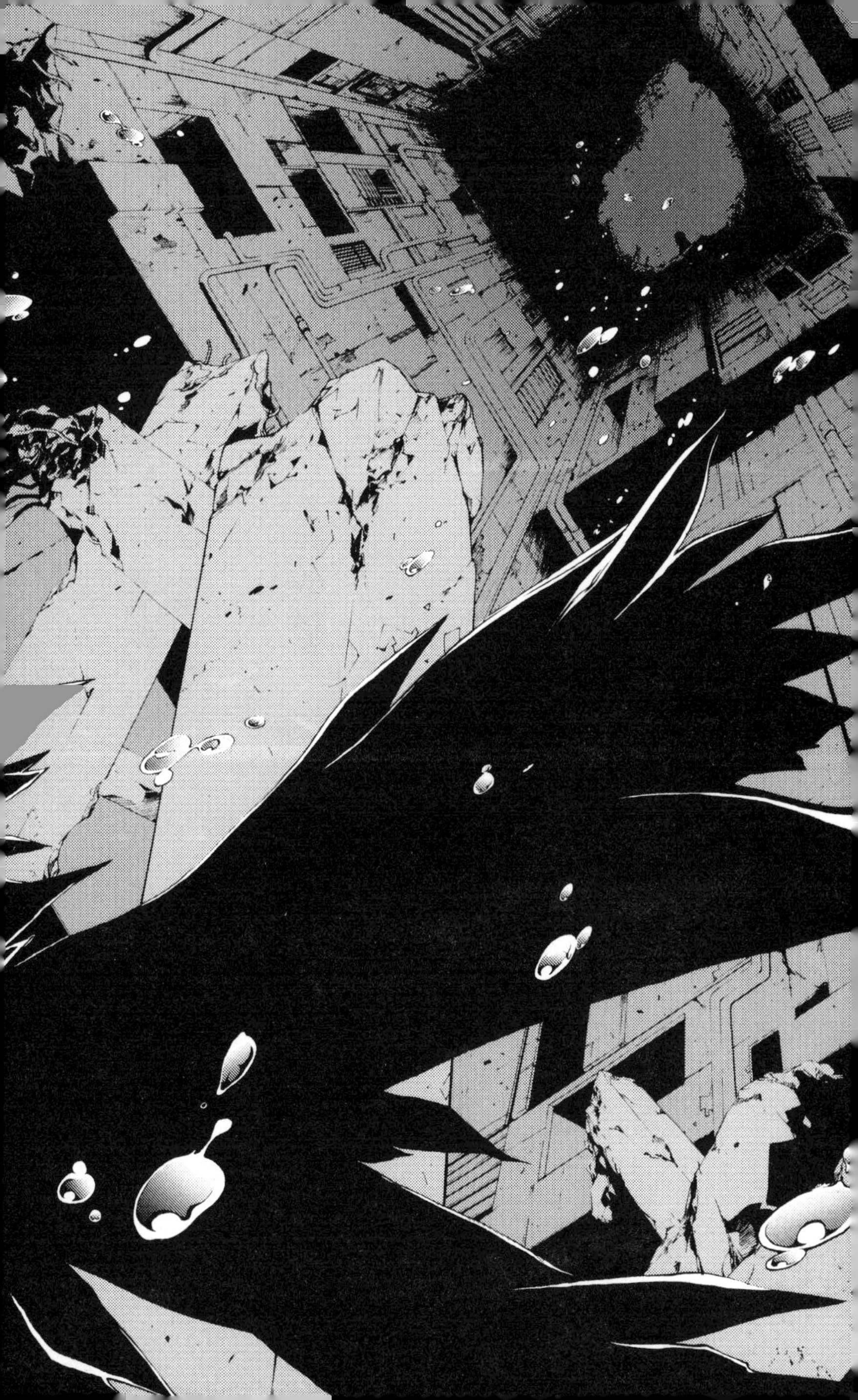

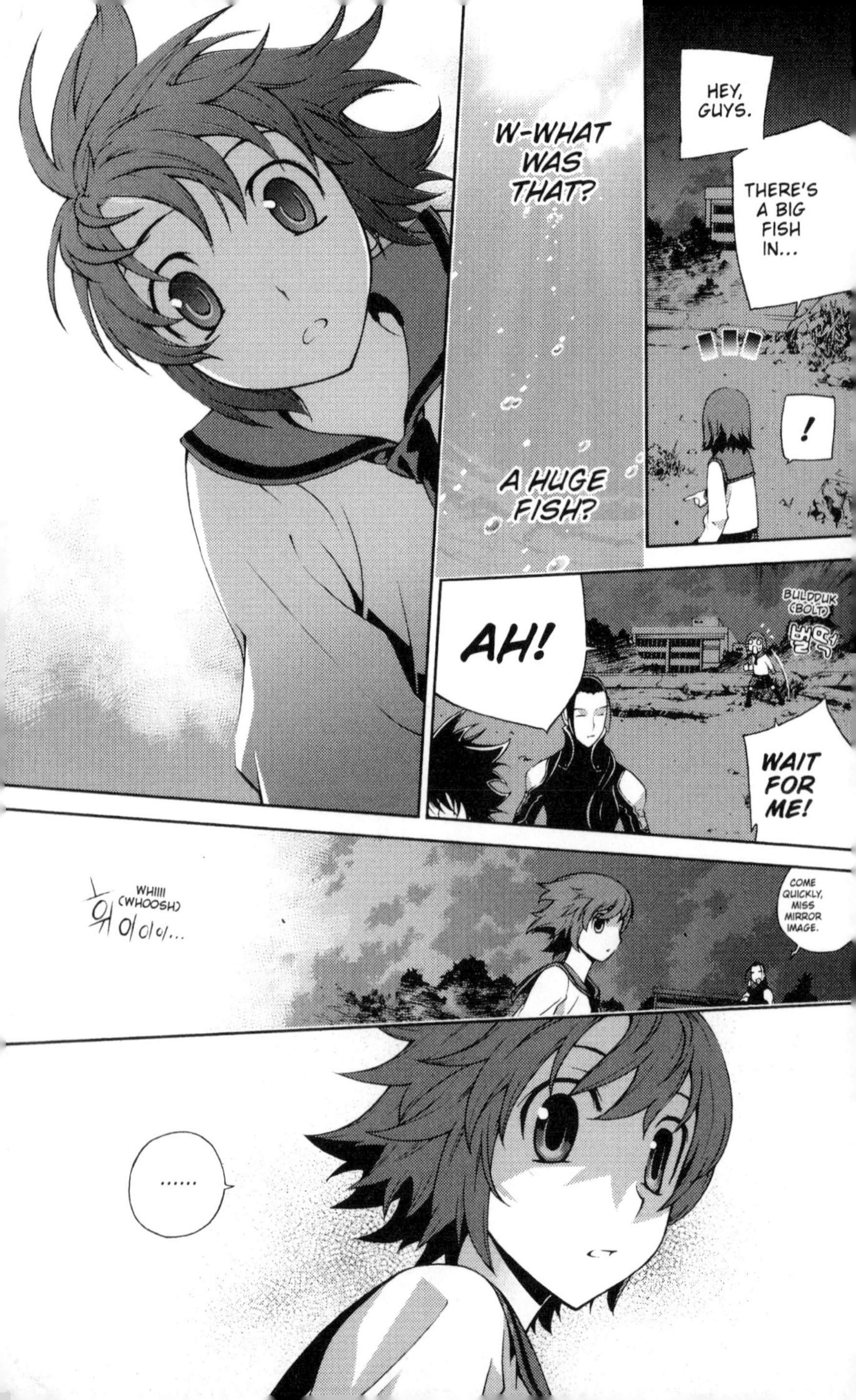

W-WHAT WAS THAT?
A HUGE FISH?
HEY, GUYS.
THERE'S A BIG FISH IN...
!
AH!
BULDDUK (BOLT)
벌떡
WAIT FOR ME!
WHIIII (WHOOSH)
휘이이이...
COME QUICKLY, MISS MIRROR IMAGE.
......

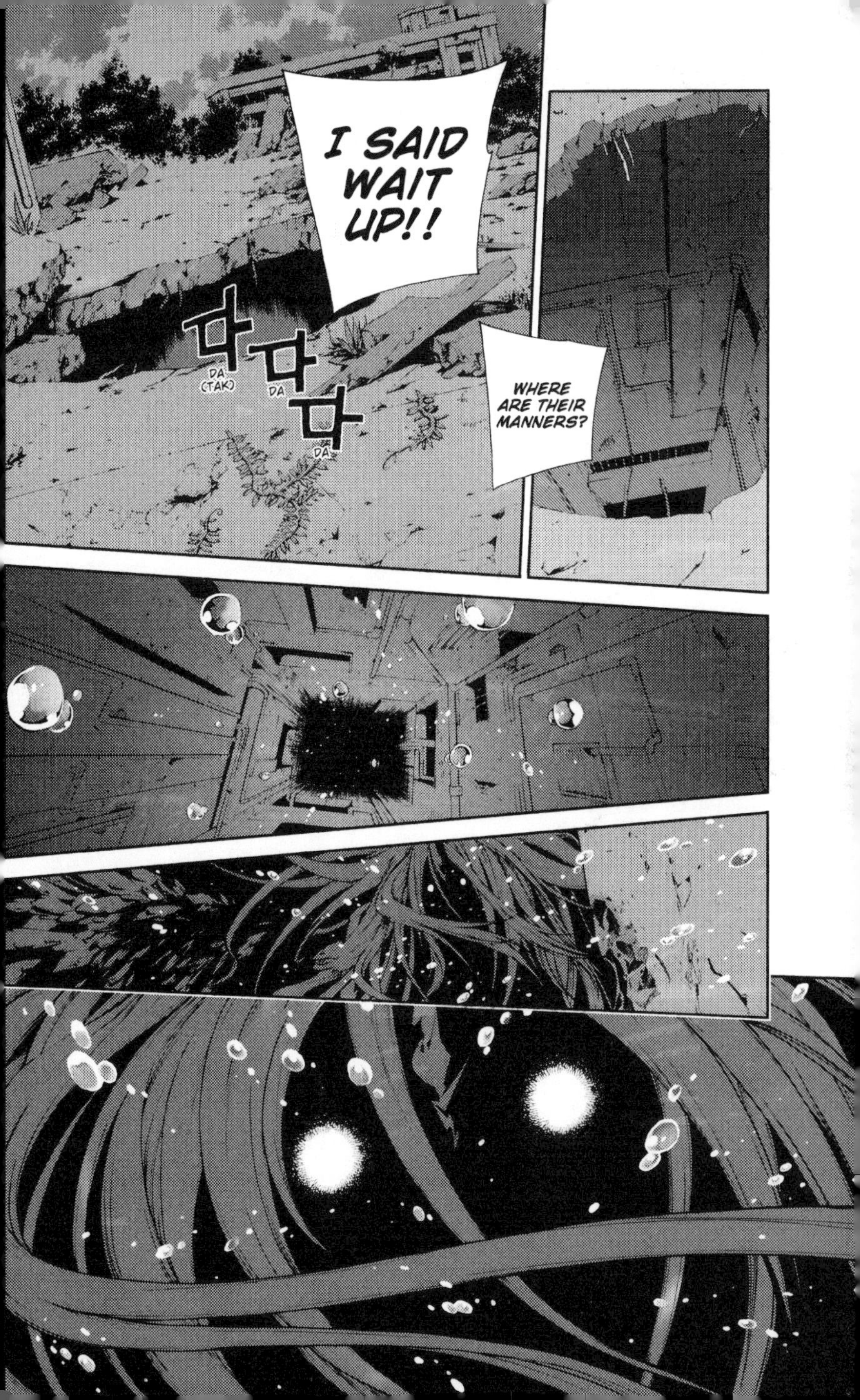
I SAID WAIT UP!!
DA (TAK)
DA
DA
WHERE ARE THEIR MANNERS?

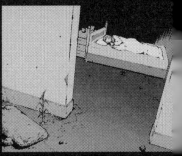

WHY DID IT HAPPEN TO ME...?

WHY, NOH-A?

WHY ARE YOU MAKING ME GO THROUGH THIS?!

TELL ME.

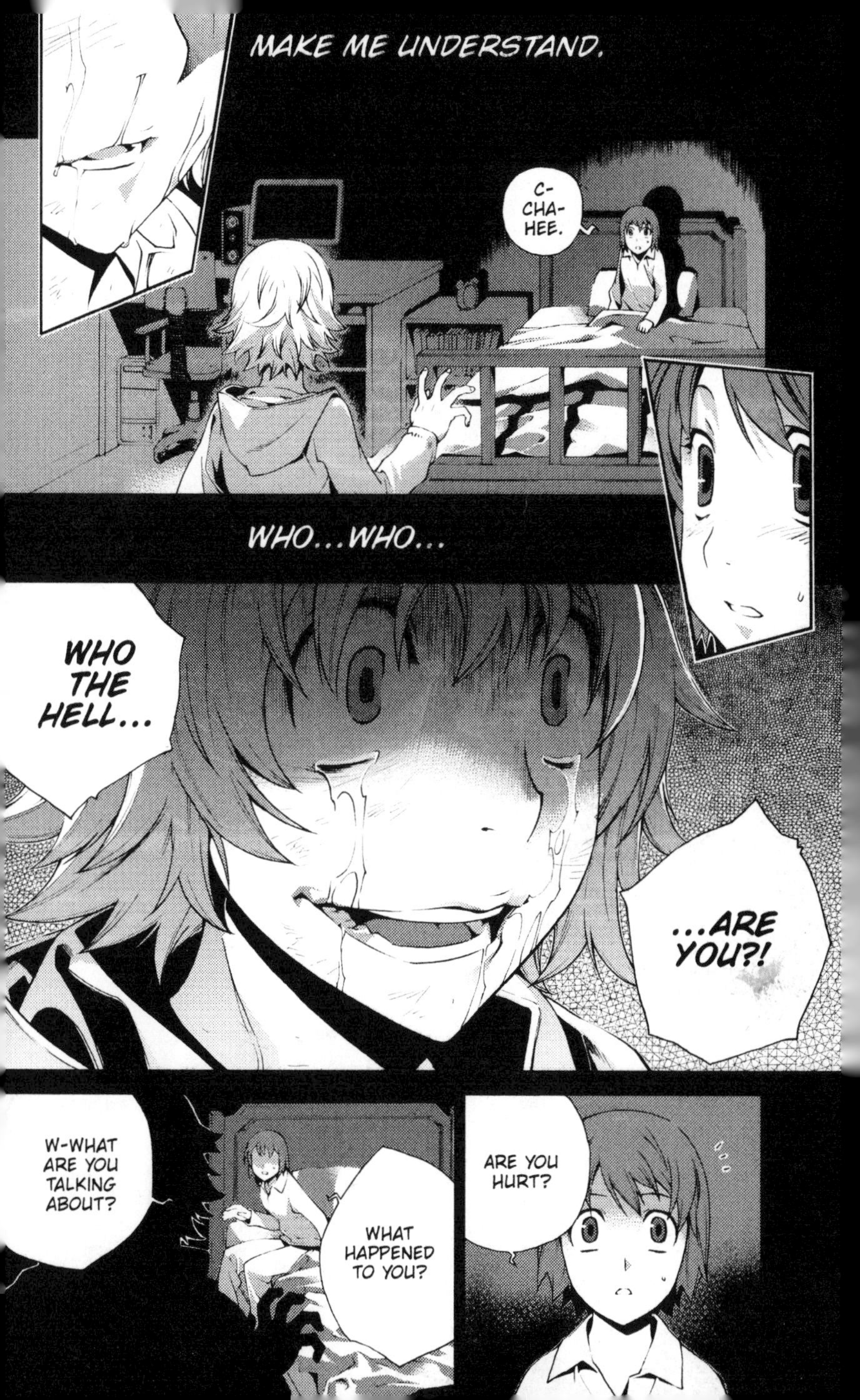
MAKE ME UNDERSTAND.
C-CHA-HEE.
WHO...WHO...
WHO THE HELL...
...ARE YOU?!
W-WHAT ARE YOU TALKING ABOUT?
WHAT HAPPENED TO YOU?
ARE YOU HURT?

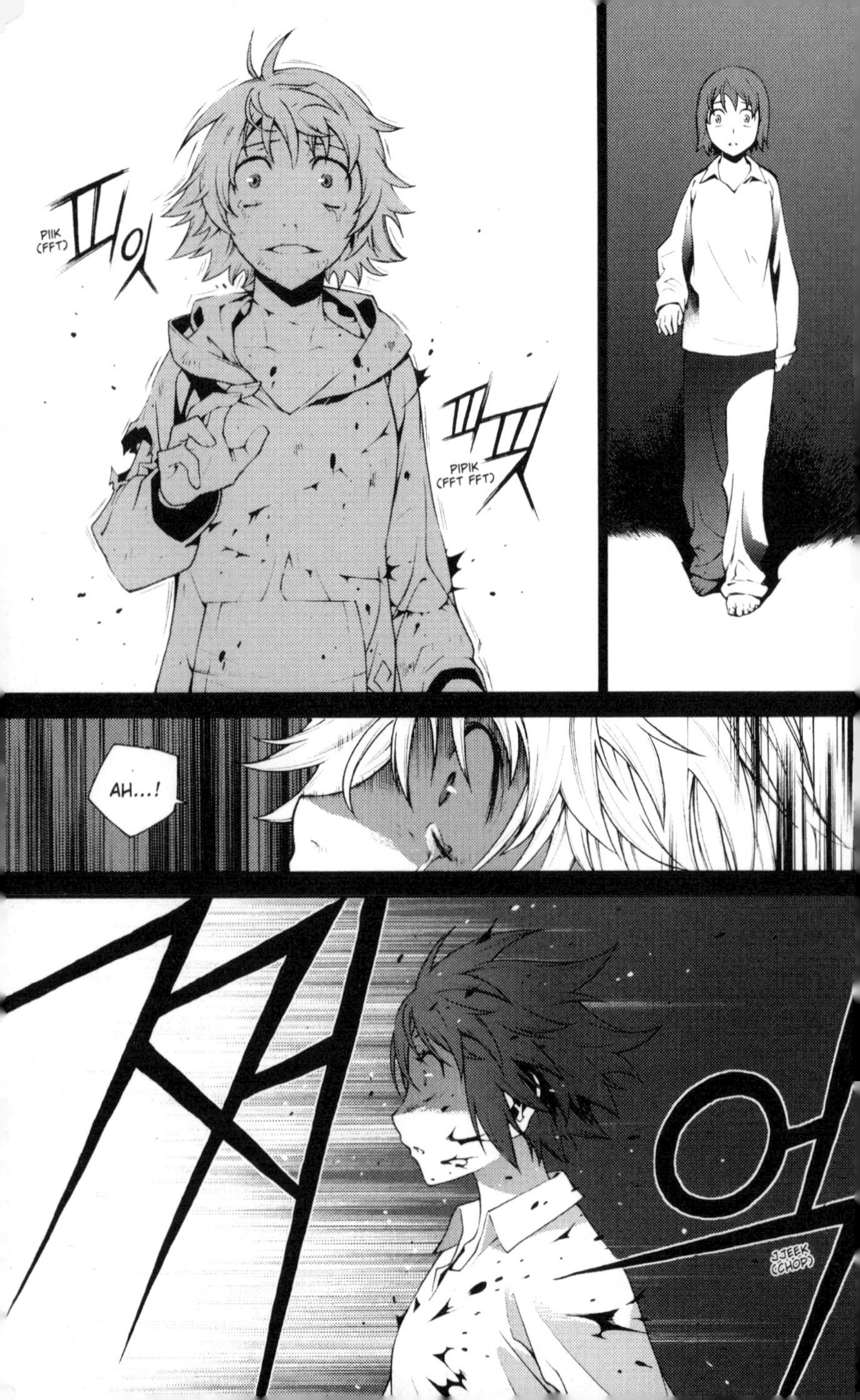

피잇
PIIK (FFT)
피피픽
PIPIK (FFT FFT)
AH...!
JJEEK (CHOP)

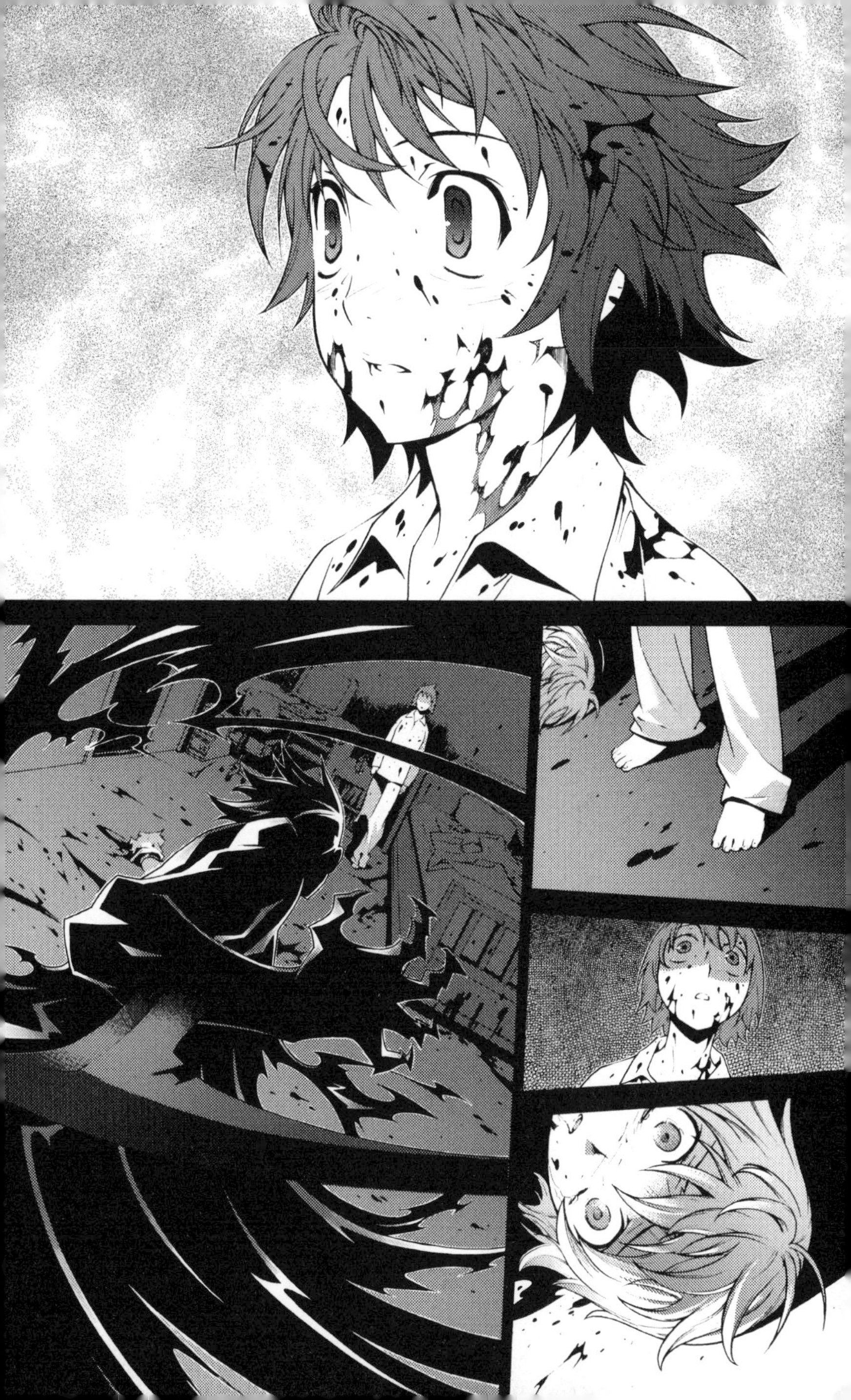

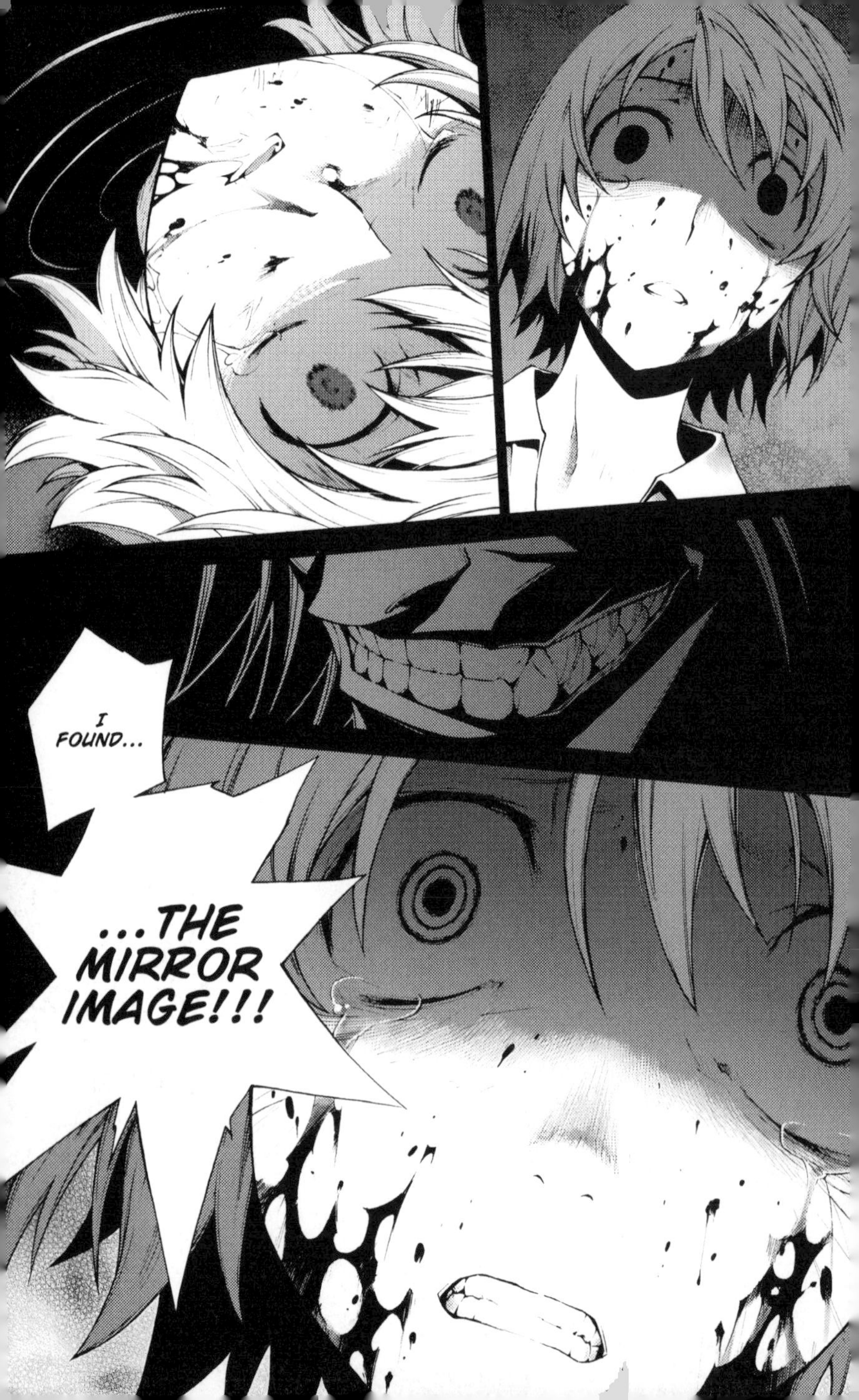
I FOUND...
...THE MIRROR IMAGE!!!

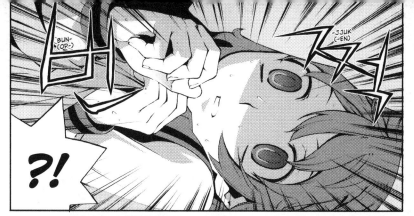

BUN
(-OP-)

?!

-JJUK
(-EN)

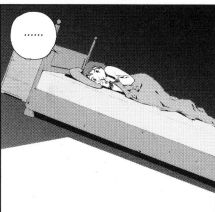

......

UGH~.

IT WAS THAT GIRL NAMED CHA-HEE AGAIN. SHE KEEPS SHOWING UP IN MY DREAMS.

SHE WAS TORN APART...

...AND THE MAN BEHIND HER WAS...

...JACK?

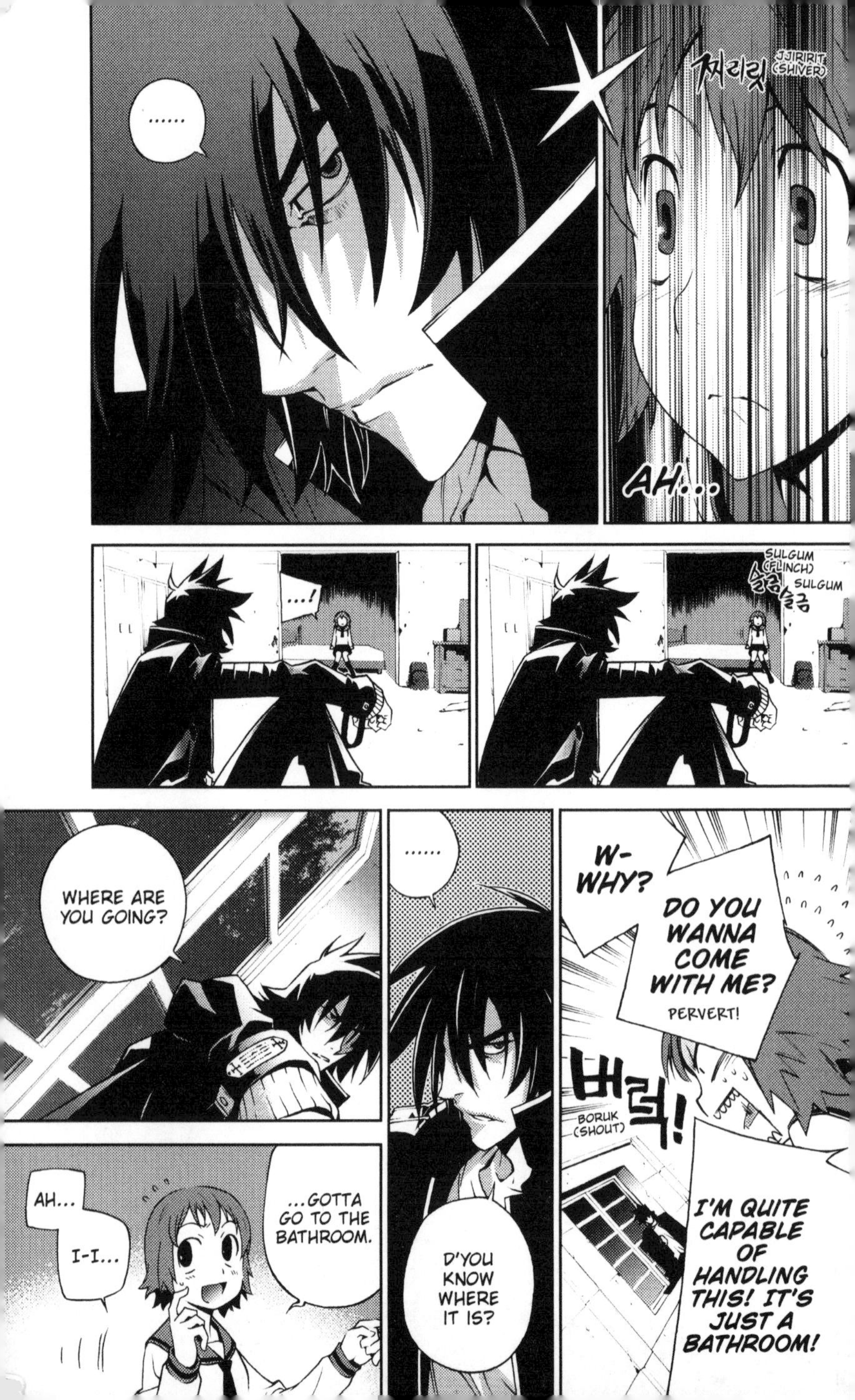
......
찌리릿
JJIRIRIT (SHIVER)
AH...
...!
SULGUM (FLINCH)
슬금슬금
SULGUM
WHERE ARE YOU GOING?
AH...
I-I...
...GOTTA GO TO THE BATHROOM.
......
D'YOU KNOW WHERE IT IS?
W-WHY?
DO YOU WANNA COME WITH ME?
PERVERT!
버럭!
BORUK (SHOUT)
I'M QUITE CAPABLE OF HANDLING THIS! IT'S JUST A BATHROOM!

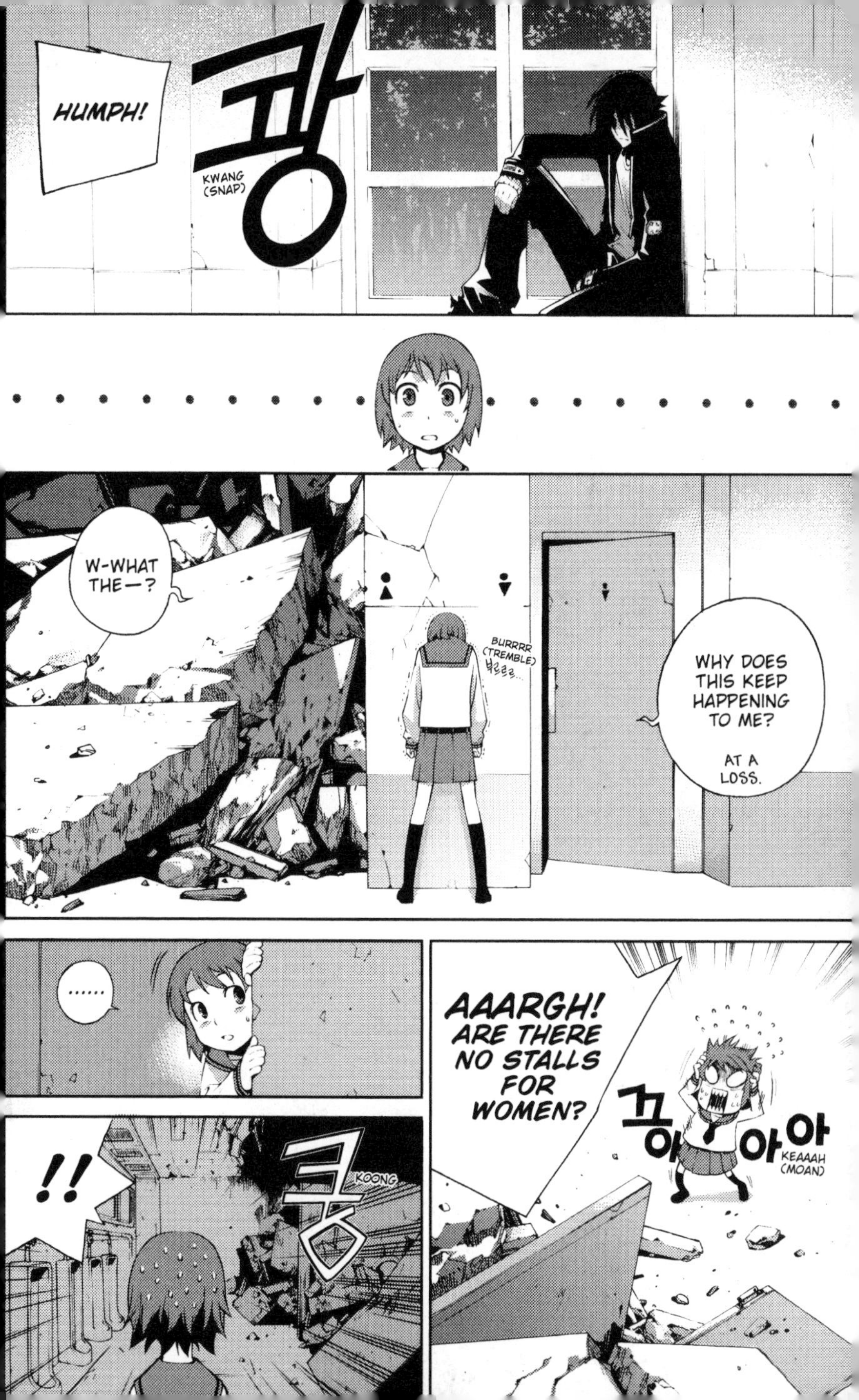
HUMPH!
KWANG (SNAP)
W-WHAT THE—?
BURRRR (TREMBLE)
WHY DOES THIS KEEP HAPPENING TO ME?
AT A LOSS.
......
AAARGH! ARE THERE NO STALLS FOR WOMEN?
KEAAAH (MOAN)
!!
KOONG

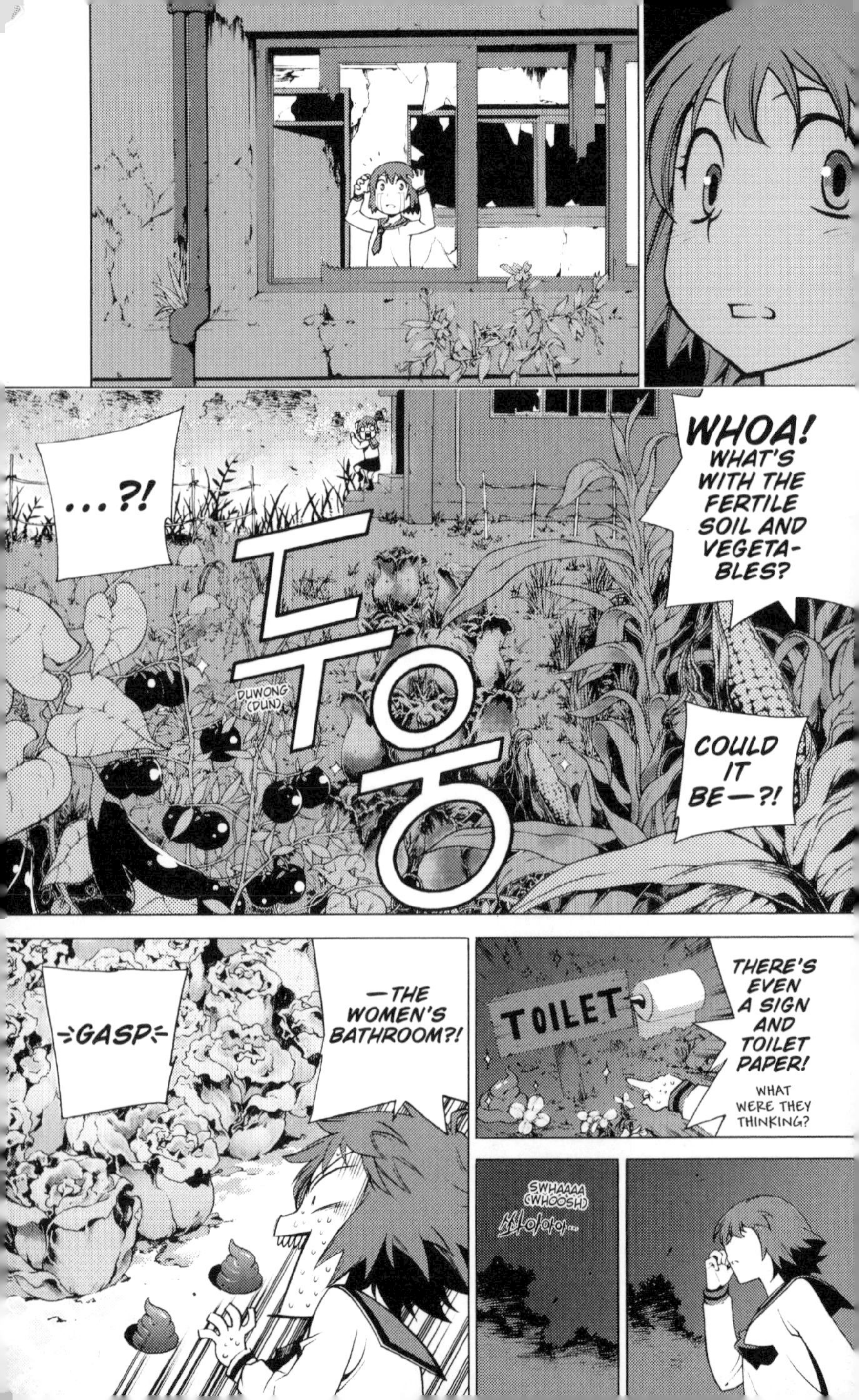
...?!
DUWONG (DUN)
WHOA! WHAT'S WITH THE FERTILE SOIL AND VEGETA-BLES?
COULD IT BE—?!
=GASP=
—THE WOMEN'S BATHROOM?!
TOILET
THERE'S EVEN A SIGN AND TOILET PAPER!
WHAT WERE THEY THINKING?
SWHAAAA (WHOOSH)
쏴아아아...

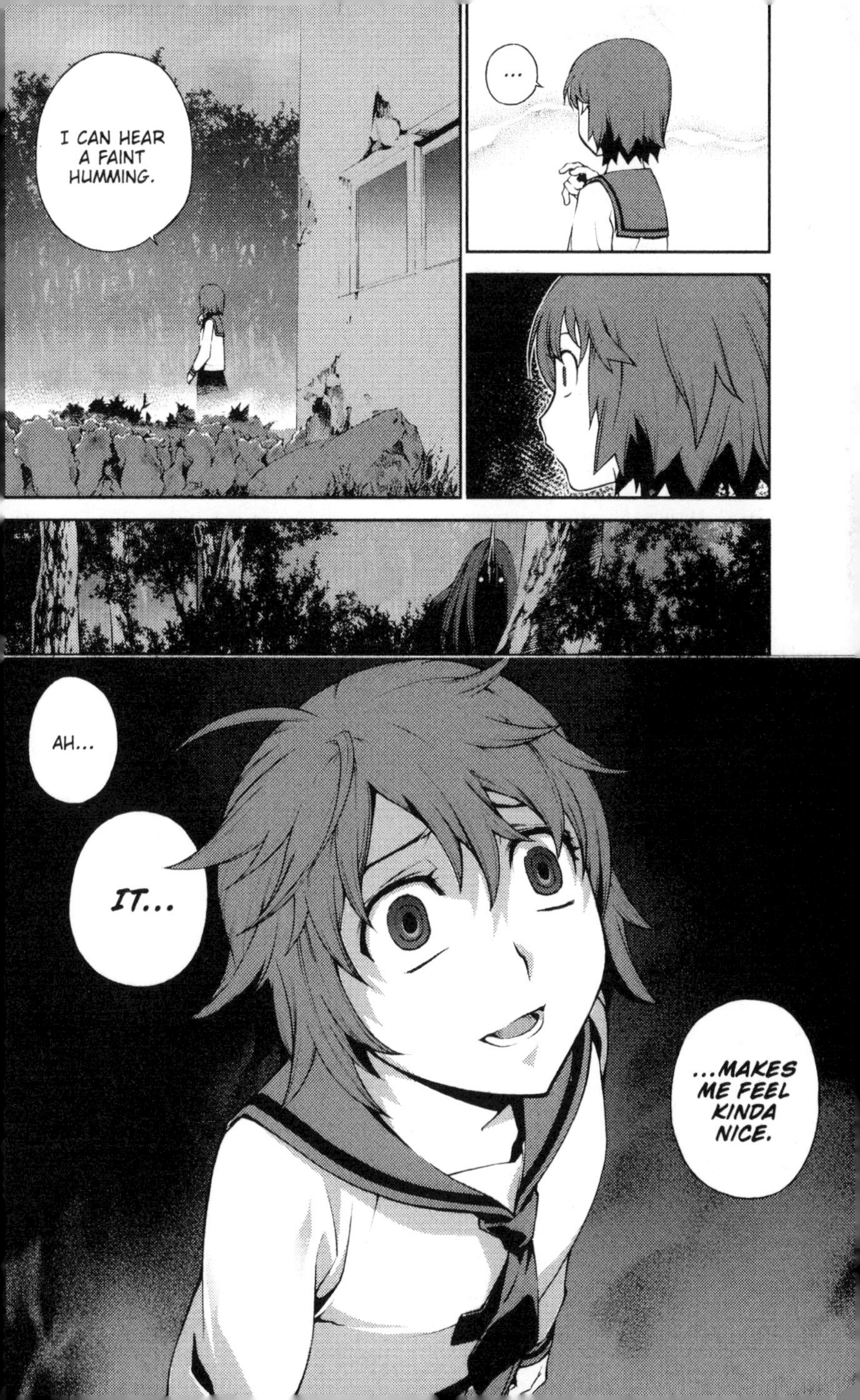
I CAN HEAR A FAINT HUMMING.
...
AH...
IT...
...MAKES ME FEEL KINDA NICE.

JACK FROST

The Amityville

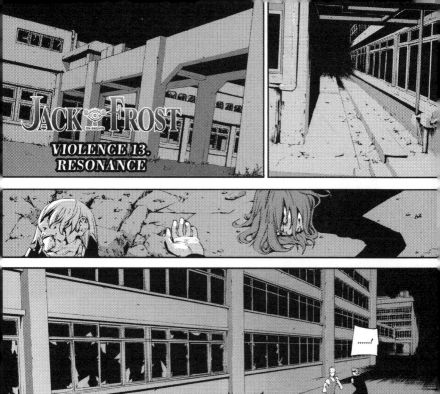

JACK FROST
The Amityville

VIOLENCE 13.
RESONANCE

......!

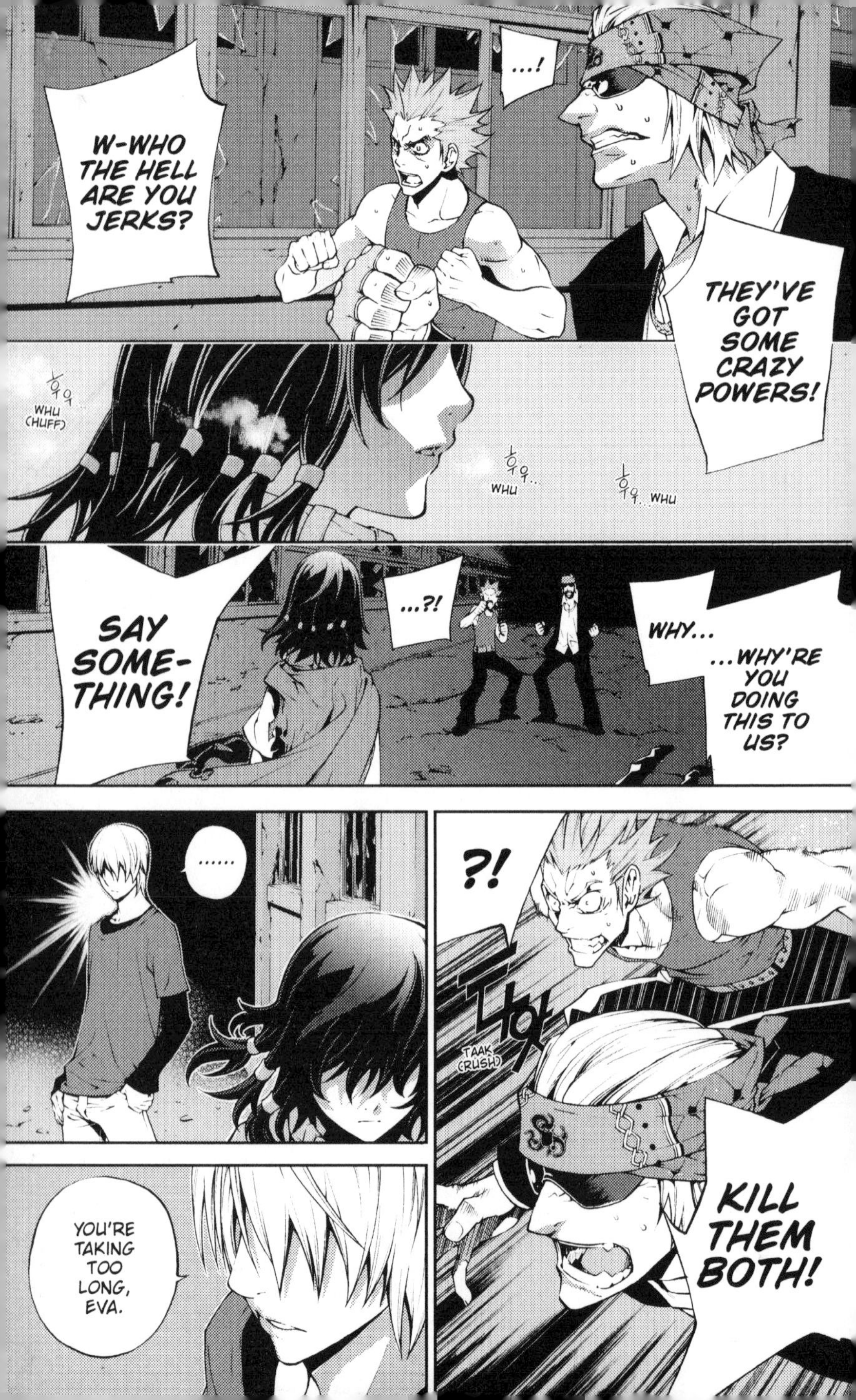
W-WHO THE HELL ARE YOU JERKS?
...!
THEY'VE GOT SOME CRAZY POWERS!
WHU (HUFF)
WHU
WHU
SAY SOME-THING!
...?!
WHY...
...WHY'RE YOU DOING THIS TO US?
......
YOU'RE TAKING TOO LONG, EVA.
?!
TAAK (RUSH)
KILL THEM BOTH!

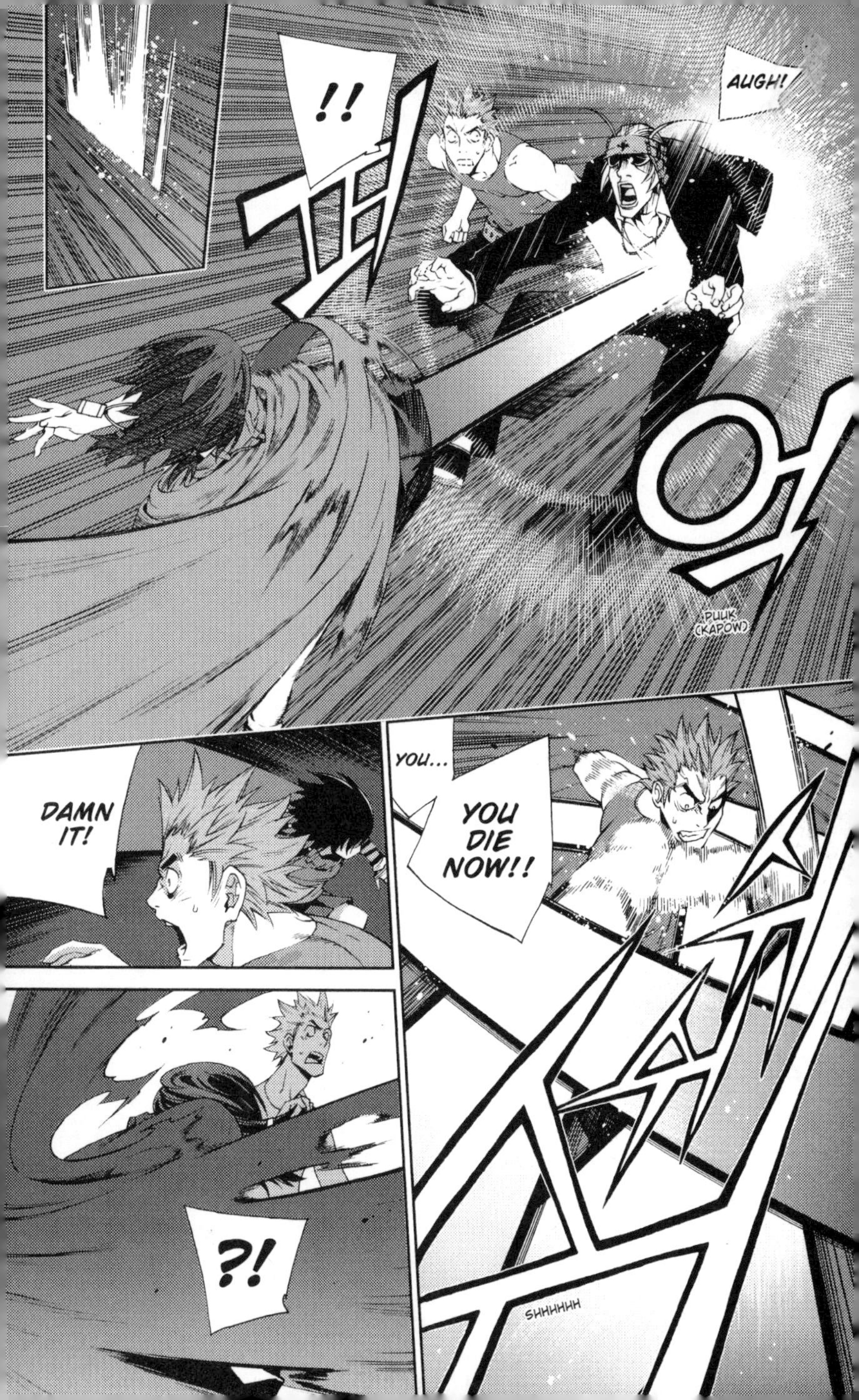
!!
AUGH!
PUUK (KAPOW)
DAMN IT!
YOU...
YOU DIE NOW!!
?!
SHHHHHH

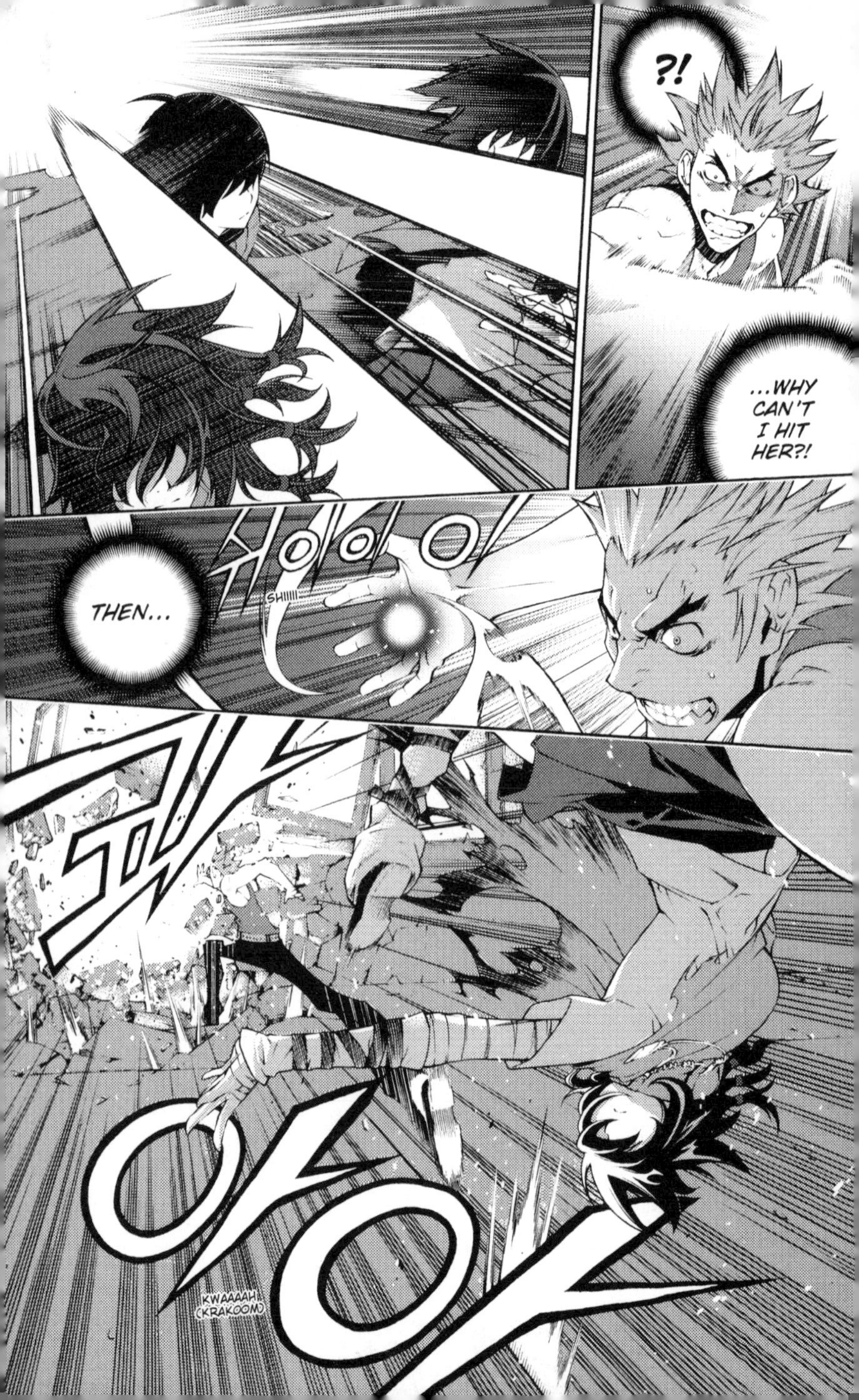
?!
...WHY CAN'T I HIT HER?!
THEN...
SHIIIII
KWAAAAH (KRAKOOM)

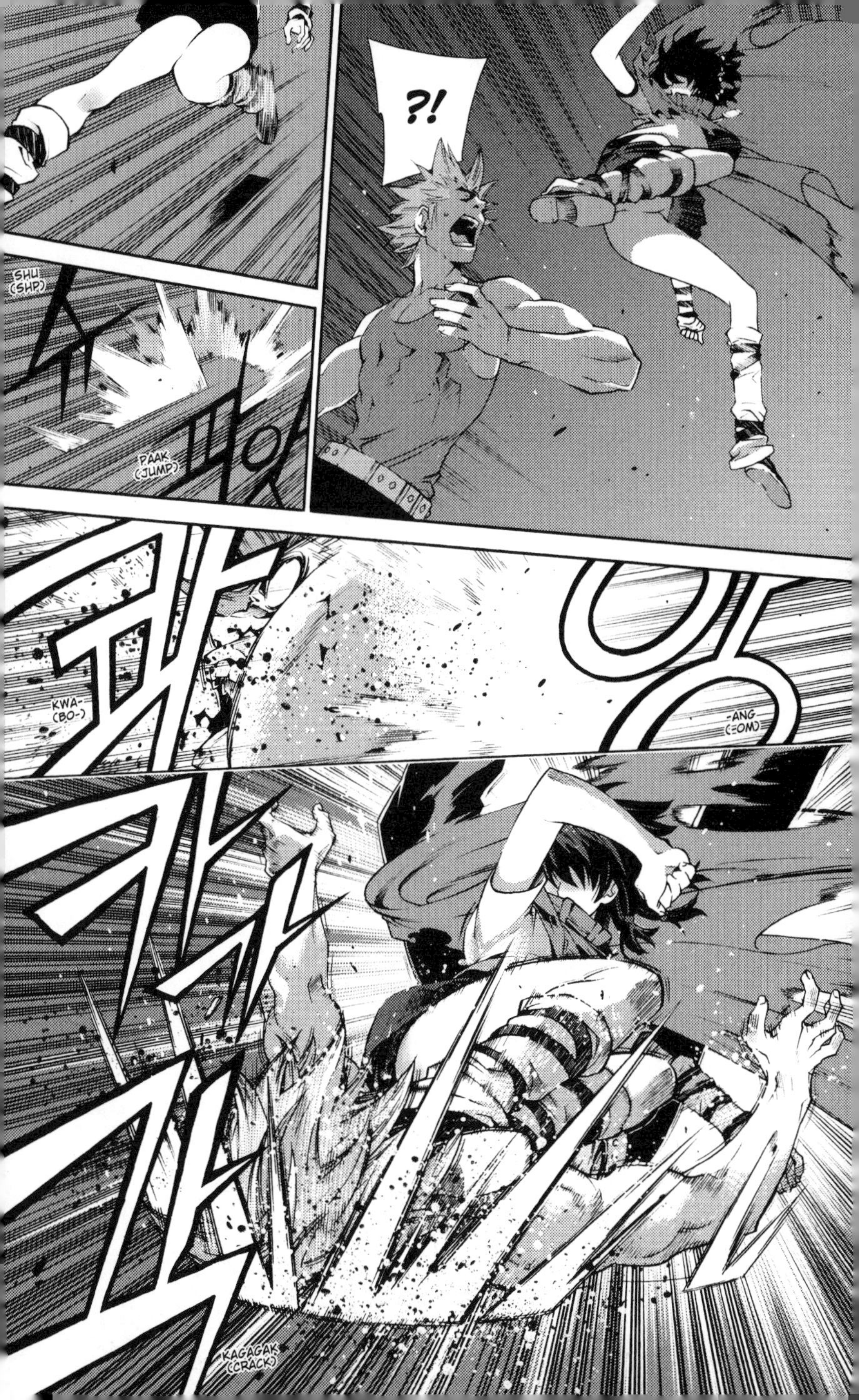
?!
SHU (SHP)
PAAK (JUMP)
KWA- (BO-)
-ANG (=OM)
KAGAGAK (CRACK)

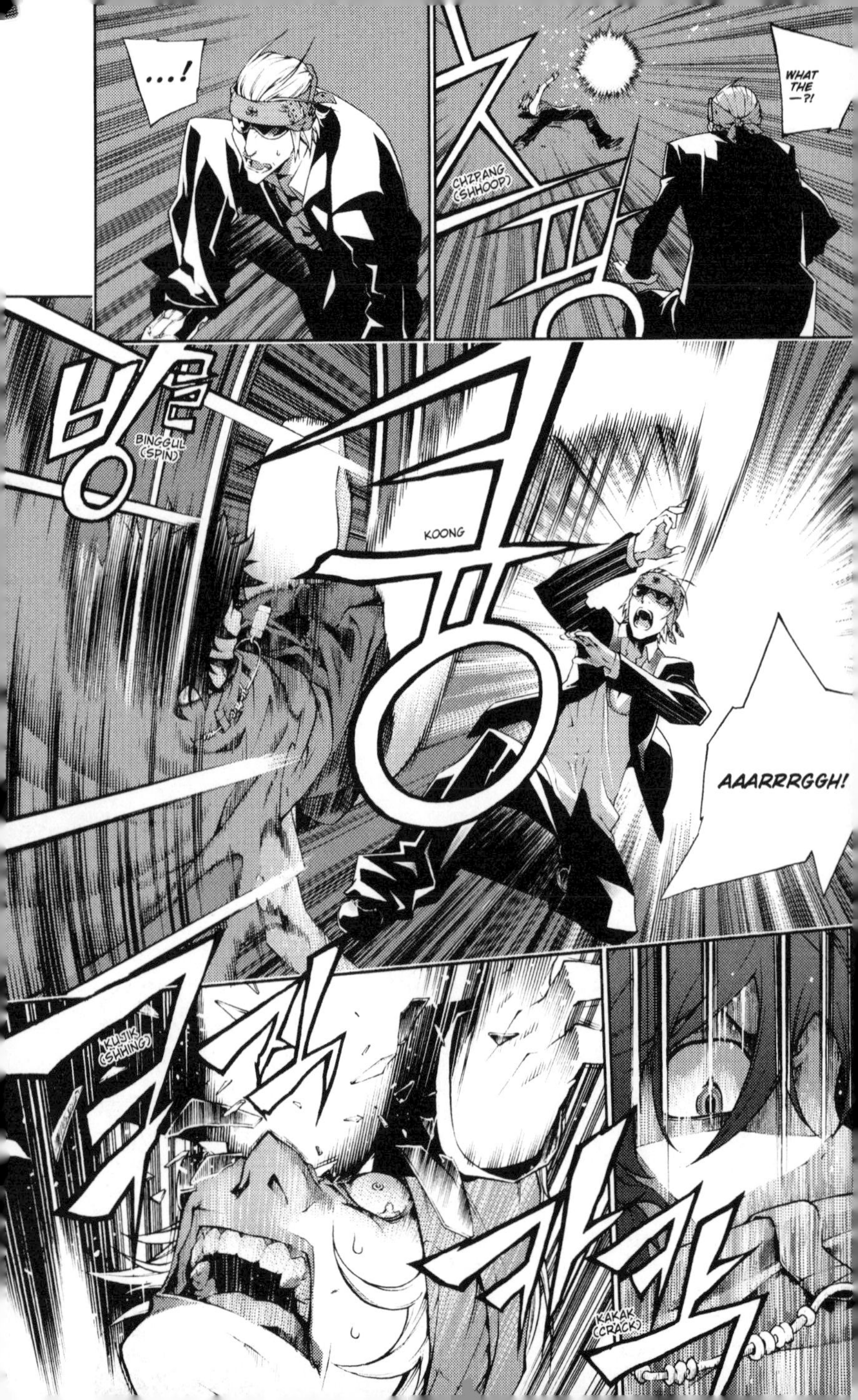
...!
CHZPANG (SHHOOP)
WHAT THE —?!
BINGGUL (SPIN)
KOONG
AAARRRGGH!
KUSIK (SHHING)
KAKAK (CRACK)

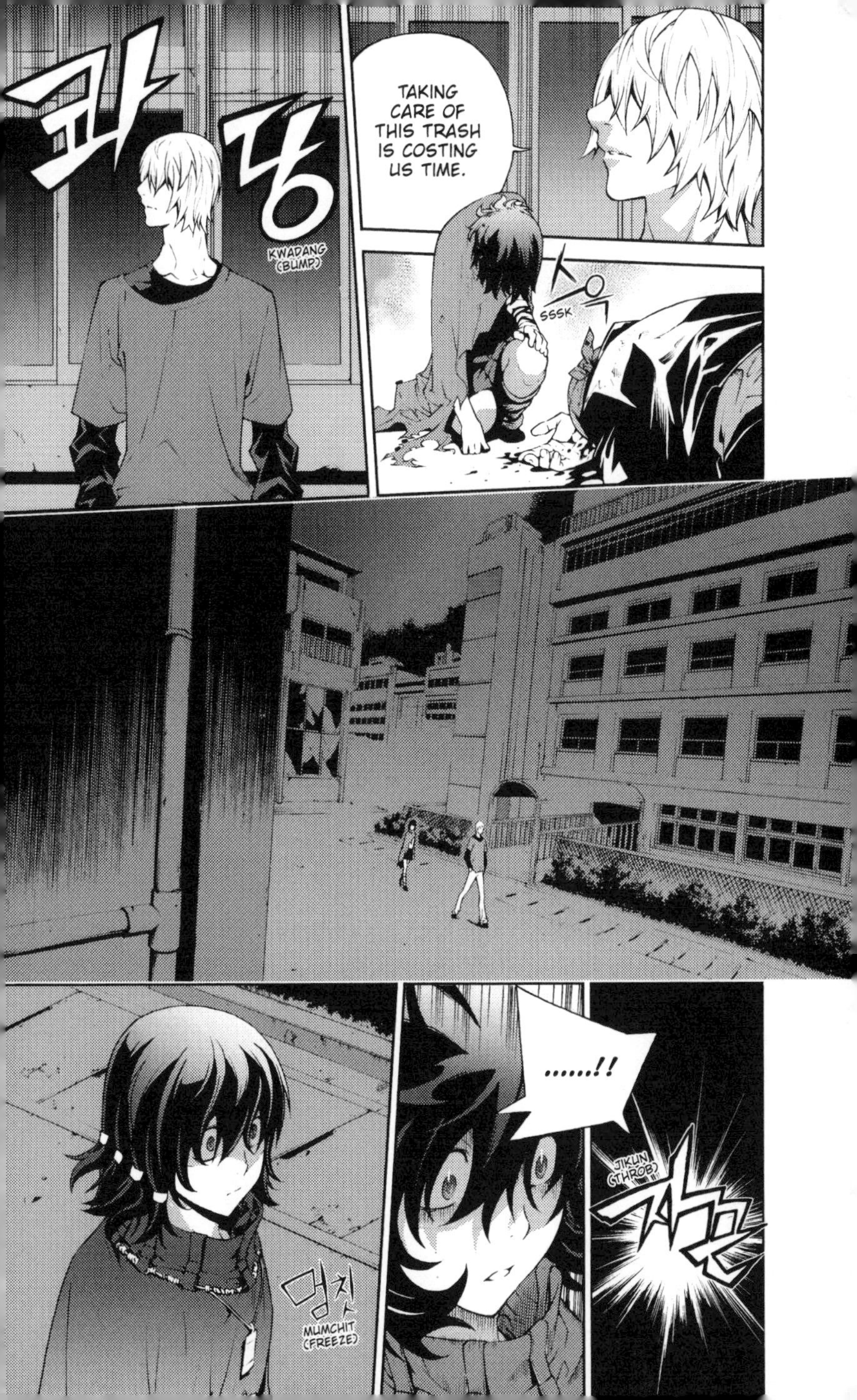

콰당
KWADANG (BUMP)
TAKING CARE OF THIS TRASH IS COSTING US TIME.
SSSK
멈칫
MUMCHIT (FREEZE)
......!!
JIKUN (THROB)

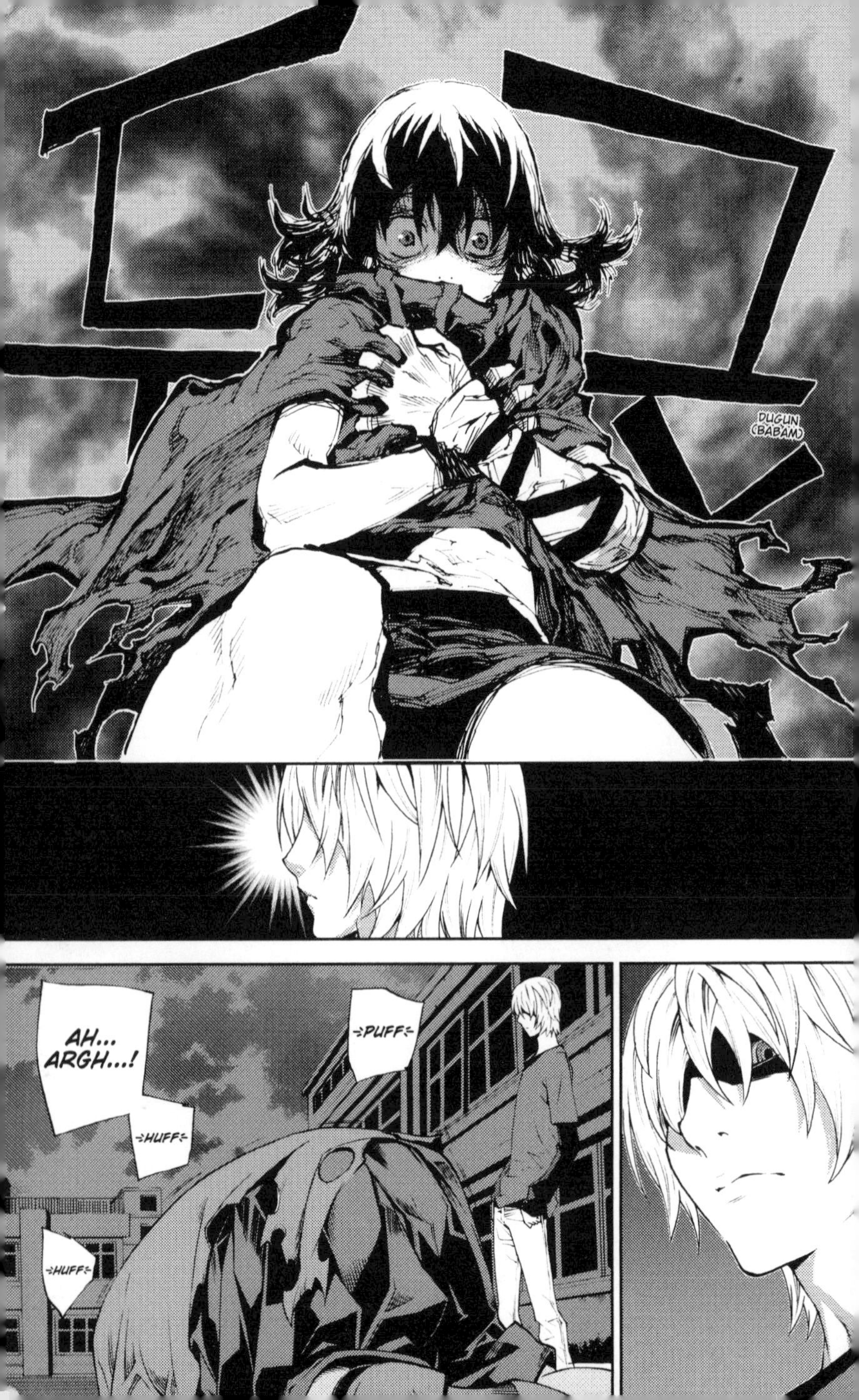

DUGUN (BABAM)
AH... ARGH...!
HUFF
HUFF
PUFF

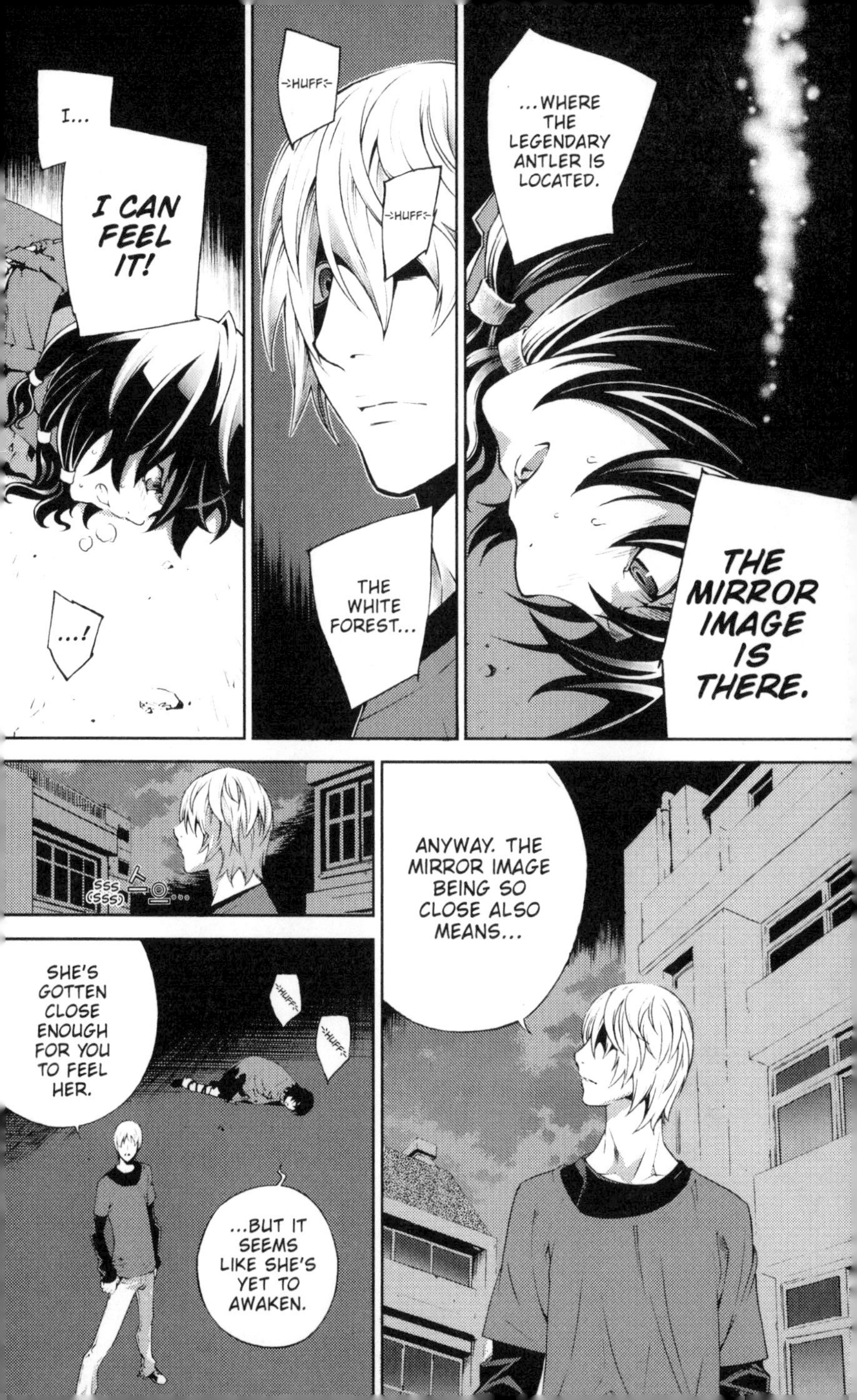

I...
I CAN FEEL IT!
...!
HUFF
HUFF
THE WHITE FOREST...
...WHERE THE LEGENDARY ANTLER IS LOCATED.
THE MIRROR IMAGE IS THERE.
SSS (SSS)
SHE'S GOTTEN CLOSE ENOUGH FOR YOU TO FEEL HER.
HUFF
HUFF
...BUT IT SEEMS LIKE SHE'S YET TO AWAKEN.
ANYWAY. THE MIRROR IMAGE BEING SO CLOSE ALSO MEANS...

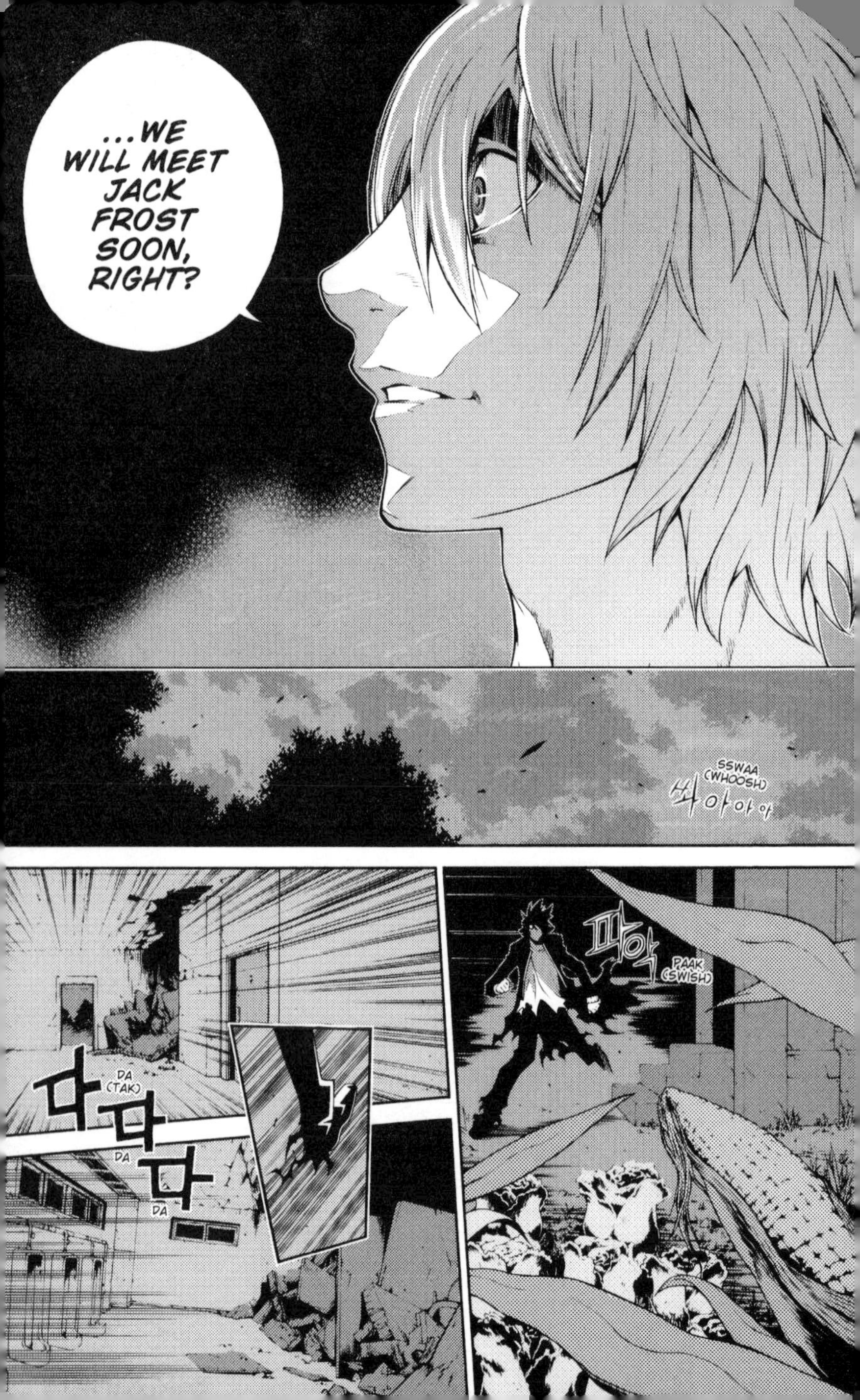
...WE WILL MEET JACK FROST SOON, RIGHT?
SSWAA (WHOOSH)
싸아아아
DA (TAK)
DA
DA
파악
PAAK (SWISH)

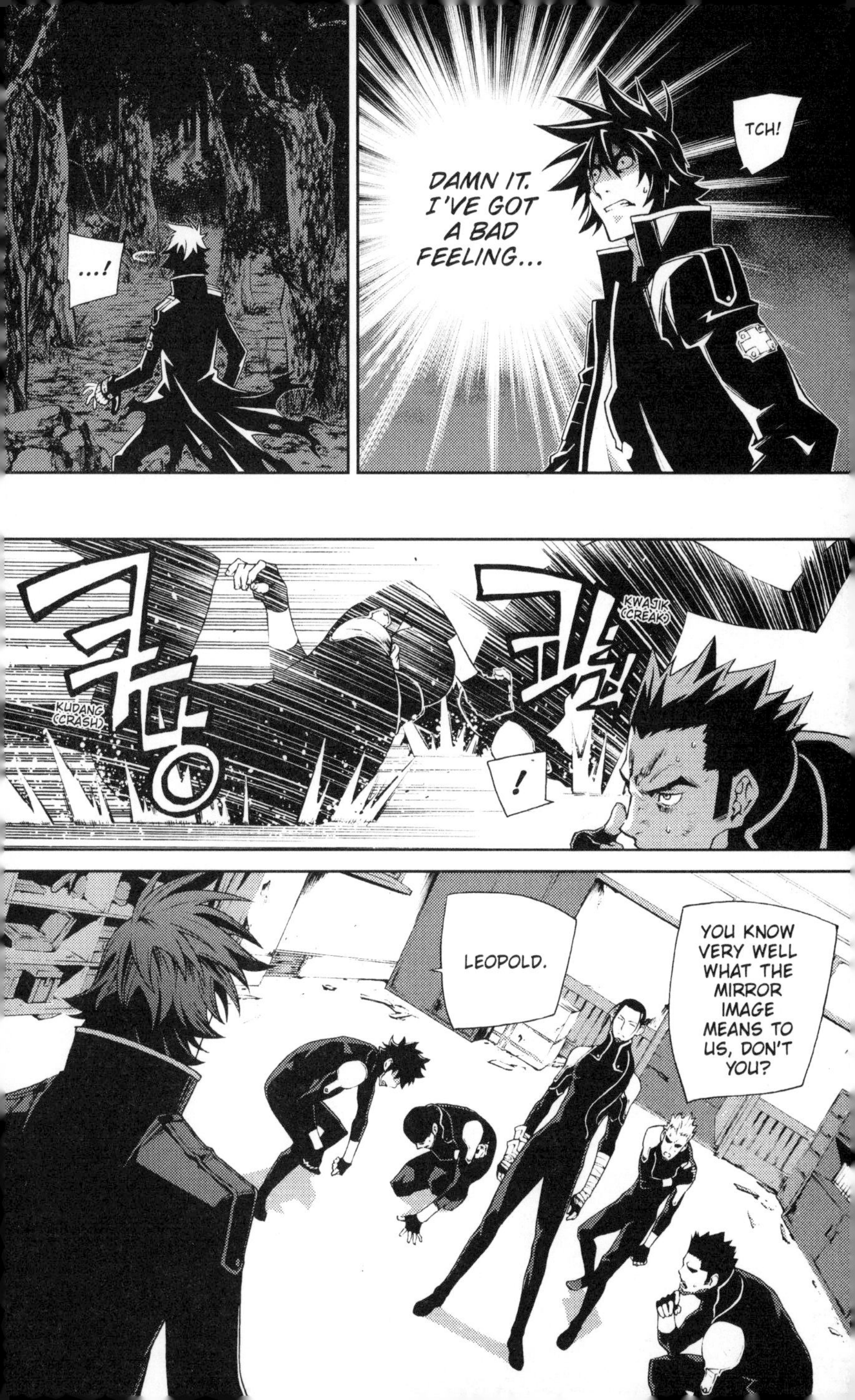
...!
DAMN IT. I'VE GOT A BAD FEELING...
TCH!
KUDANG (CRASH)
KWAJIK (CREAK)
!
LEOPOLD.
YOU KNOW VERY WELL WHAT THE MIRROR IMAGE MEANS TO US, DON'T YOU?

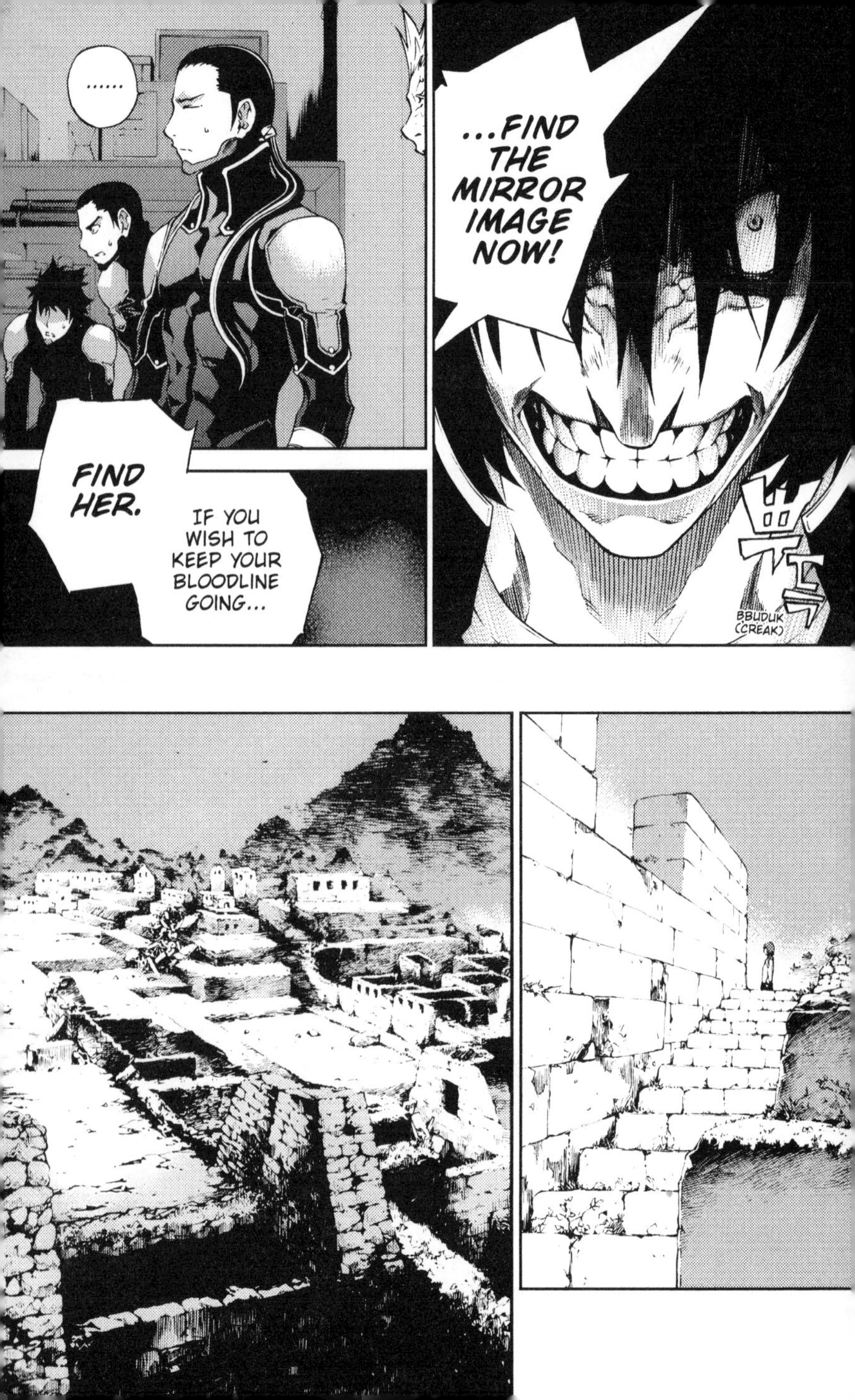
......
FIND HER.
IF YOU WISH TO KEEP YOUR BLOODLINE GOING...
...FIND THE MIRROR IMAGE NOW!
BBUDUK (CREAK)

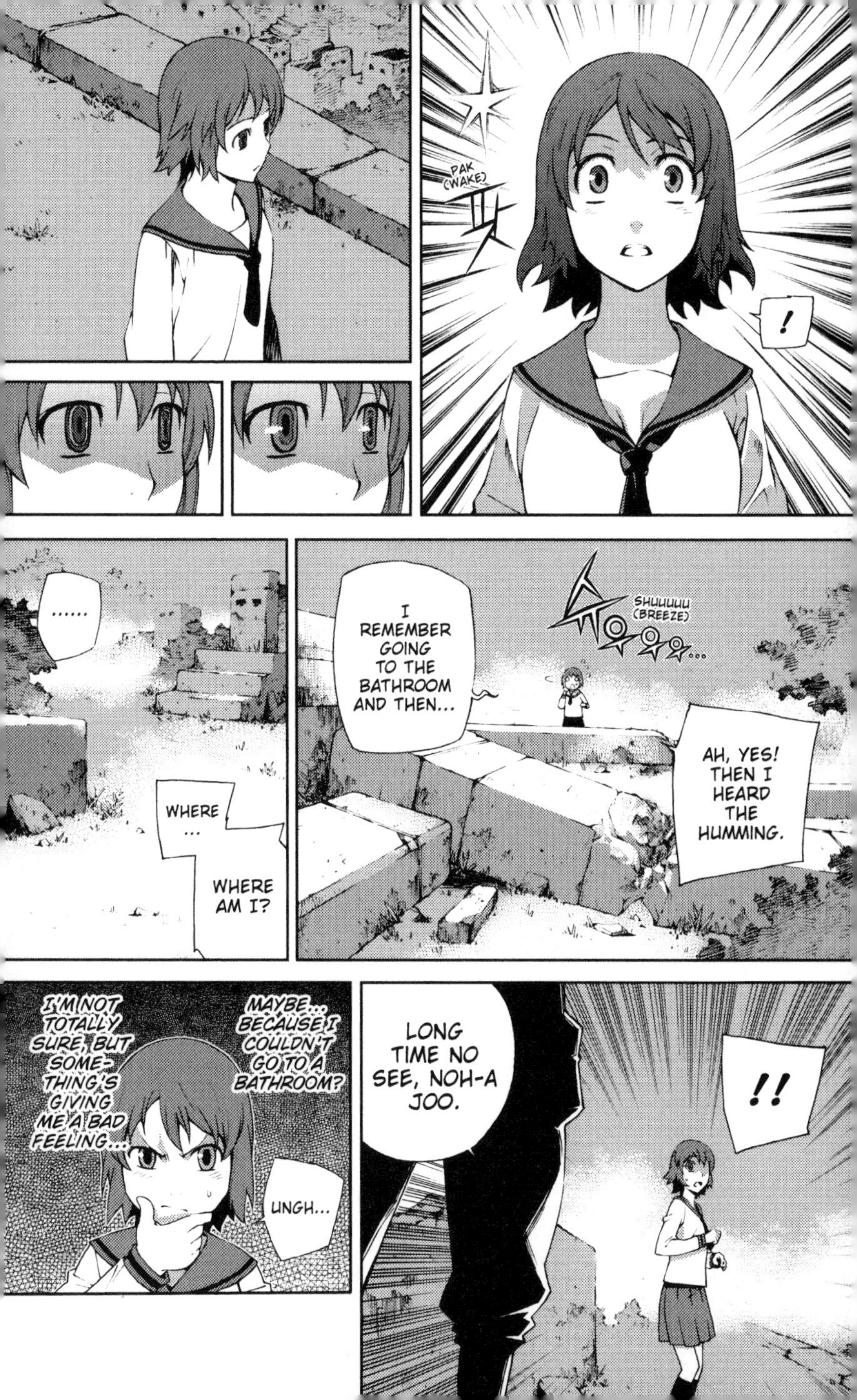
PAK (WAKE)
팍
!
......
WHERE ...
WHERE AM I?
I REMEMBER GOING TO THE BATHROOM AND THEN...
SHUUUUU (BREEZE)
슈우우우...
AH, YES! THEN I HEARD THE HUMMING.
I'M NOT TOTALLY SURE, BUT SOME-THING'S GIVING ME A BAD FEELING...
MAYBE... BECAUSE I COULDN'T GO TO A BATHROOM?
UNGH...
LONG TIME NO SEE, NOH-A JOO.
!!

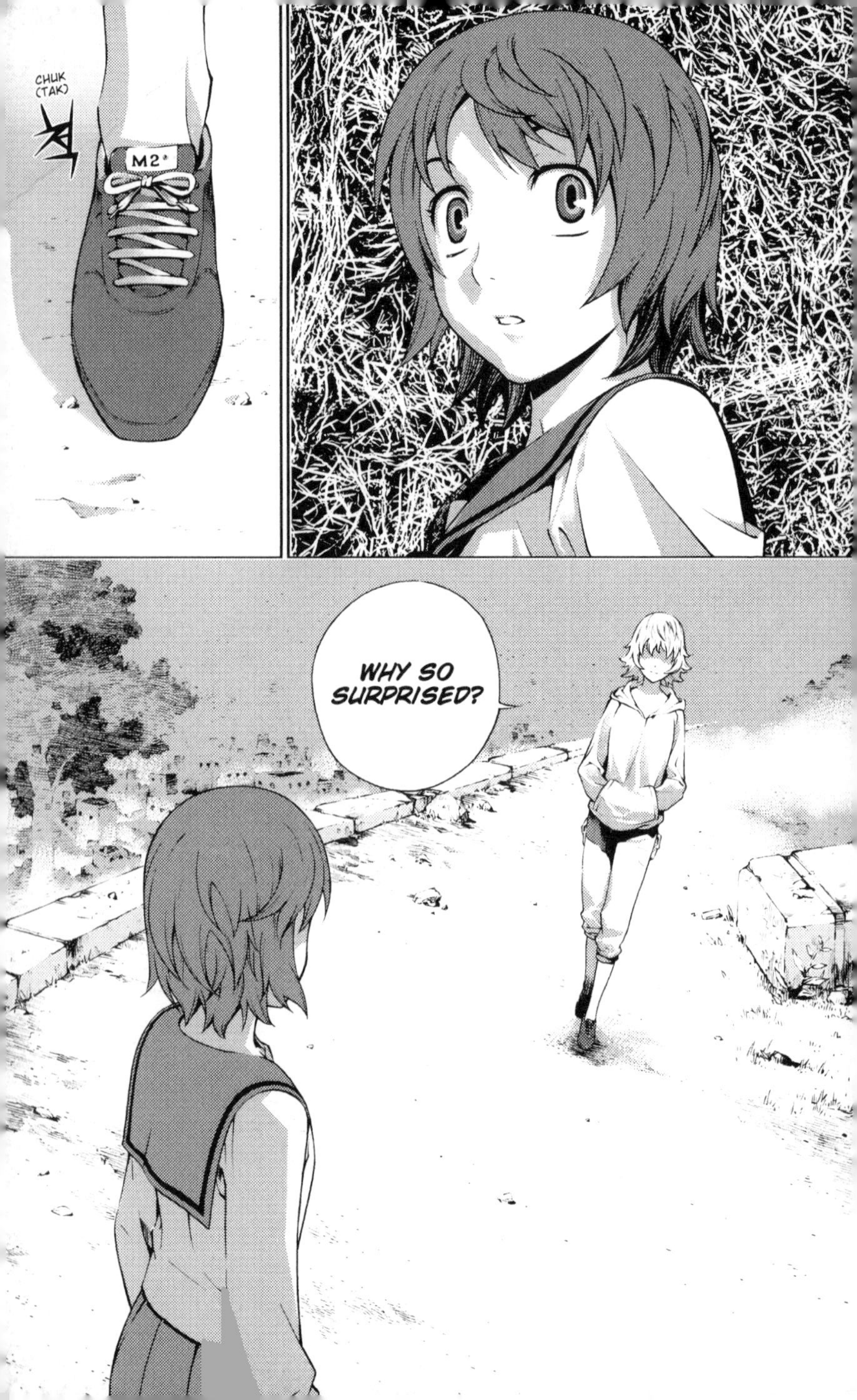
CHUK (TAK)
WHY SO SURPRISED?

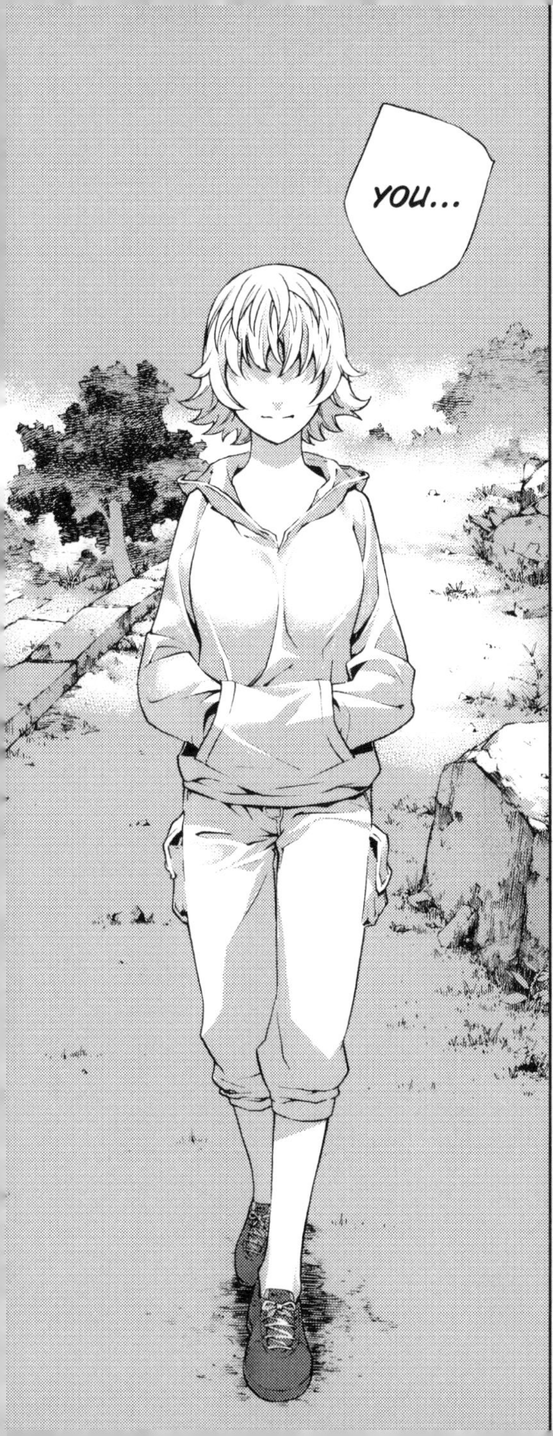
YOU...
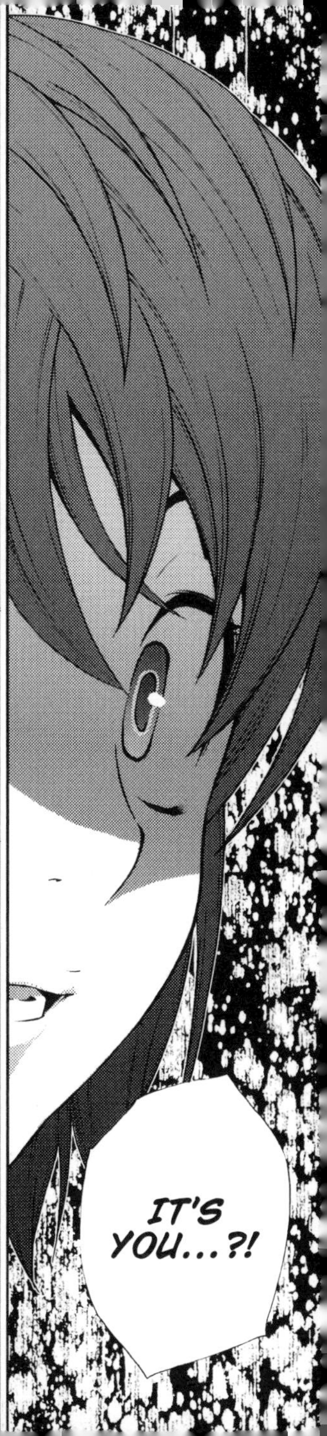
IT'S YOU...?!

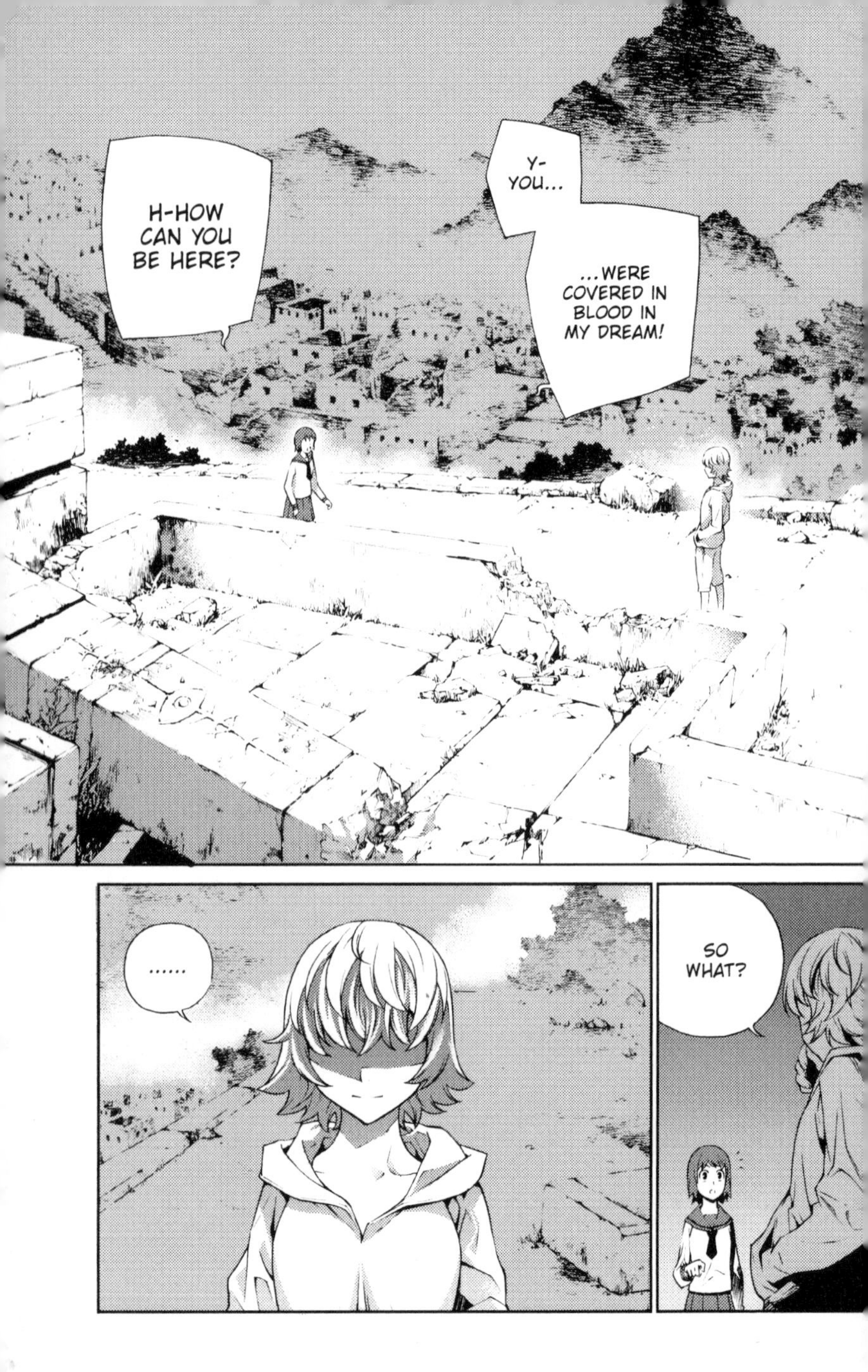
H-HOW CAN YOU BE HERE?
Y- YOU...
...WERE COVERED IN BLOOD IN MY DREAM!
......
SO WHAT?

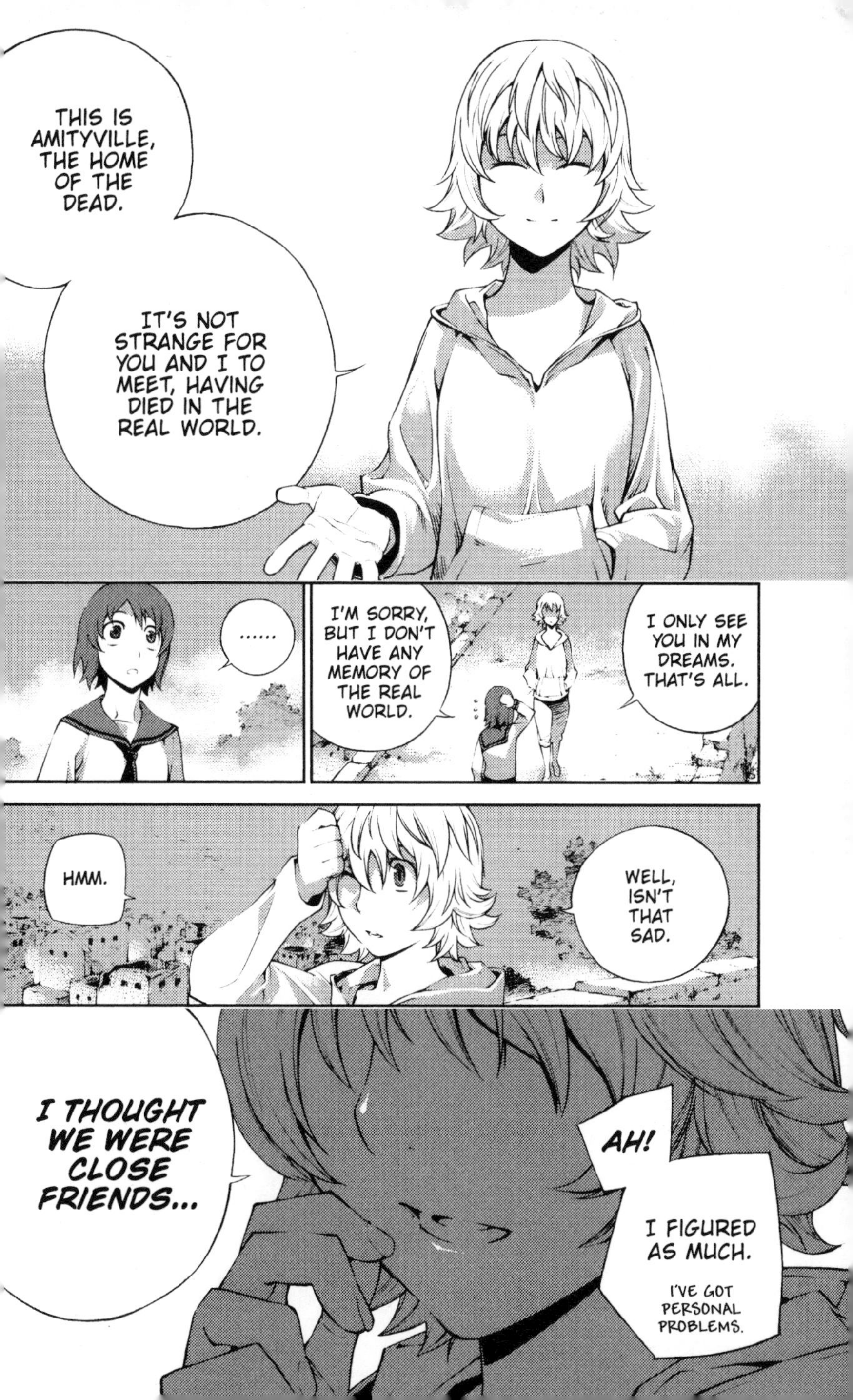

THIS IS AMITYVILLE, THE HOME OF THE DEAD.
IT'S NOT STRANGE FOR YOU AND I TO MEET, HAVING DIED IN THE REAL WORLD.
......
I'M SORRY, BUT I DON'T HAVE ANY MEMORY OF THE REAL WORLD.
I ONLY SEE YOU IN MY DREAMS. THAT'S ALL.
HMM.
WELL, ISN'T THAT SAD.
I THOUGHT WE WERE CLOSE FRIENDS...
AH!
I FIGURED AS MUCH.
I'VE GOT PERSONAL PROBLEMS.

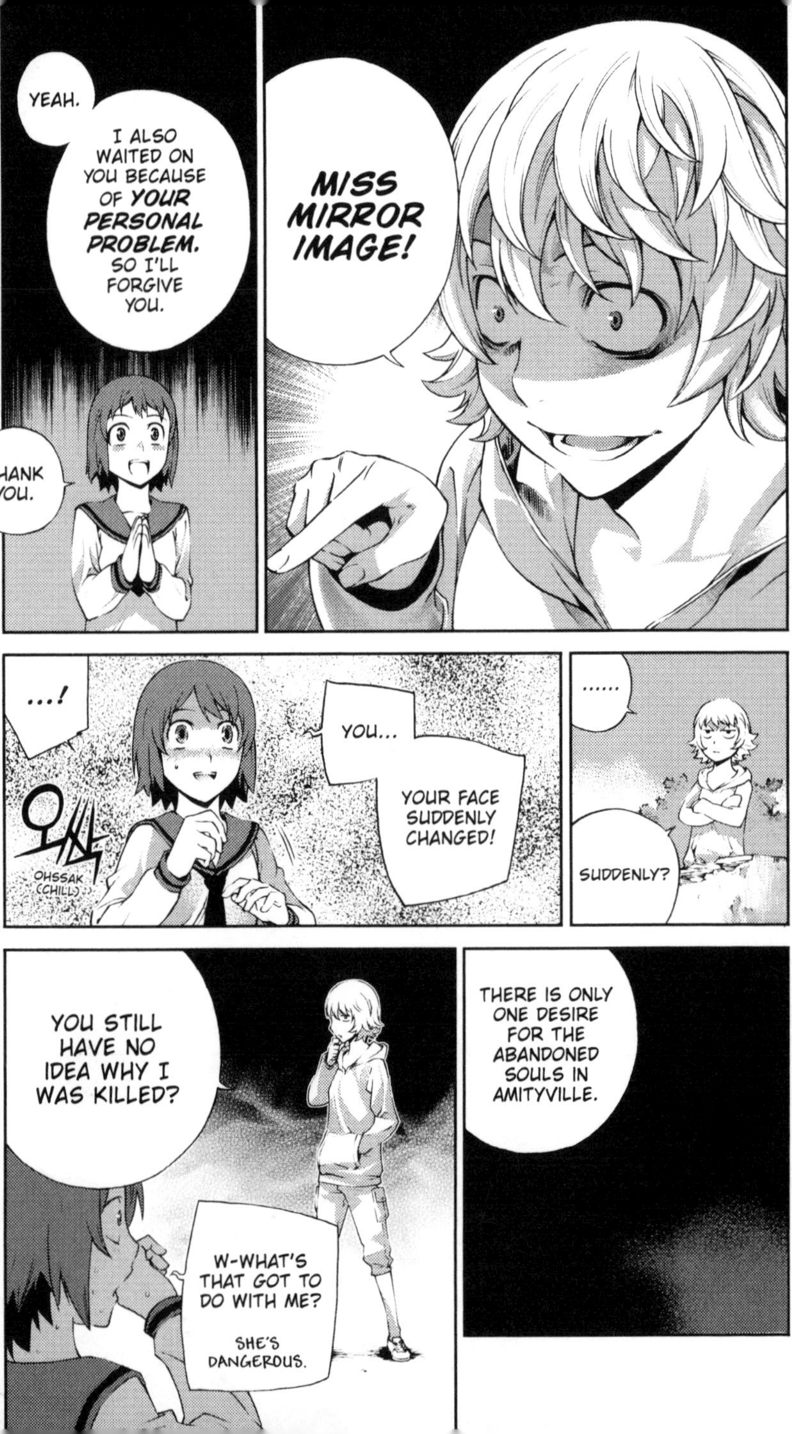
YEAH.
I ALSO WAITED ON YOU BECAUSE OF YOUR PERSONAL PROBLEM. SO I'LL FORGIVE YOU.
THANK YOU.
MISS MIRROR IMAGE!
...!
OHSSAK (CHILL)
YOU...
YOUR FACE SUDDENLY CHANGED!
......
SUDDENLY?
YOU STILL HAVE NO IDEA WHY I WAS KILLED?
W-WHAT'S THAT GOT TO DO WITH ME?
SHE'S DANGEROUS.
THERE IS ONLY ONE DESIRE FOR THE ABANDONED SOULS IN AMITYVILLE.

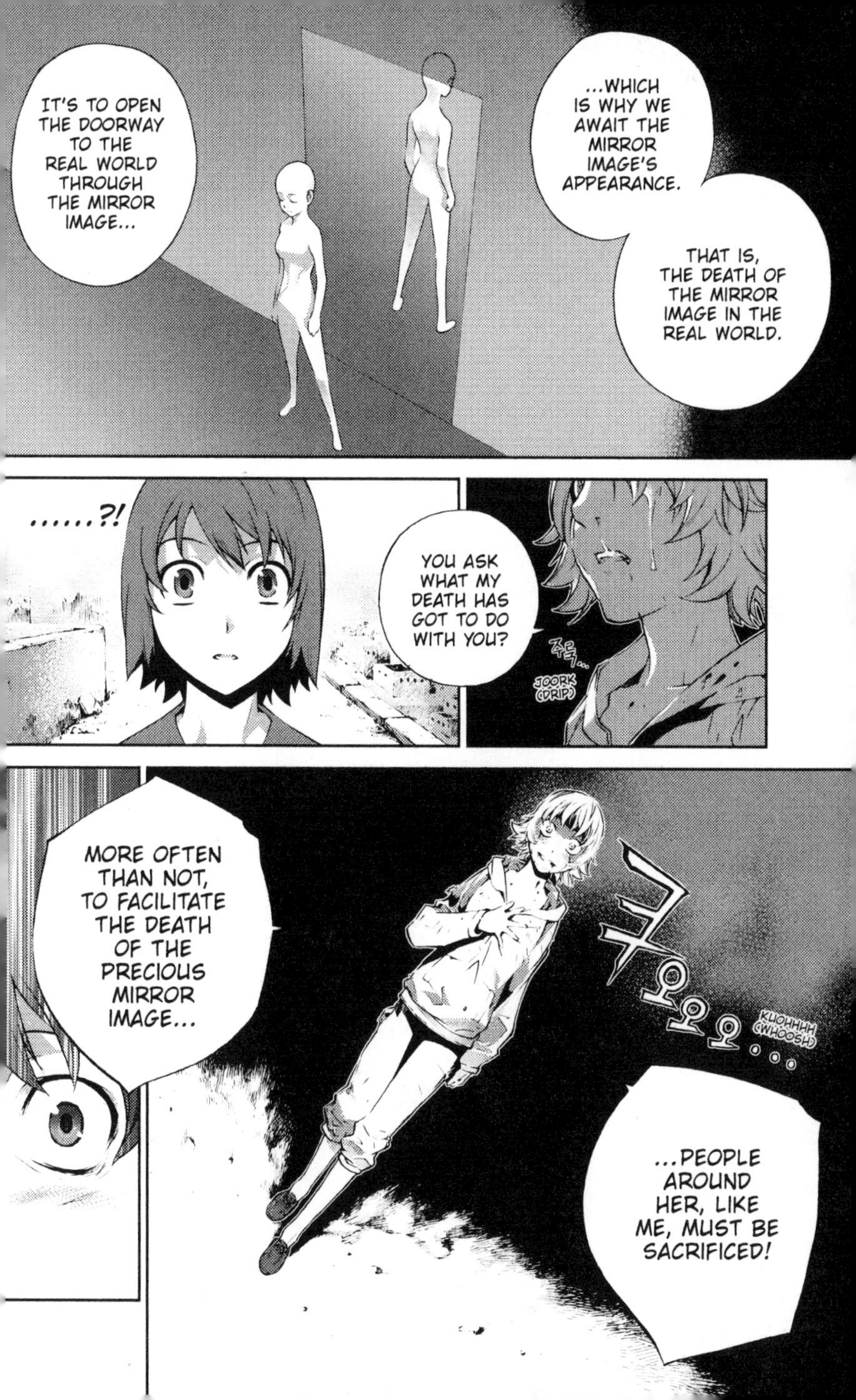
IT'S TO OPEN THE DOORWAY TO THE REAL WORLD THROUGH THE MIRROR IMAGE...
...WHICH IS WHY WE AWAIT THE MIRROR IMAGE'S APPEARANCE.
THAT IS, THE DEATH OF THE MIRROR IMAGE IN THE REAL WORLD.
......?!
YOU ASK WHAT MY DEATH HAS GOT TO DO WITH YOU?
주륵...
JOORK (DRIP)
MORE OFTEN THAN NOT, TO FACILITATE THE DEATH OF THE PRECIOUS MIRROR IMAGE...
크오오오...
KUOHHHH (WHOOSH)
...PEOPLE AROUND HER, LIKE ME, MUST BE SACRIFICED!

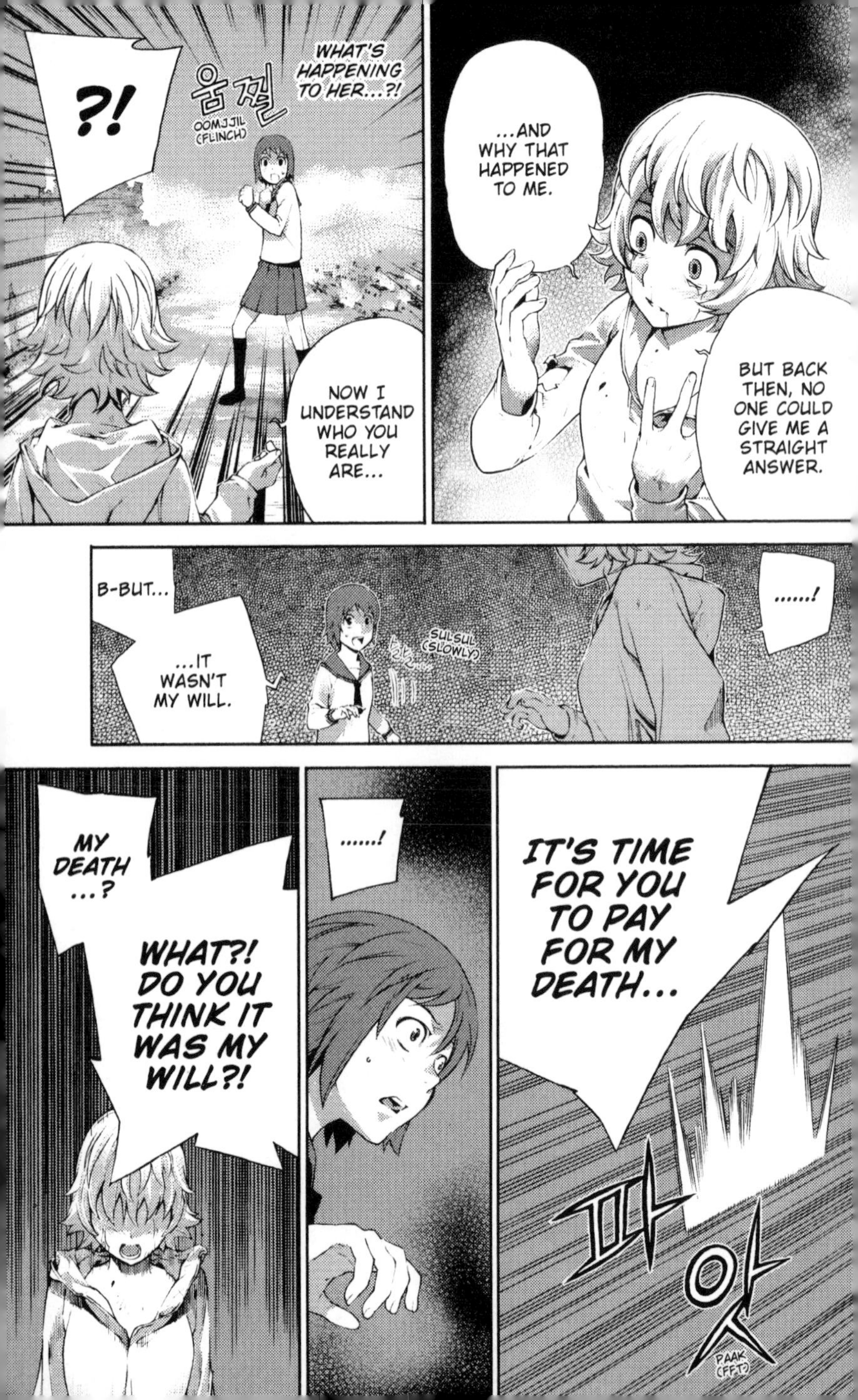
?!
움찔
OOMJJIL (FLINCH)
WHAT'S HAPPENING TO HER...?!
NOW I UNDERSTAND WHO YOU REALLY ARE...
...AND WHY THAT HAPPENED TO ME.
BUT BACK THEN, NO ONE COULD GIVE ME A STRAIGHT ANSWER.
B-BUT...
...IT WASN'T MY WILL.
SULSUL (SLOWLY)
......!
MY DEATH ...?
WHAT?! DO YOU THINK IT WAS MY WILL?!
......!
IT'S TIME FOR YOU TO PAY FOR MY DEATH...
PAAK (FFT)

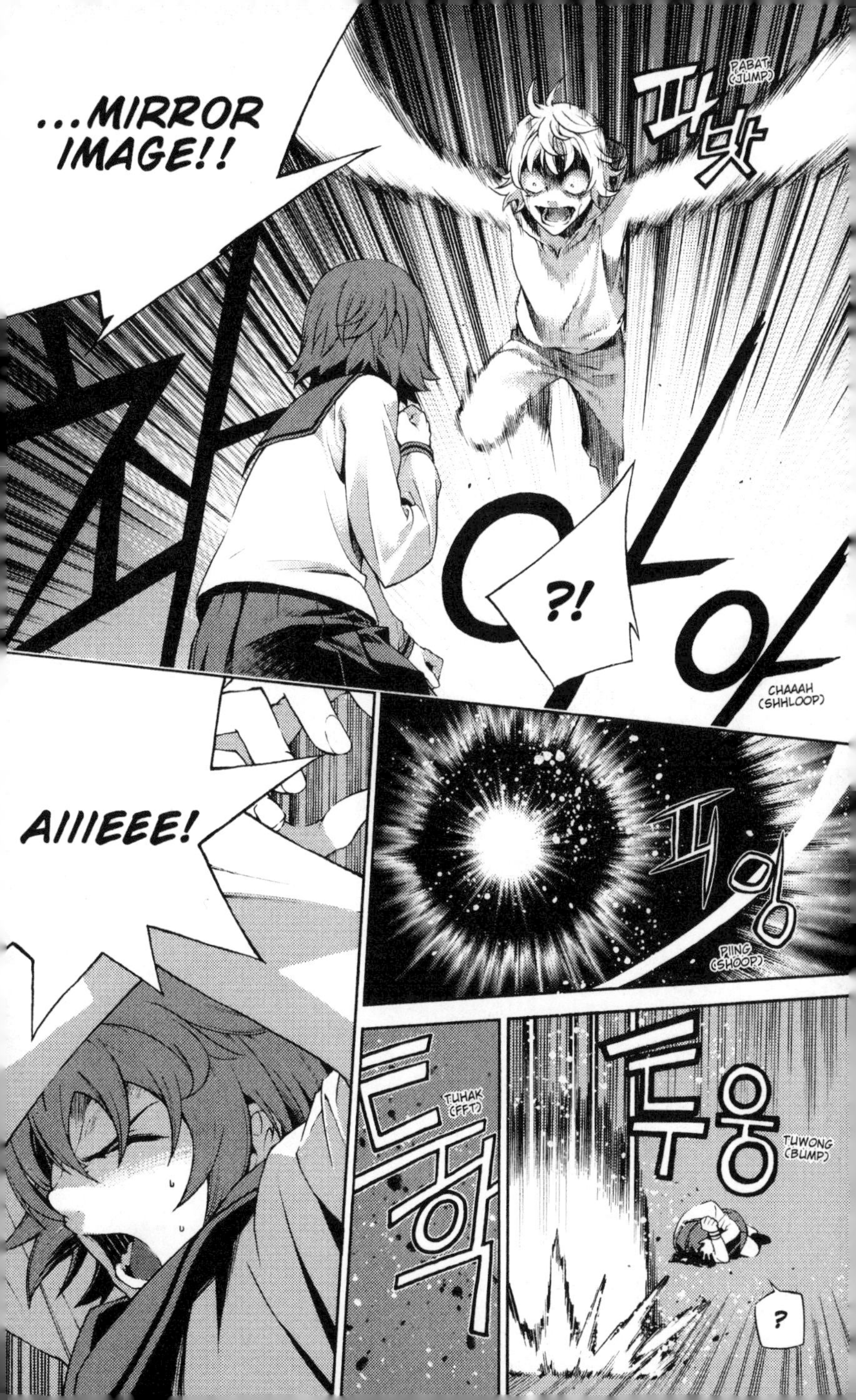
...MIRROR IMAGE!!
파밧
PABAT (JUMP)
?!
CHAAAH (SHHLOOP)
AIIIEEE!
피잉
PIING (SHOOP)
TUHAK (FFT)
투웅
TUWONG (BUMP)
?

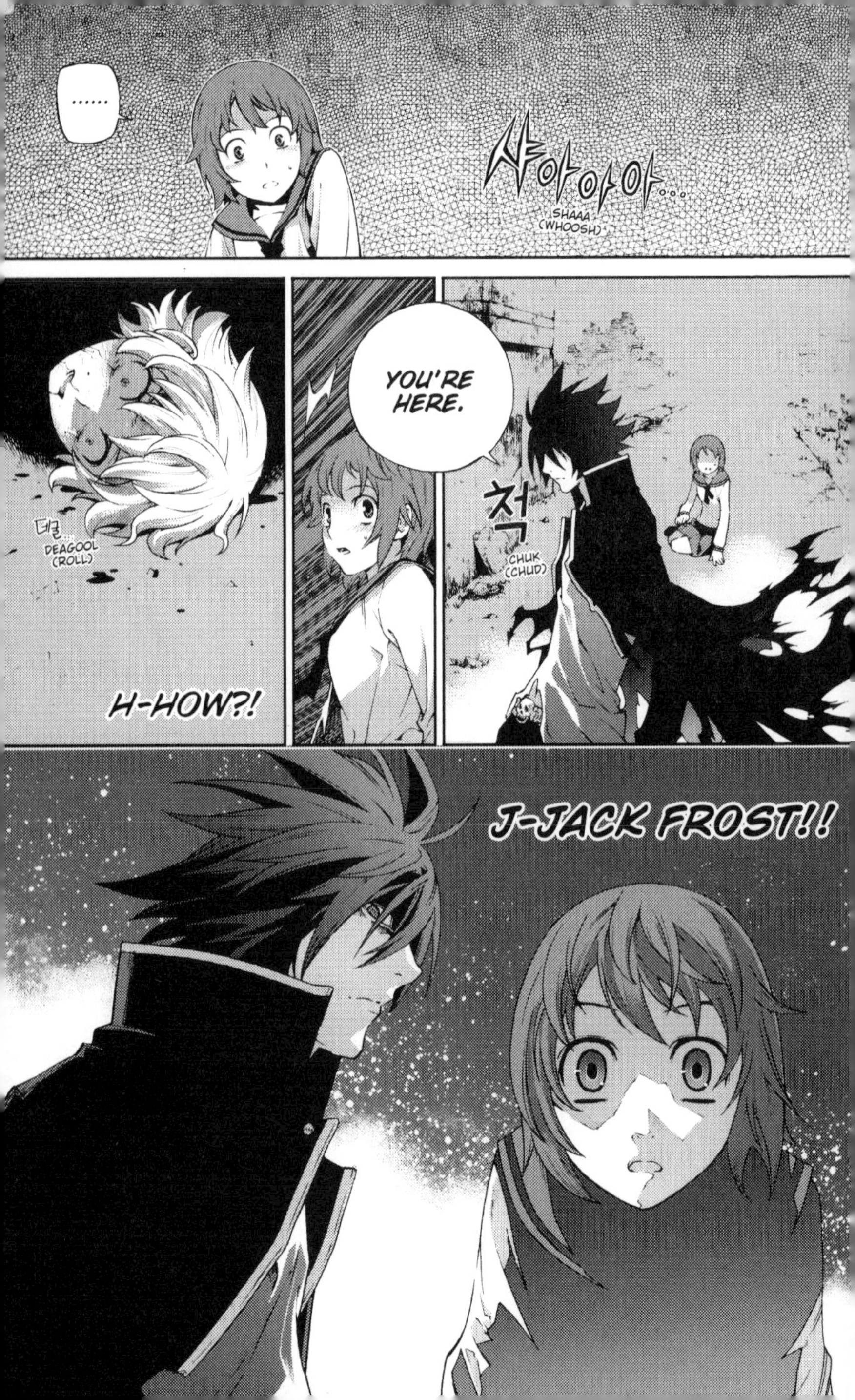
......
샤아아아...
SHAAA (WHOOSH)
데굴...
DEAGOOL (ROLL)
H-HOW?!
YOU'RE HERE.
척
CHUK (CHUD)
J-JACK FROST!!

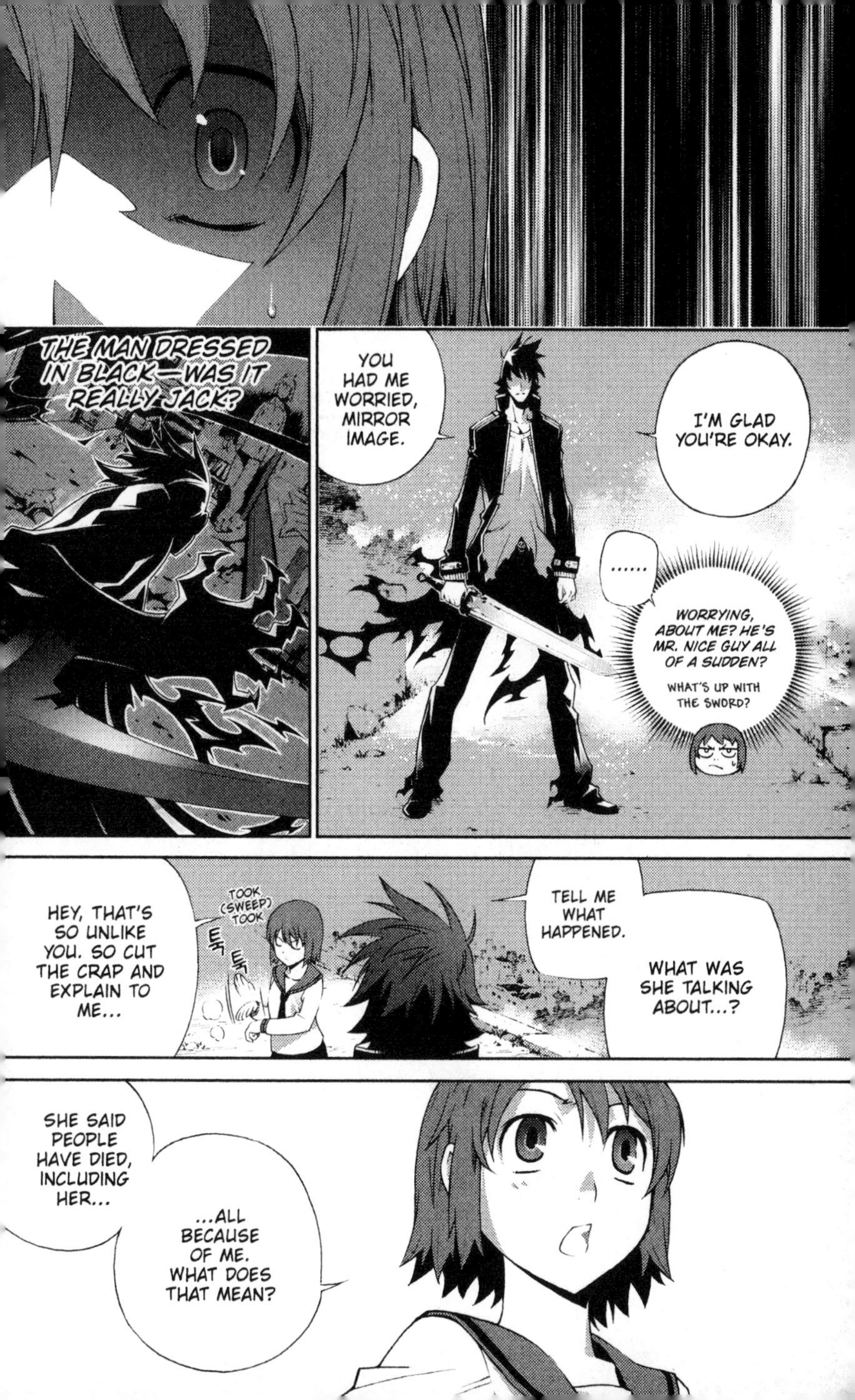
THE MAN DRESSED IN BLACK—WAS IT REALLY JACK?
YOU HAD ME WORRIED, MIRROR IMAGE.
I'M GLAD YOU'RE OKAY.
......
WORRYING, ABOUT ME? HE'S MR. NICE GUY ALL OF A SUDDEN?
WHAT'S UP WITH THE SWORD?
HEY, THAT'S SO UNLIKE YOU. SO CUT THE CRAP AND EXPLAIN TO ME...
TOOK (SWEEP) TOOK
TELL ME WHAT HAPPENED.
WHAT WAS SHE TALKING ABOUT...?
SHE SAID PEOPLE HAVE DIED, INCLUDING HER...
...ALL BECAUSE OF ME. WHAT DOES THAT MEAN?

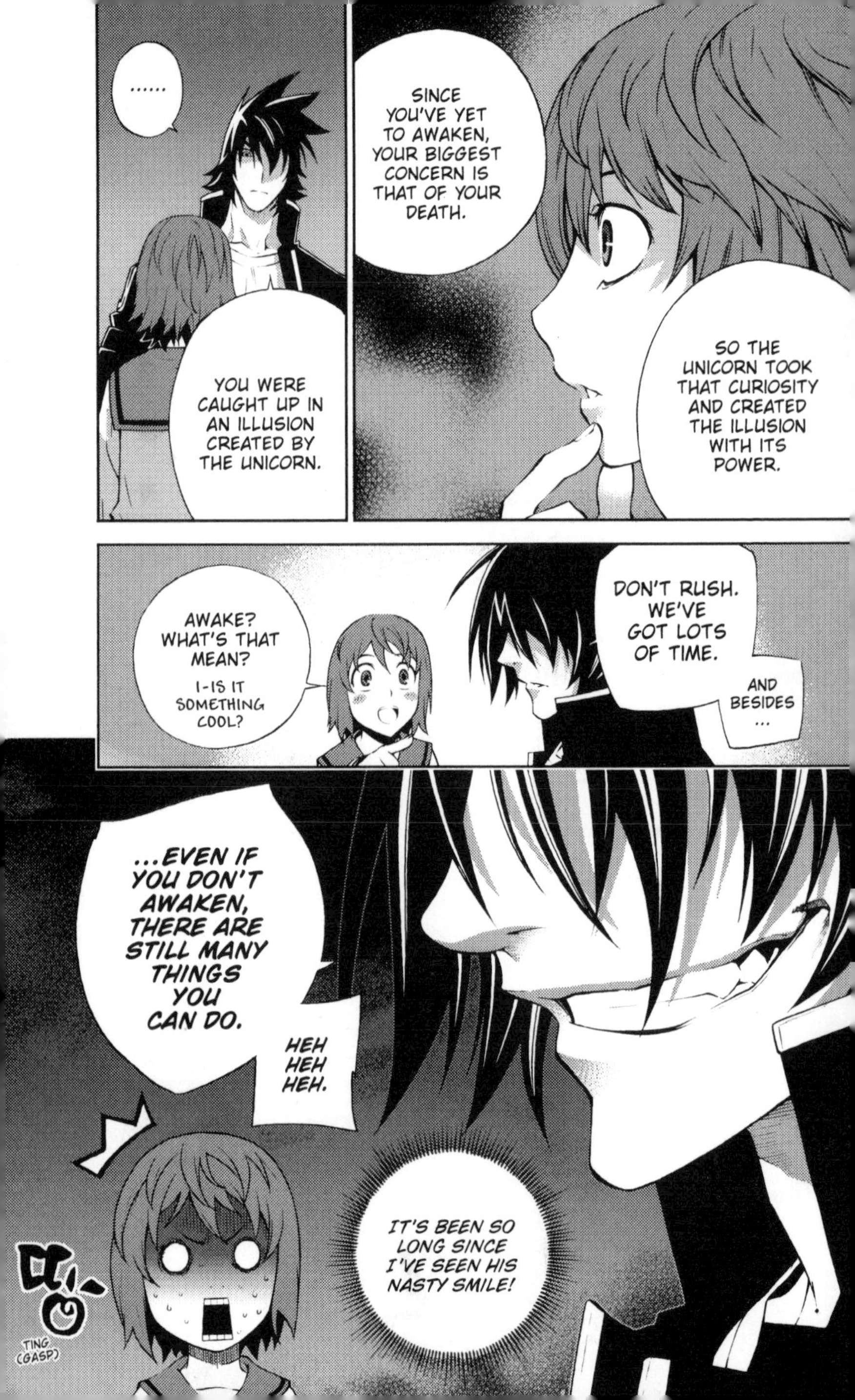
……
YOU WERE CAUGHT UP IN AN ILLUSION CREATED BY THE UNICORN.
SINCE YOU'VE YET TO AWAKEN, YOUR BIGGEST CONCERN IS THAT OF YOUR DEATH.
SO THE UNICORN TOOK THAT CURIOSITY AND CREATED THE ILLUSION WITH ITS POWER.
AWAKE? WHAT'S THAT MEAN?
I-IS IT SOMETHING COOL?
DON'T RUSH. WE'VE GOT LOTS OF TIME.
AND BESIDES …
…EVEN IF YOU DON'T AWAKEN, THERE ARE STILL MANY THINGS YOU CAN DO.
HEH HEH HEH.
IT'S BEEN SO LONG SINCE I'VE SEEN HIS NASTY SMILE!
TING (GASP)

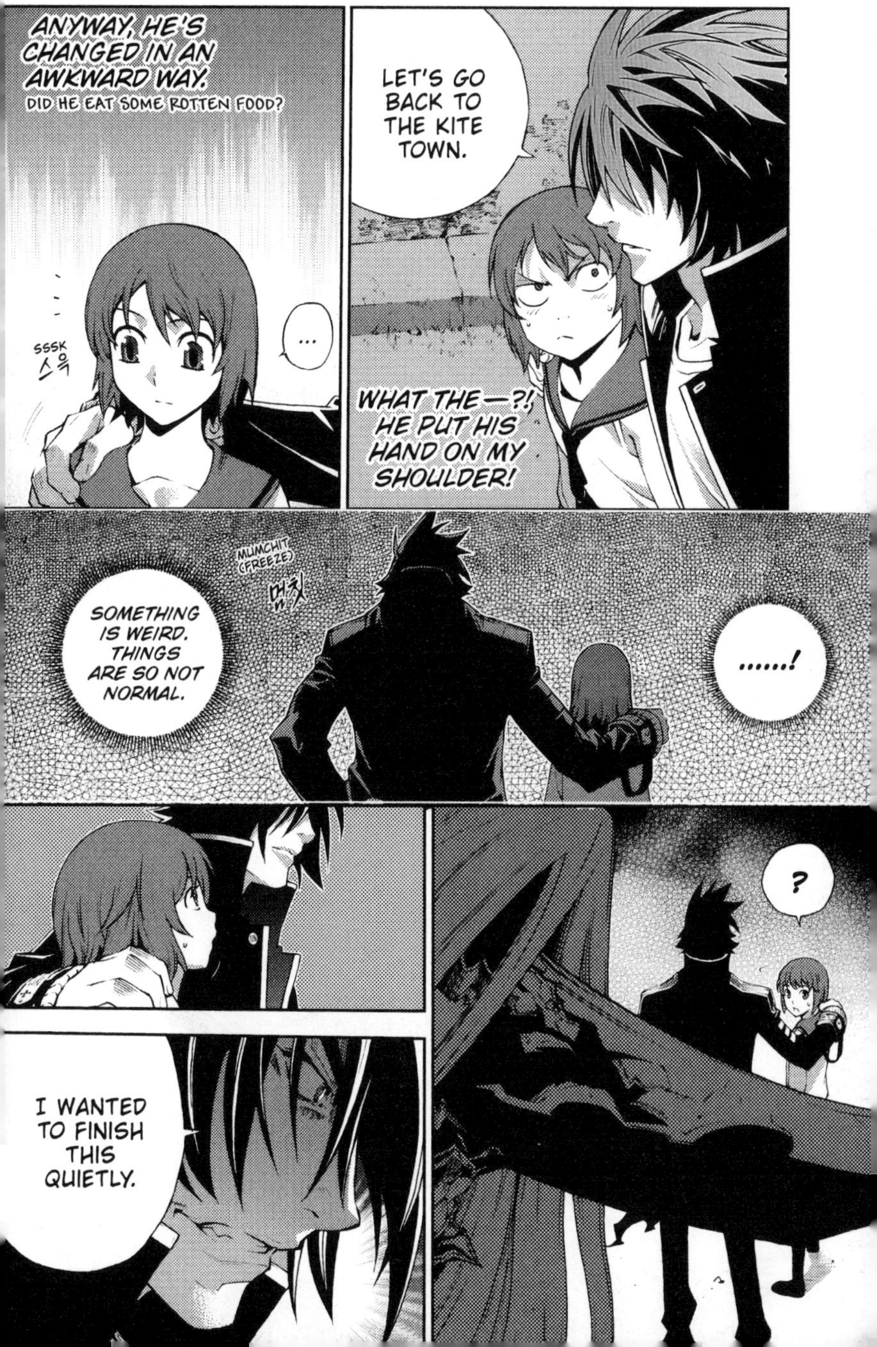
ANYWAY, HE'S CHANGED IN AN AWKWARD WAY.
DID HE EAT SOME ROTTEN FOOD?
SSSK
스윽
...
LET'S GO BACK TO THE KITE TOWN.
WHAT THE—?! HE PUT HIS HAND ON MY SHOULDER!
MUMCHIT (FREEZE)
멈칫
SOMETHING IS WEIRD. THINGS ARE SO NOT NORMAL.
......!
?
I WANTED TO FINISH THIS QUIETLY.

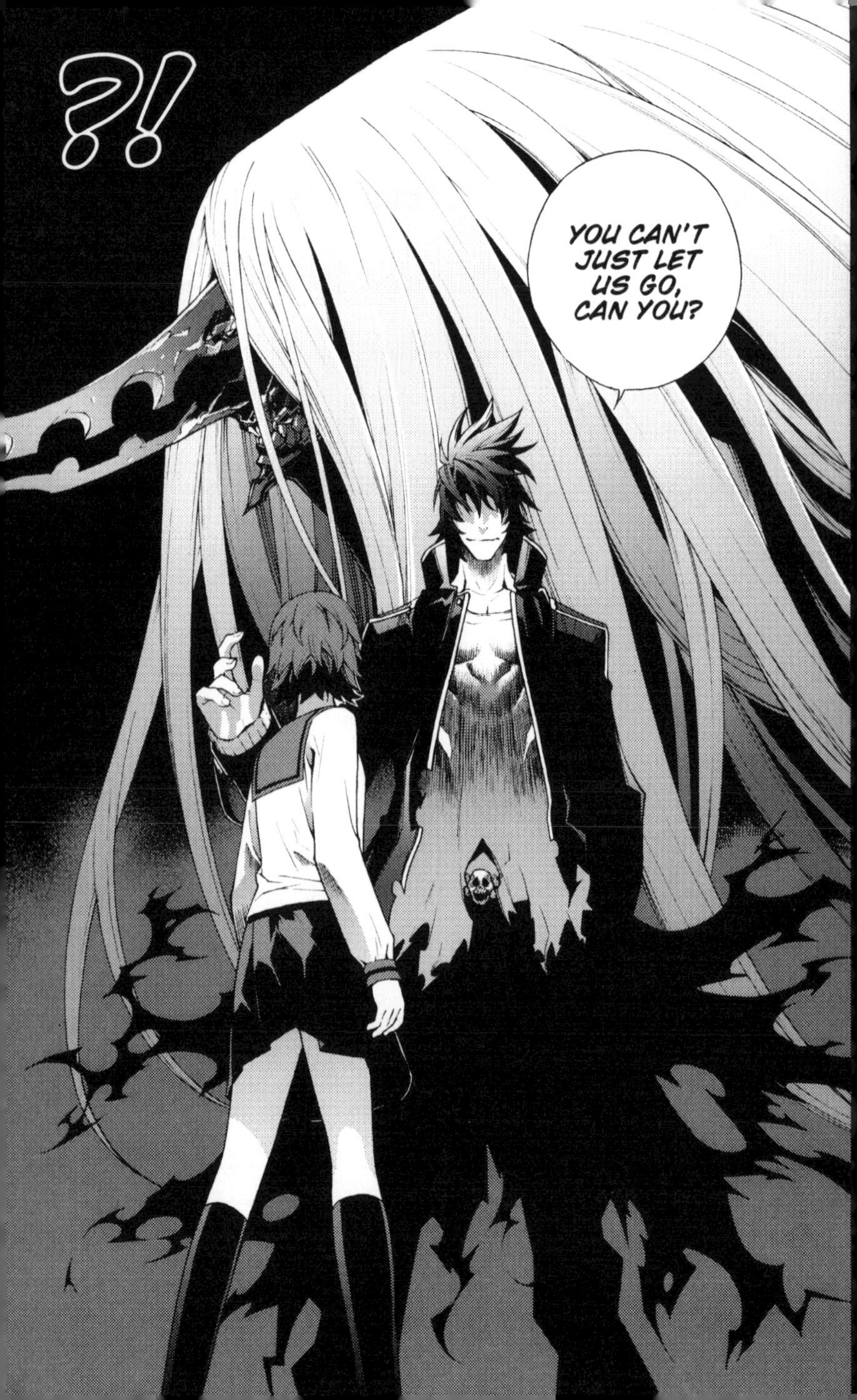
?!
YOU CAN'T JUST LET US GO, CAN YOU?

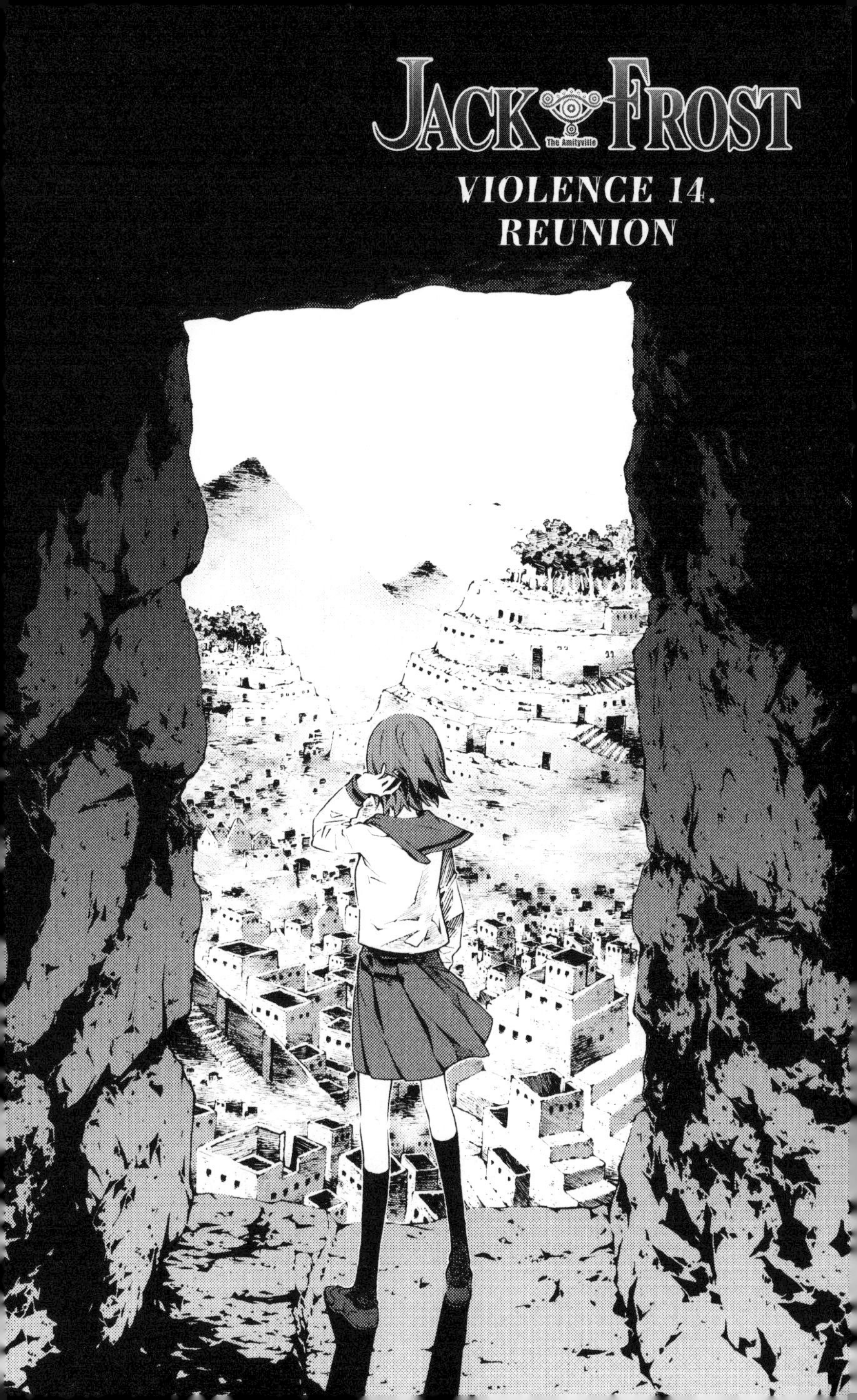
JACK FROST
The Amityville
VIOLENCE 14.
REUNION

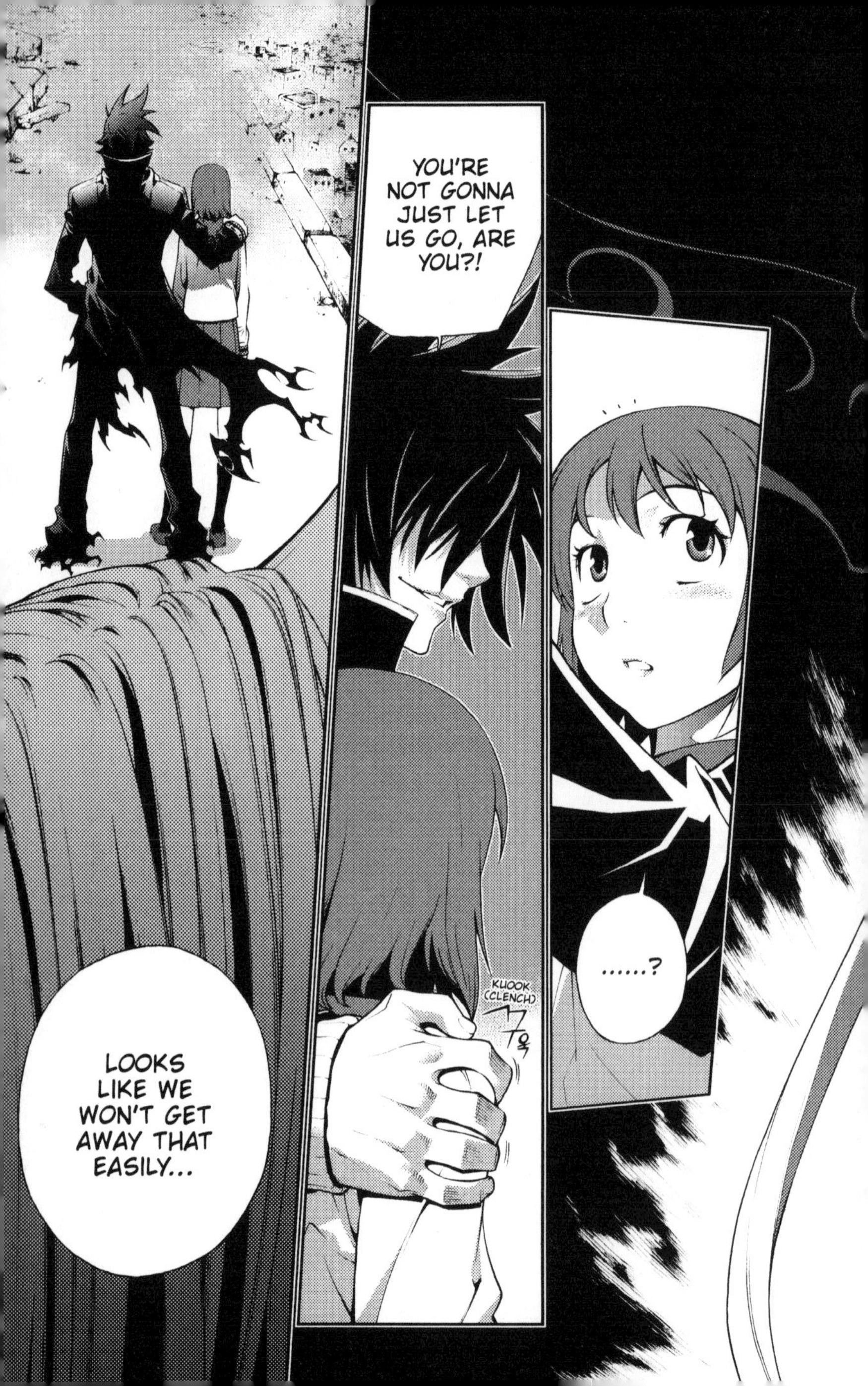
LOOKS LIKE WE WON'T GET AWAY THAT EASILY...
YOU'RE NOT GONNA JUST LET US GO, ARE YOU?!
KUOOK (CLENCH)
......?

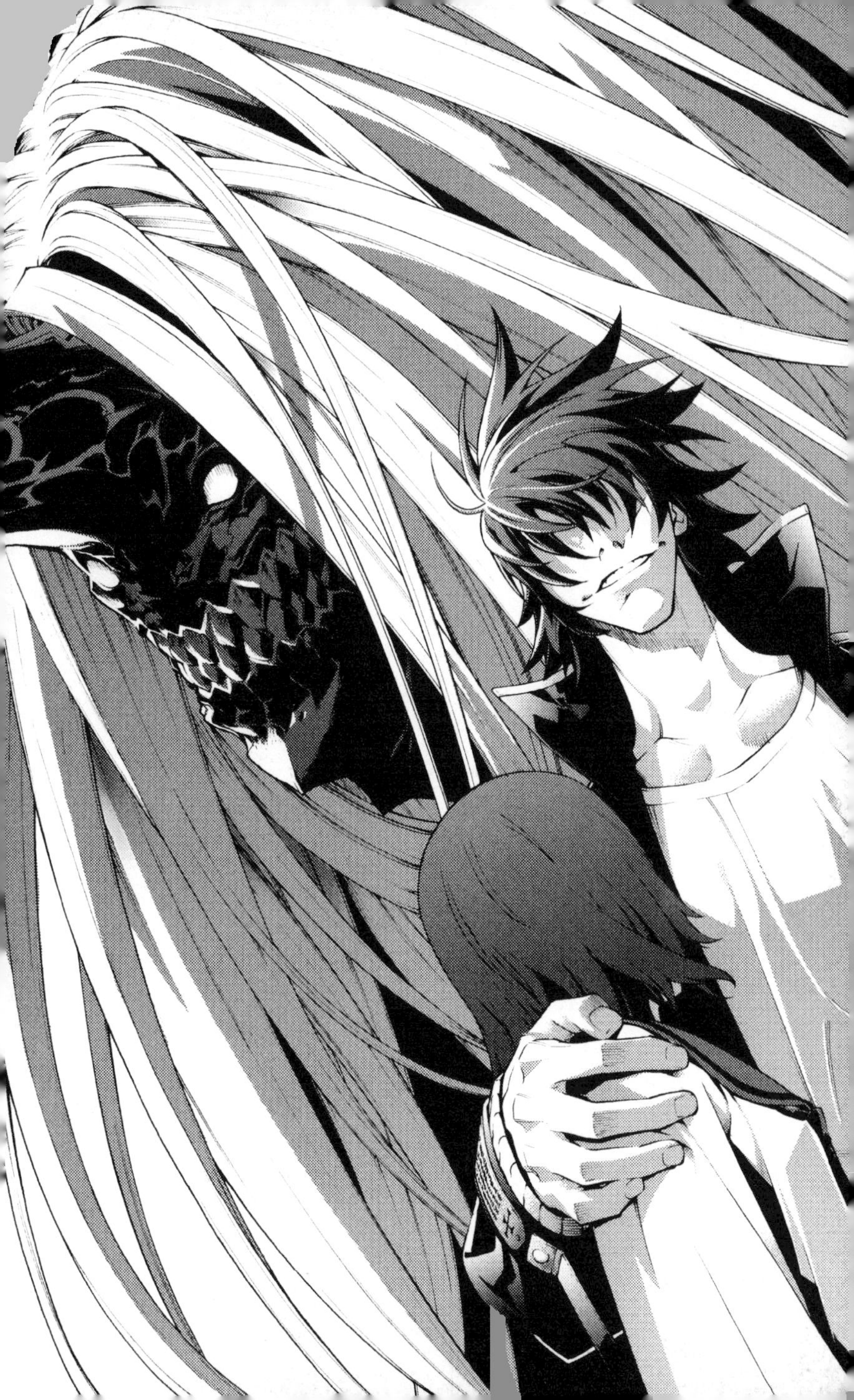

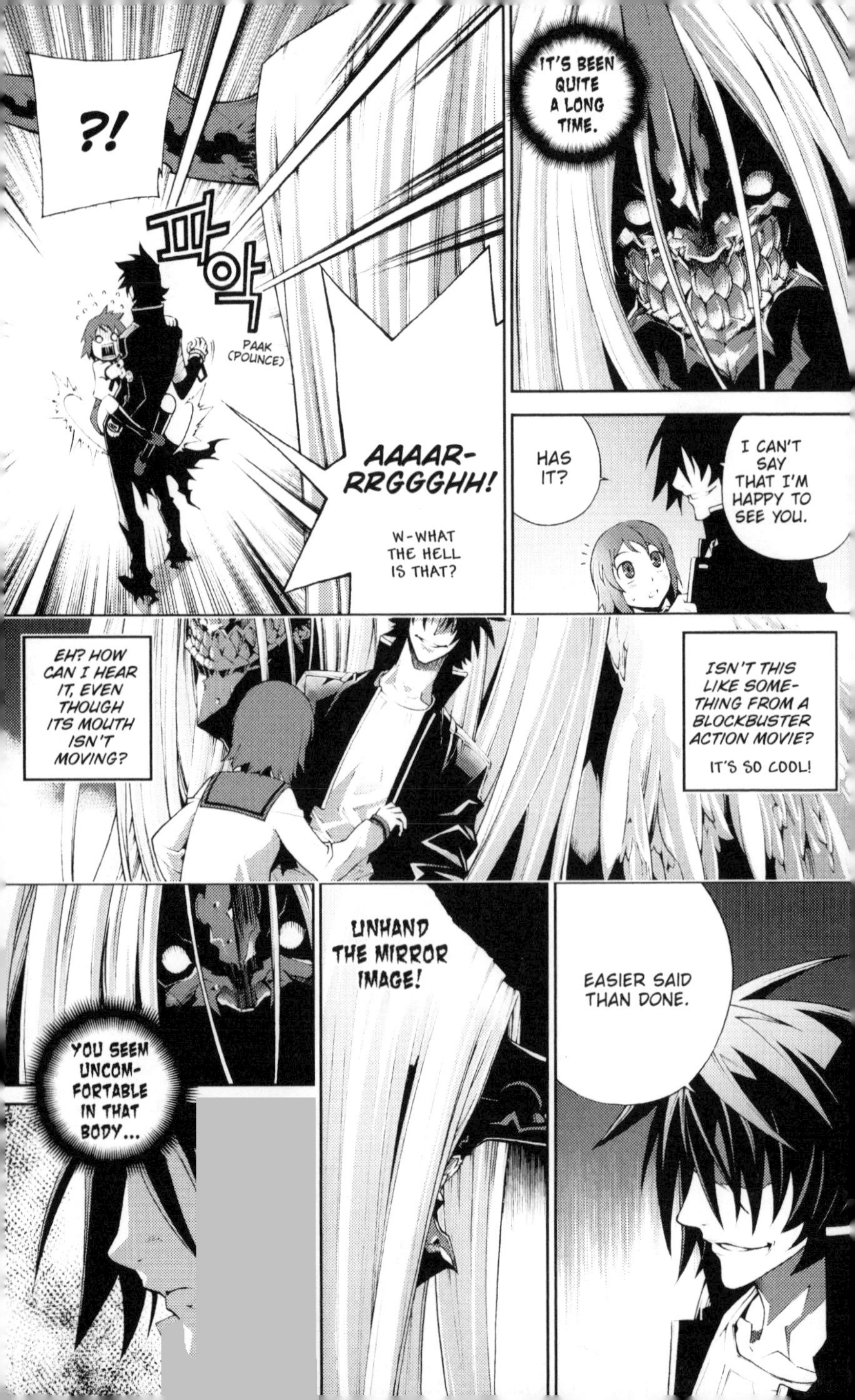
?!
파악
PAAK (POUNCE)
AAAAR-RRGGGHH!
W-WHAT THE HELL IS THAT?
IT'S BEEN QUITE A LONG TIME.
HAS IT?
I CAN'T SAY THAT I'M HAPPY TO SEE YOU.
EH? HOW CAN I HEAR IT, EVEN THOUGH ITS MOUTH ISN'T MOVING?
ISN'T THIS LIKE SOME-THING FROM A BLOCKBUSTER ACTION MOVIE?
IT'S SO COOL!
YOU SEEM UNCOM-FORTABLE IN THAT BODY...
UNHAND THE MIRROR IMAGE!
EASIER SAID THAN DONE.

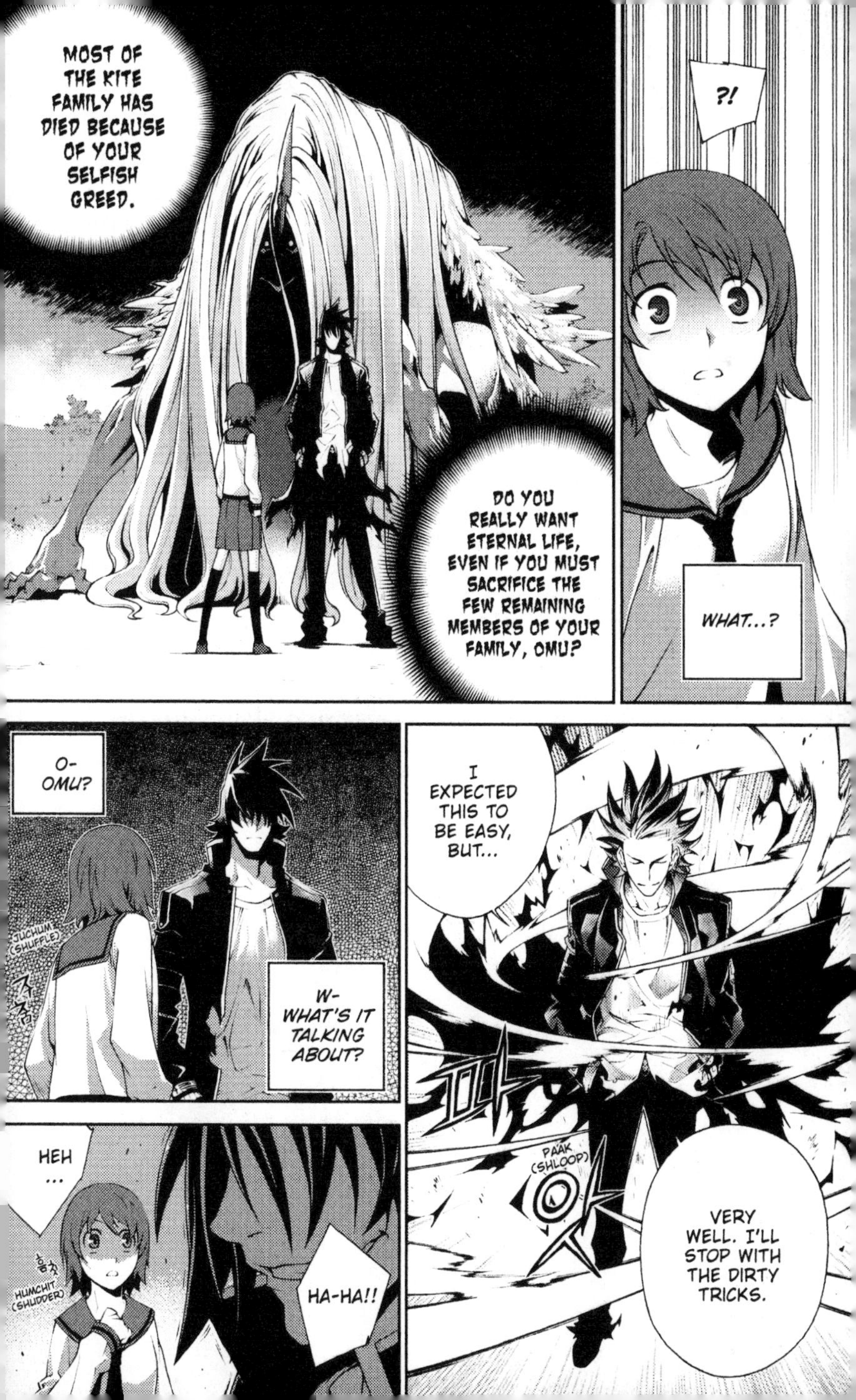
MOST OF THE KITE FAMILY HAS DIED BECAUSE OF YOUR SELFISH GREED.
DO YOU REALLY WANT ETERNAL LIFE, EVEN IF YOU MUST SACRIFICE THE FEW REMAINING MEMBERS OF YOUR FAMILY, OMU?
?!
WHAT...?
O-OMU?
JUCHUM (SHUFFLE)
주춤
W-WHAT'S IT TALKING ABOUT?
HEH...
흠칫
HUMCHIT (SHUDDER)
HA-HA!!
I EXPECTED THIS TO BE EASY, BUT...
PAAK (SHLOOP)
VERY WELL. I'LL STOP WITH THE DIRTY TRICKS.

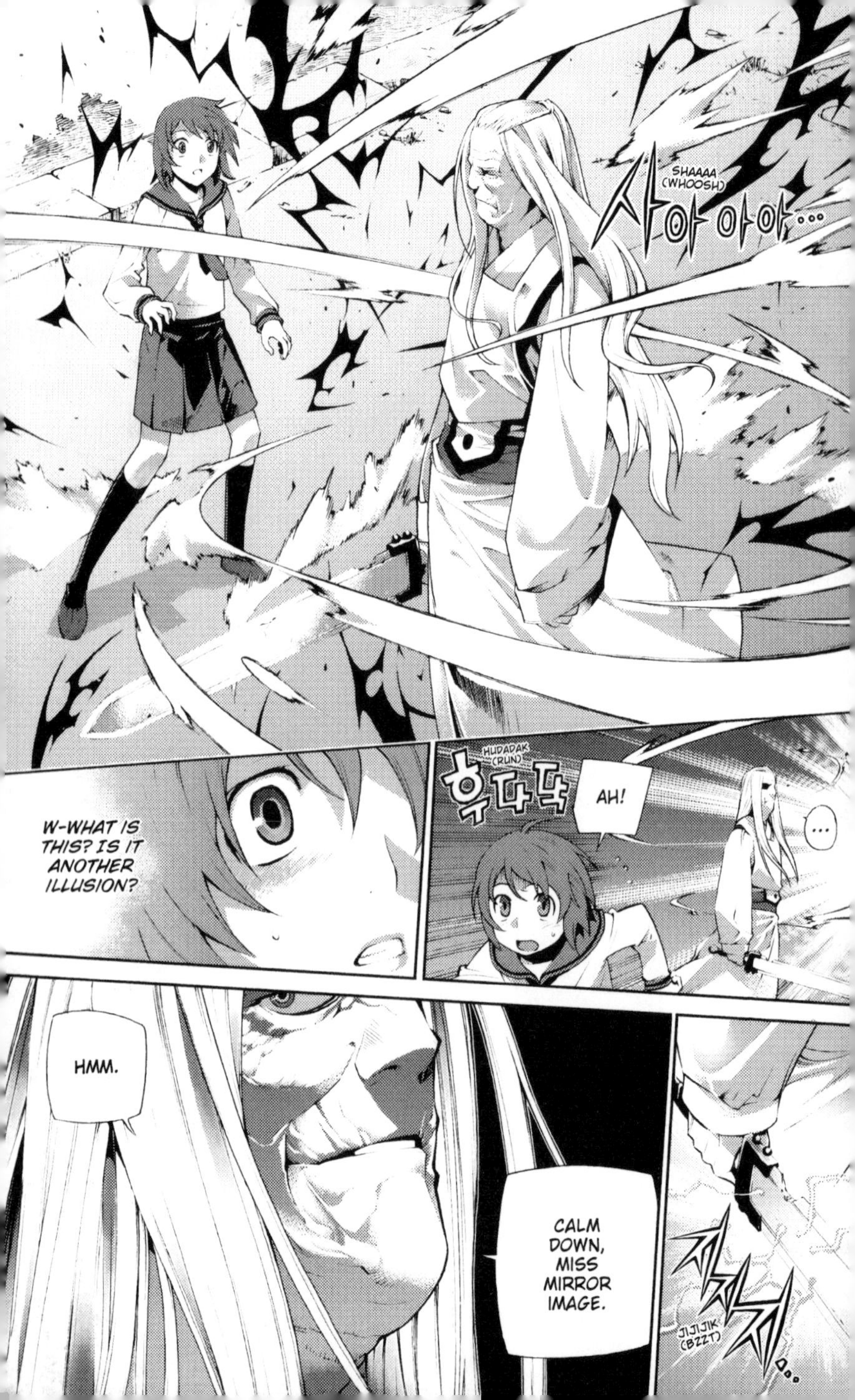
SHAAAA (WHOOSH)
샤아아아...
W-WHAT IS THIS? IS IT ANOTHER ILLUSION?
HUDADAK (RUN)
후다닥
AH!
...
HMM.
CALM DOWN, MISS MIRROR IMAGE.
JIJIJIK (BZZT)

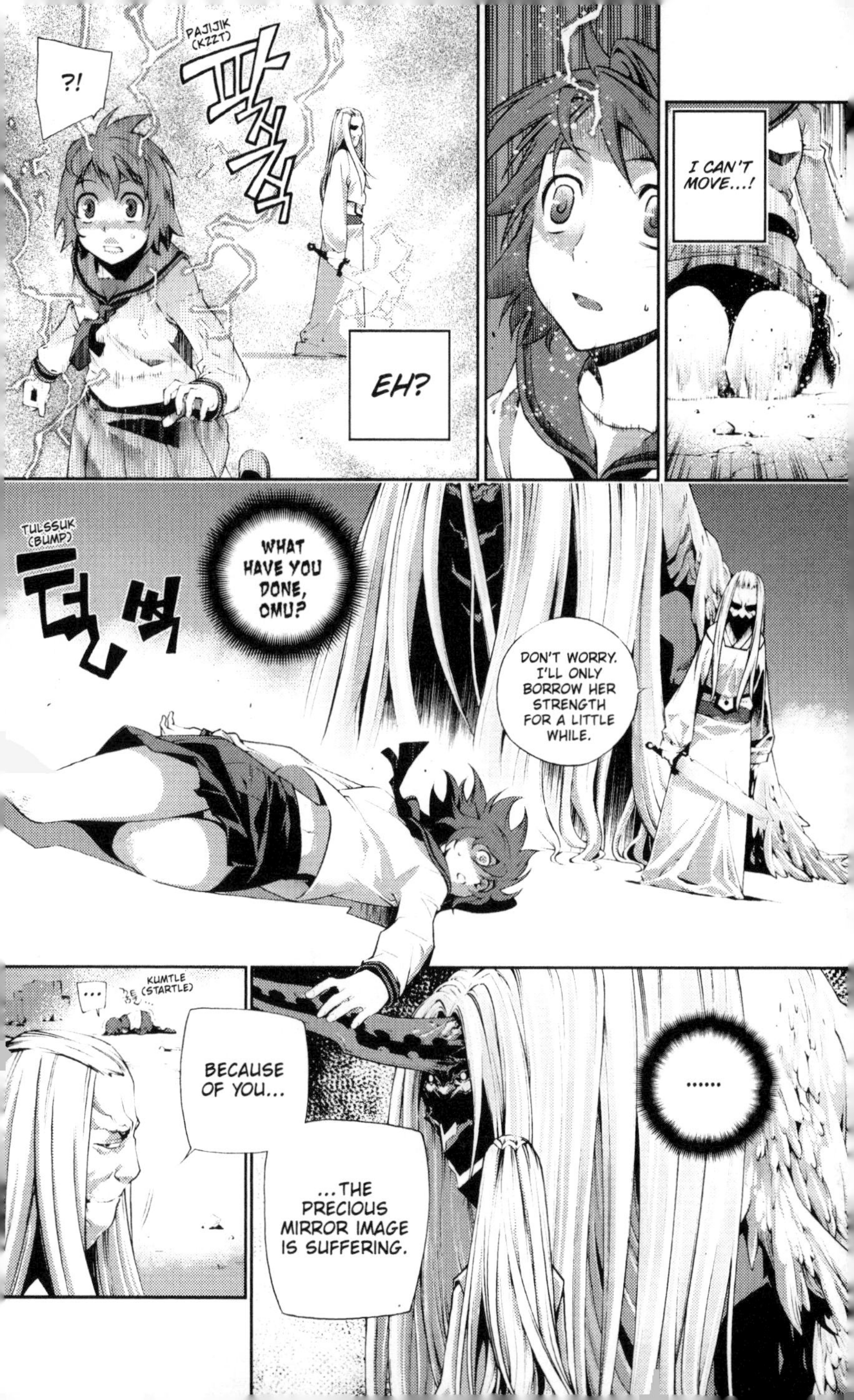
?!
PAJIJIK (KZZT)
EH?
I CAN'T MOVE...!
TULSSUK (BUMP)
WHAT HAVE YOU DONE, OMU?
DON'T WORRY. I'LL ONLY BORROW HER STRENGTH FOR A LITTLE WHILE.
...
KUMTLE (STARTLE)
BECAUSE OF YOU...
......
...THE PRECIOUS MIRROR IMAGE IS SUFFERING.

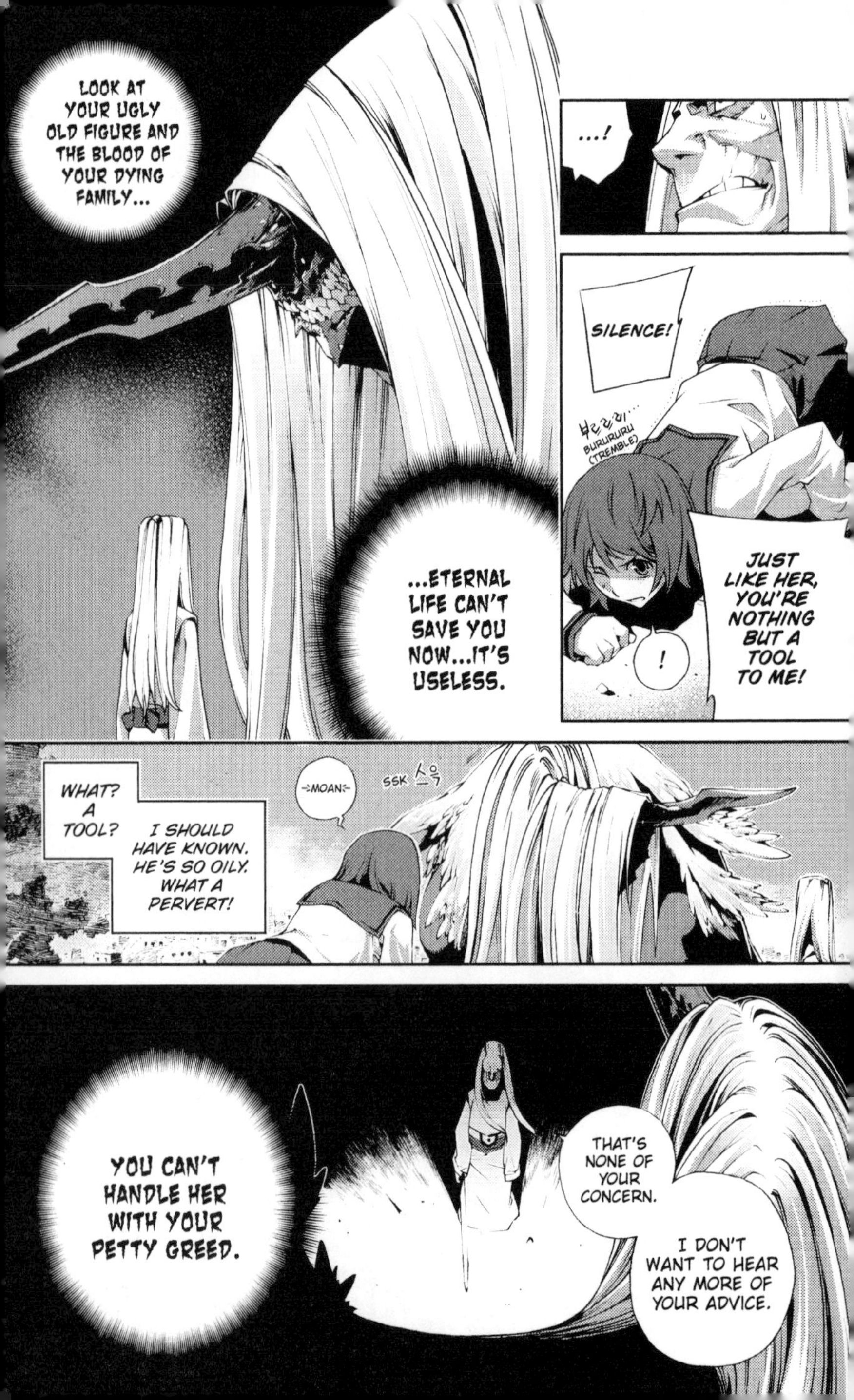
LOOK AT YOUR UGLY OLD FIGURE AND THE BLOOD OF YOUR DYING FAMILY...
...ETERNAL LIFE CAN'T SAVE YOU NOW...IT'S USELESS.
...!
SILENCE!
부르르...
BURURURU (TREMBLE)
!
JUST LIKE HER, YOU'RE NOTHING BUT A TOOL TO ME!
WHAT? A TOOL?
I SHOULD HAVE KNOWN. HE'S SO OILY. WHAT A PERVERT!
~MOAN~
SSK 스윽
YOU CAN'T HANDLE HER WITH YOUR PETTY GREED.
THAT'S NONE OF YOUR CONCERN.
I DON'T WANT TO HEAR ANY MORE OF YOUR ADVICE.

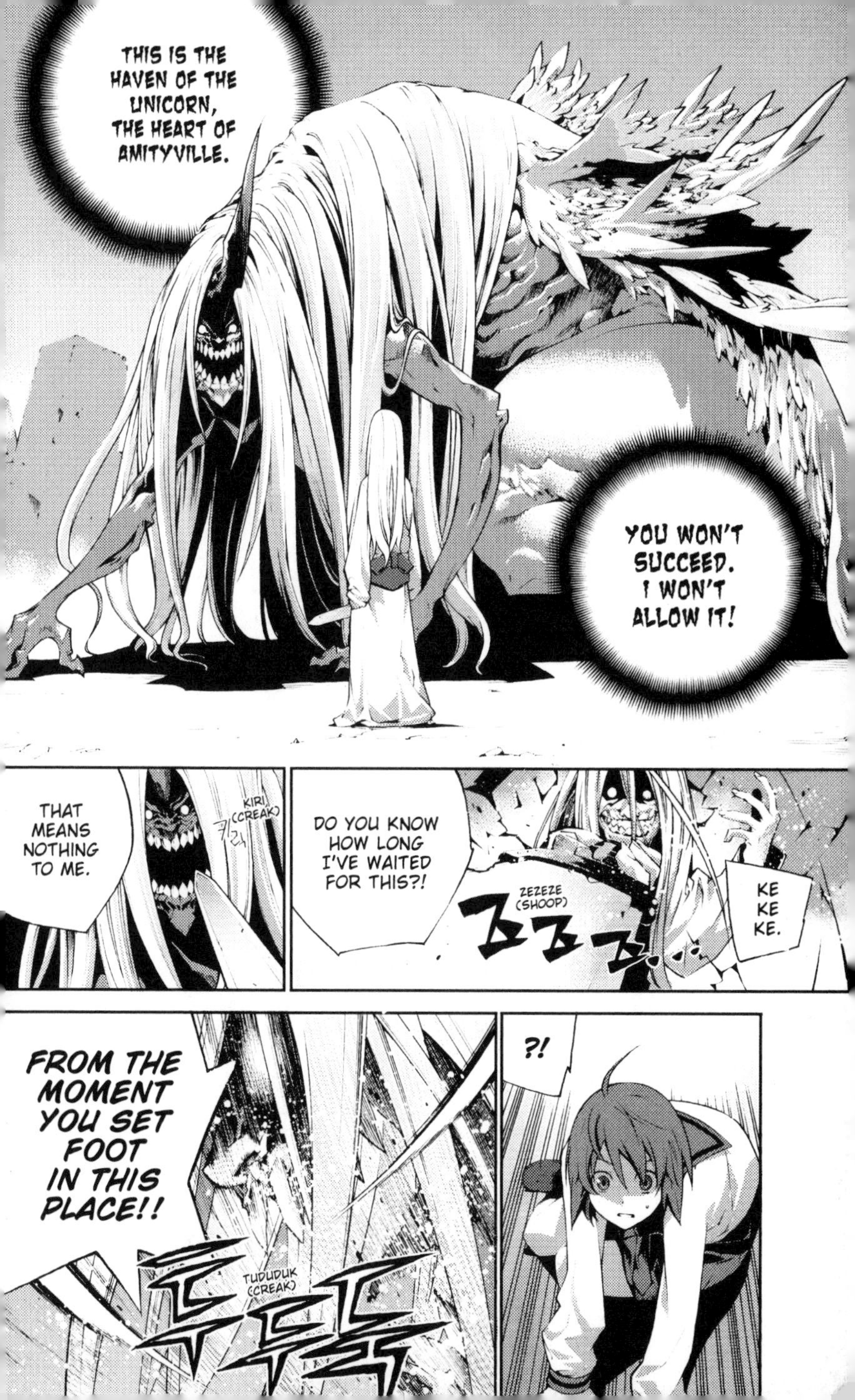
THIS IS THE HAVEN OF THE UNICORN, THE HEART OF AMITYVILLE.
YOU WON'T SUCCEED. I WON'T ALLOW IT!
THAT MEANS NOTHING TO ME.
KIRI (CREAK)
DO YOU KNOW HOW LONG I'VE WAITED FOR THIS?!
ZEZEZE (SHOOP)
KE KE KE.
FROM THE MOMENT YOU SET FOOT IN THIS PLACE!!
TUDUDUK (CREAK)
?!

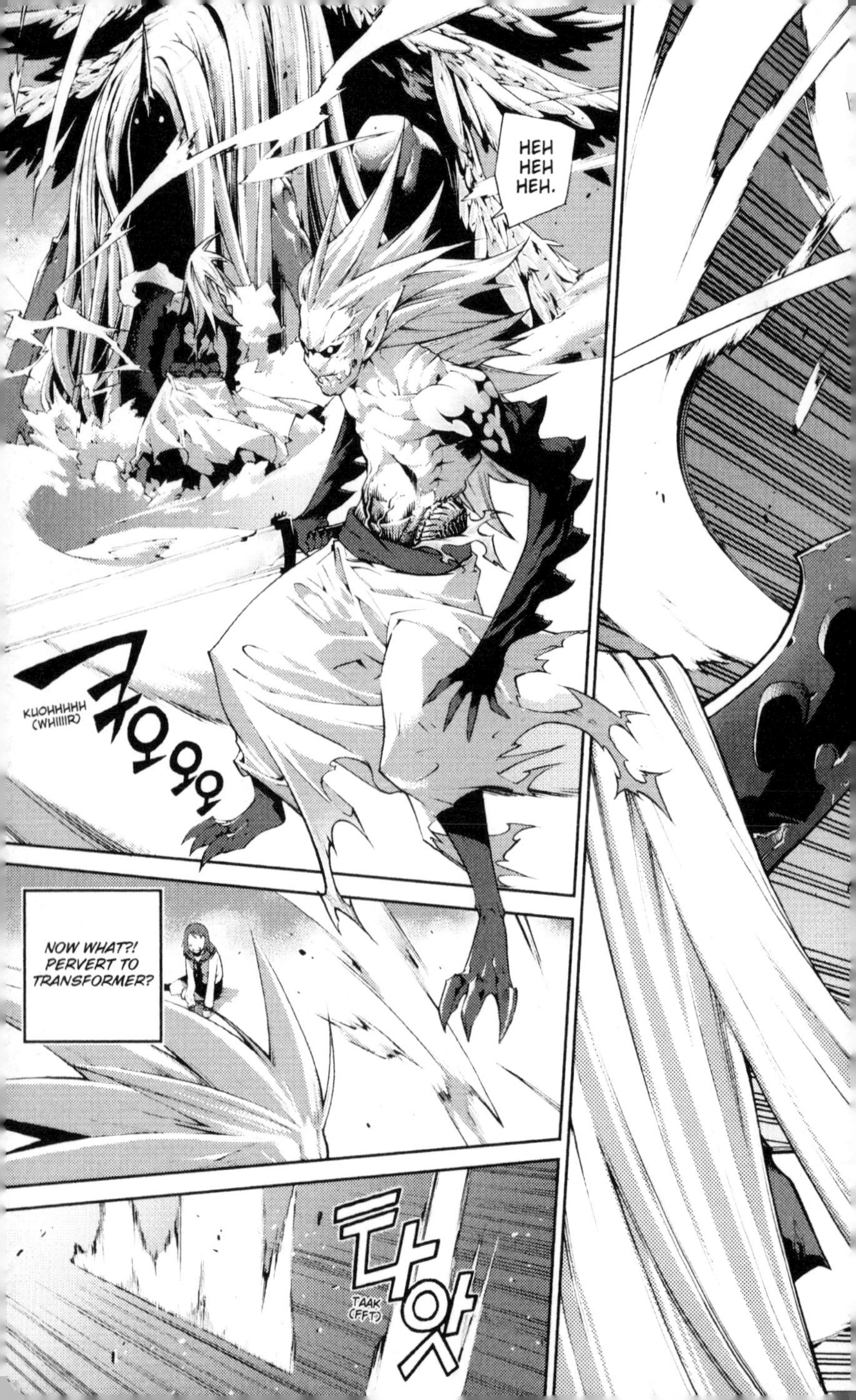
HEH HEH HEH.
쿠오오오
KUOHHHHH (WHIIIIR)
NOW WHAT?! PERVERT TO TRANSFORMER?
타악
TAAK (FF-T)

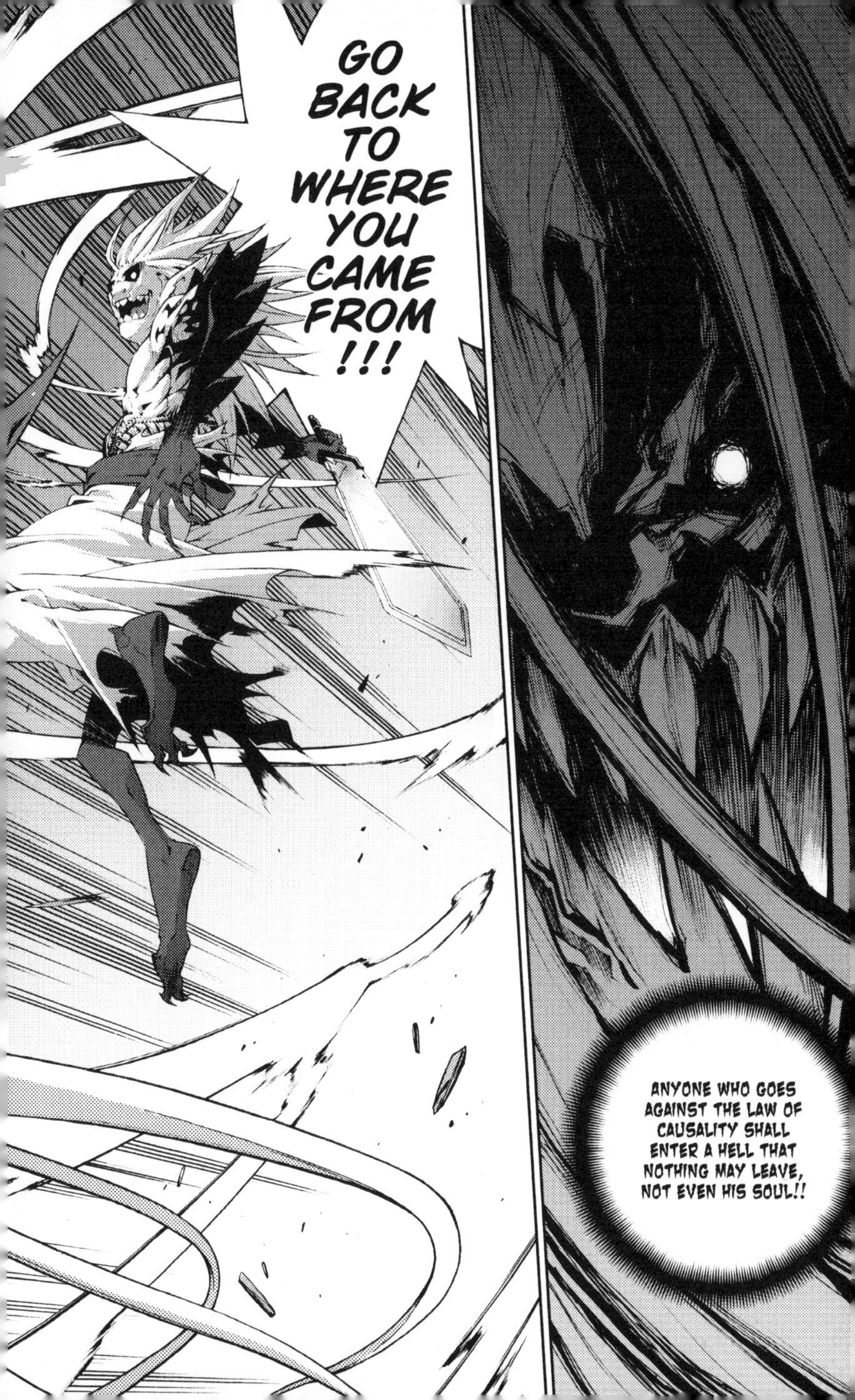
GO BACK TO WHERE YOU CAME FROM!!!
ANYONE WHO GOES AGAINST THE LAW OF CAUSALITY SHALL ENTER A HELL THAT NOTHING MAY LEAVE, NOT EVEN HIS SOUL!!

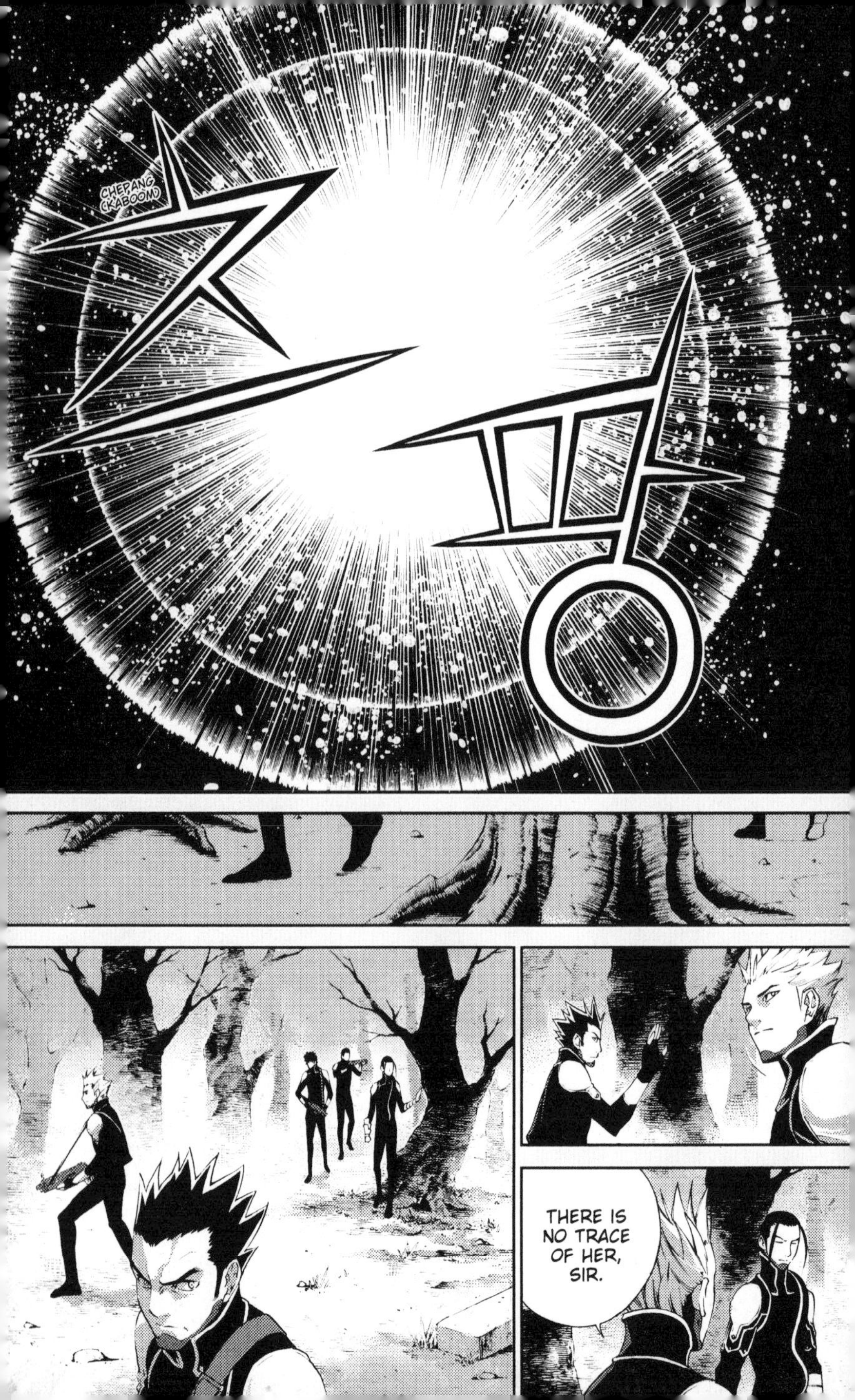
CHEPANG (KABOOM)
THERE IS NO TRACE OF HER, SIR.

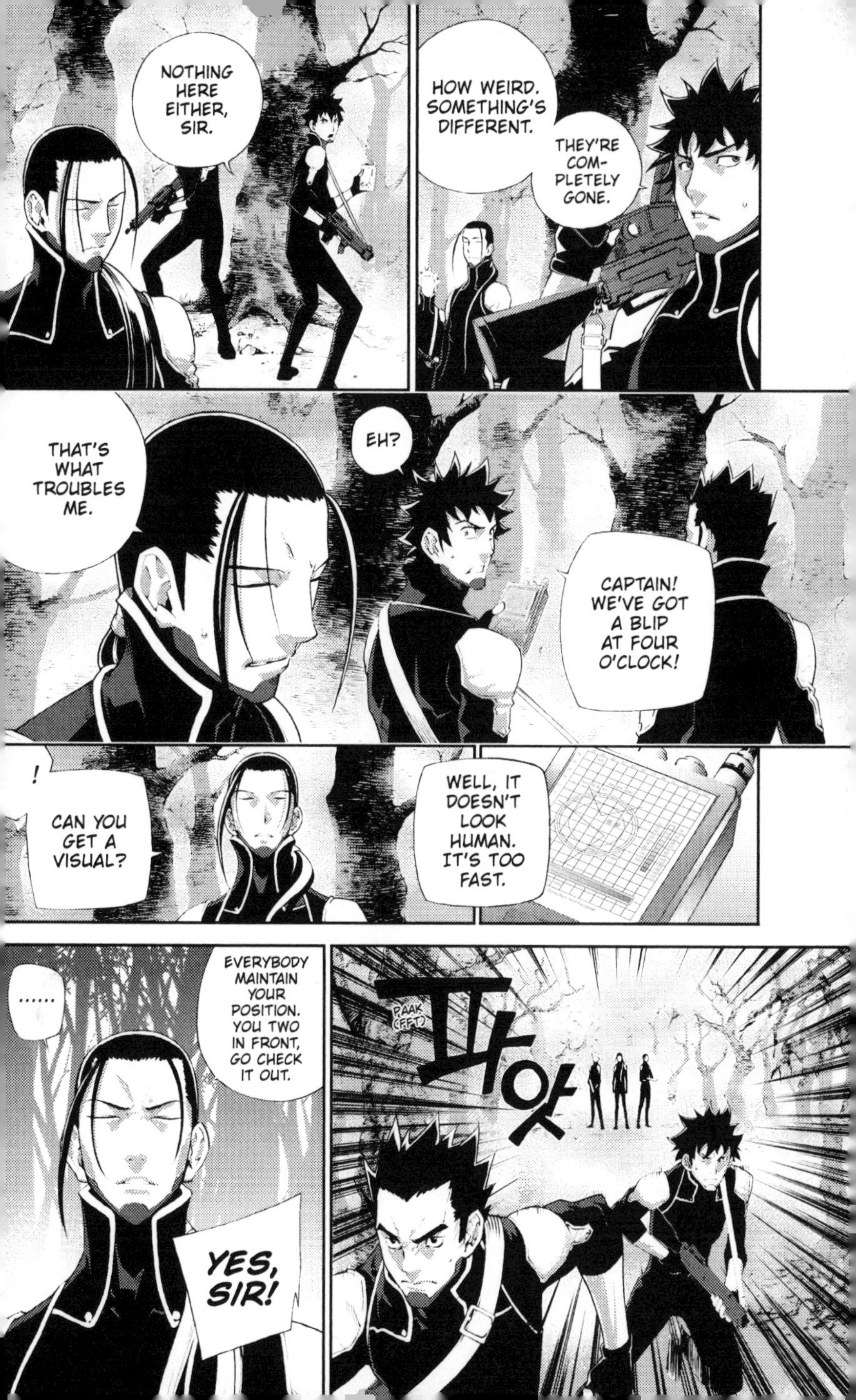
NOTHING HERE EITHER, SIR.
HOW WEIRD. SOMETHING'S DIFFERENT.
THEY'RE COM-PLETELY GONE.
THAT'S WHAT TROUBLES ME.
EH?
CAPTAIN! WE'VE GOT A BLIP AT FOUR O'CLOCK!
!
CAN YOU GET A VISUAL?
WELL, IT DOESN'T LOOK HUMAN. IT'S TOO FAST.
......
EVERYBODY MAINTAIN YOUR POSITION. YOU TWO IN FRONT, GO CHECK IT OUT.
YES, SIR!
파앗
PAAK (FFT)

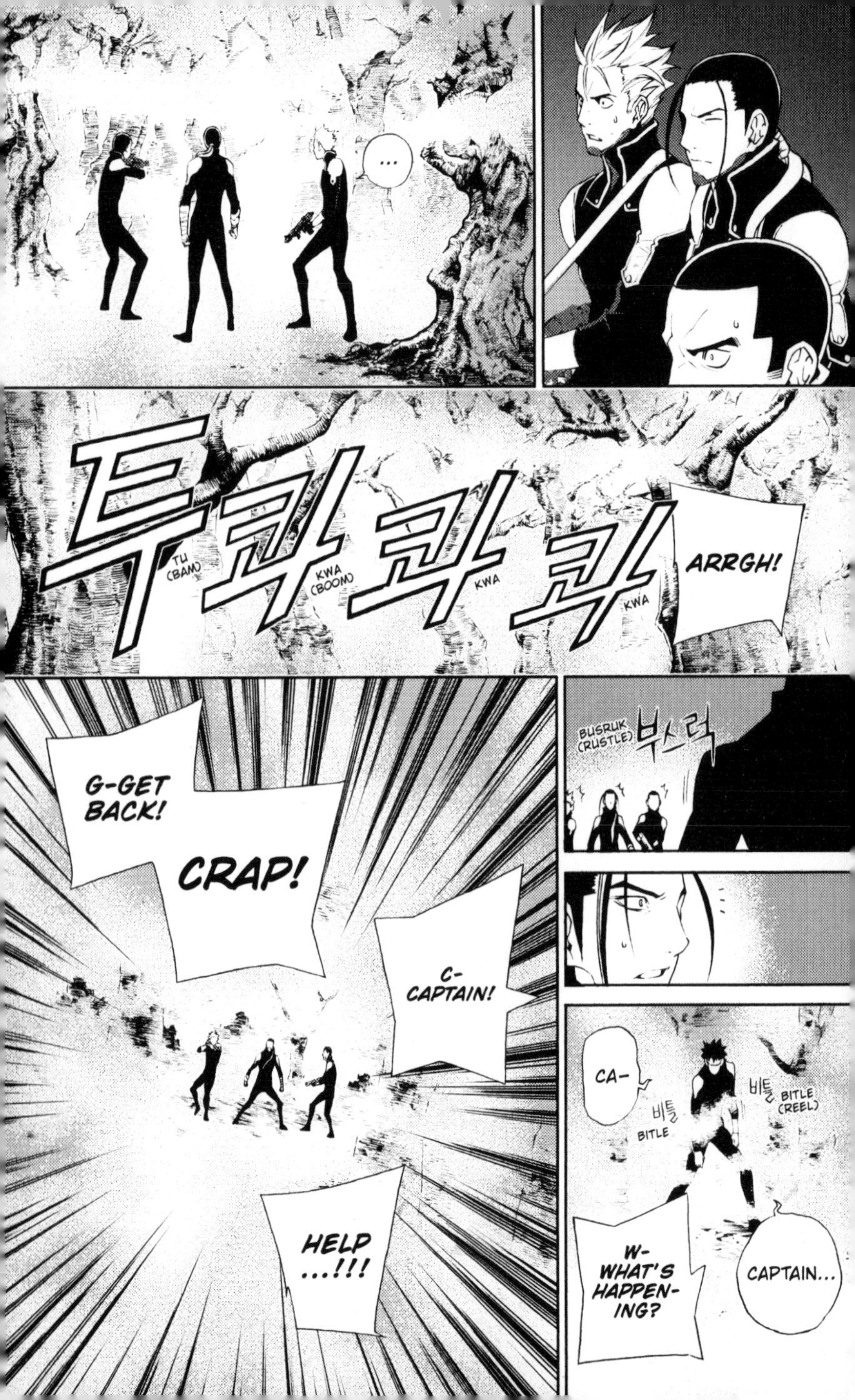
...
투콰콰콰
TU (BAM)
KWA (BOOM)
KWA
KWA
ARRGH!
G-GET BACK!
CRAP!
C-CAPTAIN!
HELP ...!!!
BUSRUK (RUSTLE) 부스럭
CA-
비틀 BITLE
비틀 BITLE (REEL)
W-WHAT'S HAPPEN-ING?
CAPTAIN...

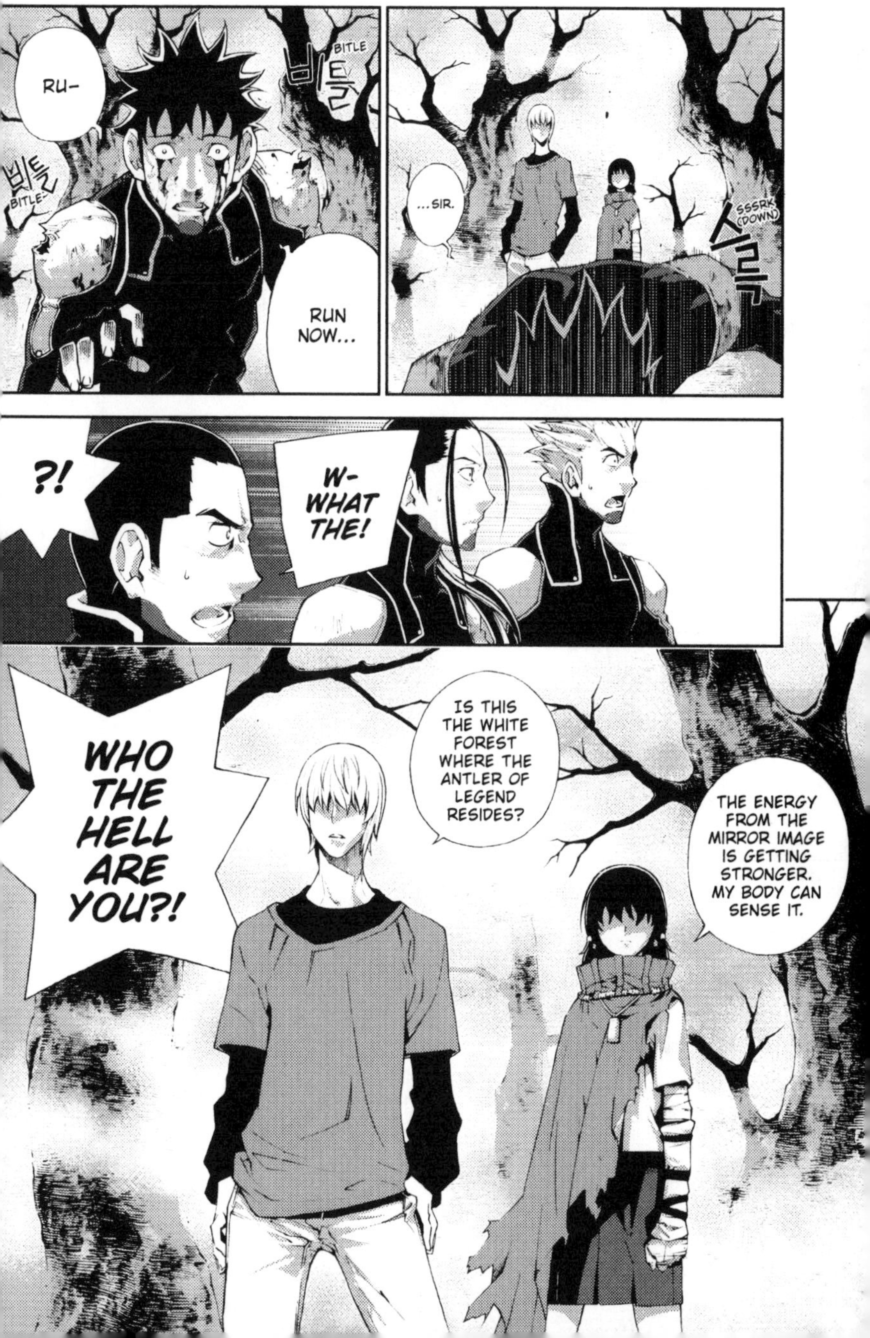

RU-
비틀
BITLE
비틀
BITLE
RUN NOW...
...SIR.
SSSRK (DOWN)
?!
W-WHAT THE!
WHO THE HELL ARE YOU?!
IS THIS THE WHITE FOREST WHERE THE ANTLER OF LEGEND RESIDES?
THE ENERGY FROM THE MIRROR IMAGE IS GETTING STRONGER. MY BODY CAN SENSE IT.

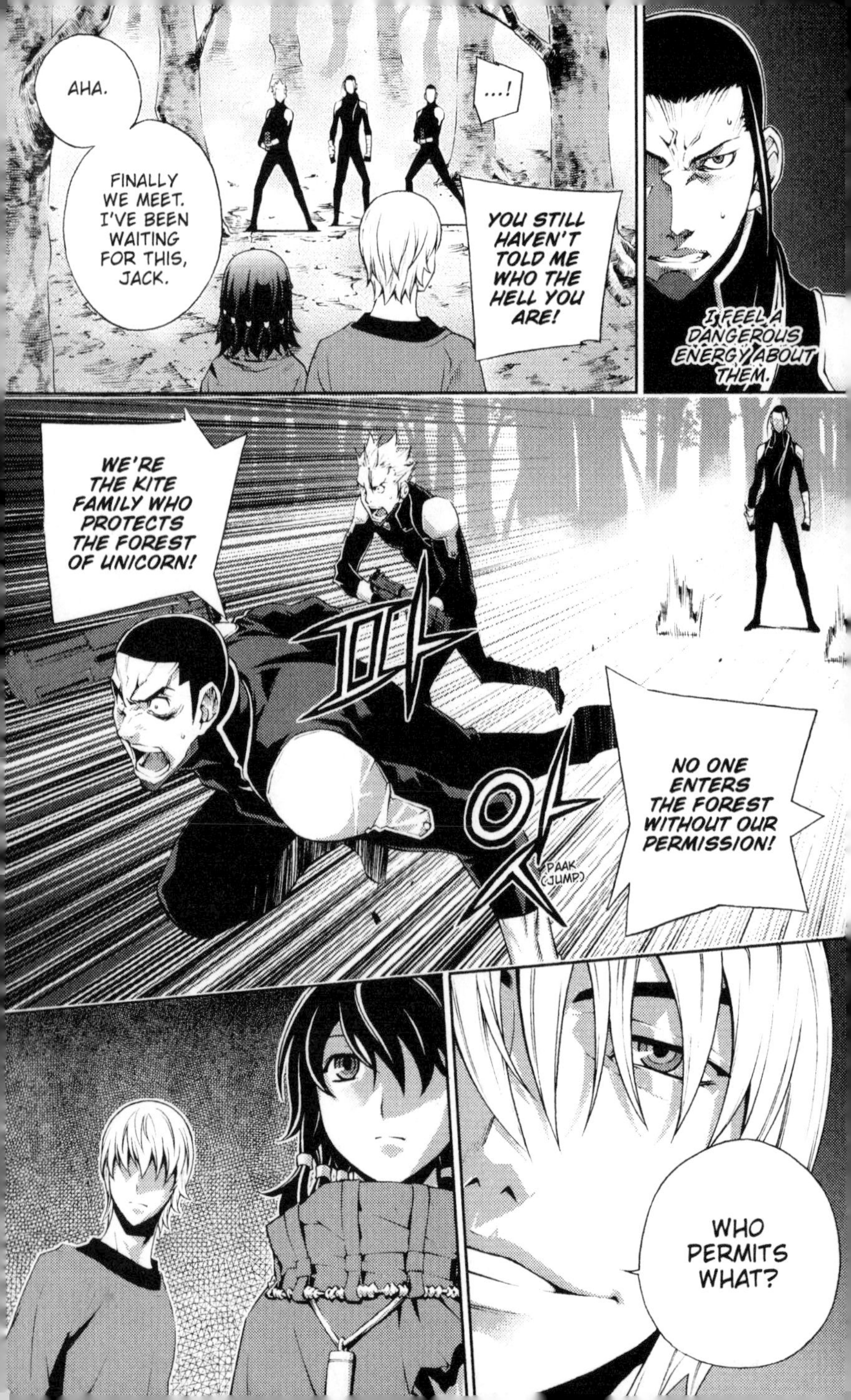
AHA.
FINALLY WE MEET. I'VE BEEN WAITING FOR THIS, JACK.
...!
YOU STILL HAVEN'T TOLD ME WHO THE HELL YOU ARE!
I FEEL A DANGEROUS ENERGY ABOUT THEM.
WE'RE THE KITE FAMILY WHO PROTECTS THE FOREST OF UNICORN!
PAAK (JUMP)
NO ONE ENTERS THE FOREST WITHOUT OUR PERMISSION!
WHO PERMITS WHAT?

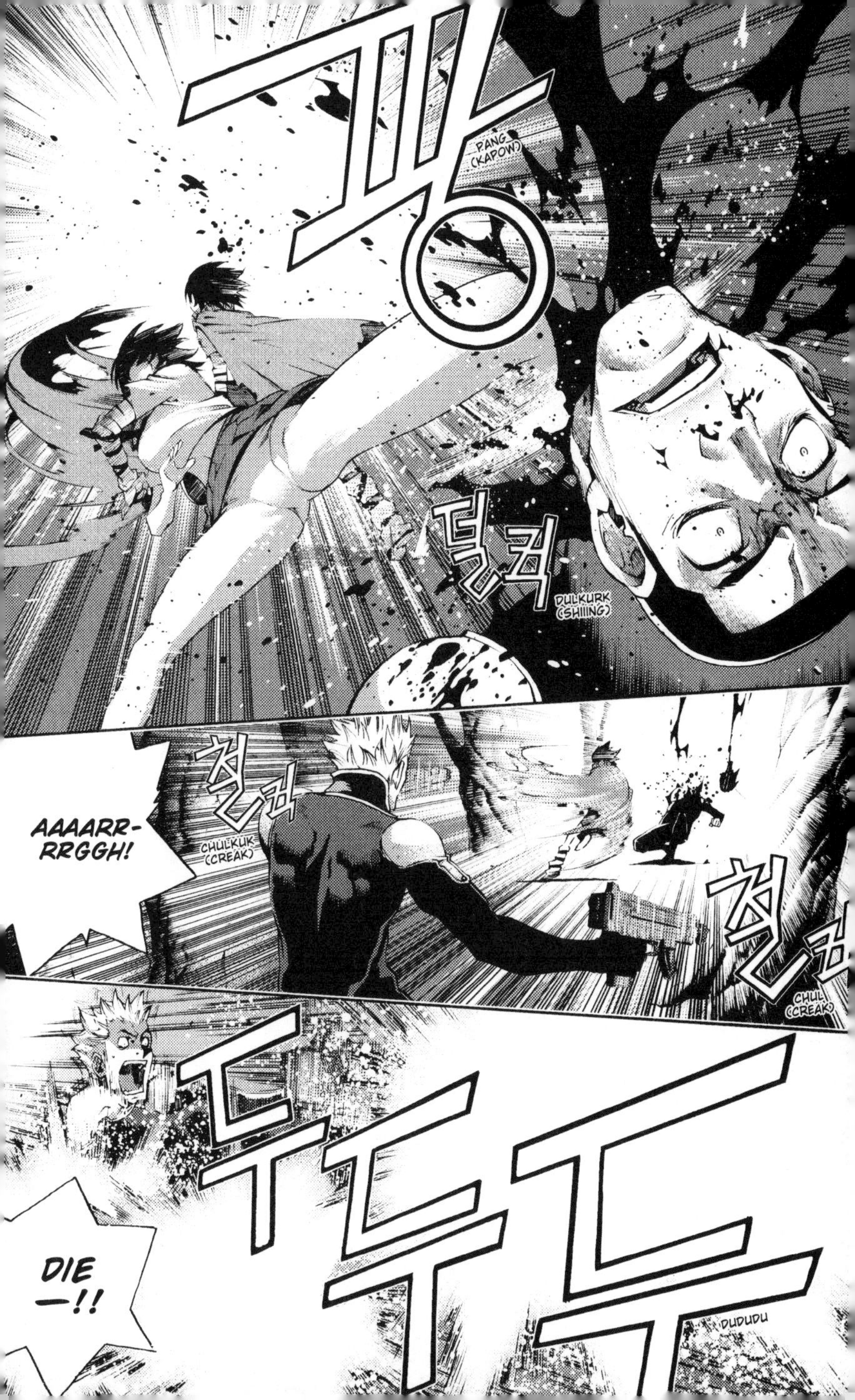

팡
PANG
(KAPOW)
덜컥
DULKURK
(SHIIING)
AAAARR-
RRGGH!
철컥
CHULKUK
(CREAK)
CHUL
(CREAK)
DIE
—!!
두두두
DUDUDU

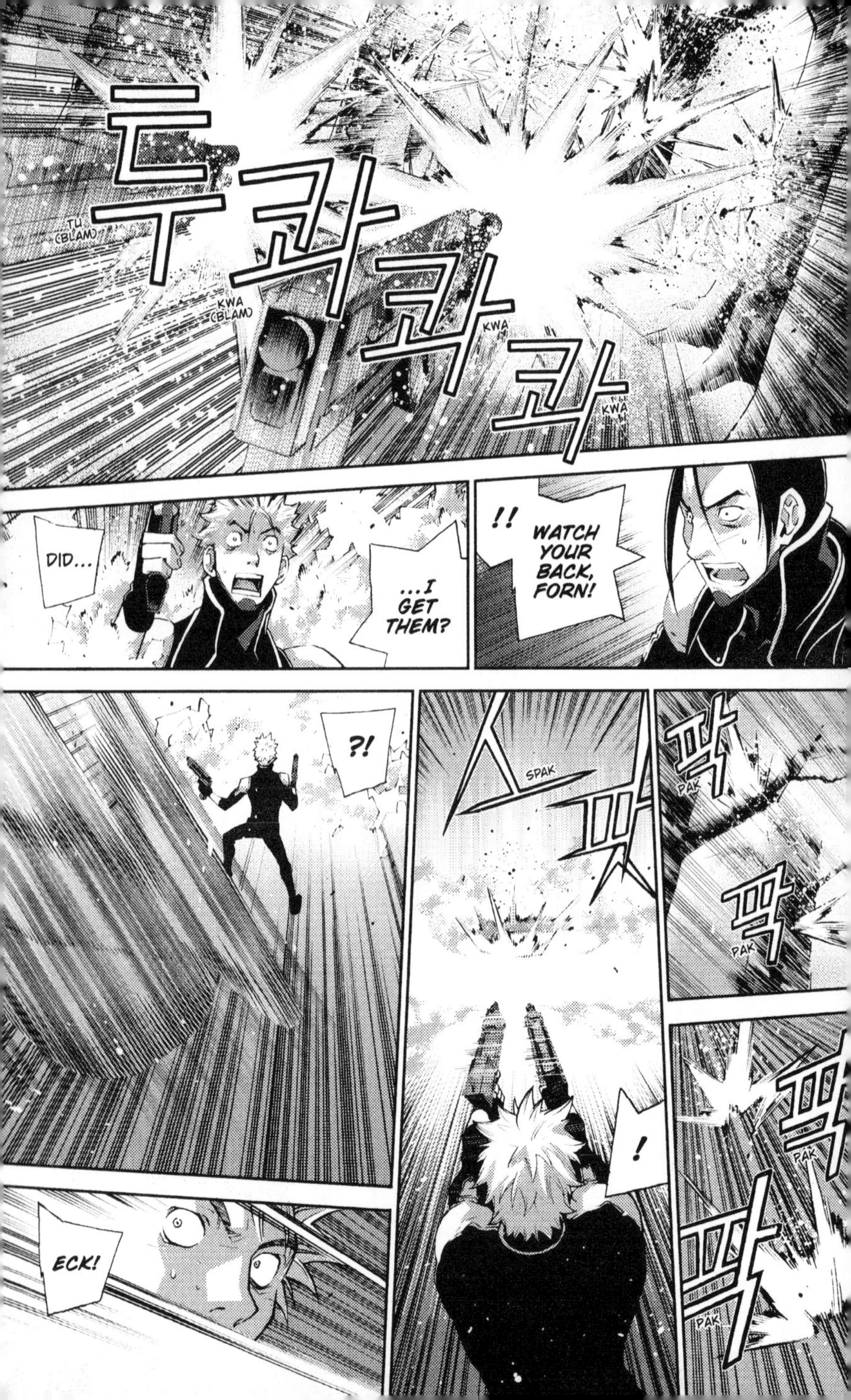

투
TU
(BLAM)
콰
KWA
(BLAM)
콰
KWA
콰
KWA
DID...
...I GET THEM?
!!
WATCH YOUR BACK, FORN!
?!
ECK!
스팍
SPAK
!
팍
PAK
팍
PAK
팍
PAK
팍
PAK

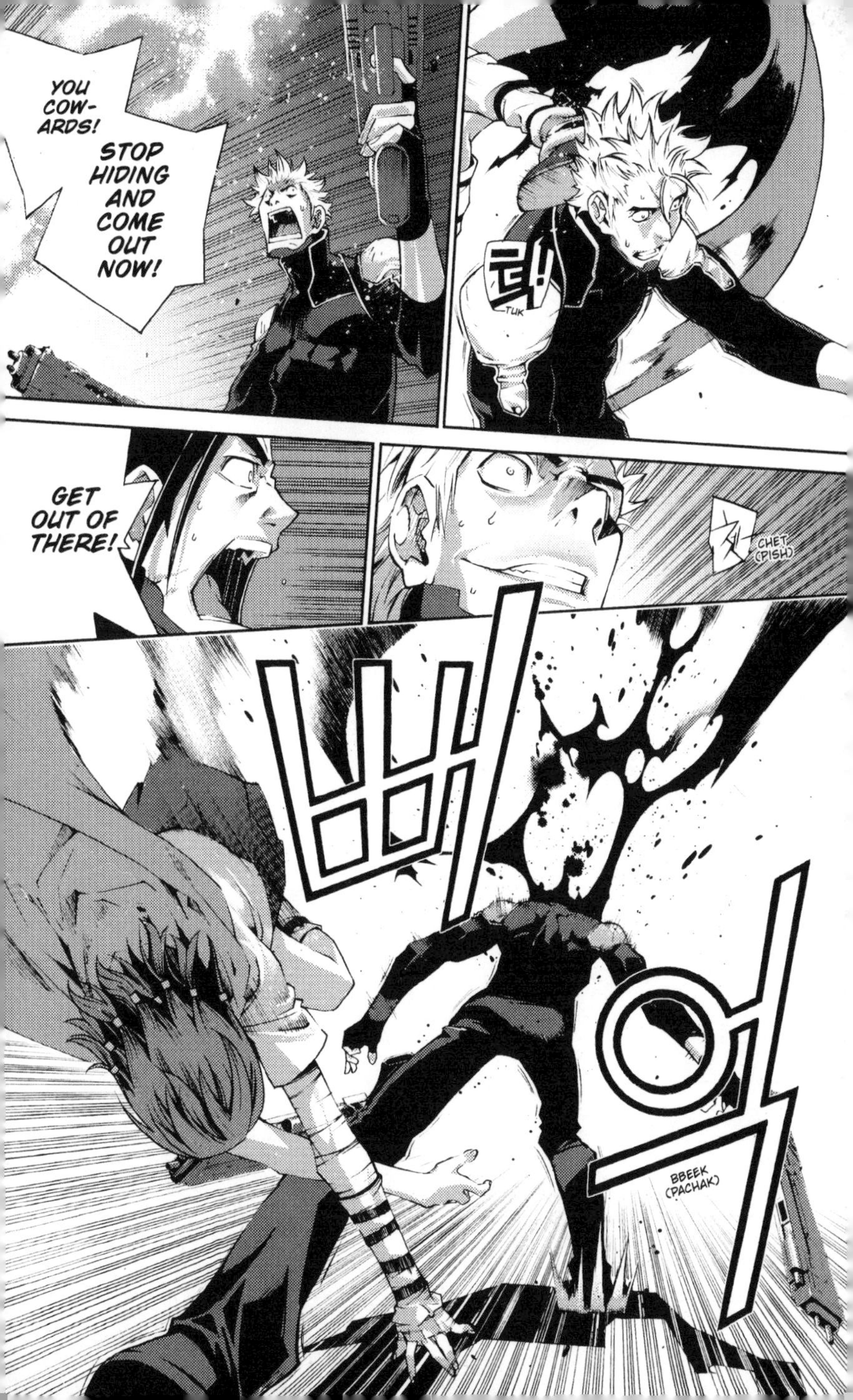
YOU COW-ARDS!
STOP HIDING AND COME OUT NOW!
TUK
GET OUT OF THERE!
CHET (PISH)
BBEEK (PACHAK)

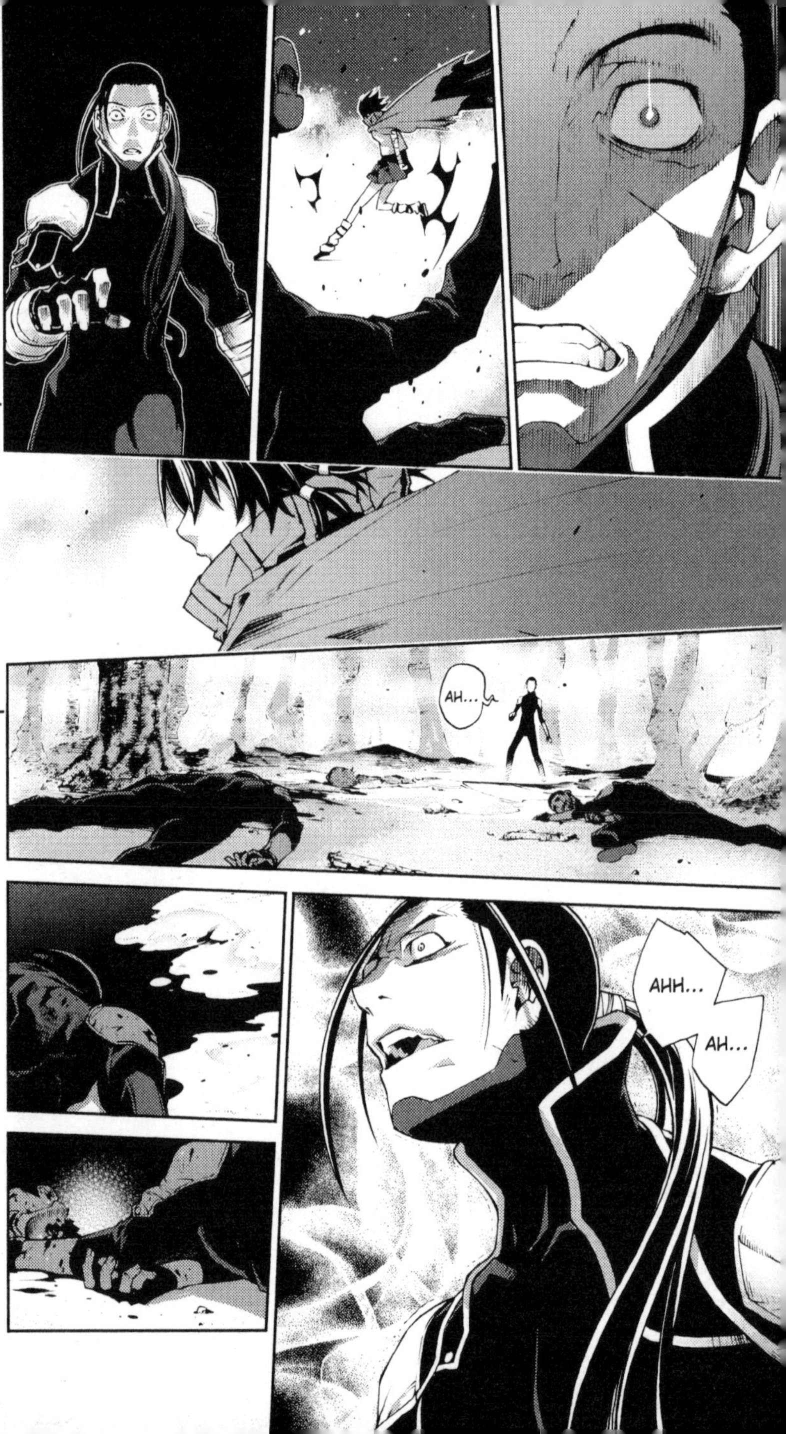
AH...
AHH...
AH...

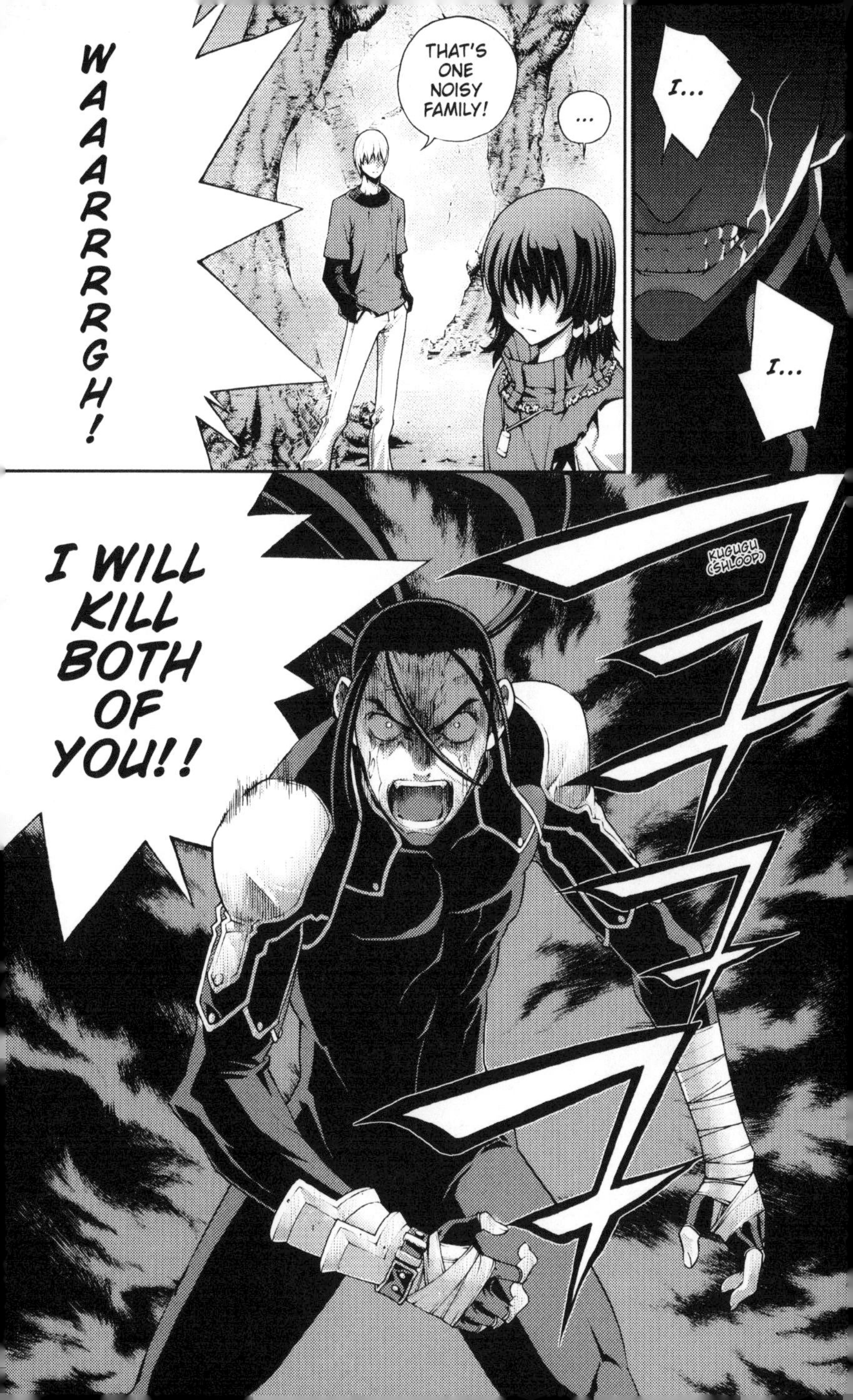
WAAAARRRRGH!
THAT'S ONE NOISY FAMILY!
...
I...
I...
I WILL KILL BOTH OF YOU!!
KUGUGU (SHLOOP)

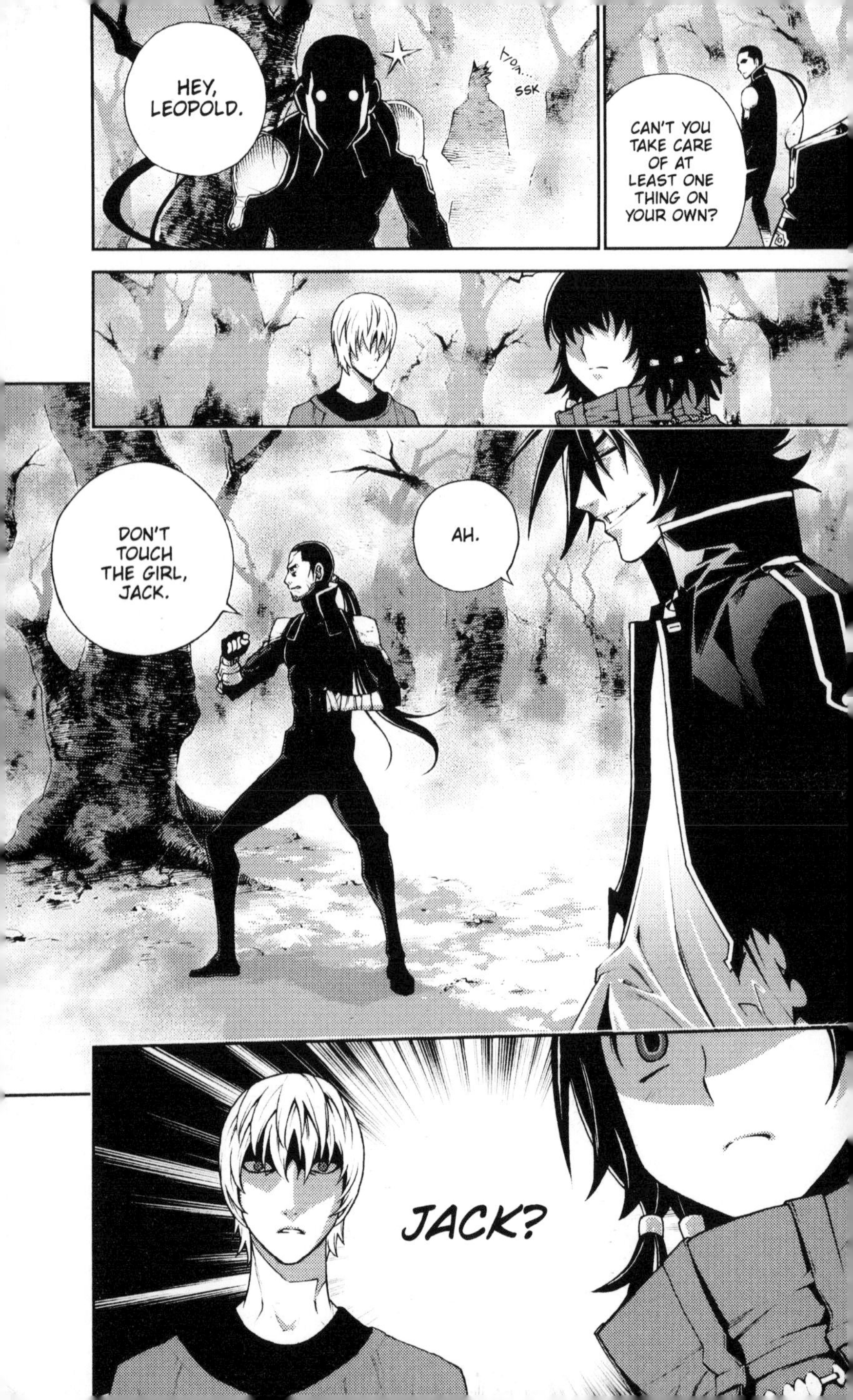
HEY, LEOPOLD.
SSK
CAN'T YOU TAKE CARE OF AT LEAST ONE THING ON YOUR OWN?
DON'T TOUCH THE GIRL, JACK.
AH.
JACK?

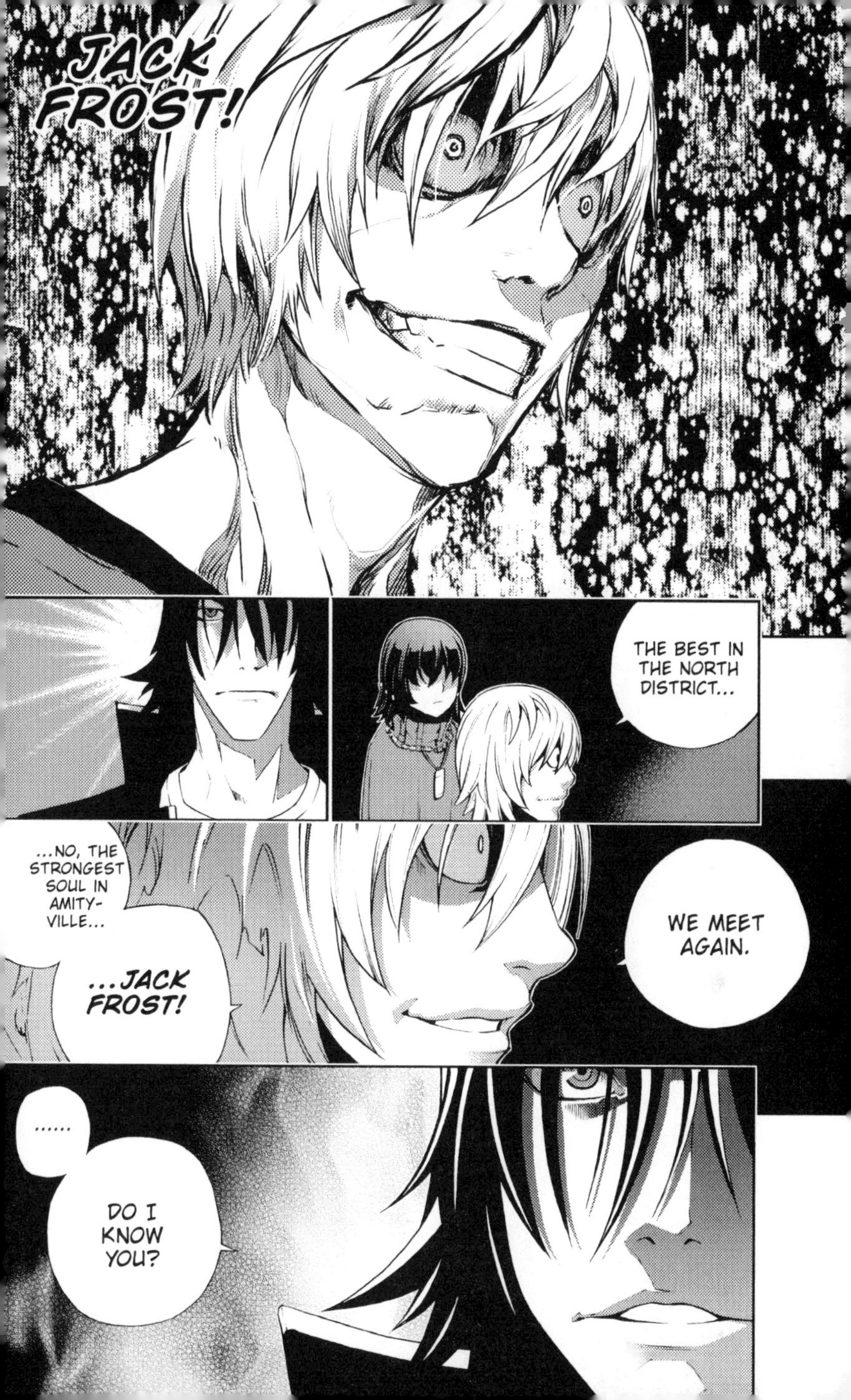
JACK FROST!
THE BEST IN THE NORTH DISTRICT...
...NO, THE STRONGEST SOUL IN AMITY-VILLE...
...JACK FROST!
WE MEET AGAIN.
......
DO I KNOW YOU?

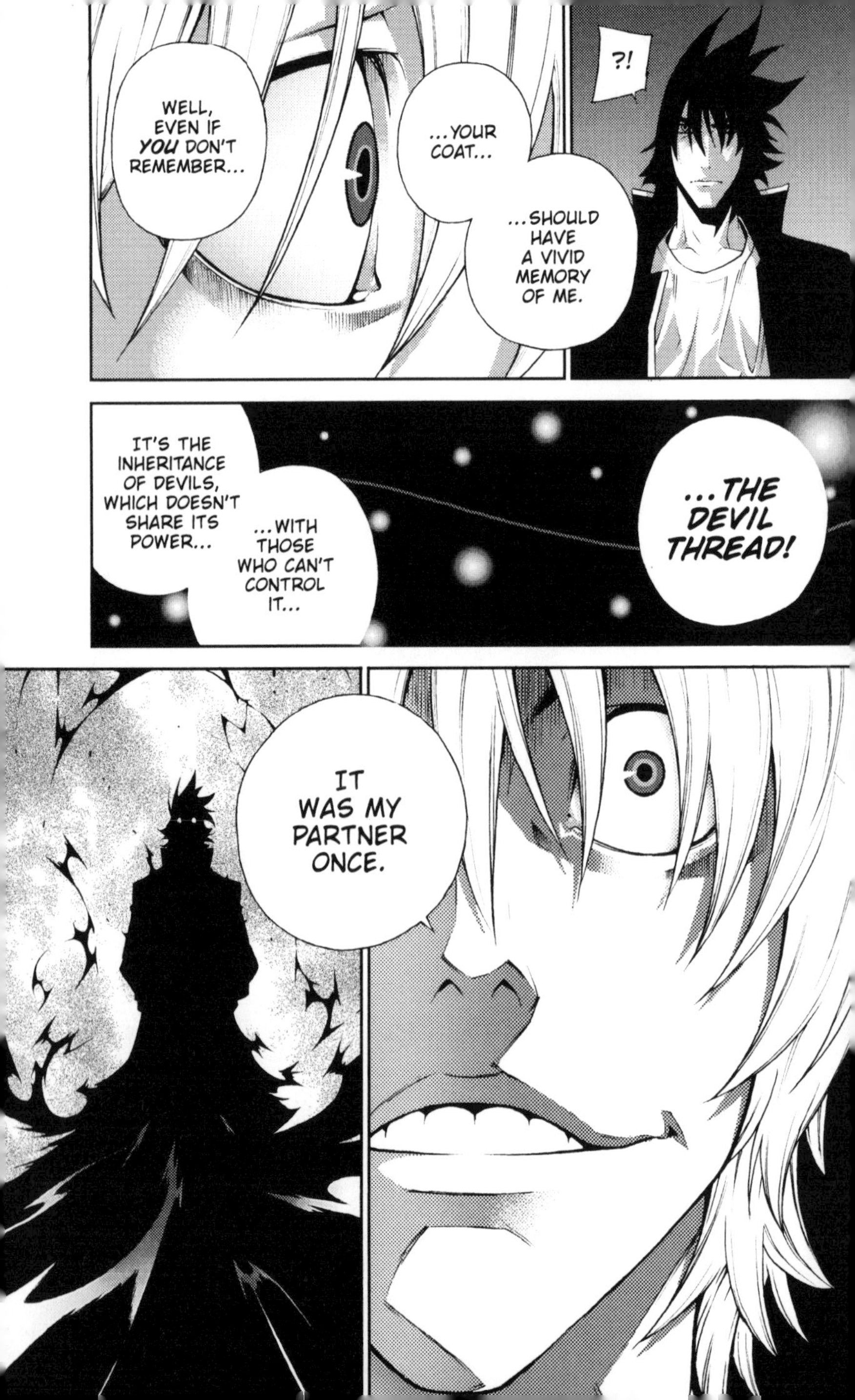
WELL, EVEN IF *YOU* DON'T REMEMBER...
...YOUR COAT...
...SHOULD HAVE A VIVID MEMORY OF ME.
?!
IT'S THE INHERITANCE OF DEVILS, WHICH DOESN'T SHARE ITS POWER...
...WITH THOSE WHO CAN'T CONTROL IT...
...THE DEVIL THREAD!
IT WAS MY PARTNER ONCE.

JACK FROST

The Amityville

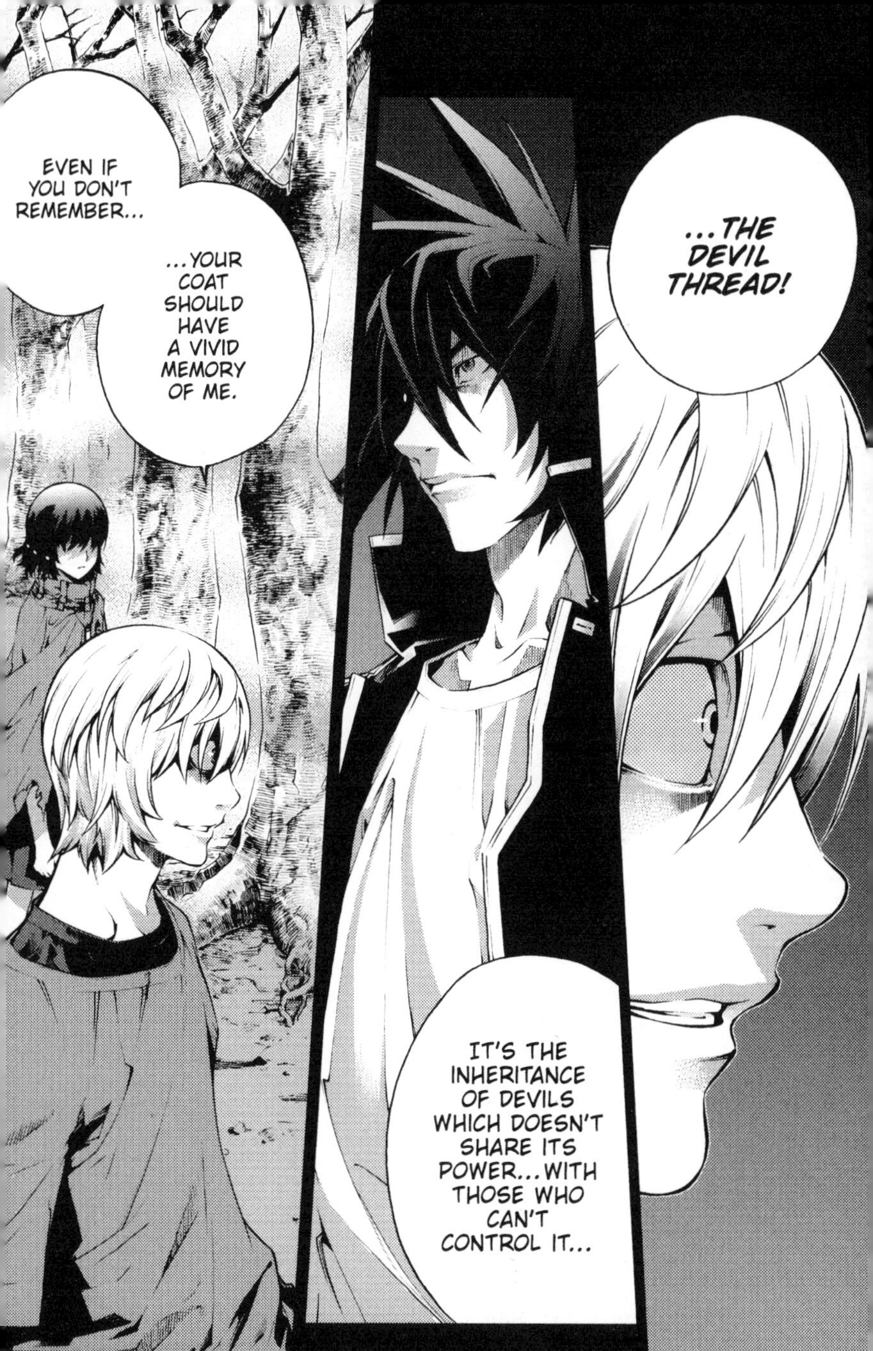
EVEN IF YOU DON'T REMEMBER...
...YOUR COAT SHOULD HAVE A VIVID MEMORY OF ME.
...THE DEVIL THREAD!
IT'S THE INHERITANCE OF DEVILS WHICH DOESN'T SHARE ITS POWER...WITH THOSE WHO CAN'T CONTROL IT...

VIOLENCE 15. DEVIL THREAD

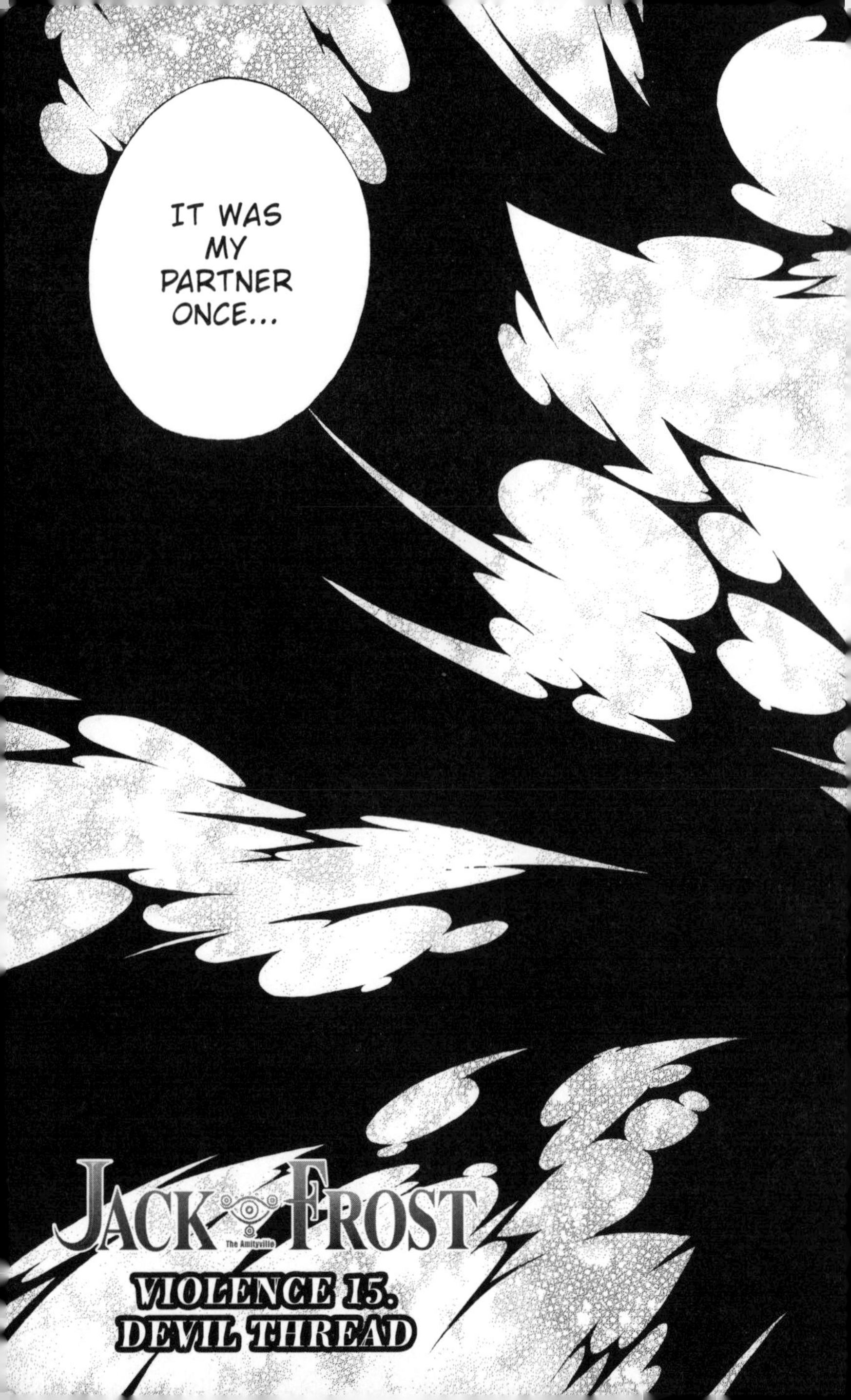
IT WAS MY PARTNER ONCE...
JACK FROST
The Amityville
VIOLENCE 15. DEVIL THREAD

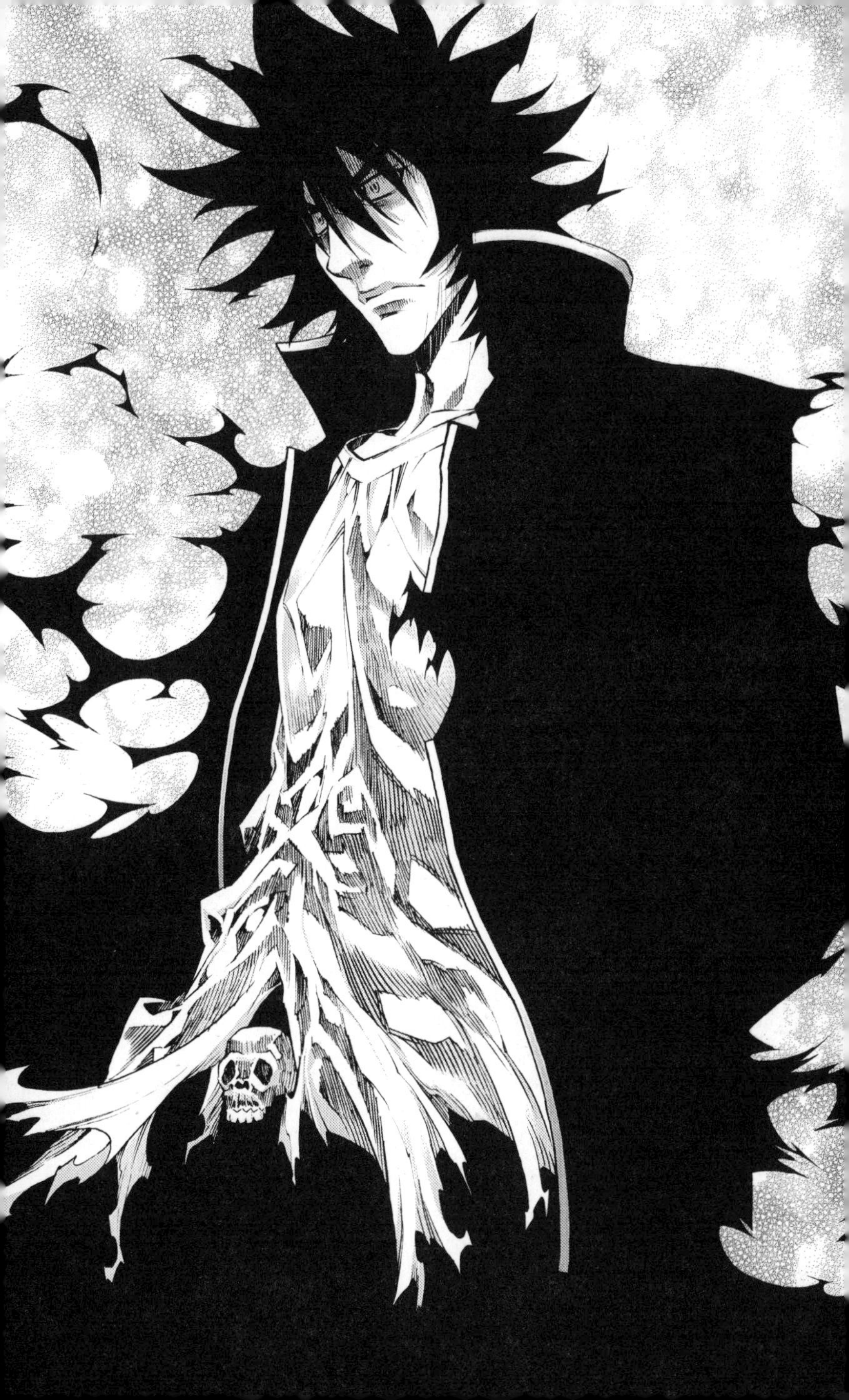

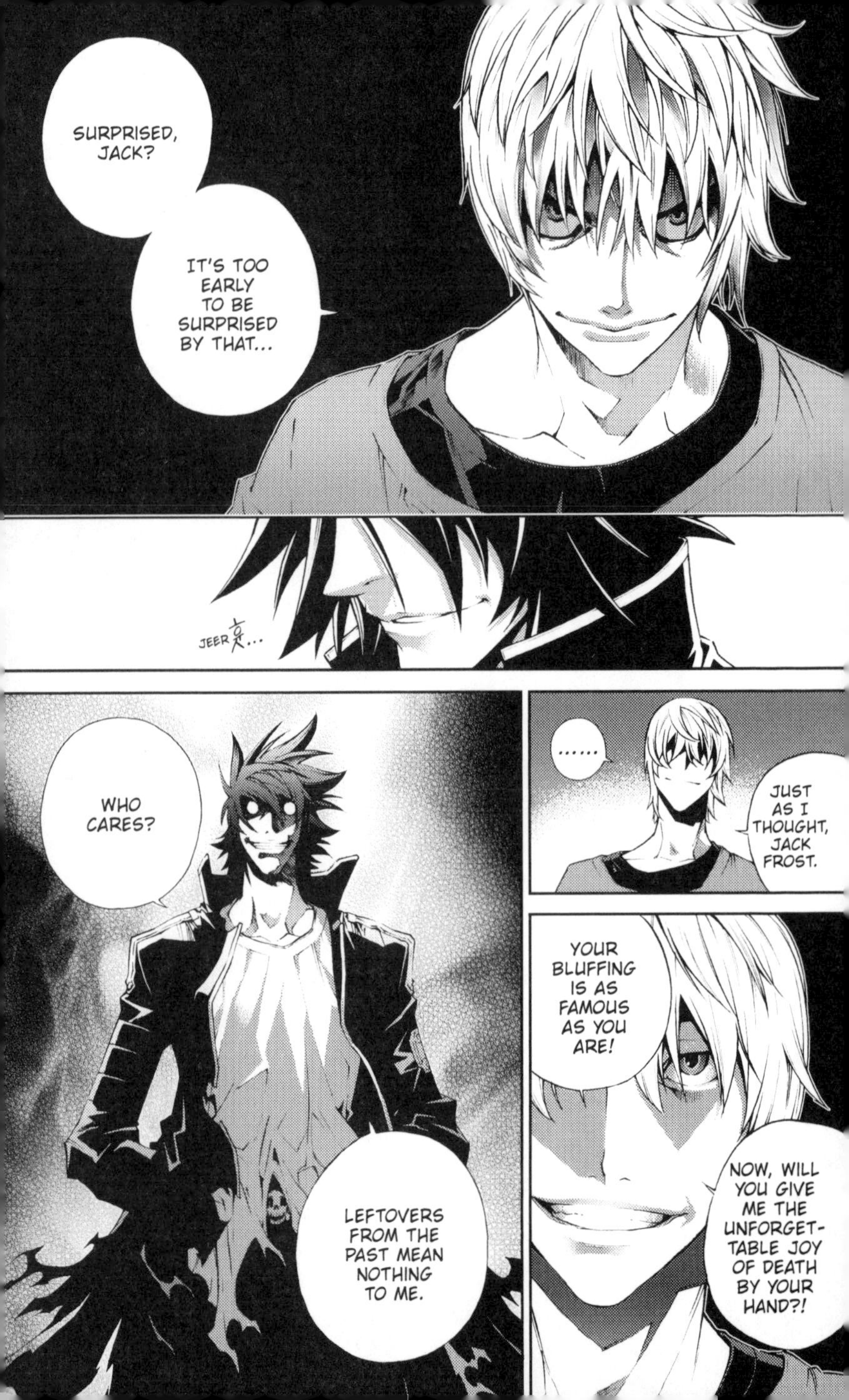
SURPRISED, JACK?
IT'S TOO EARLY TO BE SURPRISED BY THAT...
JEER...
WHO CARES?
LEFTOVERS FROM THE PAST MEAN NOTHING TO ME.
......
JUST AS I THOUGHT, JACK FROST.
YOUR BLUFFING IS AS FAMOUS AS YOU ARE!
NOW, WILL YOU GIVE ME THE UNFORGET-TABLE JOY OF DEATH BY YOUR HAND?!

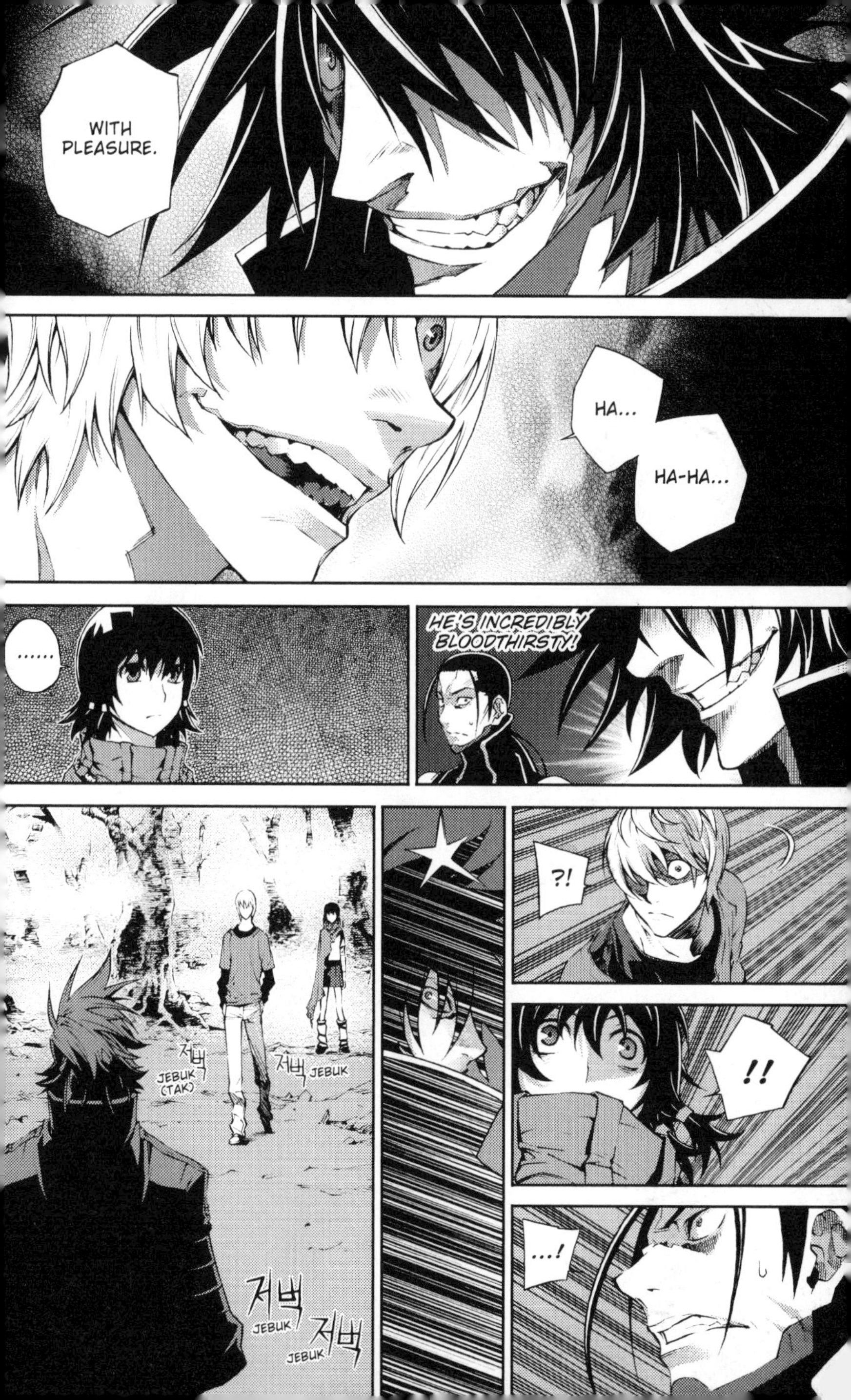

WITH PLEASURE.
HA...
HA-HA...
......
HE'S INCREDIBLY BLOODTHIRSTY!
저벅
JEBUK (TAK)
저벅 JEBUK
저벅
JEBUK
저벅
JEBUK
?!
!!
...!

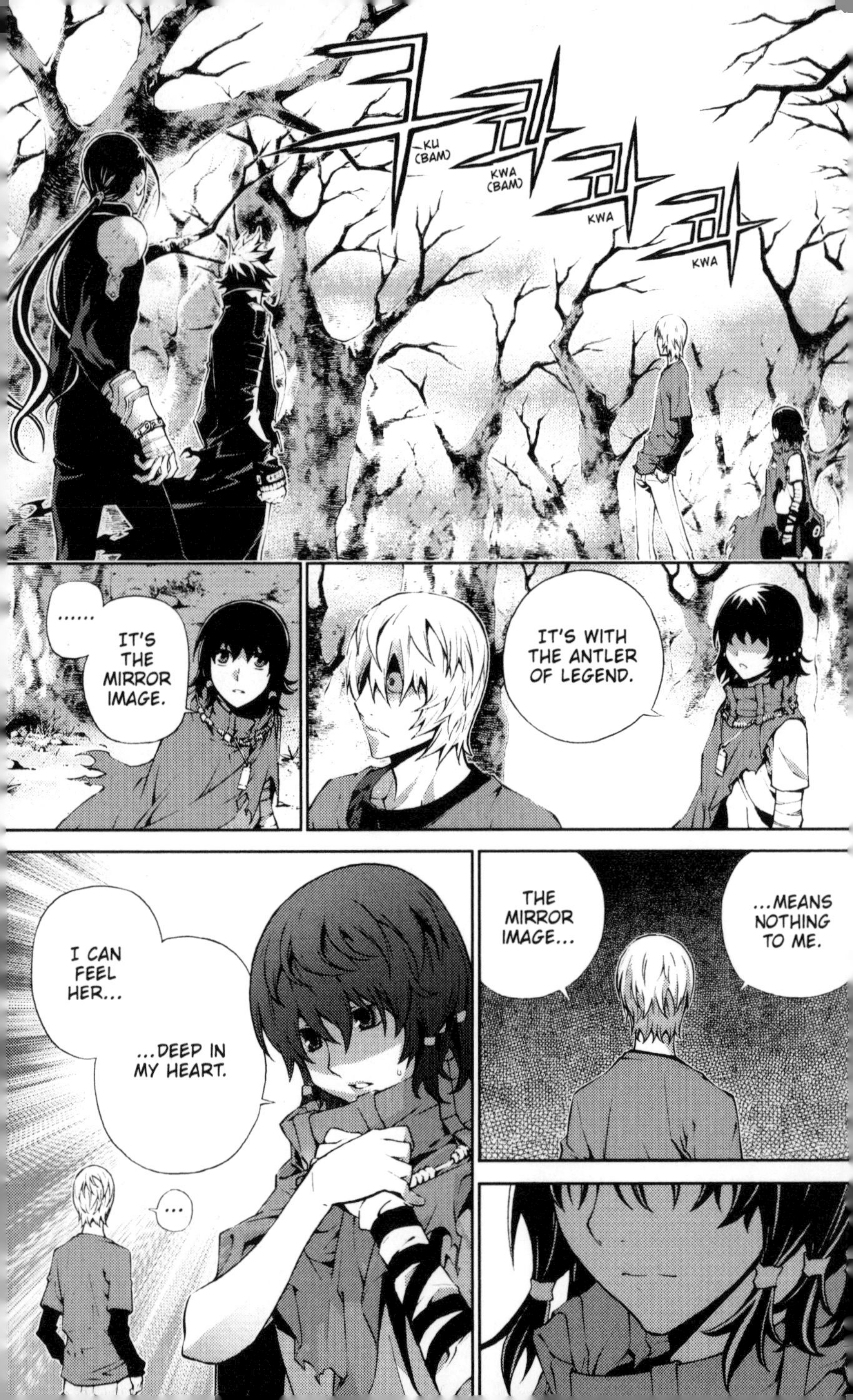
KU (BAM)
KWA (BAM)
KWA
KWA
......
IT'S THE MIRROR IMAGE.
IT'S WITH THE ANTLER OF LEGEND.
I CAN FEEL HER...
...DEEP IN MY HEART.
...
THE MIRROR IMAGE...
...MEANS NOTHING TO ME.

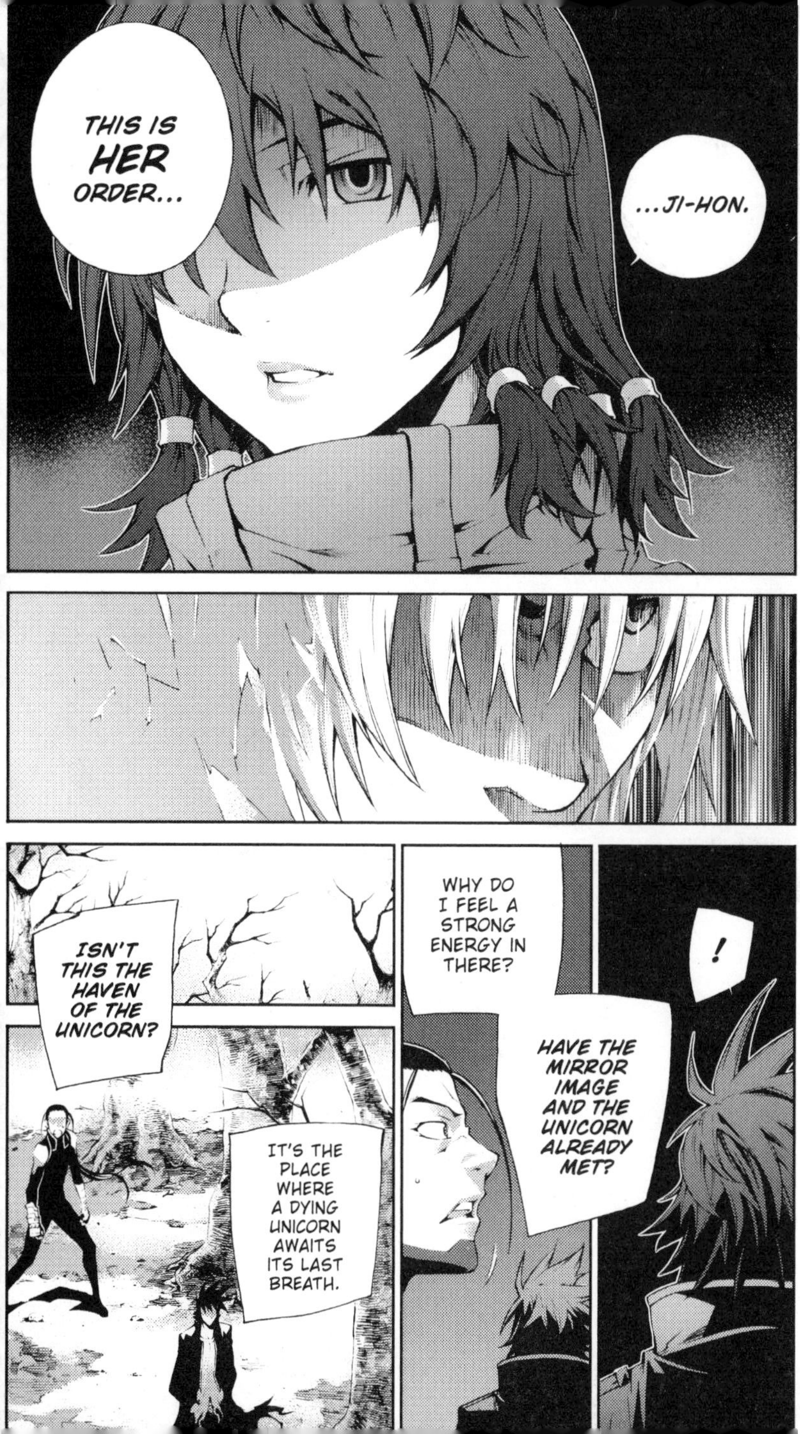
THIS IS HER ORDER...
...JI-HON.
ISN'T THIS THE HAVEN OF THE UNICORN?
IT'S THE PLACE WHERE A DYING UNICORN AWAITS ITS LAST BREATH.
WHY DO I FEEL A STRONG ENERGY IN THERE?
HAVE THE MIRROR IMAGE AND THE UNICORN ALREADY MET?
!

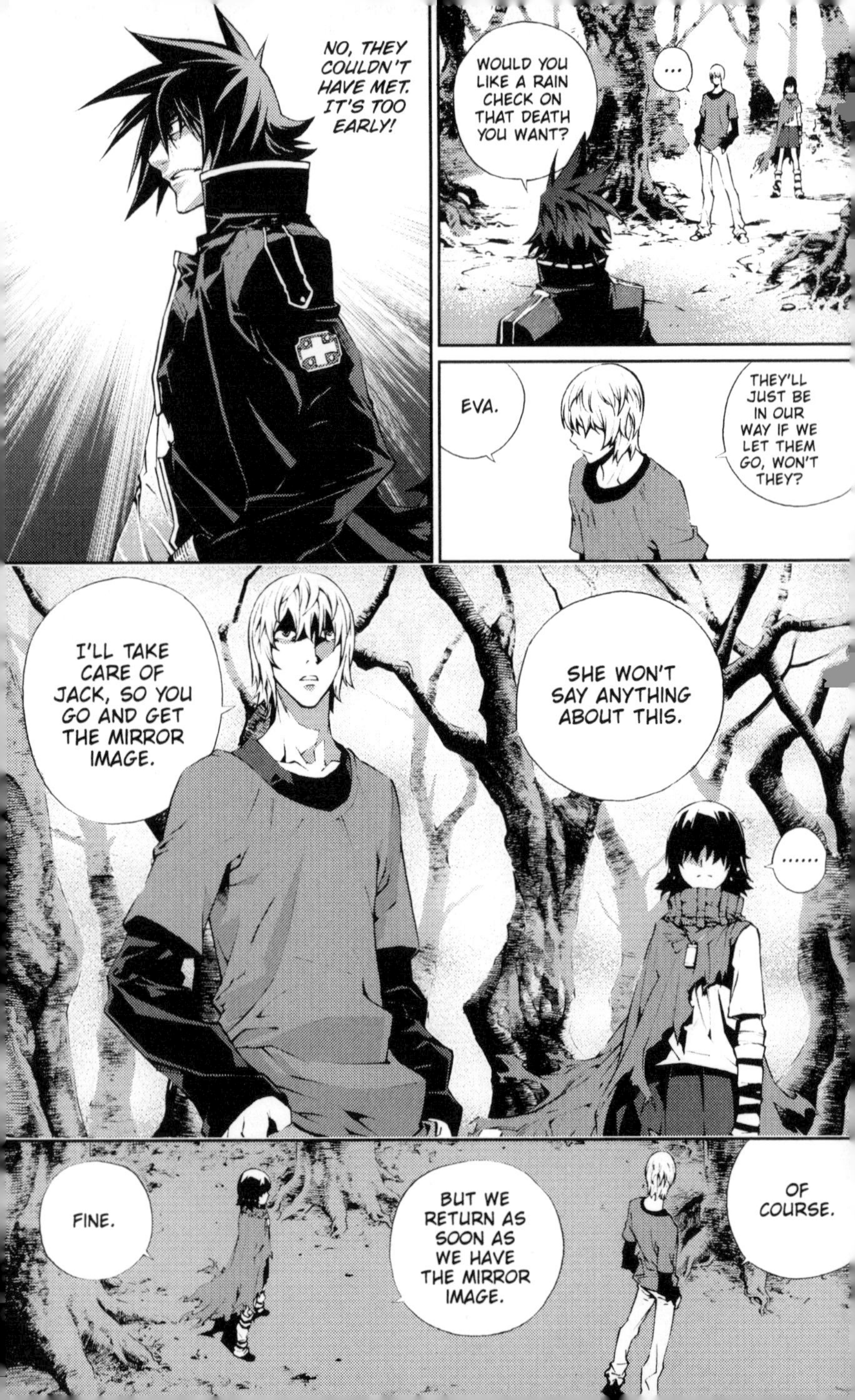
NO, THEY COULDN'T HAVE MET. IT'S TOO EARLY!
WOULD YOU LIKE A RAIN CHECK ON THAT DEATH YOU WANT?
...
EVA.
THEY'LL JUST BE IN OUR WAY IF WE LET THEM GO, WON'T THEY?
I'LL TAKE CARE OF JACK, SO YOU GO AND GET THE MIRROR IMAGE.
SHE WON'T SAY ANYTHING ABOUT THIS.
......
FINE.
BUT WE RETURN AS SOON AS WE HAVE THE MIRROR IMAGE.
OF COURSE.

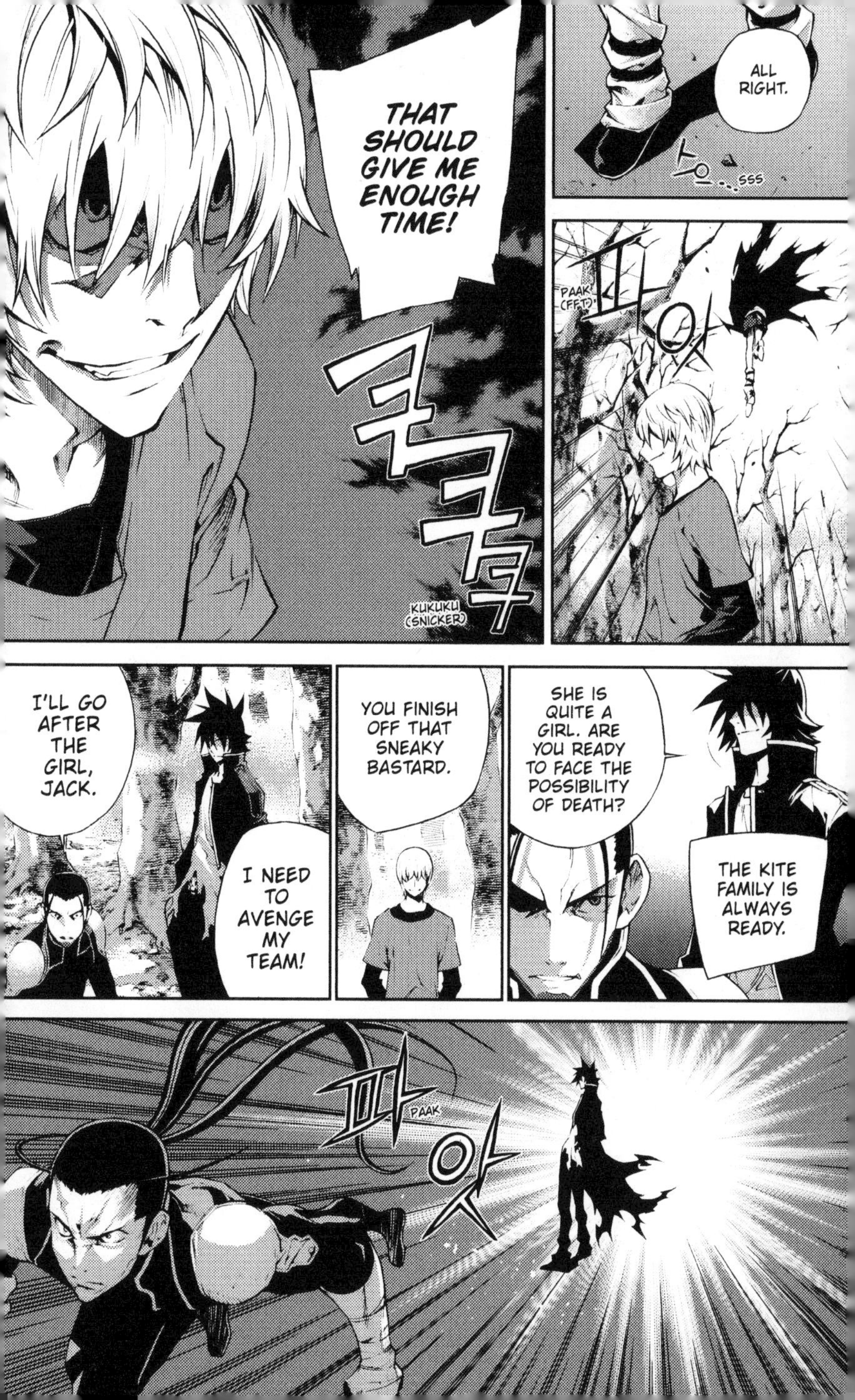
THAT SHOULD GIVE ME ENOUGH TIME!
KUKUKU (SNICKER)
ALL RIGHT.
SSS
PAAK (FFT)
I'LL GO AFTER THE GIRL, JACK.
I NEED TO AVENGE MY TEAM!
YOU FINISH OFF THAT SNEAKY BASTARD.
SHE IS QUITE A GIRL. ARE YOU READY TO FACE THE POSSIBILITY OF DEATH?
THE KITE FAMILY IS ALWAYS READY.
PAAK

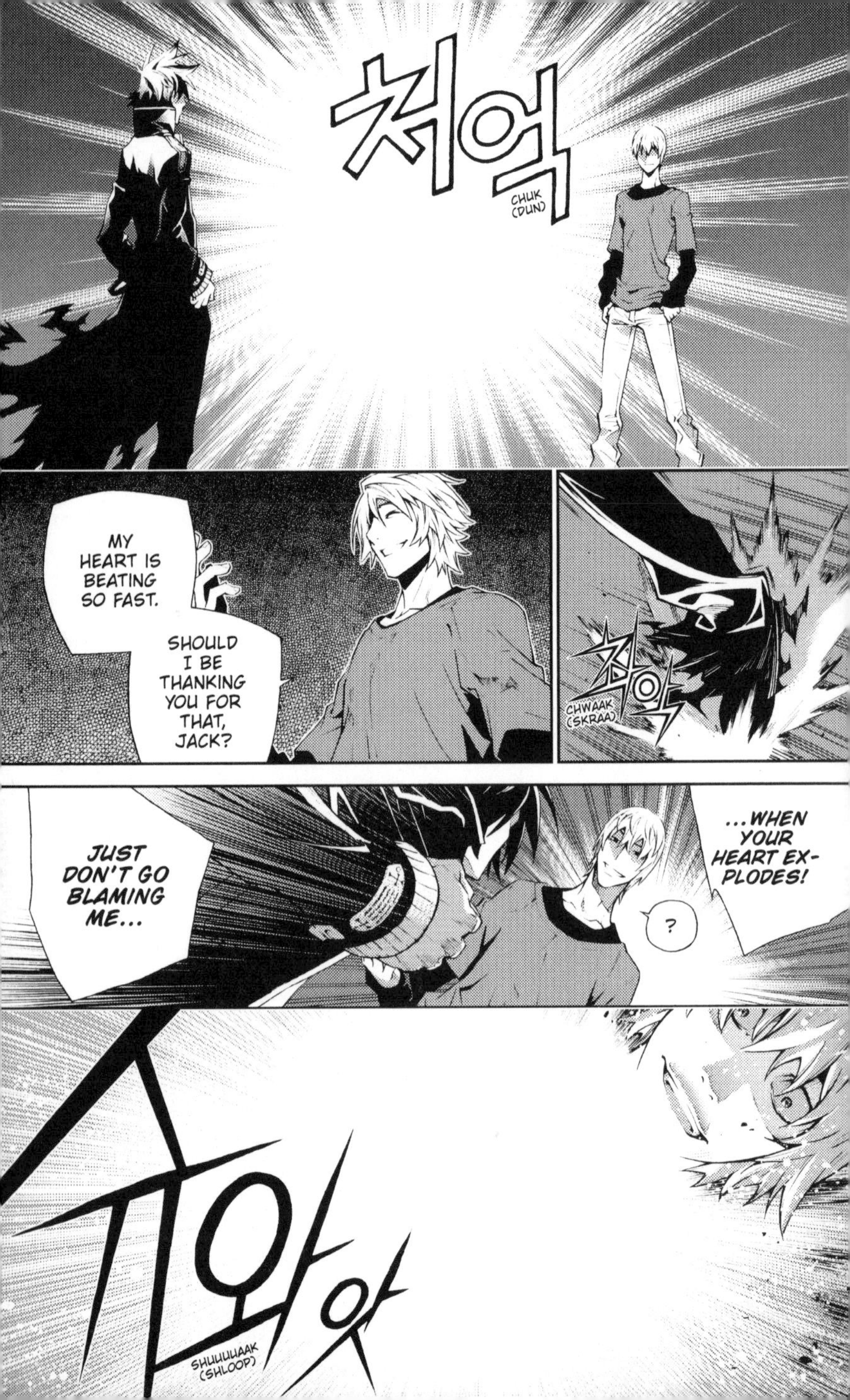

처억
CHUK (DUN)
MY HEART IS BEATING SO FAST.
SHOULD I BE THANKING YOU FOR THAT, JACK?
촤악
CHWAAK (SKRAA)
JUST DON'T GO BLAMING ME...
?
...WHEN YOUR HEART EXPLODES!
솨악
SHUUUUAAK (SHLOOP)

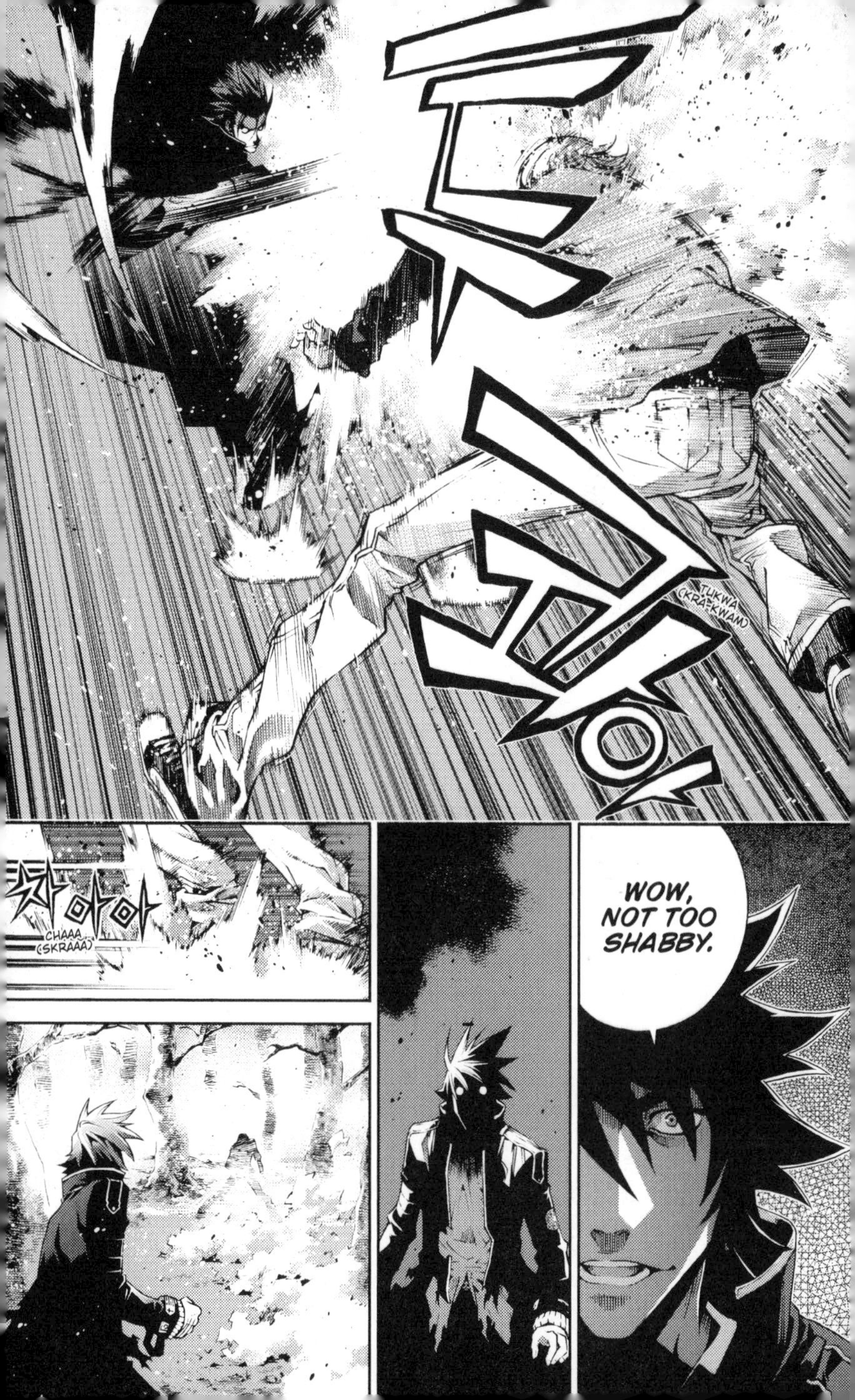
TUKWA
(KRA-KWAM)
CHAAA
(SKRAAA)
WOW, NOT TOO SHABBY.

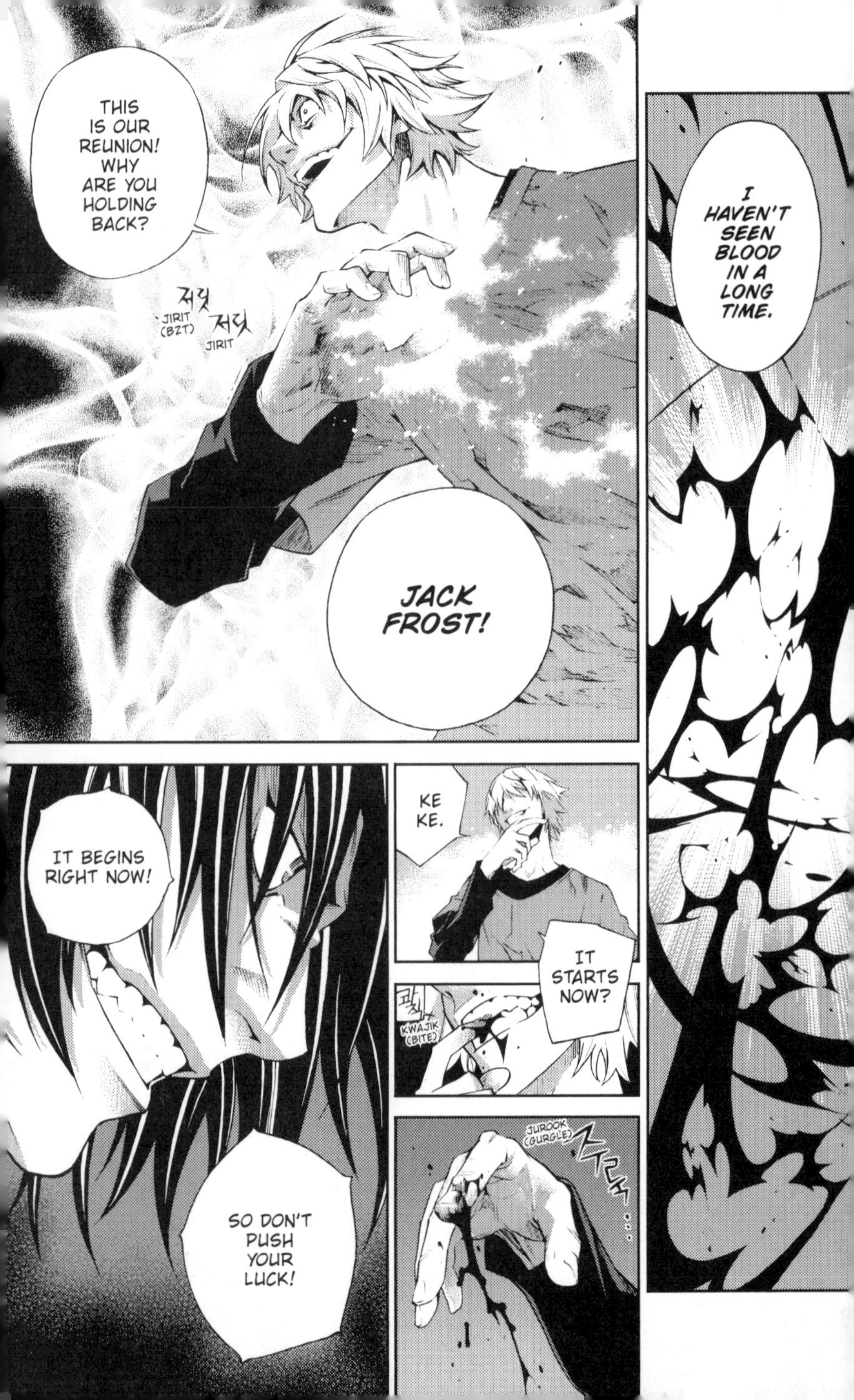
THIS IS OUR REUNION! WHY ARE YOU HOLDING BACK?
JIRIT (BZT)
JIRIT
JACK FROST!
IT BEGINS RIGHT NOW!
SO DON'T PUSH YOUR LUCK!
KE KE.
IT STARTS NOW?
KWAJIK (BITE)
JUROOK (GURGLE)
I HAVEN'T SEEN BLOOD IN A LONG TIME.

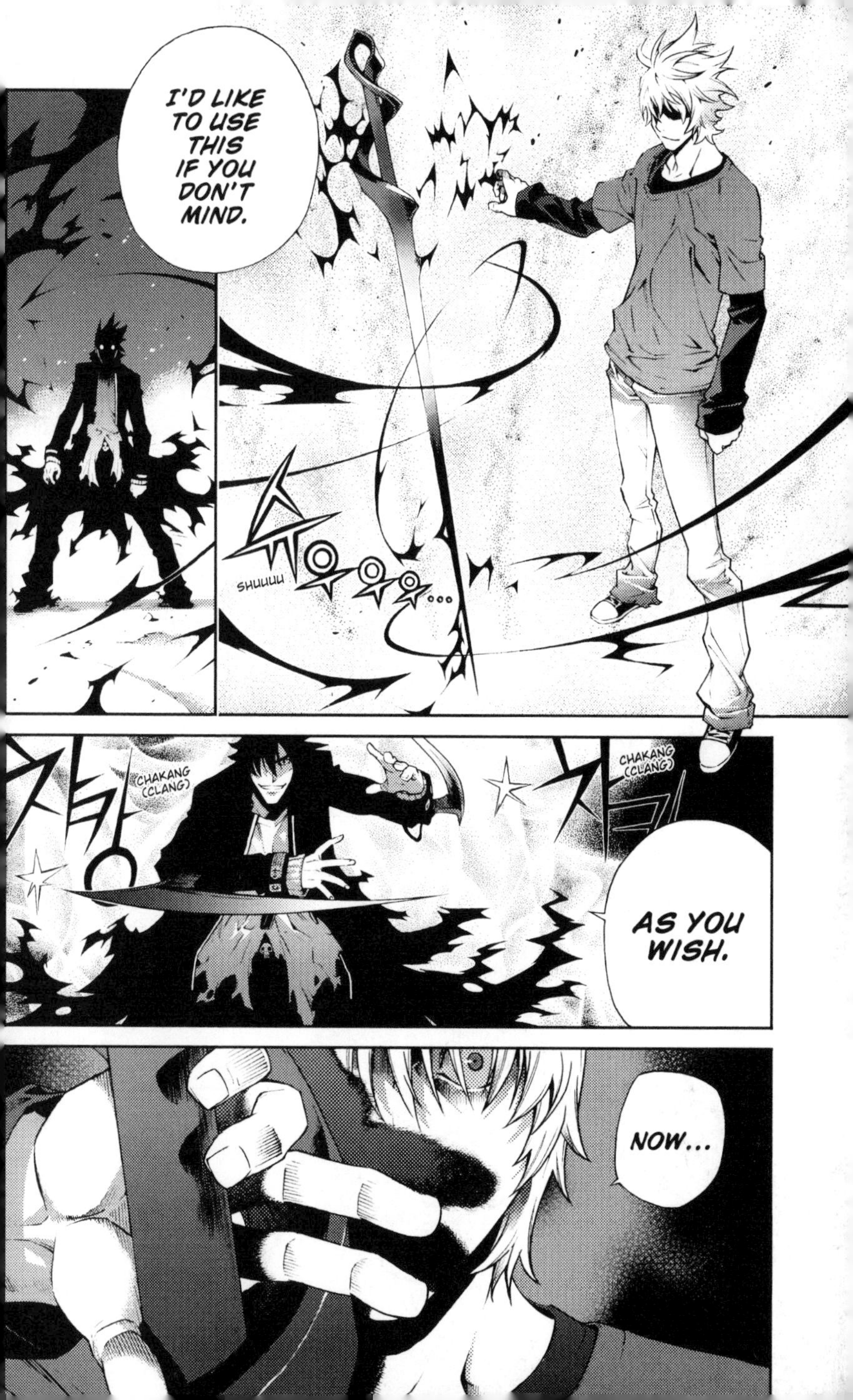
I'D LIKE TO USE THIS IF YOU DON'T MIND.
SHUUUU
CHAKANG (CLANG)
CHAKANG (CLANG)
AS YOU WISH.
NOW...

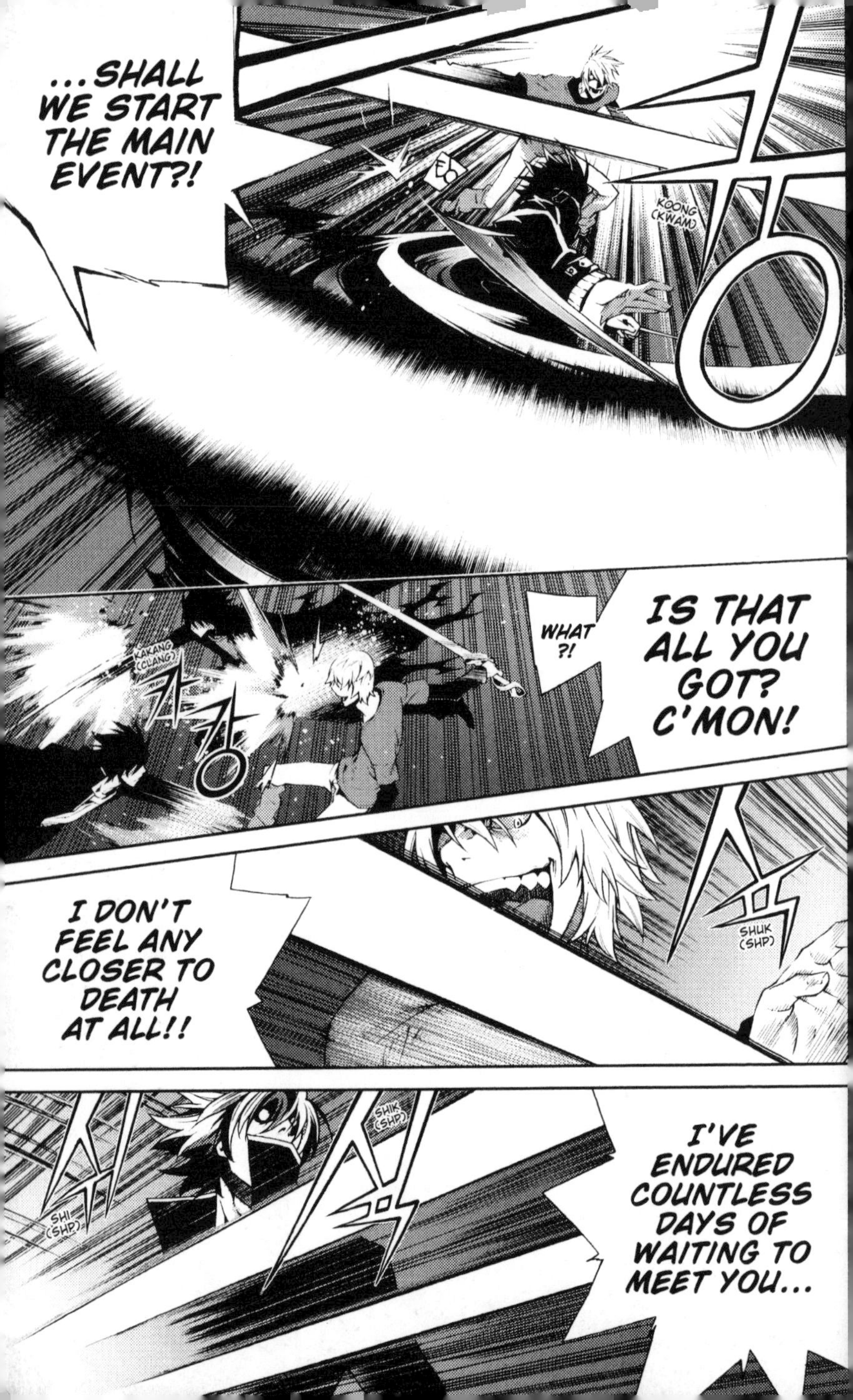
...SHALL WE START THE MAIN EVENT?!
KOONG (KWAM)
KAKANG (CLANG)
WHAT?!
IS THAT ALL YOU GOT? C'MON!
I DON'T FEEL ANY CLOSER TO DEATH AT ALL!!
SHUK (SHP)
SHI (SHP)
SHIK (SHP)
I'VE ENDURED COUNTLESS DAYS OF WAITING TO MEET YOU...

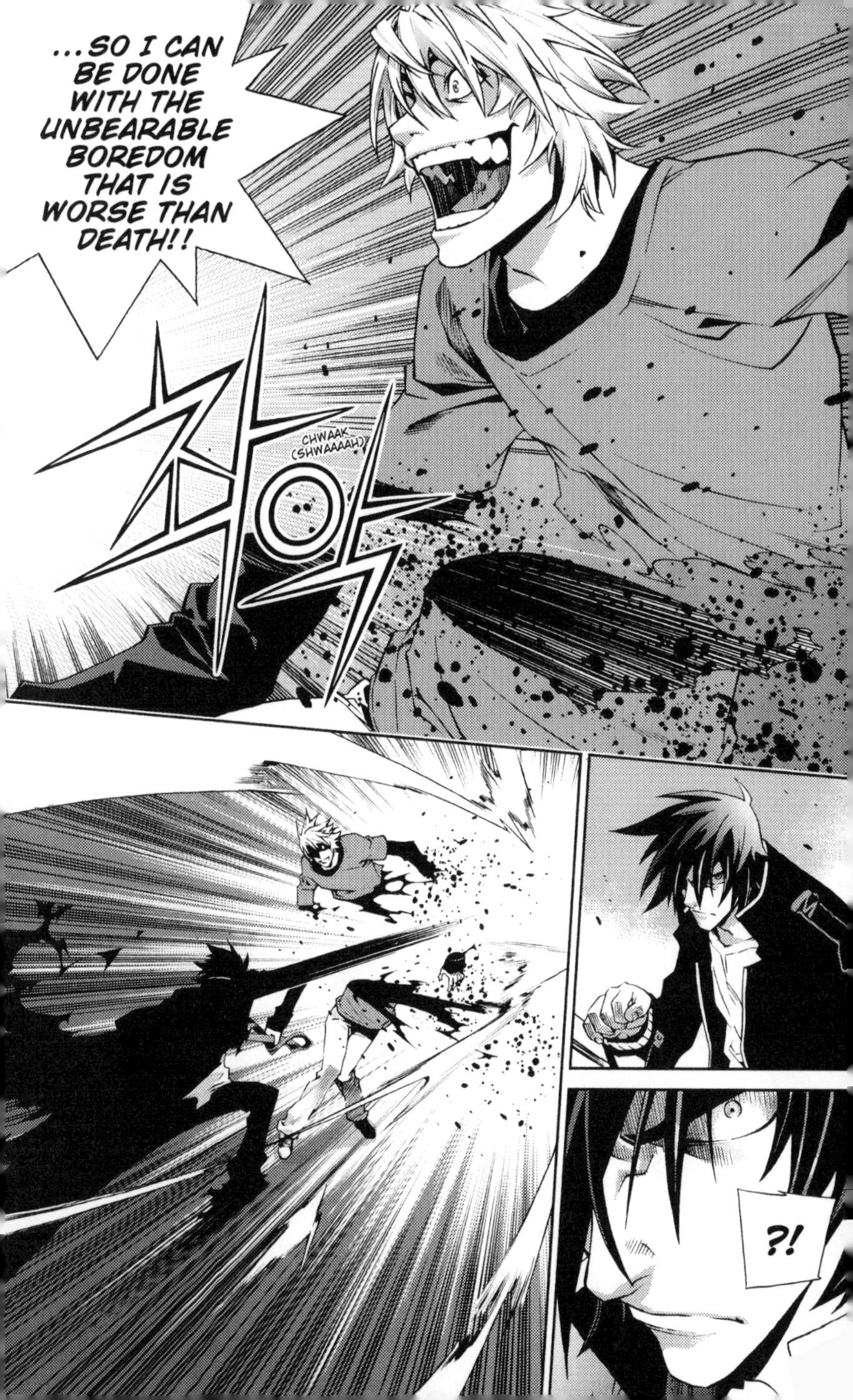
...SO I CAN BE DONE WITH THE UNBEARABLE BOREDOM THAT IS WORSE THAN DEATH!!
CHWAAK (SHWAAAAH)
?!

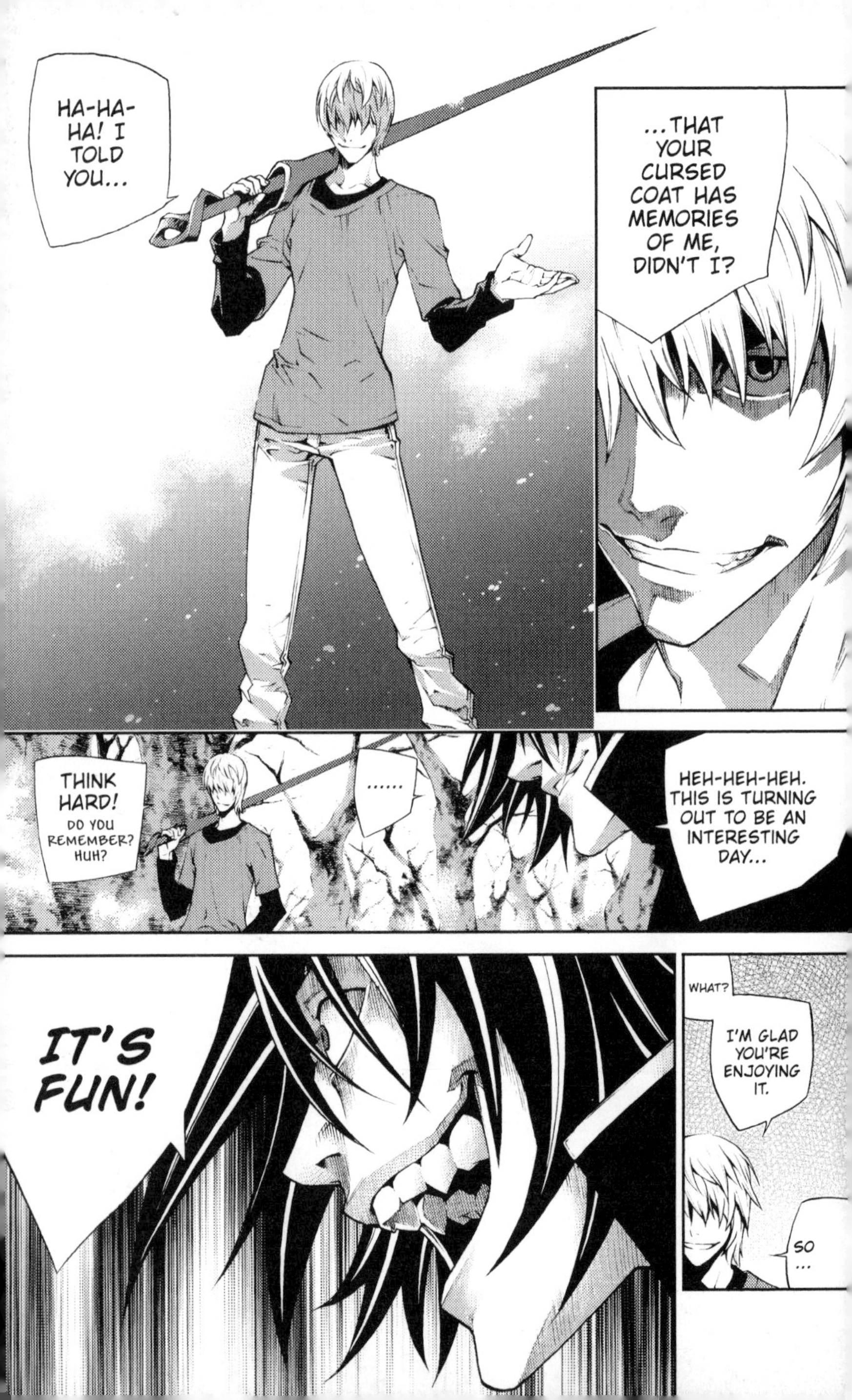
HA-HA-HA! I TOLD YOU...
...THAT YOUR CURSED COAT HAS MEMORIES OF ME, DIDN'T I?
THINK HARD! DO YOU REMEMBER? HUH?
......
HEH-HEH-HEH. THIS IS TURNING OUT TO BE AN INTERESTING DAY...
IT'S FUN!
WHAT?
I'M GLAD YOU'RE ENJOYING IT.
SO...

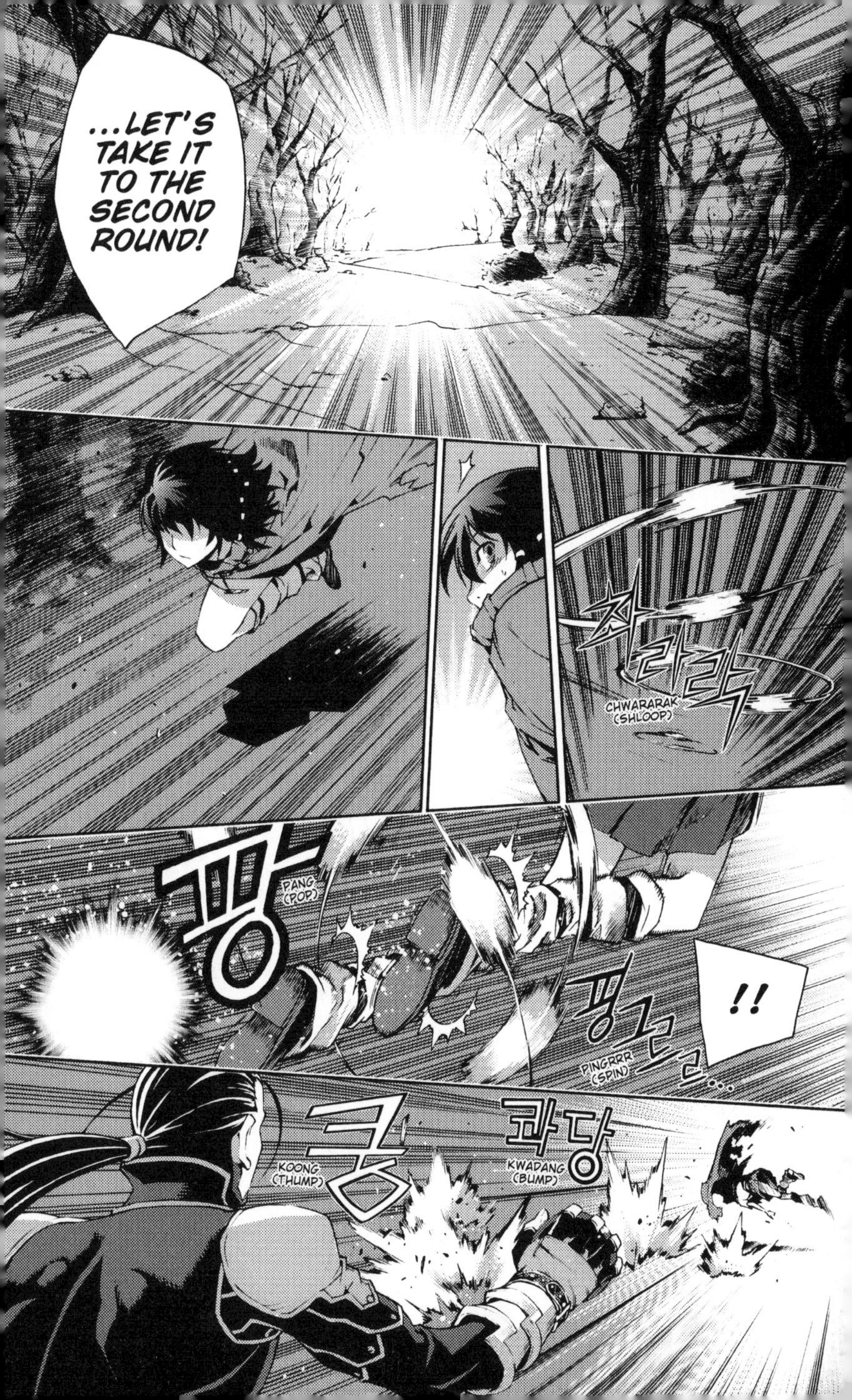
...LET'S TAKE IT TO THE SECOND ROUND!
좌라락
CHWARARAK (SHLOOP)
팡
PANG (POP)
핑그르르...
PINGRRR (SPIN)
!!
쿵
KOONG (THUMP)
콰당
KWADANG (BUMP)

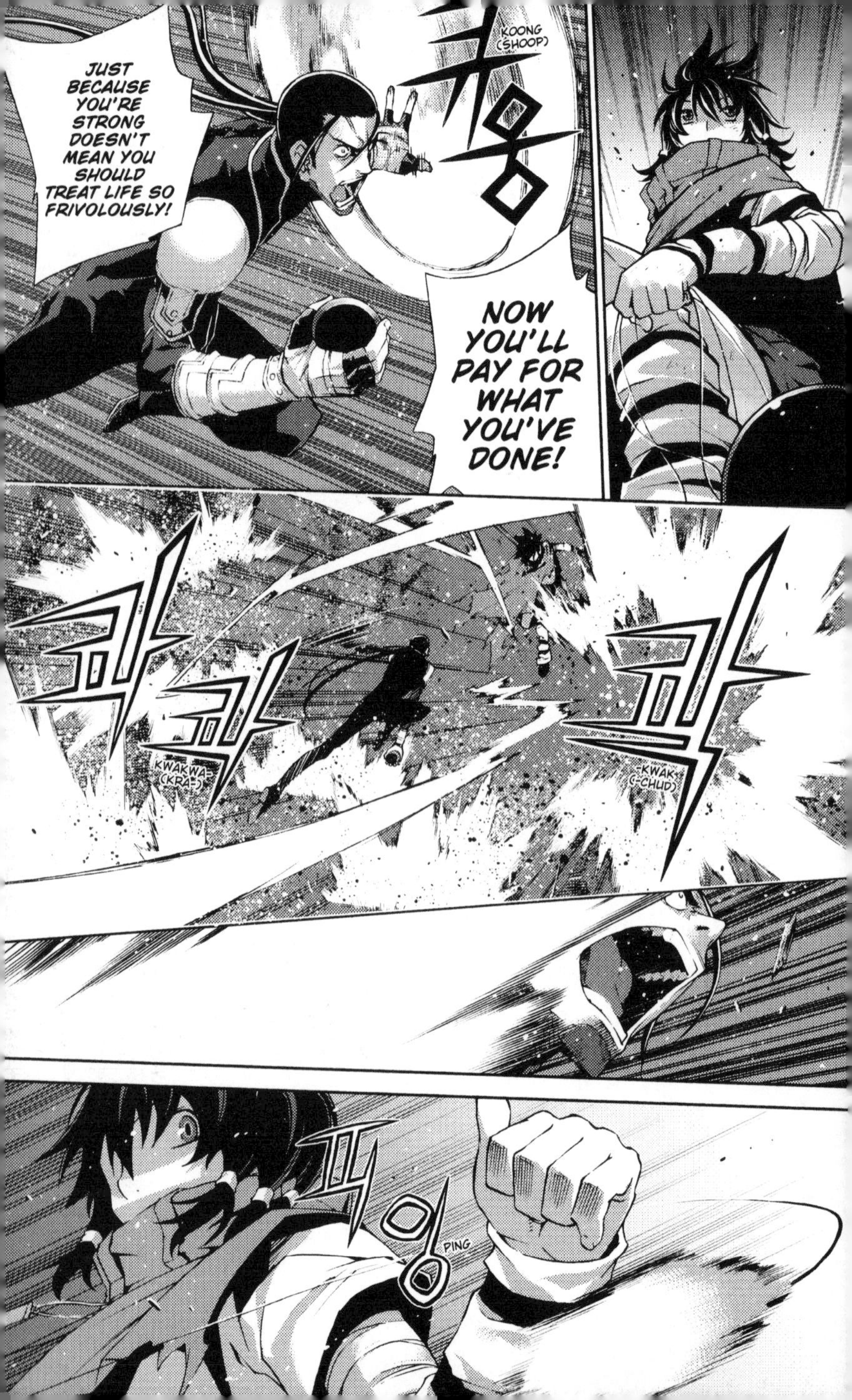

JUST BECAUSE YOU'RE STRONG DOESN'T MEAN YOU SHOULD TREAT LIFE SO FRIVOLOUSLY!
KOONG (SHOOP)
NOW YOU'LL PAY FOR WHAT YOU'VE DONE!
KWAKWA- (KRA-)
-KWAK (-CHUD)
PING

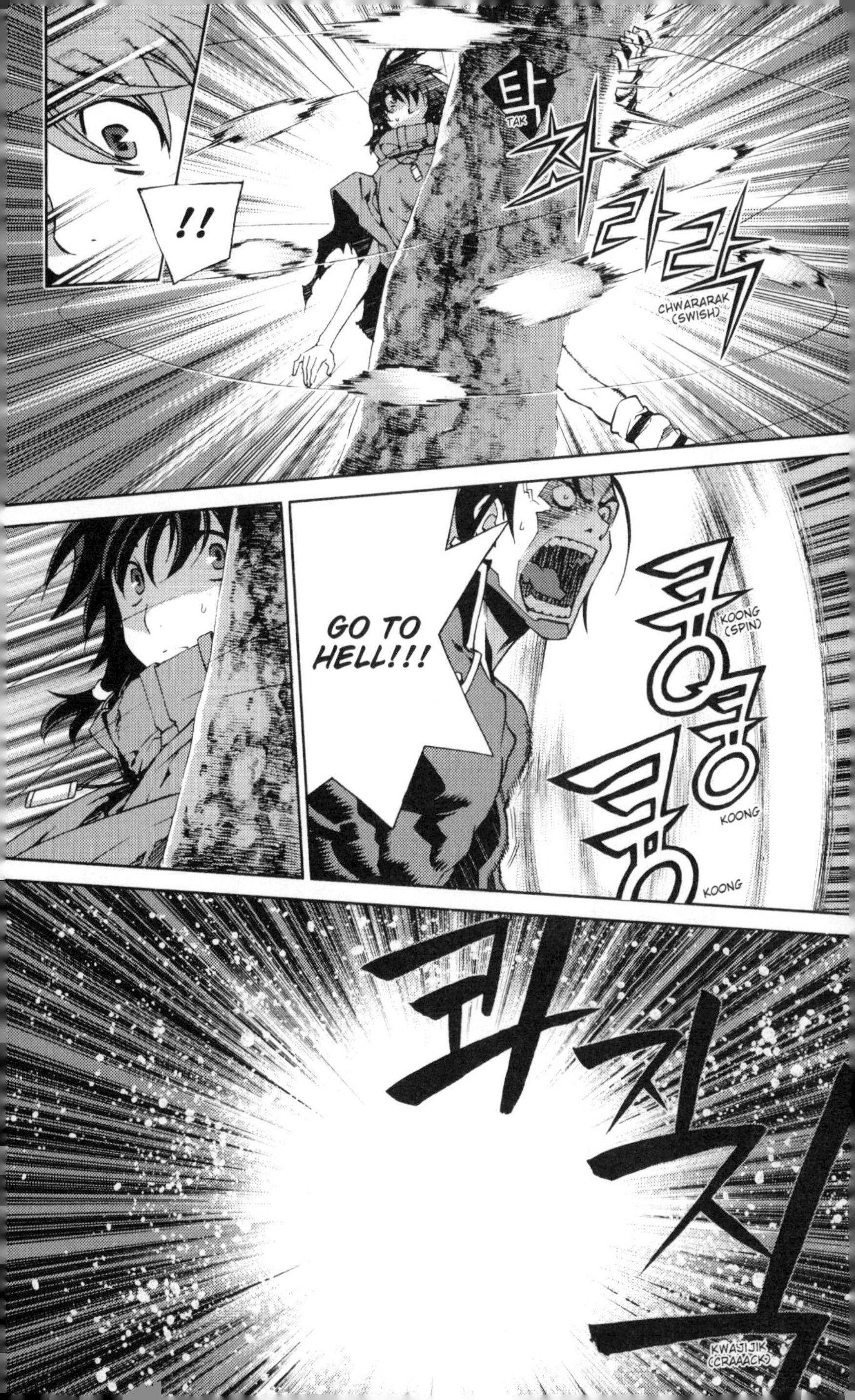
!!
탁
TAK
CHWARARAK
(SWISH)
GO TO HELL!!!
KOONG
(SPIN)
KOONG
KOONG
KWAJIJIK
(CRAAACK)

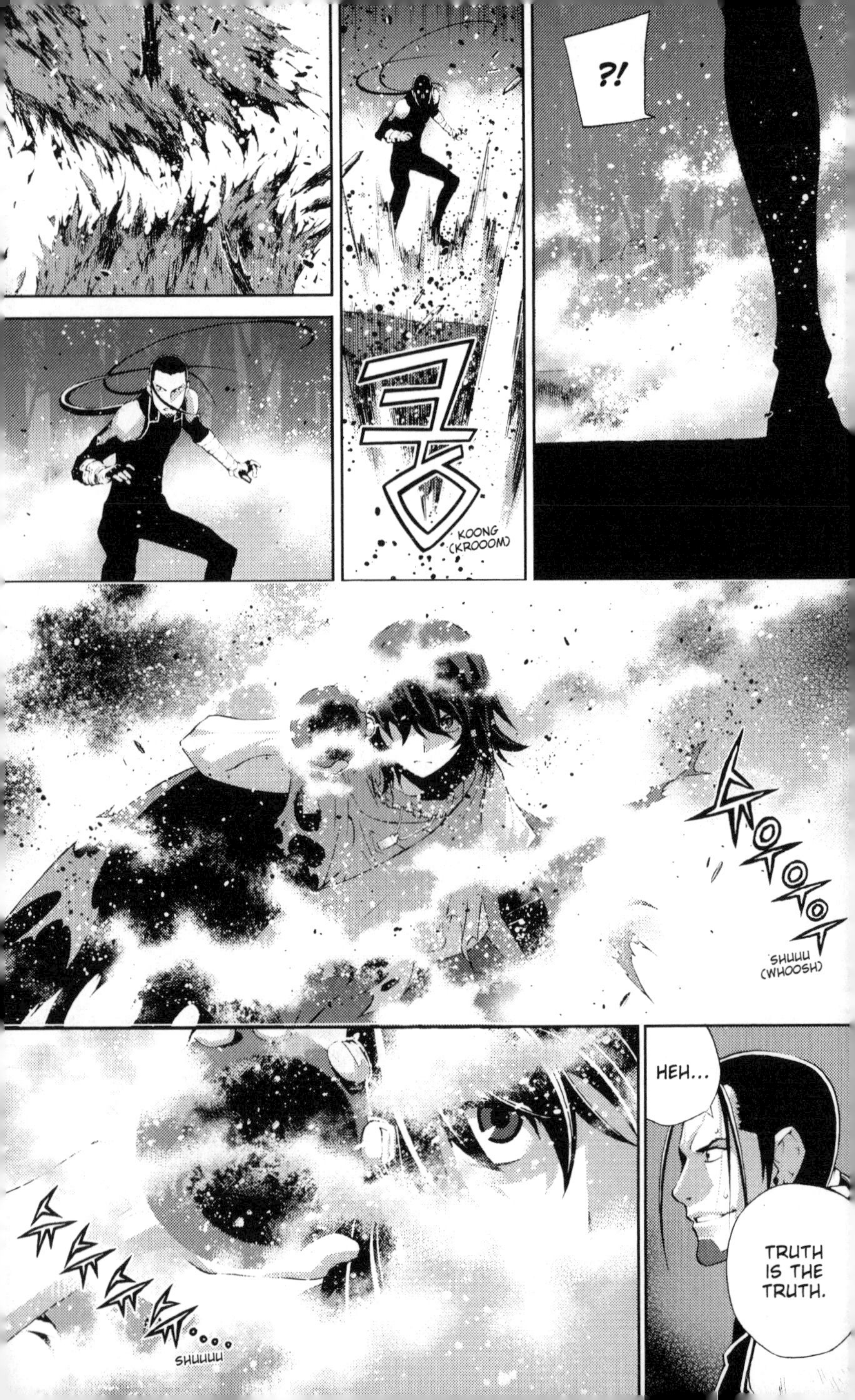
KOONG (KROOOM)
?!
SHUUU (WHOOSH)
SHUUUU
HEH...
TRUTH IS THE TRUTH.

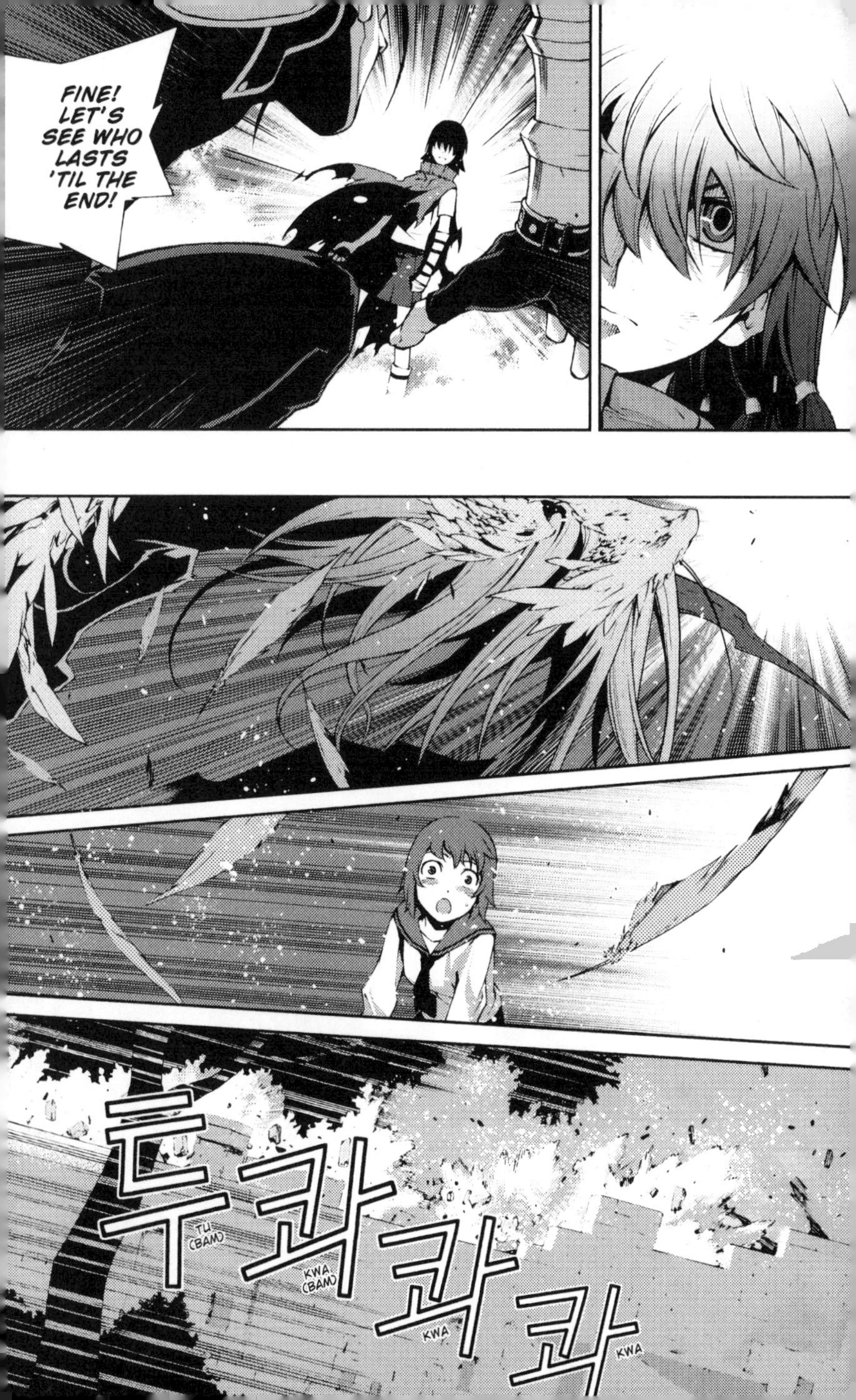
FINE! LET'S SEE WHO LASTS 'TIL THE END!
투
TU (BAM)
콰
KWA (BAM)
콰
KWA
콰
KWA

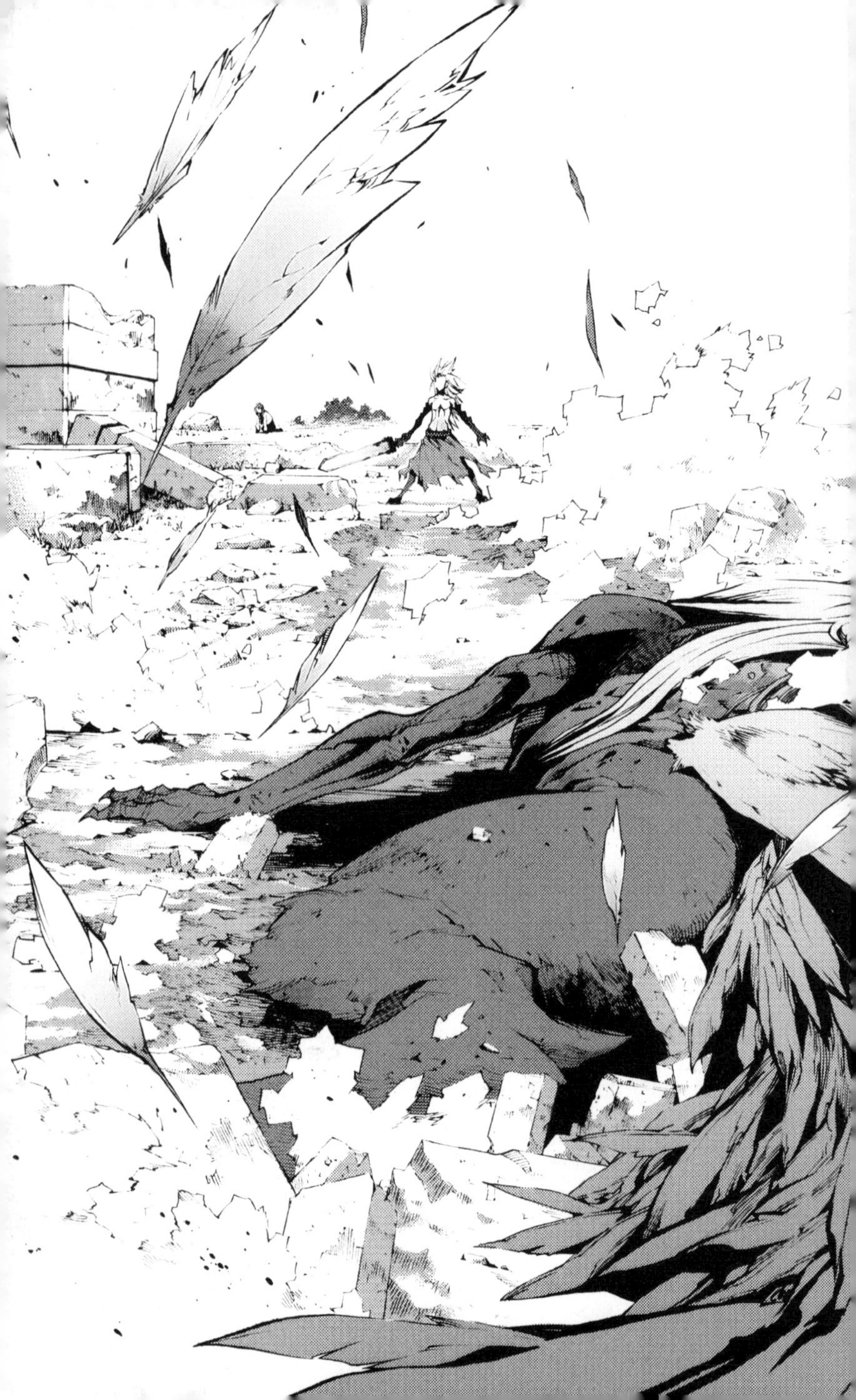

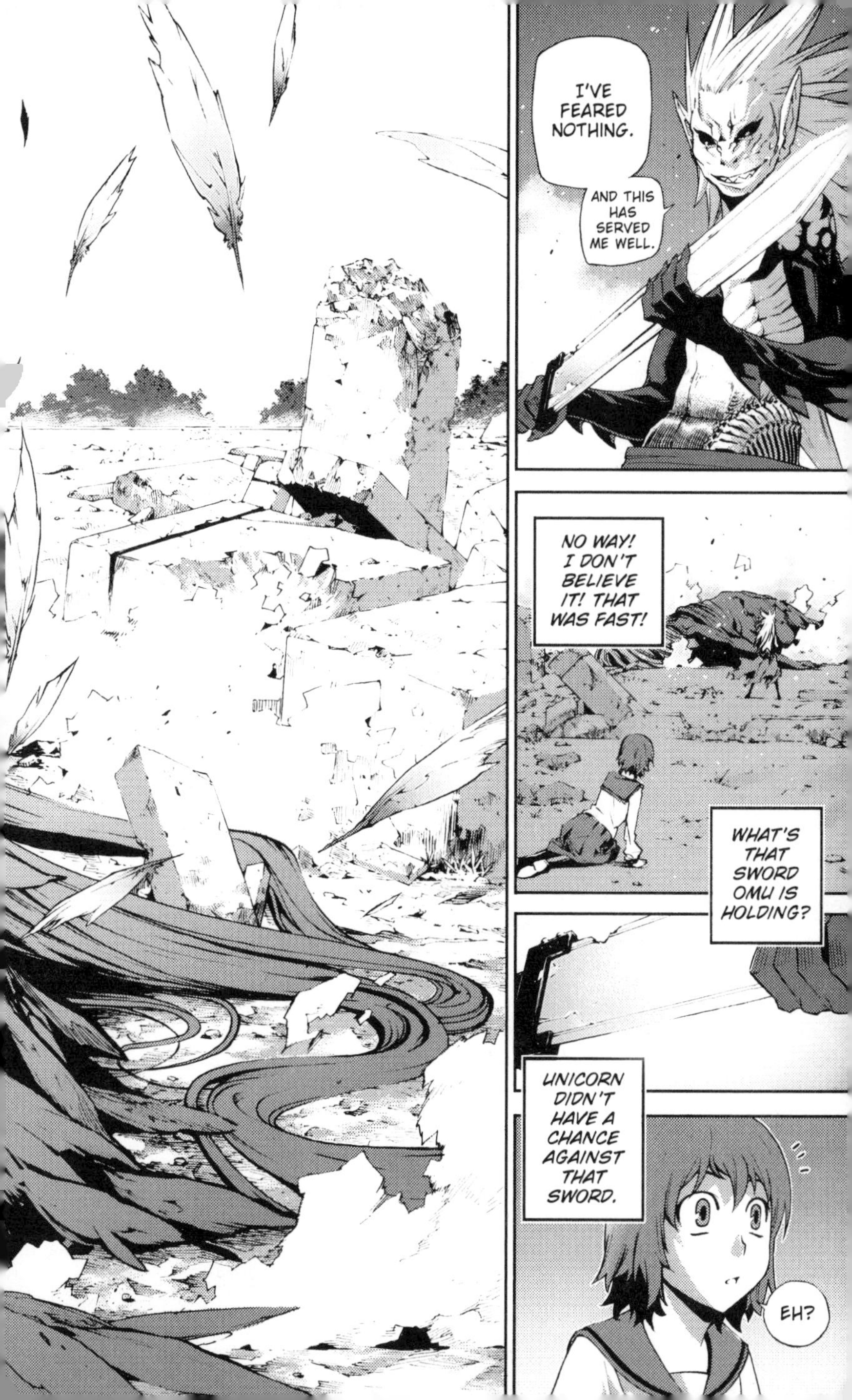
I'VE FEARED NOTHING.
AND THIS HAS SERVED ME WELL.
NO WAY! I DON'T BELIEVE IT! THAT WAS FAST!
WHAT'S THAT SWORD OMU IS HOLDING?
UNICORN DIDN'T HAVE A CHANCE AGAINST THAT SWORD.
EH?

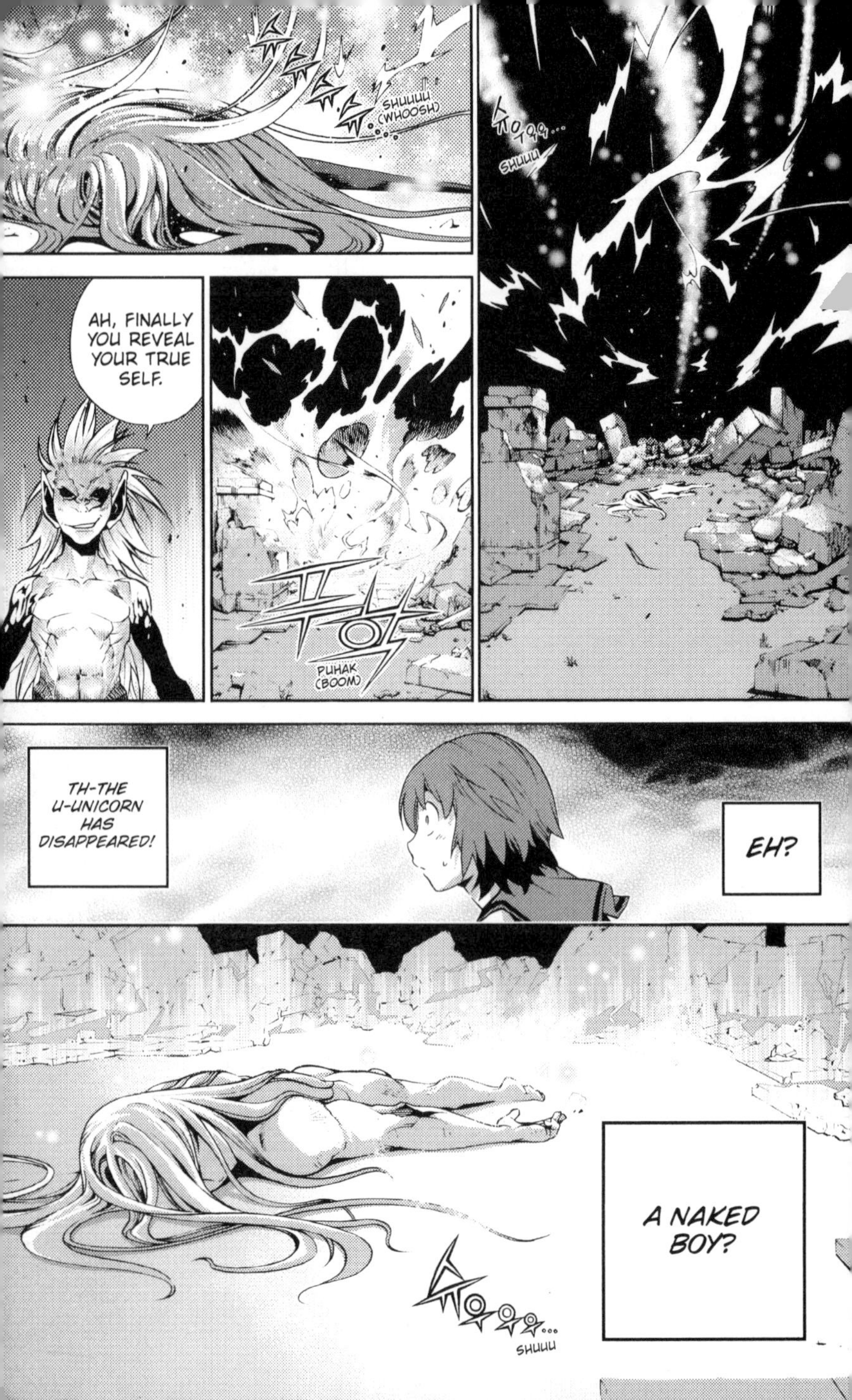
SHUUUU (WHOOSH)
AH, FINALLY YOU REVEAL YOUR TRUE SELF.
PUHAK (BOOM)
SHUUU
TH-THE U-UNICORN HAS DISAPPEARED!
EH?
A NAKED BOY?
SHUUU

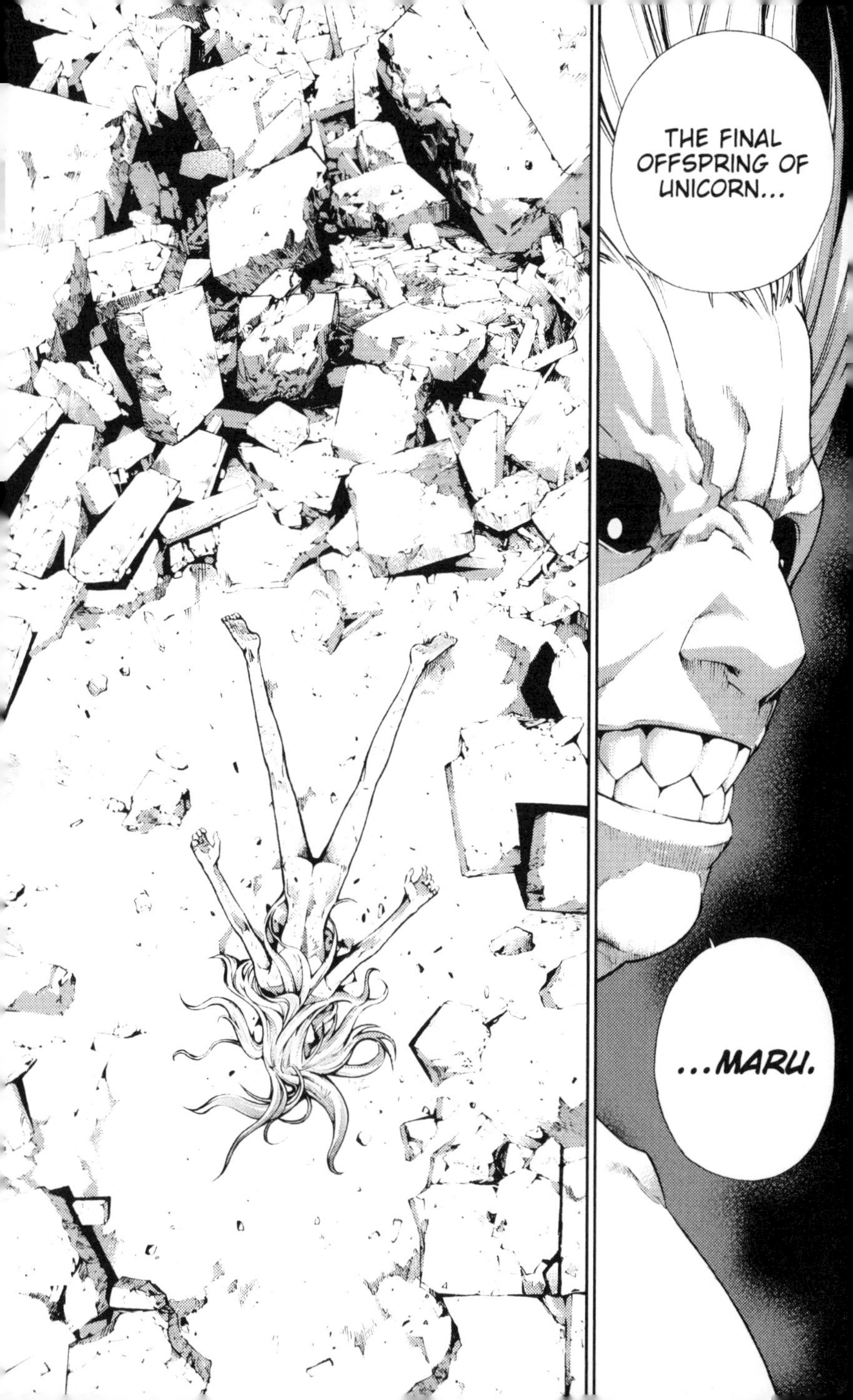
THE FINAL OFFSPRING OF UNICORN...
...MARU.

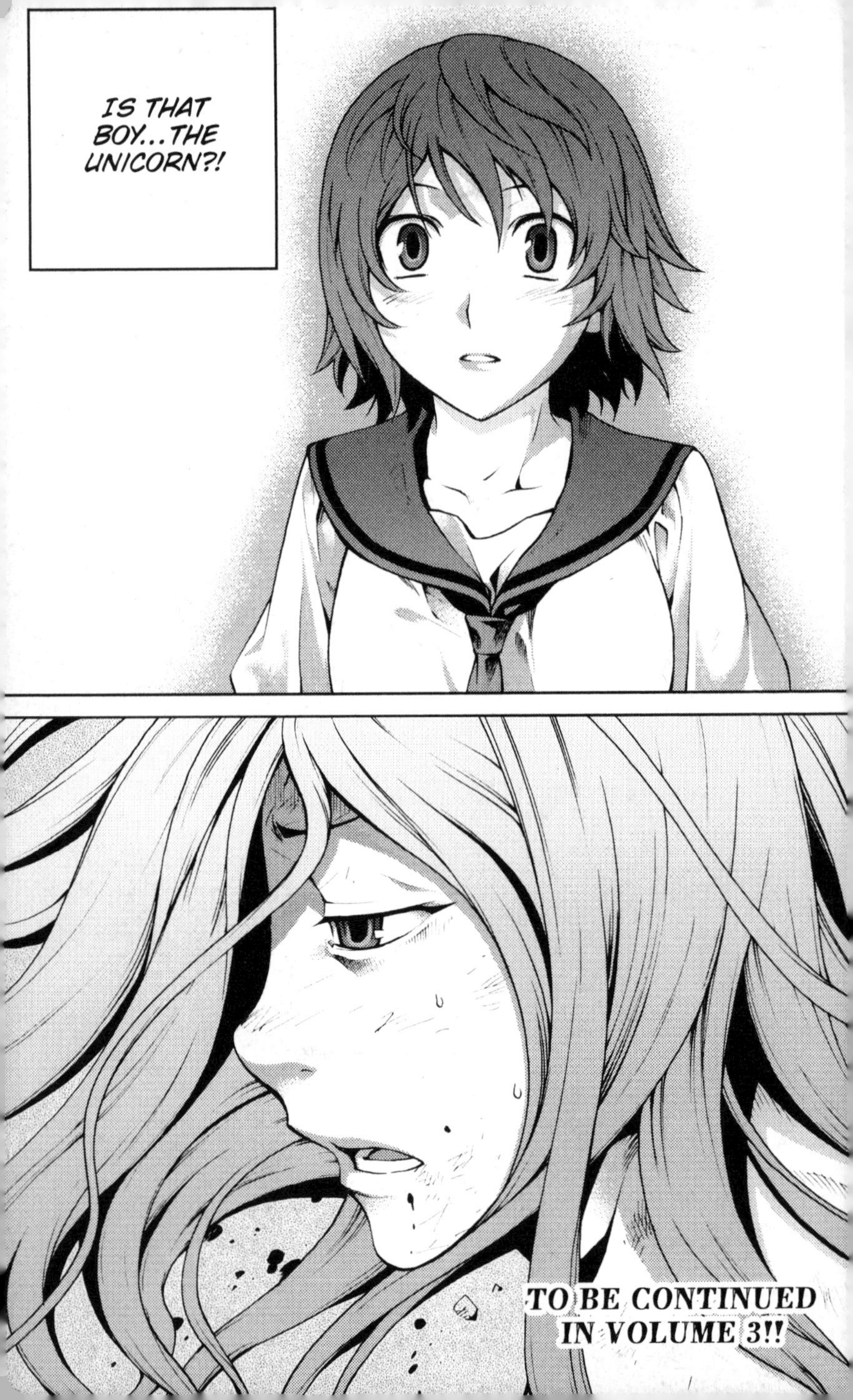
IS THAT BOY...THE UNICORN?!
TO BE CONTINUED IN VOLUME 3!!

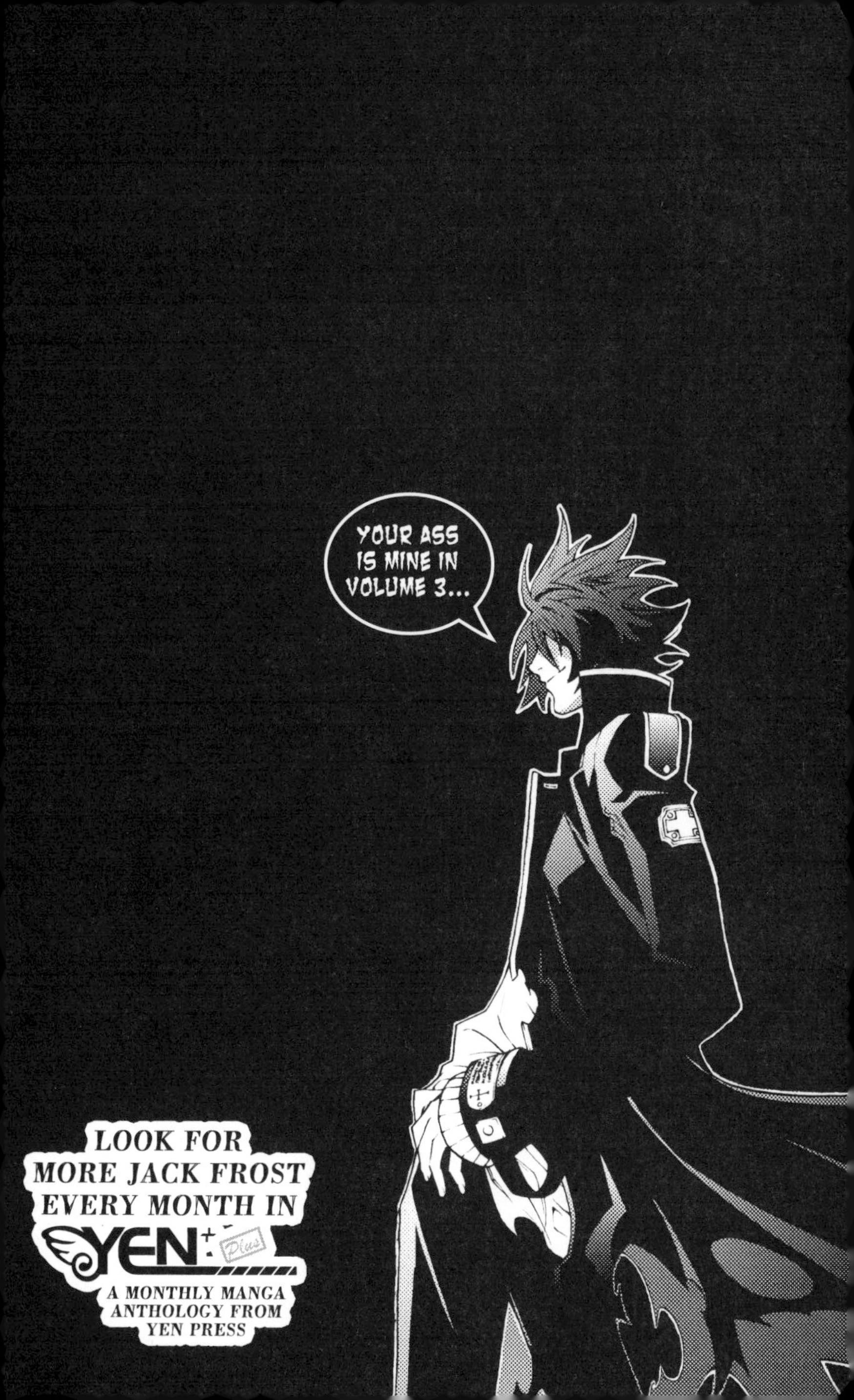
YOUR ASS IS MINE IN VOLUME 3...
LOOK FOR MORE JACK FROST EVERY MONTH IN
YEN Plus
A MONTHLY MANGA ANTHOLOGY FROM YEN PRESS

JACK FROST ②

JINHO KO

Translation: JiEun Park
English Adaptation: Arthur Dela Cruz

Lettering: Jose Macasocol, Jr.

Jack Frost Vol. 2 © 2007 JinHo Ko. All rights reserved. First published in Korea in 2007 by Haksan Publishing Co., Ltd. English translation rights in U.S.A. Canada, UK, and Republic of Ireland arranged with Haksan Publishing Co., Ltd.

English translation © 2009 Hachette Book Group, Inc.

Yen Press
Hachette Book Group
237 Park Avenue, New York, NY 10017

www.HachetteBookGroup.com
www.YenPress.com.

Yen Press is an imprint of Hachette Book Group, Inc.
The Yen Press name and logo are trademarks of Hachette Book Group, Inc.

First Yen Press Edition: November 2009

ISBN: 978-0-7595-2953-3

10 9 8 7 6 5 4 3 2 1

BVG

Printed in the United States of America